If My Boss Calls...
Get His Name

If My Boss Calls... Get His Name

A *Big Business Adventure*

Jerry Shaff

CLEAR LIGHT PUBLISHERS
SANTA FE

© 1999 Jerry Shaff

Clear Light Publishers
823 Don Diego, Santa Fe, NM 87501
WEB: www.clearlightbooks.com

First Edition
10 9 8 7 6 5 4 3 2 1

Library of Congress Cataloging-in-Publication Data

Shaff, Jerry.
    If my boss calls—get his name : a big business adventure / by
Jerry Shaff.
        p.   cm.
    ISBN 1-57416-018-4. — ISBN 1-57416-019-2 (pbk.)
I. Title.
PS3569.H295144   1998
813'.54—dc21   98-30830
                                                                    CIP

Cover photograph by © Bo Zaunders
Cover design by Marcia Keegan
Typography by V.S. Elliott

Printed in Canada.

Contents

Dedication

This book is dedicated to my wife, Carole, my loving partner in life...and the best boss I ever had.

Acknowledgments

I would like to thank the professionals who helped me turn my experiences into a book. My editor, Valerie Shepherd, taught me to have pity on my readers and not burden them with technical details. She made this poor engineer into a writer.

My copy editor, Sara Held, helped me make the story and the characters more believable and much more interesting.

Marcia Keegan and Harmon Houghton guided me through the complex maze of the publishing business...which might also make a good book.

1. The Professor

"For Chrissake why would you go to Leon for a muffler?" Henry asked, as he pulled out of the parking lot and up to the light. "He screws you on price and doesn't give you a guarantee. You should do business with Midas." He honked emphatically at a woman driver in front of him who pulled out to get into the turn lane. He bit the tip off an expensive cigar and reached for the lighter.

Ray watched his brother-in-law pull on the cigar until the end went red. He could see how Henry's impressive athletic frame and know-it-all manner might intimidate some of the people he did business with. Ray was sure these traits contributed to Henry's success as a contractor and developer.

"I always go to Leon," Ray answered patiently, "because they know my car and they do good work. And as far as I know Leon's honest."

Henry laughed. "Come on, Ray." He screeched the wheels of his new '76 El Dorado convertible as he turned up Western Avenue. "Honest my ass. I know the type. He talks a good game and gets hold of a bunch of simpleton customers like you so he can spend his winters in Florida."

Ray Pendleton was not a simpleton. You did not get to be a Harvard professor by being a simpleton, even a hard-working assistant professor. He was up for promotion to associate and he intended to make full professor by 1980. It would take a lot of honest, hard work to get there, but he could do it.

Ray knew that his brother-in-law saw his belief in honesty and hard work as a simple-minded illusion of no use in the real world.

Ray knew that Henry found him "unimpressive" in other ways as well.

While not as tall as Henry, who had played football for a year at Boston College, Ray was still above average at 5'11". His brown eyes hid behind unobtrusive horn-rimmed glasses, and his brown hair had receded slightly. Ray was not concerned with his appearance. He wasn't handsome, but he wasn't bad looking either. There was nothing memorable about him physically, and his personality was equally forgettable. He could be included in any business or social event at the Harvard Business School, or he could be left out. It didn't seem to make much difference.

This did not bother Ray very much. He knew he was impressive enough in the classroom to have to turn away students from every class he offered. He was satisfied with his life. But at this moment he was not entirely satisfied with himself. He was not using his intelligence. Once again he was letting Henry get to him.

"How about this baby," Henry said, as he drove toward the campus. "Cost me over 17 grand, but it's a good investment. They stopped making convertibles—this'll be worth a fortune."

"Yeah. Beautiful car," Ray agreed, without much enthusiasm.

"You should get a car for Dorothy. She deserves it. I'm talking a new one, not another clunker."

"The Bel Air is OK to get me to work...uh...usually. But we're ready to get a new car." Ready yes, but could they afford it?

"One of these?" Henry grinned at him pointedly and slapped the leather-covered dash.

Ray gritted his teeth. He saw where Henry was headed. "No, Henry, not one of these."

"Not on a professor's salary, huh?" Henry flipped his barely smoked cigar back over the trunk, muttering something about "third-rate leaf." He went on, "Not on any salary if you ask me. If you were a CEO with a multimillion-dollar package—but that's not salary, that's a package, percentage of profits, stock options, you name it—that's where they get the real money." Henry was warming up to his pet subject. "You know as well as I do Ray, anyone on pure salary just isn't going anywhere in life." He glanced at Ray. "Nothing personal, you know, but that's a fact."

Henry had left college his sophomore year to go into his father-in-law's small general contracting business in Waltham. He was successful in his business, less successful in persuading Ray that anyone who wasn't in business for himself was nothing more than a flunky.

"Come on Ray," he said. "Are you going to slave away for forty years and think you're doing great when you finally make $50,000 a year—then you and Dorothy retire on a stinking little pension?"

This really bothered Ray. The average wage for teachers was $13,000, and Ray was making twice that much—nowhere near $50,000—and Henry knew it. And Ray didn't know where he would be when it came to retiring. He thought of the raise that would come with his promotion, but that was not an argument to make to Henry. "Life isn't only about money," Ray said. "Job satisfaction is important, so is being part of a prestigious professional community and publishing your work and—"

"I'll tell you what job satisfaction is," Henry said, jabbing his finger at Ray. "You get a development started with a hundred homes going at 60 grand and up, and every time someone moves in you put 5–10 grand in your pocket." He jutted his big chin and adjusted his masterful grip on the steering wheel. "That," he said, "is job satisfaction."

Money is everything: This was what Henry's philosophy amounted to. Ray advised himself to remember that the next time Henry started to get under his skin. He took a deep breath. "Some of the faculty do consulting," he said. "That would be very rewarding."

"Agh chicken feed."

Ray laughed. "I wasn't talking about money. But they do get paid of course."

"How you gonna afford a new car? I've been telling you, you should come in with me. I need someone in Brookline. There'll be a shitload of new homes in Brookline, and I can't trust half the people I got working for me."

Ray laughed. "What would I do—build houses? Install bathtubs? Toilets?"

Henry frowned doubtfully. "I'll think of something," he said. "Family is family."

Ray's eyes opened wide—Henry was serious. "Well thanks for the offer, Henry. Really. But I think I'll stick to what I know. Which is teaching."

"Well if you'd rather drive that old Bel Air."

Ray paused before answering. He would not get into a ridiculous argument with his brother-in-law. "No, Henry," he said. "But frankly I don't care that much about the car. I want to teach, that's all."

Henry glanced over at him and shook his head, frowning, as if Ray were a hopeless case.

"It's my profession and I'm good at it." Ray could feel his patience cracking. "Students don't cut my classes; they get serious. They practice dealing with real world business situations. They learn to be one step ahead of the game, to analyze and debate all sides of a question, they learn there's no one black-and-white ready-made answer to business problems."

"Analyze? *Debate?*" Henry looked at Ray in evident disbelief. "That's what you do at Harvard? They waste their money on that kind of crap? How much do they pay?"

"They pay plenty," Ray said, struggling to keep his voice calm. "And they get plenty. You talk about CEOs. There are twice as many CEOs from Harvard as from any other school. We teach them the financial side, the marketing side, how to run companies right. When they leave here—"

"How the hell can you teach them to run a business? What do you guys know about business? You tell them stories about business and you teach them finance. Finance, hell. All you need is to know how to count. My accountant counts for me, but he couldn't run a hot dog stand. And neither could any of you professors."

Ray could feel his jaw tighten. He didn't trust himself to answer Henry.

Henry glanced at him and seemed surprised at the expression on his face. "Look Ray," he said, "I know you believe in what you're doing, and you like teaching and all that, and maybe it helps other people who want to teach. But come on. Let your students follow me around for a few days and they'll learn more than you guys could ever teach them. How to look someone in the eye to see if he's lying, or just how much he'll pay, or how to tell if you're being cheated on your material. That's the real world. If any of you guys were dropped into the real world, you wouldn't last six months."

Ray took a long breath to calm himself down. "You're entitled to your opinion," he said.

■■■

When they finally got to the school, Ray got out of the car, thanked Henry for picking him up, and walked across the campus. Henry had gone too far this time. It was bad timing for Ray, who had to be up for teaching a particularly important class. Ray didn't have much respect for Henry, but he had to admit that he could be right. In fact Ray had no way of knowing whether his knowledge and abilities would be enough to keep him afloat in a corporate setting.

Ray hardly noticed anything as he walked to his office. The winter of 1976 was over and it was officially spring. The ice was gone from the Charles River and the students were out celebrating the first really warm day. Some threw Frisbees back and forth. Others were lying on blankets and studying or just sunbathing. A small group followed the slow, alien motions of a tai chi instructor.

The celebration was wasted on Professor Ray Pendleton as he plodded along thinking about surviving in the real world of business. And about providing for his family. Shouldn't he get into a better-paying field? Not according to Dorothy. "Don't listen to Henry," she'd said. She always knew when Ray had been talking to him. "He's my brother, so I love him, but sometimes he's not too smart. He talks big but he doesn't believe half of what he says himself. And he hasn't a clue about what you're all about—what *we're* all about." Ray knew Dorothy was proud of her Harvard professor husband. "I'm happy with the way things are," she said.

But would she always be? Would he?

■■■

Ray walked up the steps to his office in the Baker Library.

The class coming up was Business Strategies, given to graduating students who would be the new rookies in industry in a few short months. The material to be taught could have come right out of the textbook, which would have made it easier for the professor to prepare and easier for students to forget. Ray preferred to tackle his case study in a game he called "reverse advocacy."

As he walked into class, he knew exactly how he would start. They had been studying the Bulova case for three weeks, and it was time to set the game in motion.

"Miss Granger," he said. "Just where do we stand? What's going on in the watch industry?"

Betty Granger could be depended on to cover the facts. She would have complete notes on everything they had covered and could talk about them in an organized manner. Ray was not disappointed.

"Well, we're on the marketing staff of Bulova Watch Company," she started, pulling out her notes. "And we have to present a strategy in response to the new marketing campaign from Timex."

"The invasion of Timex," Jim Orlowski interrupted. Orlowski was a strong proponent of meeting the Timex challenge head on. He was very emotional about it, almost as if he was at war.

Granger ignored the interruption and continued. "In recent years, Timex has made fantastic inroads in the watch industry by using modern engineering and manufacturing techniques to produce a low-cost, adequate quality product line. Their selling approach is also modern, in that they are aiming at the mass market through drugstores, discount stores, and other low-cost outlets. The traditional channel of distribution in the industry, the conventional jewelry store, is being bypassed."

She glanced at her notes. "Some of the questions to be considered are:

"—Should Bulova...should we abandon our classical link to the consumer through the jeweler?

"—Should we fight the drugstore approach?

"—If so, how?

"—Should we use both approaches, with an added line of inexpensive watches for the drugstores and jewelry watches for the jewelry stores?

"—Would the cheap watches ruin our reputation with the jewelers, leaving us out of both markets?

"—Would..."

"OK, very good," Ray interrupted. "There are a lot of things to consider. And what's our assignment?"

"We have to prepare a strategy to present to the Board."

"Good," Ray agreed. "Now let's see where to start. I think we've already got an idea where Mr. Orlowski stands." The class giggled. "What about you, Mr. Rasche?"

Phil Rasche was his traditionalist ultraconservative. "What do you think we should do?" Ray asked. "We have a critical situation here."

Rasche's response was predictable. "Bulova," he said, "has built a whole system based on manufacturing a quality watch and selling it as jewelry. When someone buys our watch they aren't looking for an efficient way to tell time, they're investing in an expensive jewel that also tells time. There always will be a market for them and it is through our jewelers. That's where we should stay. If Timex has found a market for cheap watches, there's nothing Bulova can do about it. Nor should we even try. It would be like going into a new business."

"But if our business is becoming obsolete," Ray asked, "don't we have to go into a new business?"

"Maybe," Rasche answered, "but we would be better off going into the bracelet business than cheap watches."

Ray smiled at that. It was a good answer and showed real understanding. He could see Orlowski squirm, wanting to debate. Rasche would be successful in the business world, without a doubt. But Ray wanted to test his sensitivity. "Let's be fair," he said. "You can't dismiss the problem with the argument that Bulova is in the watch business. They have to meet competition and consider new technology."

"Sure," Rasche answered. "They can't run away every time there's a threat, but—"

"OK, let's let someone else answer that question." Ray had heard enough—Rasche would be all right. "Mr. Orlowski, you're almost jumping out of your seat. I suspect you might have an opinion on this."

Orlowski responded quickly. "The Timex approach is a direct threat to Bulova. If we ignore it, we'll be wiped out just like Bic wiped out the pen companies in Europe. The only course of action is to catch up with the Timex technology and compete in the same markets. The companies that don't, won't be around."

Ray was a little startled by Orlowski's vehemence. He knew what Orlowski's opinion was, but thought he might have some flexibility. Another test was in order. "But even if Timex takes the low end of the market, can't Bulova still do well in the jewelry end?"

Orlowski would have none of that. "No way!" he answered. "There won't *be* any jewelry end. The whole watch industry will be the inexpensive end, and Timex will have it all."

That did it. Orlowski could not be his man. He was too polarized. Ray had miscalculated in choosing him, but had discovered it before it was too late. He had to change plans.

Turning to Sylvia Gregory, he hopefully probed, "Miss Gregory, you've also been leaning toward direct confrontation. Do you agree with Mr. Orlowski?"

Gregory nodded and added, "Yes, I think Bulova can compete in the low-price end. I mean, they're—we're not a bunch of dummies. But I'm not sure it's a life-or-death matter."

This sounded good. Ray probed a little further. "What about the argument that the jewelers would rebel if Bulova sold a cheap product through the drugstores?"

"Well, that has to be considered. I suppose it depends on how we go about it. Maybe if we used a different name or something."

Ray had heard enough. Sylvia Gregory would do just fine. He continued the debate for about five minutes, getting opinions from several others. Then he outlined his surprise. "We've covered the situation from about every direction," he said, "and it doesn't look like we agree on any one solution. But, in real life situations, that's what we should expect. In a big company, it is highly unlikely that everyone will agree on one approach. It looks like we'll have to prepare two separate courses of action for the Board. One will present the reasoning for meeting the Timex threat head on. The other will propose concentrating on the higher-priced field through jewelers."

Ray stood up. "We'll make up two teams." He smiled, looking around the class. "Miss Gregory, you will head up the team advocating staying with the expensive jewelry-type product."

"But I think we should go the other way," she corrected him.

"I know, but a professional marketing executive should be able to objectively present the facts to support any logical course. And you've heard a great deal of logic on both sides."

"I would much rather put together what I believe in."

"And that's exactly what you should do in the end," Ray responded. "But to do a good job you should thoroughly understand all the opposing arguments, maybe better than your own.

And what better way than to present the opposing view?"

"I don't know if I can," she protested, but very weakly.

"Just present what you think Mr. Rasche would present," Ray said grinning and looking over at Phil Rasche. "Only do it better."

A murmur spread through the class and a few smiles started to appear. Orlowski looked dubious.

"And Mr. Rasche," Ray continued, "I think you should present the case for total war against Timex."

Rasche had seen that coming and grinned. "OK, but I don't know if I could really put my heart into it."

"Don't worry, you'll have help. Mr. Orlowski will be your number one assistant."

With that, even Orlowski joined in the laughter, and Ray knew he was home free. He gave out several more assignments, making sure the vehement advocates stayed on their own side, but switching others as much as he could. The class was noisy but smiling as he instructed them on the details of the presentation:

"—Remember, the board members are responsible to the stockholders.

"—Don't forget, your proposal has to be financially realistic.

"—Prove that Bulova is capable of doing what you propose."

As the class filed out, they were kidding each other, especially Phil Rasche and Sylvia Gregory. Jim Orlowski began instructing Rasche as they went out the door.

■■■

The following Tuesday Dorothy dropped Ray off at school. "I might be a little late," she said. "Leon says he can replace the pump while I wait. But he can't start on it 'til 2:30."

"No problem," Ray assured her. "Just give me a call from Leon's."

He kissed her and started to get out. He stopped. "Why don't we look for a new car. You deserve something better than this. Henry's right about that at least."

"Henry has a few good ideas at that," she said. "We can trade this in next year—after the 250,000-mile checkup."

Ray laughed. If the odometer hadn't stuck at 97,000, the Bel Air might be in the record books by now. "We'll keep this," he told Dorothy, "for sentimental reasons. And to get me back and forth from work—when it's not in the shop."

He kissed her again and opened the door. "We'll go car shopping this weekend."

"How about that," she grinned. "Mr. and Mrs. America."

She could poke fun at the idea, but he saw her eyes light up. That made everything worthwhile.

Ray gave her a thumbs-up as she drove away.

He slowed his brisk pace across the campus, wondering if he had spoken too quickly. Things were a little tight already, and he hadn't done his homework—he didn't know if they could afford car payments. Ray sighed. His class wouldn't think much of him as a model if they knew how careless he could be with his own finances.

He made up his mind to look into doing some consulting. He thought of the executives who had taken his summer seminar. Several of them told him he could help them in their operations— an open-ended invitation he could follow up on. "The guy from GF," Ray thought, "and the loud guy from the glass company." Then there was the fat man from the automotive industry. "No, probably not him," Ray said to himself. He remembered the man who had sat in the back in a special wide chair, shooting aggressive questions at him—the sort of "big shot" executive his students would look on as the ultimate bad guy, a big fish ready to swallow the small ones. He was a "heavy" all right, from shark-infested corporate waters. "Could I handle that?" Ray wondered. "And just how long does Henry think he would last in that world? Henry doesn't know shit about big business."

Ray felt himself begin to tense. "Forget Henry," he muttered under his breath. He had to concentrate on the game. The success or failure of the semester's work was riding on it, and the outcome of a game was never predictable. Today was the big day.

When he arrived, everyone was waiting for him. He took his seat as Chairman of the Board and asked Sylvia Gregory to present her case. She covered all the reasons for staying with the traditional product line and distribution channel, and she came up with the idea of expanding the Bulova line to include other "pricey" items to be sold by Bulova outlets. Everything was objective and thorough, but it was obvious she really did not believe all that she presented. And to make things even more difficult, after almost every statement there would be a groan from Jim Orlowski in the back.

Phil Rasche got up to present the other side. Using Orlowski's arguments, he attacked many of the statements that he himself had made, and really seemed to be enjoying himself.

After the presentations, Ray asked the students who made up the Board for questions and comments. The predictable questions were easily fielded by Rasche and Sylvia Gregory. Then Orlowski could not contain himself any longer. He asked Sylvia how much sales would go down by letting Timex take the low-cost market. As she started to answer, he interrupted.

"How can you defend this position?" he asked her. "You know that not taking aggressive action is going to ruin the company. Sales will drop drastically and lots of employees will lose their jobs."

She was taken aback by the intensity of Jim's attack. "Hold on," she said. "I'm just presenting one side."

"But you don't believe what you're saying. It's like selling out."

"I'm not selling out," she protested. "I'm doing what Professor Pendleton asked. It's really just a game that we're—"

"Well, I don't like this game," he interrupted. He turned to Ray. "Are you telling us that we should say what we don't believe? Forget our principles. Is that what we're learning?"

Ray was not surprised by Orlowski's vehemence—it was why he had decided against using him in the first place. But by changing the focus from the case itself to Ray's teaching methods, Orlowski could destroy the momentum Ray had been building. He had to get things back on track.

"Hold on, Mr. Orlowski," Ray said, holding up his hand. "Hold on. In no way am I suggesting you do something against your principles. I respect your principles."

"But you're making Sylvia—"

"I'm *asking* Miss Gregory to present the case for the other side. And I think she did a very good job." Ray smiled at Gregory and asked, "But I don't think that you've changed your position, have you?"

"No, I haven't," she replied, clearly relieved to be rescued by the professor.

"And you still agree with Mr. Orlowski?"

"Yes," she replied, but then added, "but he may be in the process of changing my mind."

Everyone laughed except Orlowski, who muttered, "I still don't like this game."

Ray could feel that Orlowski was becoming isolated. He looked for a way to get this holdout student into the game.

"Jim," he asked. "You follow football? The Patriots?"

"Yeah, sure."

"Ok. Let me use this as an example. Every week the Patriots have to prepare for Sunday's game. How do they do it? What do they do first?"

Orlowski answered hesitantly, "Well, first they come up with a game plan. Then—"

"Before that. Before they make up their plan."

"Well, game films. They look at game films."

"Of the other team, right?"

"Yeah, but their own team too."

"And they do that to understand the other team's strengths and weaknesses...and their own, right?" Ray did not wait for an answer. "Because they want to know what the other team is going to do. They even have a squad to run the other team's offense...and defense. And they even try to simulate the way individual players will act. And if they find a weakness in their own team, they'll have that squad exploit that weakness over and over again."

Orlowski seemed to be rethinking his opposition. "So you're having us switch sides as a way to find our own strengths and weaknesses?"

"And your opponents."

"Not just to learn to tell the boss what he wants to hear?"

Ray laughed. "No, absolutely not. But that might not be a bad idea."

"Oh, c'mon," Orlowski protested.

"Just kidding," said Ray. "Look, Jim—everybody. The best way you can serve your boss is to tell him exactly what you think. Be perfectly honest. That's what you're getting paid for. But the boss, or his boss, or someone higher up will not always agree with you. Then you have two choices. Either actively work to make this other idea work, or quit your job. And that decision could come up in every job you get."

He stopped to let that thought sink in.

"Can't you just decline?" Granger asked. "Just stay off that project?"

"No," Ray answered, glad to see someone other than Orlowski getting in on the discussion. "That would be...like...well, let's go back to the football team. The quarterback calls a play and the right tackle doesn't agree. So he says to run the play without him."

The class laughed.

A student in the back asked, "But can you really say that a corporation is like a football team?"

Another student answered, "Sure it is. Take Bulova. Suppose they decide to go after Timex. Then everyone has a job to do. The engineers, the salesmen, everyone. They have to be a team."

"That's right," Ray agreed. "And any salesman who was against it will have to come up with something to tell their present customers. He can't tell them he was against it or the company will look terrible. He'll have to give the company line and make it convincing." Ray paused and looked around. Everyone was listening. "In business," he said, "sometimes you have to do things you don't really want to do. That's the real world."

Ray did not realize how important that statement would be for him in the future. But for now, he felt he had given the class some worthwhile direction. Henry might not think so, but this was real practical knowledge. Ray was doing his job.

Ray had little more to do. The students took over the discussion, asking and answering good questions. Rasche was explaining how Bulova was going to sell their new watches through the drugstores, when Orlowski suddenly hit Rasche with a challenging question. "What do you mean, sell through the drugstores? Sell who? Bulova doesn't have anyone who knows about selling in that market. They wouldn't even know who to call on."

The class was stunned. Here was Orlowski hitting on a key weakness in his own position. There was a moment of silence and then several started talking at once. Ray grinned. Orlowski had joined the game.

Ray's students began to generate one pearl of wisdom after another. Without exception, everyone in the class knew the facts, the issues, and most everyone had opinions. Ray just sat back and listened. Things were going even better than he expected. He could have stepped in to tell them there was always the other side to consider; or that they should always be objective when making business decisions; or there was never the one perfect answer. But the students were covering just about everything on their own.

Outside the classroom, spring was in full bloom. The sun was shining brightly, warming the grass and trees, preparing them for another glorious summer. Out on the lawns, students were talking, studying, and in some cases loving. In his office, the Dean was talking to an alumnus and his son, who would be starting school next fall. Down the hall a student was being interviewed by a representative from a multinational company. Off campus, Dorothy Pendleton was on the phone with Emil Gross, the President of Amsaco, a large automotive parts company. All sorts of people were doing all sorts of things, but none of them were aware of what Ray Pendleton had accomplished. And if they had been, they would not have considered it very important.

But Ray Pendleton did not care what what anyone else might have thought at this moment. He sat back with his hands clasped behind his head, listening to the beautiful music coming from his students.

2. Emil

Many miles away from Harvard, in Jackson, Michigan, Emil Gross, President of Amsaco, could not sit still at his desk. He had to lean way forward and push hard with his arms and legs in order to raise his heavy frame out of his chair, but when he got excited, he could not sit still. As he stepped toward his office window, he was not happy. He was angry with Dennison and Procino and annoyed that so much effort was required just to get up from behind his desk. While he was fully capable of handling Dennison and Procino, he knew he had a real battle against the personal cross he had to bear, his weight.

Gross was a big man in every way. He had worked his way up the ladder at Amsaco through the sales route, from a Sales Rep, to District Manager, Regional Manager, to Vice President of Sales, all within a ten-year span. Once into the home office, it had taken only two years to get his boss's job as Executive Vice President of Marketing, and three more to take over as President of the whole company. In the six years he had been President, since 1970, Amsaco had enjoyed good growth in the automotive aftermarket, although the last two were not so good.

Unfortunately, as Emil's career had grown, so had his body. Customer entertainment and good living could not be controlled. His body grew from a heavy, but acceptable, 240 pounds up toward 300 and beyond. As he approached the 400-pound mark, his personal lifestyle required minor but significant change. Bowling was the first thing to go, but since he had little time for that as his career grew, that loss was not attributed to weight. Even the end of golfing could be attributed to career. With customers he had played golf regularly. At the home office, however, he would schedule meetings during the golf outings and participate afterward in the eating, drinking, and card playing. He did not correlate the end of golf with his weight.

But the personal details could not be ignored. He could no longer fit into a normal seat. The company aircraft had a special seat belt extension for his use. Tying his shoes was next to impossible. Reaching parts of his body in the shower or on the toilet was extremely difficult. When he lost sight of his genital area, he could no longer deny the fact that he was abnormal, and he did not like it.

As he turned away from the window, weight was not his primary concern, but it was an irritant in the back of his mind. Of immediate importance was to put Dave Dennison in his place. He went over to his desk, picked up an artist's sketch of an ad. "Dave, this is just the same crap you had in here last year, warmed over."

Dennison had prepared himself for trouble. Emil had gotten up from his desk without speaking to him—that was never a good sign. Dennison answered calmly, "That's not true, Emil. We've changed the whole approach. We're hitting the do-it-yourself portion of the market through the jobber publications. Some of the graphics are similar, but they're going to a different audience, with a different message. You have to look at the total program and how each segment supports—"

"You don't have a total program," Emil interrupted. "All you do is run a few ads. You spend the budget every year, but for the life of me, I don't know if it does any good."

"Of course it does," Dennison countered, thinking, "Here it comes." Ever since Emil had attended a marketing seminar at Harvard Business School, he had kept agitating for a "total marketing plan."

Emil stepped up his attack. "If it does do any good, it's purely by accident. There's no total plan, no coordinating of merchandising...and product line engineering...and the field force.... I tell you Dave, we don't have a marketing strategy or a plan. We just repeat last year's program over and over and over."

Dennison and Procino stood in front of Emil's desk feeling foolish, looking like a comedy team from an old movie. Dave Dennison, who had succeeded Emil as Executive Vice President of Marketing, was like a smaller version of Emil. Standing only 5'6", he had to be pretty round to reach his 220-pound weight. Friends described him as a ball of fire, which he was, except when he was with Emil.

Vince Procino was a tall, slender, quiet man. His thin moustache and shy smile made him attractive to women, but caused some unacknowledged jealousy with the men, including Emil. He worked for Dennison as the head of Advertising and Promotion, doing a capable, workmanlike job.

Both men were silent as Emil walked back from the window, calming down a little. Emil was breathing heavily from the effort of moving his large frame.

"When I was at Harvard," he said, "there was a Professor Singleton or something. He had us go through cases to analyze marketing plans, business plans, strategies, everything. All sorts of companies, Kodak, Bulova, American Motors; all of them, with strategies and plans. Makes us look like amateurs."

"We're not exactly amateurs," Dennison countered. "We're the second-biggest shock absorber company in America—in the world probably. We've got 20 percent of the market. Is that right, Vince?"

Procino quickly responded, "19.2 percent."

"Close enough. We're doing pretty good, turning a profit every year, growing bigger."

"Depends on what your goal is," said Emil. "Blackwell Manufacturing is twice our size." He glanced over at Procino.

"They have 41.6 percent market share," Procino injected, "from our best estimate on last quarter's figures."

"More than twice as big," Emil continued, getting angrier, as if Dennison had questioned his statement. "And they make more than twice our profit. Why the hell aren't we first?"

Dennison did not answer. There was no answer. Blackwell was first because they had more money, more customers, more plants, more salesmen—more everything. And this brought them more profit, which reinforced the whole cycle. Without worrying about Blackwell, Amsaco was fighting like hell to keep ahead of Crane Automotive, who were third and getting closer.

Gross was well aware of this and it made him even angrier. "If we just try to hang on, keep looking over our shoulder, we'll end up further behind. You guys are going to have to change your style. Be more creative, more aggressive."

"But Emil," Dennison countered, "we have a damned aggressive program this year. Vince has put together a very creative package, if we hit the market at the right time. And we have to let the agency get going on it this week, or we're going to have nothing for our National Sales Meeting."

There was silence for a moment, then Emil conceded. "OK, goddamn it, there's nothing we can do. We're stuck with it for now. But I'm telling both of you, I want to see something new, something better—something that will pick up market share. Maybe you guys ought to take one of those marketing seminars."

This stung both Dennison and Procino. They were professionals who *gave* seminars. They were not students. But Dennison said nothing. He had worked for Gross long enough to know when not to argue. He had gotten approval for the program, and it was best to leave. He and Procino gathered up the material and started for the door.

"Will you and Marilyn be able to make our shindig next Saturday?" Dennison asked.

Emil was not in the mood for friendly talk. "Yeah, Marilyn's planning on it," he said without smiling. "Send Betty in."

Before they could get out the door, Betty Johnson, Emil's young secretary, came in with her steno pad. It was obvious she had heard their conversation from her office. She was a good-looking woman in her late twenties, with classic Scandinavian features, blonde hair, blue eyes, and a tall, slender figure. She had started in Customer Service and was promoted to a public relations job before she caught the attention of the boss.

Emil had forced his old secretary to retire in order to take on this good-looking young newcomer. No one suspected a romantic involvement between Emil and Betty Johnson—his excess weight ruled that out—but he was severely criticized for humiliating his old secretary, who had served him well for years. Actually, Betty's good looks were a major factor in her getting the job, but her efficiency, intelligence, and thoroughness were equally as important. She was a good secretary.

Betty just nodded to Dennison and Procino as they left. Vince would usually joke around with her, but this was not the time. She took a seat in front as Emil eased his large frame into his special chair behind the desk.

"Did you get me into the Breakers?" he asked.

"Yes, but it was a problem. They are all filled. Harry Fitzimmons got you the room adjoining the suite. They will have to play musical rooms with our sales staff, and someone will have to double up, but Harry is real glad you can make it. He wondered if you could get down there tonight and play golf with Bob Sanders tomorrow morning. I checked with the hangar, and they can fly you down tonight. The only problem is you're supposed to go to the symphony."

Emil thought for a moment. Although he would not be playing golf, he would much rather be in Florida than to a damn symphony. Marilyn would be mad though.

"Yeah, tell the hangar to have the Falcon ready about 4:00. And tell Harry I'll be down tonight, but no golf. Tell him to set up breakfast with Sanders. I'll call Mrs. Gross. And tell Burch I want to see him. I want the flash figures for the month."

Betty wrote a few notes and left. Emil watched her leave, knowing that everything would be taken care of. There would be a good meal on the plane; Harry Fitzimmons would pick him up at the airport; there would be a bottle of Chivas Regal in his room—everything. Those who had given him a hard time when he put Betty on were wrong. She was as capable as any secretary he had known. And she had a nice ass, besides.

Emil gave a melancholy sigh, picked up the phone, and dialed home. As expected, Marilyn was not happy with the change in schedule.

"I knew you would find some excuse," she said angrily. "I just knew it. The least you could have done was to let me know a week ago, and I could have planned something with someone else."

"Can't be helped," Emil answered. He knew he would get chewed out and he knew he could not talk his way out or intimidate Marilyn in any way. She knew him too well after twenty-seven years. She knew he loved to get on the plane, be served a fancy meal, be met by subordinates, be the center of attention, and live well at a fancy hotel. She knew it, and he knew she knew it. What was worse was that he had no control over her. He could not discipline her and he could not fire her. Not that divorce hadn't been considered. He had thought about it many times when they were battling, but it was basically too much trouble. He needed a wife occasionally for social purposes. She managed the house well, and they were each too set in their routines to separate.

Marilyn seemed content, living her own separate and comfortable life. They had a workable truce, marred occasionally by inconsiderate acts on his part. These acts were accepted at the office because he was the boss, but not at home. This did not stop him from being inconsiderate, but he had to pay the price, which he was doing.

"And don't give me that hard work routine either. Where are you going this time?"

"Down to the Universal Auto Parts meeting—"

"Where are they meeting?"

"This is their annual—"

"Where?" she demanded.

"At the Breakers, Palm Beach."

"Ha!" she shouted. "I really feel sorry for you. Well, go on to your damn hardworking meeting." And she slammed down the phone.

Emil sat with the phone to his ear, feeling foolish and angry. She had no right to hang up on him. "Damn her," he thought. If she was going to act that way, he might as well stay an extra day or two and really enjoy himself.

As he was thinking, Ralph Burch came in carrying two copies of the month's flash report. His position of Vice President of Finance fit like a glove. He was a thin man, in his early fifties, short-haired and—by Emil's standards—excessively neat. He seldom smiled, had no apparent sense of humor, and seemed incapable of emotion of any kind.

Burch was a keen observer, well aware of the emotions and politics going on all around him. Indeed, he had used these to get to his present powerful position.

Amsaco was wholly owned by United Tire in Dallas, and contact with the parent company was with Emil and Ralph. Ralph had direct dealings with the financial people at United and therefore, indirectly, with Emil's boss, Max Simpson. He was really reporting on how good a job Amsaco, and therefore Emil, was doing. It was a sensitive and peculiar job, and it fit Ralph Burch perfectly.

"It doesn't look good at all," he said as he handed a copy of the report to Emil. "Europe is running at less than 50 percent of budgeted profit and it's not getting any better. And U.S. sales are weak. That's really the big problem. If sales don't turn up pretty soon, we won't have a chance to make goal."

Emil looked at the figures. "I don't see how it's going to improve. Dennison is just planning to repeat what we did last year. I don't think there's been a new idea in sales since I left the field."

"Aren't we going after the jobber direct this year?" Burch asked. "Dennison was saying something about—"

"It's the same old crap," Emil said disgustedly. "How is this outfit ever going to come up with something new? I was thinking of maybe going outside. Get some new blood."

"Good marketing men are scarce...and expensive," said Burch cautiously.

"I'm thinking of a college professor—the young man who gave that seminar at Harvard. He knew everything about every company you could imagine. Maybe we could use some outside thinking."

"I don't know," Burch said slowly. "His theories might be great, but putting them in action is another thing."

"I'm not thinking of putting him in charge," Emil countered. "Just let him feed new ideas into the system. Let him work for Procino. It might work. Anyway, I'm just thinking about it." Burch had an odd expression on his face—actually a smile. "What are you smiling about?"

"You're thinking of letting a *college professor* loose in this place? I doubt he could survive."

"Maybe not. But if he does, we might develop a new species, an intelligent marketing man." Emil laughed and Burch's smile became more pronounced.

Emil got them quickly back on track. "What about Europe? Does Griebe have control of that operation?"

"Control is the word. We can't get him to do anything. He should be cutting back right now, but he won't. Says they've never had a layoff and things will improve. He's a bleeding heart, that Kraut, and I don't trust him."

Emil thought for a moment, then called Miss Johnson. "Betty, get me Hans Griebe on the phone. If he's left the office already, get him at home."

Turning to Burch he asked, "Where do we stand on the five-year plan? I have to call Simpson this morning."

"We're in trouble," Burch responded quickly. "If sales don't pick up this year, we can't show such a major increase in the next year, so we have to reduce our projections each year of the plan. It could be embarrassing."

"Goddamn it Ralph, don't you have any good news?"

"Not while sales are down."

"OK, damn it. Well, get me the preliminary five-year figures. And compare them to last year's plan. I have to call Simpson and let him know what's coming."

As Burch left, Emil yelled, "Betty, get me Max Simpson on the phone."

"Before I get Mr. Griebe in Frankfurt?" she asked.

"Whichever line comes first."

The foreign lines were busy and the call to Max Simpson came through first. Emil was not anxious to give bad news to his boss at United, and his mood was getting worse the more he thought about it. When he told Max of the trouble with sales, his fears were confirmed.

"I don't like the sound of that at all, Emil," Max said slowly in the Texas drawl he had acquired since being promoted to Dallas. "This slump is lasting a little too long."

"I don't like it either, Max. It's starting to affect the five-year figures."

"Oh? That's even worse. I want the details on that. The long-range planning committee is meeting on Thursday, and I need your best estimates on what the final plan will show. They don't like to be surprised. I need you and Ralph down here tomorrow. We have to go into it in depth."

"Sure Max. Ralph is putting the figures together right now. We'll have a pretty good feel by tomorrow."

"Good. Get in by noon. We'll have lunch first."

"OK. Sounds good," said Emil. "By the way, Max," he added. "I've got Dennison working on a plan for boosting U.S. sales. That's the key. And we may go outside for extra help."

"Good," said Simpson "Do what you have to do. You have to get things turned around."

"OK, see you tomorrow. Bye."

There was no response from Simpson before he hung up. Emil did not like that, or the tone of the whole conversation. And he definitely did not like going to Dallas to go over bad news with his boss, rather than to Palm Beach and a sales meeting.

He called in his secretary and told her about his change of plans. "Tell the hangar we'll leave at 8:00, Burch and me," he said. "And call my wife and tell her I'll be home tonight, but too late for the symphony." Emil was in no mood to speak to Marilyn about his bad luck.

"And, oh yeah, cancel out my lunch with Chessman. I'll be going over the five-year plan with Burch."

"Should I get you some sandwiches?" asked Betty. "An assortment?" This was an undiscussed code that allowed Betty to get three sandwiches, without asking him the embarrassing question of how many he wanted.

"Yeah, and see what Burch wants."

As Betty left, Emil dialed Dave Dennison on his speakerphone and, in a loud voice, filled him in on tomorrow's meeting. "I told Simpson you're working on a new marketing plan, something to get us out of this rut, and damn it Dave, I want something on my desk by Friday."

He was about to elaborate when Betty buzzed him on the intercom to tell him the call to Germany was ready.

Hans Griebe had just come home from a well-organized day as Managing Director of the Amsaco European operations. He was relaxing with a glass of his favorite Mosel, looking forward to a nice meal with his family.

Emil continued to vent his anger, this time on the unsuspecting Griebe.

"Damn it Griebe," he started, by way of saying hello, "I just went over the month-end results with Ralph Burch, and you're not doing well at all. You're not holding up your end."

Hans did not know exactly what Emil meant by "holding up your end," but he understood the basic message. He answered carefully in precise, accented English, "I realize, Emil, that we are not doing as well as we hoped, but all of Europe is slow...and we are still profitable."

"Profitable?" Emil yelled. "Profitable may be good enough for you, but it's not for me. I have to go down to Dallas tomorrow and tell Max Simpson that you're running at 50 percent of budgeted profit, and he isn't gonna like it. We didn't build up the European operation to break even. We have a lot of money invested and we need our forecasted return. Otherwise, we look like amateurs."

"I understand," said Hans quietly.

"Well, what are you gonna do? If sales aren't gonna pick up, then you have to cut costs. And that means heads."

"Emil, that is very difficult to do in Germany," Hans explained. "We have government regulations, which do not let us do many of the things you do in America." He had of course been over all this before with the American parent company.

"Bullshit, Griebe. You find some way."

There was silence for a moment. Then Emil continued. "I don't know how to operate in Europe, Hans. That's why you're there. That's why we pay you so much. You find a way to get your costs in line with sales. You understand?"

"Yes," said Hans slowly, "I understand. We will determine a plan."

"I'd like to see that plan, along with next month's flash report. And it should show just exactly how you're going to meet forecasted profits."

"We will, Emil. We will find some way."

"Good. Now we are communicating."

As Hans Griebe hung up the receiver, he turned to his wife and said deliberately, "That Emil Gross is a madman."

Emil was not mad, but he was still angry. He struggled to lift his weight from his chair and walked slowly to his private bathroom.

"Goddamn Kraut," he thought. "He doesn't intend to cut any heads. All he'll give me in the plan will be garbage."

Crossing over to the toilet, he cursed his poor luck. "And Dennison won't have any marketing plan worth a damn either. That son of a bitch doesn't have an ounce of creativity, and he thinks he can do my job yet. No doubt about it, I've got to bring in that Professor Singleton, and shove him down Dennison's throat if I have to. I'll call him tomorrow. No, damn it, I'll be with Simpson tomorrow."

He thought about his disrupted plans as he slowly unzipped his extra-length fly from his belly to his crotch. "And a helluva lot of sympathy I get from Marilyn. She thinks I just have one ball around here, goddamn her."

As he fumbled with his underwear in that unknown area below his belly, his frustration increased. "And goddamn it, I can't even see what I'm doing when I take a leak."

3. The Corporate Wife

This was the kind of trip Ray thought was a perk available only to football recruits and rich alumni. He and Dorothy were flying back first class, after two days of wining and dining with the executives of Amsaco in Jackson, Michigan.

On the first day, they toured the plant with Bob Simpranian, head of Engineering, looked at homes in Jackson with Vince and Ruth Procino, and dined at the Jackson Country Club with Emil and Marilyn Gross and Dave and Ann Dennison. The dinner at the club was first class, with three different wines served with six courses.

The second day, Vince Procino made Ray a job offer that had to be taken seriously. Now, at 35,000 feet, Ray leaned back comfortably in his first-class seat, smiled, and raised his champagne in a toast to his wife. She returned his toast and his smile, and sipped the champagne. "I could get used to this," she said.

"It sure beats flying coach," he agreed.

"And going by bus." It was true, they had made many trips by bus. Not only was it the only way to get to some of the other schools throughout New England, but it was a prudent and practical way to travel on an Assistant Professor's salary.

Ray watched his wife as she leaned back and closed her eyes, holding her glass of champagne on the arm of her seat, a dreamy smile on her face. Although motherhood had added a few inches here and there, Dorothy was still attractive, and in Ray's mind, getting prettier. After going through all the crazy hairdos of the sixties, she now wore her sandy-colored hair cut short. This simple, unsophisticated look matched her face—with her tiny nose, beautiful green eyes, and impish smile. It matched her personality as well. The hairdo was honest, and so was Dorothy.

"I suppose you could get used to the country club, too," he said, teasing her.

Dorothy opened her eyes. "That was some meal. I thought I'd die when they brought out that Beef Wellington."

"Me too," Ray said, laughing. After the shrimp and oysters with champagne, and then Mosel wine with trout, Ray and Dorothy were ready for dessert. But out came the main course—and more red wine.

"And the desserts," she added. "If that's the way executives eat all the time, I'll weigh 200 pounds. And you'll be as big as Mr. Gross."

"I don't think we have to worry. We wouldn't be eating at the club very often."

"Would we be expected to join?"

"Depends on priorities, but I think we could afford it. Pretty soon, if I can move up the proverbial corporate ladder." He thought for a moment and added, "I suppose that's why they took us there, to show what we could expect if we accept."

"I suppose so," she said, closing her eyes again. "Weird," she murmured. It was all unexpected, unreal. She had become comfortable with their life at school and never thought about such a drastic change. Her plans for the future had revolved around Ray's academic career and raising their two children. Ray had talked about doing some consulting—after the kids grew up. They could travel together and she could be his assistant. Or they might start a business.

Dorothy had worked as an editorial assistant for a nonprofit organization. Her degree was from Smith, with a major in English, and she had intended to pursue a career in publishing. Those thoughts faded when she married Ray and became immersed in raising children, running the home, and the social life connected with being a faculty wife.... This potential change was major... and she was scared.

They knew no one in the Midwest. New England was their home. Dorothy's mother lived in Newton and her brother Henry and his family lived in Waltham. Even visiting her sister Gloria in Brattleboro, Vermont, seemed quite a trip. Going to Michigan would be like leaving the country.

Ray's parents had retired to their summer home on Cape Cod.

Taking the kids away would be hard on their grandparents. And what about the kids? Paul was eleven and Barbara was nine. They had lived most of their lives in their present home. They had a lot of friends in Boston, none in Michigan. "A move like this could be tough for the kids," she pointed out.

He dismissed the idea. "Nah. Kids are resilient. In a month they'll have new friends and will have forgotten Boston."

"What about their grandparents? They would miss their grand-parents."

"Yeah, that's true," Ray agreed. "But look on the bright side. We'll be a thousand miles away from your brother."

Dorothy laughed a little, but added, "But I'd miss Emily and the kids. Paul and Barbara really do love their cousins."

"Yeah, but it's not like we'll never see them. We'll still visit them and they'll visit us. It might even be more fun that way."

"Yeah...it might," Dorothy half agreed. She sipped her cham-pagne and thought some more. It could be just a grand adventure for the kids. The Midwest was different from New England. They would learn from new teachers and new friends. It would broaden their perspective, add another dimension to their experience. And they could show off their New England knowledge. It could be good for the kids. Then why was she holding back?

Maybe it was fear for herself. Ray would have his work and the kids would have their friends from school, but she would be alone. She was good at making friends, but her new friends would be wives of executives—instead of professors' wives and old friends she'd known for years. Would she have anything in common with "corporate" midwesterners?

It was scary. She had to think this through. "Aren't you scared at all?" she asked.

Ray answered the question as if Dorothy had asked about the job. "Sure, a little," he said. "But it seems they really want me. You should have heard Mr. Gross introduce me to Vince. 'Vince, this is Ray Singleton, the college professor who's gonna make you a hero.'"

"Singleton?"

Ray laughed. "I corrected him, but that seemed to annoy him. 'Now look...*Pendleton*,' he said, 'Vince is the best damn advertising man in the industry.' He talked about what a powerful combination they'd have with my planning and strategy combined with Vince's experience. He told me, 'Don't let these guys scare you away with stories about how tough it is here, or how hard we have to work. We work hard sure, but we get paid good too. And we have fun doing it.' Then he told Vince to show me around. He said, 'All I want to know is when he's going to start.' So Vince and I spent the morning together. I liked him. What did you think?"

"He really didn't say much." Emil and Dennison had done the talking. "But he seemed nice."

Ray nodded in agreement. "And I think he's honest."

"Why do you say that?"

He told me that at first he wasn't too happy about me coming aboard. That it was kind of an insult to him and Dave Dennison for Emil to go around them. And they certainly had no need for a lot of crazy ideas. They were having enough trouble with their jobbers now."

"Jobbers?"

"That's their customers. It's confusing. They sell to the WD, the Warehouse Distributor, who sells to the Jobbers, the auto parts stores, who sell to the garages and service stations. I guess business is a little slow and they're getting a lot of flack."

"If business is bad, why are they hiring?"

"Well, they're looking for some new ideas. Something to increase their market share."

"Can you do that?"

"I don't know," he answered. "I mean, I know my field. I'm a good teacher. But Harvard is a hell of a way from the automotive aftermarket. And 'doing' is a lot different than 'teaching.' But I might know a lot of things from other company success stories that I can apply here." He paused and looked at Dorothy. "That's what I told Vince...that I was apprehensive. I think that's when we started to hit it off. He probably was expecting some sort of 'lesson' from the teacher. He told me he was apprehensive too, and so was Dennison. But then he said, 'Who knows? Maybe this sort of marriage really will give us something no one else has.' When he finally made me the job offer, I think he really wanted me to accept."

Dorothy was still not convinced, but Ray continued as the meals were served. "The money has got to be considered," he pointed out. "Forty thousand dollars a year...that's almost a 50 percent raise. And if I move up, there'll be a hell of a lot more."

Dorothy said nothing and he continued. "And the rest of the package—profit sharing, insurance, pension, it's all there. Plus expense account, the company plane, the meetings at fancy resorts, and stuff I never even thought of." He grinned at his wife, "If our friends could see us now."

She smiled back, paused thoughtfully, and asked, "What about the work, Ray? It seems strange that you can work all these years teaching, gaining that experience, and then step into a new career where you have no experience, and make all that money—it's like something Henry would dream up. Doesn't any of this worry you?"

Ray had been thinking the same way. His colleagues and students had been ridiculing and condemning the "enemy world" of business for years. Business caused pollution and poverty and wars. Businessmen were insensitive to the people they were supposed to serve and only looked for ways to improve profits. Besides that, they were ruthless and cunning in their own small political world. Ray was poised to enter this enemy world and was not even sure he could do the job. If he couldn't, he would be left without income, job, or contacts in Michigan. Even worse, how could he go back to teaching others, if he couldn't do the job himself? To leave the safety of his present environment was frightening.

"I don't know, hon," he said, sipping his champagne. "It's scary all right. But, if I can't do the job, why are they offering it to me? Why do they want me?"

Dorothy looked seriously at her husband. "I got the feeling that Mr. Gross wants you and thinks you can do the job. I didn't get that feeling from Mr. Dennison."

Ray half smiled. "Well, if it can't be unanimous, I would rather have the President on my side."

"Ann Dennison told me her husband was next in line to succeed Mr. Gross. And, I hate to say this, but with Mr. Gross weighing so much, I hate to depend on him for very long."

Ray sat back and thought. Dorothy was right in bringing this up. Ray knew how rapidly things changed in the business world. There certainly was little security in making such a move. That had to be considered.

Still, it was not as if they were leaving civilization. Corporate executives were still human beings, with talents, ambitions, and morals, like people in the academic world. True, they seemed more ruthless, more subject to emotional decisions, and quicker to act. But what could really happen? What was the worst that could happen?

"What could really happen if it didn't work out?" Ray said thoughtfully. "All they could do is fire me. It would be a blow to my ego, but that's the worst." They looked at each other. He gulped down the rest of his champagne and continued. "But, what if I could get a leave of absence for a year or two? To do research in a real company, in real time, under real conditions. I'll bet I could sell the school on that. If it doesn't work out, we go back to Harvard. Then that becomes the worst...and that's where we are right now."

He sat up straighter. "But that's not what will happen, Dot," he said enthusiastically. "I can do this work. I know what I'm doing, and this is my chance to do something myself, rather than just talking about it. My work will become the case study."

He was staring straight ahead now, not really talking to his wife. "If I don't take this chance, I'll wonder the rest of my life if I could have done it. It's a challenge that may never come up again. I can put all my knowledge to use, not just teach it to students. I can put plans to work. I can change things. What would Henry say about that? And I know what I'm doing. I've taught business executives and studied their styles. I've—"

Dorothy Pendleton watched her husband as he went on. She was surprised at his exuberance and a little frightened. He had never shown much emotion about his work. She did not know this side of him. He did not seem to be the quiet college professor she knew, carefully viewing the world. She still was not sure he was making the right choice, but it was clear the decision was his: she no longer had any say in it. Dorothy was about to become a corporate wife.

"Ray," she said and touched his arm to get his attention.

He stopped mid-sentence and blinked at her in surprise.

"Let's rent for a couple of years before we think about buying a house," she said.

4. The American Barrel

Ray reported for work on June 1, 1976. As he sat in the lobby filling out personnel forms, he felt what it was like to be a complete stranger. He watched people walking by. These people knew their jobs. They were confident and secure. Ray, however, had never worked for a large company before. He was not even sure what he was supposed to do in his job. He might be expected to know things that he did not know. Maybe he would come up with ideas that people would laugh at. Maybe he would just be that "foolish Professor." Maybe Henry was right after all.

The thought of Henry saying "I told you so" was in his mind when he entered Vince Procino's office. Luckily that was his first stop. Had he spoken to Emil Gross first, he might have gone right back to Boston.

"Welcome to the rat race," Vince said, smiling.

"Its good to be here," Ray answered, looking around. Vince had a good-sized desk of cherry, a high-backed swivel chair, three big files, and enough room for three chairs on the other side of his desk. The linoleum floor had a small rug at the doorway.

Vince introduced Ray to the others in the department. They each had a title of "Manager" and a cubicle in the area outside Vince's office. There were managers for Customer Service, Product Planning, Advertising and Promotion, Pricing, and Sales Administration. Janet Holden was Department Secretary. There were a few jokes about being ready to learn from the professor and who would be awarded the dunce cap. Overall though, he was greeted warmly and welcomed into the department.

"We gave you Stanley's desk," Janet said as she showed Ray his cubicle.

"Stan Bronski is a Territory Manager in New Jersey," Vince explained. "We'll find some place for him when he comes in next fall. Why don't you just get settled. Then c'mon in and I'll fill you in on who's who at Amsaco. Emil wants to see us at 11:00. Then we can talk about what you'll be doing."

"Yeah. I've been wondering about that."

"Emil's got a lot of people reporting to him," Vince explained. "Here, let me show you on the organization chart." He pulled out a looseleaf book and opened to the first page.

AMSACO ORGANIZATION

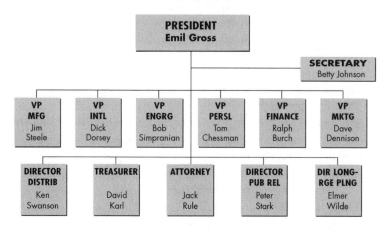

"That's twelve people reporting to him," Vince continued. "It gives him tight control over everything that's going on."

"Seems like a lot of people," Ray mused. "Who are the key ones?"

Vince smiled. "That's a good question. And it's hard to answer. But we think of Dave Dennison as the second in command. He's followed the same path as Emil, and he knows the customers. Then there's Jim Steele, who runs internal operations. Bob Simpranian runs Engineering and is always fighting with Jim. Bob's strictly an engineer, and he wants us to have the best product in the industry. Jim argues that we can't afford to be so good. We have to compromise and make shocks that are easier to manufacture. They're both good men, but I think Jim's got Emil's ear. He usually gets his way." Vince paused, then added, "We usually side with Simpranian."

"And lose?" Ray joked.

"Yeah, because accounting's always against anything that costs money. Dave tells me about the battles in Emil's staff meetings and—"

Just then a short, stocky man with a friendly smile came into the office, interrupting Vince. "Sorry to butt in," he said, "but Janet said the professor was in here."

"Sure is," said Vince. "Ray, this is Al Goldman. I asked Al to come meet you and help me give you the inside scoop on Amsaco. Al's the only friend we have in Accounting."

Al shook hands with Ray and laughed. "I'm not really a friend. A bean counter and a salesman can't be friends. I'm just the only one in accounting who'll tell Vince *why* he's wrong."

There was a friendliness about Al Goldman that Ray could feel. He smiled and said, "Well, that's what friends are for."

Goldman sat down and asked Ray, "What kind of misinformation is Vince giving you?"

Ray pointed to the organization chart and answered, "Vince is filling me in on who's important in the company. We were just talking about Jim Steele and—"

"Don't worry about them," Al interrupted. "Tom Chessman is the only one you need to know about."

Vince laughed, and so did Al.

"What do you mean?" Ray asked. "Chessman's in charge of Personnel, right? But Steele has a bigger job, runs all of Manufacturing. And Dennison runs Marketing."

"Not to mention he's our boss," Vince added.

"And Burch handles all the finance," Al agreed. "But none of them play gin with Emil every afternoon." He stopped to let that thought sink in, then continued. "Suppose Steele thought you were real smart, and Burch thought you were doing a good job. Then one day Tom Chessman tells Emil he doesn't trust you, that you're were hiding the real numbers to make your project look good. You'd be on the defensive the next time you saw Emil. And nothing you'd say would help, because he would suspect anything you said."

"But what about Steele or Burch?" Ray asked.

"They don't care," Al answered. "If Emil's against you, why should they risk defending you?"

Vince was grinning. Ray wondered for an instant if it was all a joke. "But how can Chessman have that much power?"

Al said, "I've heard Emil say if he really wants to know what's happening, he asks Tom."

Vince looked at Ray's shocked expression. "Don't worry. Tom's got an unusual management style, but all you have to do is get him on your side."

"How do I do that?"

Vince and Al both laughed as Al said simply, "Just say nice things about Personnel...and Tom." He looked at Vince and got a little more serious. "Some people don't know this and complain about the poor job Personnel is doing. The next thing they know, their department is being investigated for something or other. Tom always knows where a few skeletons are hidden and operates on the theory that a good offense is the best defense. Most managers know this. We're just telling you all this as a friendly gesture. Have you met Tom yet?"

"I have an appointment tomorrow morning."

"Good luck. Now, that takes care of lesson number one. Who else do you want to know about?"

Vince showed Al the organization chart. "We're just going over the chart. We covered Steele and—"

Al looked at the chart and ran his finger across the names. "Simpranian is an engineer, 100 percent engineer. And Dennison is 100 percent salesman. Swanson is...I don't know that he's 100 percent anything, but he's competent running Distribution."

"How about Burch?" Vince asked with a smile. "Your boss. Is he 100 percent accountant?"

"At the very least. He lives and breathes finance. Is friendly with no one. I'm Manager of Budgets, but we don't say three words a day to each other. The gals in the office joke about his 'budgeted' sex life, and his two children as his 'return on his investment.' They can be awful."

Al started to laugh. "You probably haven't heard this yet Vince, but you will. The other day in the lunchroom..." He leaned closer, as did Ray. "You know Darlene in Payables...well you probably don't. Anyway, she's been trying to become pregnant, without any success. So her buddies take this jar, fill it halfway with liquid soap, and put on a label that says, 'Please contribute to Darlene's sperm bank.' Then they had a sign-in sheet with three names signed in so far, Richard Nixon, George Wallace, and Ralph Burch."

Vince and Al laughed loudly. Ray looked surprised.

Vince looked at Ray and laughed again. "Here's another piece of advice. Stay away from the lunchroom during break. I bet they don't teach that at Harvard."

"You guys are scaring the hell out of me," Ray said, going along.

Al looked at Ray and said more seriously, "But don't think of Ralph as a buffoon. Never underestimate him. Also, don't underestimate my boss, Dick Wise, our Comptroller."

Vince put both hands in the air and said, "Amen."

"Dick is like Ralph's voice," Al went on. "He thinks the same way, but he talks all the time. His philosophy of business is simple: Only accountants know how to run a business. Manufacturing people only want more and more equipment to make sure they can always deliver the product, no matter how much they screw up. They have no concept of what return on investment really means. Engineers only want a beautiful, long-lasting, high-performance product, no matter what it costs. They have no concern for profitability. The salesmen are even worse, always trying to give the product away at the lowest prices, coming up with expensive merchandising programs, high-cost advertising and long payment terms. Sales volume and market share are all they care about. Dick tells this to anyone who walks into his office, at sales meetings, at management meetings, and anywhere he can get an audience."

Ray smiled. "I ought to be writing this down."

Al stood up and looked at the organization chart. "We're giving you good information. Now, who else do you want to know about? How about Dorsey?"

"The international guy?"

"Yeah, everyone likes to help Dick. You wind up with a free trip to South America or someplace. But to understand Dorsey you have to know the history of the Livingstons and the old American Shock Absorber Company. You see Mel Livingston was—"

Vince interrupted. "Maybe we better get into that some other time. Emil wanted to meet with Ray this morning."

"Oh, I don't want to get in the way of that. Emil probably wants to get your priorities straight. The old 'your ass belongs to me now' speech."

"What do you mean?" Ray asked.

"You'll see. Nothing special. Just that you're not supposed to let anything get in the way of your job—like families, or sleeping, or unimportant stuff like that. It's a compliment, actually. Emil only gives that speech to important guys."

■ ■ ■

Goldman was right. Emil spent the first five minutes telling Ray that by accepting his paycheck, he was agreeing to absolute allegiance to Amsaco, twenty-four hours a day, seven days a week. "That doesn't mean you work all the time," Emil explained. "I understand the importance of family. But at any time, if Amsaco needs you, that's your first priority. Saturdays, Sundays, evenings, whatever's necessary. The guys that make it with us are willing to pay the price. You understand?"

"Sure," Ray answered, although Emil had never mentioned that when he was being recruited. No one had. "I've always done all the work necessary to get the job done."

"Good. Now figure on working twice as hard as that and you'll get somewhere at Amsaco."

Ray thought it was best not to argue. He looked over at Vince, who just nodded in agreement.

"Now, let's get specific," Emil continued. "What I want from you is another American Barrel."

Ray looked confused. "An American Barrel?"

Emil looked at Vince. "You haven't told him about the American Barrel?"

"He just started an hour ago," Vince said defensively.

"Well then, you've already wasted an hour," Emil scolded Vince. He turned toward Ray and said very slowly, "If you understand the American Barrel, you'll know what I want from you… from Marketing, period."

Vince squirmed as Emil continued. "In the replacement shock absorber business, we're running a poor second—almost third. What are the market share figures Vince?"

"Blackwell's got the biggest share, a little over 40 percent. We're a little under 20 percent. And Crane is around 16 percent."

Emil banged his fist on his desk. "I don't like it. We can't make any money with Blackwell controlling the market. We can't raise prices unless they do. We can't get the best accounts like NAPA because they'll send in a hundred men to nurture them. They advertise much more and much better than we do. And we're always on the defensive, protecting against losing our accounts rather than taking theirs. They're first, and we're last, and I don't like it."

"Actually, Crane's last," Vince corrected him.

"Crane's got more than just shocks," Emil replied angrily. "They've got hard parts and filters. They've got Sears and a bunch of discount warehouses, and they're happy. And Blackwell's the leader in shocks so they're happy. But all we have are shocks and we're not the leader. I'm not happy." He looked at Ray. "You understand?"

"Yeah...uh—huh," Ray stammered. "But the American Barrel? What's that?"

Emil calmed down and smiled. "Twenty-five years ago, back in the fifties, we were in a similar position. Even worse, because no one was buying replacement shocks. If people did replace shocks, they went back to the car dealers. I was out in Kansas City trying to make a living selling shocks to warehouse distributors. The distributors tried to sell them to the jobbers, who sold them to the service stations. But customers weren't buying. People were driving with worn-out shocks for years. I figured I had to find a way to sell them or go into some other line of work."

Emil paused to think, and Ray looked around the luxurious office. It was obvious that Emil had found a way.

Emil continued. "I was complaining one day to Ed Rifkin, a Jobber in Osawatomie, and we decided we had to do something. We had to show those bastards why they needed shocks. I think you call that educating the consumer. Anyway, we got a local machine shop to mount two shocks on top of a barrel, one a worn shock, the other a new Amsaco one, with a long handle to let you push the shocks in and out. He painted the barrel with Amsaco's blue and white, and we talked a local garage into trying it out. The mechanic would let the customer try it out, feel the difference in the resistance of the worn-out shock and the Amsaco. Then he would explain how the new shock would keep the car from bouncing up and down when it hit a bump or took a sharp turn. This would mean a much better ride, and longer life to the tires.

"The local garage tried it. In the first month, they did five shock jobs. Shocks were no big deal for them, but hell, they had *quintupled sales*. I spent my own money to build twenty-five more barrels. Rifkin placed them around the area, and we taught the mechanics how to use them. I gave it the name 'American Barrel.'

"The results were fantastic. Ed's shock sales tripled. I put it in all over my territory and made 'Salesman of the Year.' When I moved up to District Manager in the Northeast I did the same thing there. Then I was called into the home office to develop a national 'American Barrel' program."

Emil sat back and smiled. "That was Amsaco's moment of glory. The total replacement shock market grew tremendously every year, and we had the major share. Eventually, Blackwell came into the after-market with a copy of the program. With their big field force and their money, they took back a good portion of the market. Crane Automotive also came in and took a minor share. The beauty of the program, though, was that the total shock market grew enough to make all three companies better off. We had made salesmen out of thousands of mechanics, all over the country. We built up an industry."

"Wow," was all Ray could say. He was impressed—this would make a great case study. Then the thought hit him. "And that's what you want me to do?"

"Damn right. That's exactly what I want. Damn right." He looked at Vince. "I don't want the same old ad campaign, the same old crap warmed over. I want something new, something that will change things, something that will give us a bigger market share." He looked back at Ray. "That's why you're here. You gotta come up with something to set the industry back on their ass."

Ray sat with his mouth slightly open and said nothing.

Emil picked up some papers on his desk, indicating the meeting was over. "It's a great opportunity," he said looking down at the papers. "Welcome to Amsaco."

■ ■ ■

"How can he expect me to just come up with something that will change an industry?" Ray asked Dorothy that night. "What does he think they teach at Harvard?"

Dorothy was cooking supper after chasing all over town to get the kids enrolled in school, meeting with the realtor who had found the house they were renting, stocking up on groceries. There were boxes all over the living room and in the bedrooms. She had just finished clearing a space in the kitchen for the four of them to sit down and eat. She did not want to hear any bad news, but she could see the worry on Ray's face and she tried to make him feel a little better.

"This was just the first day," she reasoned. "It's got to be a little scary. Things will get better. Tomorrow will be better."

Ray thought of tomorrow's meeting with Tom Chessman. He knew from Goldman and Vince that he had to say nice things about Tom and his department. And maybe he could discuss some interesting personnel cases from Harvard. Maybe he could find out more about Emil and what he really wanted. Chessman was a personnel man. He had to know psychology and the personalities of other key people. Ray would ask questions rather than try to impress him. This all made sense to Ray's logical mind. In no way was he prepared for Tom Chessman.

5. Chessman

Tom Chessman greeted Ray with a booming, "So you're the goddamn college professor who is gonna teach this goddamn company how to operate."

Although Chessman spoke from behind his desk in his private office, Ray was sure he was heard right down the whole row of executive offices of Amsaco, and probably into the parking lot as well. Ray was taken back, but smiled hesitantly, as he continued to approach the desk with his hand outstretched. "Yes, I'm Ray Pendleton." As they shook hands he continued, "The goddamn college professor, but I'm not going to teach anyone anything."

Chessman was a good-looking man, with a full head of dark hair that was beginning to grey at the temples. He was developing a paunch that could no longer be restrained and that bulged over his belt. Despite a few excess pounds, he looked fairly athletic. He grinned at Ray. Then, as if the first test was passed, said, "Good! Sit down."

Ray exhaled and smiled uneasily as he settled into a chair facing Tom. He had been prepared for an interesting reception from Chessman, but no one had told him exactly what to expect. His aggressive greeting was not designed to put Ray at ease.

Emil had told him, "Tom knows everything that's going on, everywhere. Whenever I want to know what's happening, I ask Tom." Emil described his tactics as "a little unusual" and said he made enemies of the "deadbeats," but he got the job done. "I depend on Tom," Emil had told Ray.

Vince Procino referred to Tom's "unusual management style." Even the department secretary, Janet, would only say, "Yes, Mr. Chessman is different. He scares most of us."

Ray would have to tread carefully. He would have to work with

Chessman. He couldn't afford to make an enemy of him or be labeled a "deadbeat."

Ray took a breath and launched an opening statement. "Emil said I should be sure to talk to you as soon as I started. He figured if I'm to be successful as Manager of—"

"There's no way you can tell if a Manager is going to be successful until you drop him in and let him sink," Tom interrupted. "I hear more goddamn talk about this guy can't do the job, or that guy will fail for some damn reason, and they don't know. Every manager feels that he's the only one that knows how to do the job. How the hell did he ever learn?"

Tom looked at Ray as if only an idiot would disagree, and paused. Ray said, "I certainly wouldn't disagree with that. At Harvard my department head—"

"Their big problem," Tom interrupted again, "is they don't pay what they should. They let their best men leave because they have no imagination. They're afraid." Tom turned and pulled out a computer run from the credenza behind him. "I checked this out. You know we pay less than the fortieth percentile on our pay grade. That means if a guy has a range of twenty-four to thirty thousand a year, we're paying on the average, less than twenty-seven." He punched a few numbers into his calculator. "Less than twenty-six four."

Tom pushed the printout toward Ray and called to his secretary in the outer office. "Marge, get me Ralph Rizzo down in Jacksonville. And bring in some coffee for this guy." He turned to Ray and asked, "You want some coffee?"

Ray didn't know whether to get back to his opening statement or comment on the computer printout in front of him. He just said, "Thanks, I'll have it black."

Tom yelled, "Black," and walked over to the closet. Ray just watched with a frozen half-smile as Tom reached into the rear of the closet and pulled out a golf club. It looked like it was a pretty expensive driver. Tom gripped it and whipped the head carefully across the top of the plush carpet. It was obvious he knew how to handle the club.

"This damn thing costs me five strokes a round," said Tom. "I hit the damn ball 300 yards and when it strays I have a hell of a time breaking 75. I'm going to get a graphite one."

Ray was not sure if he should believe Tom. He was a pretty good golfer himself, but had to play well to stay in the 80s. And the idea of a graphite club did not fit.

"If you hit the ball so far, wouldn't a graphite club make you stray even more, and get you in even more trouble?"

Tom looked up, annoyed. "You have to know how to swing a graphite," he answered. "Most guys swing too hard."

He swished the club back and forth as his secretary came in carrying a cup of coffee. "Mr. Rizzo is on line one," she said as she placed the cup in front of Ray. She was a good-looking, well-built woman in her early thirties. She looked at Ray with a hint of mischief in her eyes. She smiled courteously and left.

Tom pushed a button on his speakerphone, and leaned toward it as he said, "Ralph, how ya doin'?"

The voice came back from the speaker, "Hi, Tom. I suppose you're checking on your club."

"Yeah. This one I got is killing me. I missed the fairway eight times Sunday."

"It ain't the club, Tom. I'll bet you're still swinging from the heels. Just slow down your backswing and you can save $100."

"What's this $100?" asked Tom. "Are you taking a commission? A good graphite shouldn't go more than $75. Tell Pierce to send it up here. I'll get a check down for $75, but tell him to move his ass. I'll have a ten handicap before he gets it packed."

"He mailed it Thursday," said Rizzo, laughing. "Send him a check for $87.88. You know the address?"

"Yeah, Marge has it. How's negotiations going? Gonna have a walkout? If your high-priced shipbuilders at the Yards walk, it sends a bad message to our poor autoworkers."

Ray figured Ralph Rizzo must be at Commerce Yards, a big shipbuilding company also owned by United Tire.

"No, it looks pretty good," Rizzo said. "We gave them a good package, including the start of dental. Unless they just want to be mean, they should ratify. Calio says he can control them."

"Can he?"

"Not really, but we made him look good with this package. Even gave them dental."

"Well, you guys have plenty of money. Might as well pass it

around. Will you be at the management meeting at Doral this year?"

"Yeah. Maybe we can chase your ball around, if we can keep it in sight. See you there."

"Great! See ya. Thanks, Ralph."

"Bye."

Tom turned to Ray and said, "Rizzo's a patsy. He didn't have to give them dental. Dental coverage is the most expensive benefit you can give. Everyone who hasn't been to the dentist in years goes and gets his whole mouth redone. But Rizzo's so afraid of a strike, he just gave them everything. They might go out anyway, just to show who's running the place. Rizzo wouldn't last a year in this place. He doesn't understand people."

Ray sat there. He couldn't think of anything to say that made sense. His academic background was based on logic, and he hadn't come across any since he entered Tom's office. Luckily, all he had to do was to sip his coffee with his half-smile frozen on his face as Tom continued.

"I studied under Kaufman at NYU, and he was the best in labor negotiations. He could tell what the final contract would be after two meetings. Knew exactly what everyone wanted, and what they would give up, and how to get them to do it. Taught me more than any of those *professors*." Ray was confused, since of course Kaufman was a professor. And Chessman evidently expected Ray to respond to his challenge—he peered at him over the top of his glasses.

Ray put down his coffee cup and said, hesitantly, "Well...uh, of course getting someone to do something you want him to do is what managing is all about. Uh, whether the person is working directly for you or not." He looked at Tom, but Tom just stared at him over the rims of his glasses, so he continued, "You have to... uh, understand what motivates them. Whether it's pride or money or fear or—"

Ray stopped as he saw a smile creep over Tom's face. Tom kept smiling and peering over his glasses, and finally said, "You want to see why people really do things?" He stood up and started for the door, motioning Ray to follow him. "C'mon, let me show you an experiment."

As they passed through the secretary's office, Tom told her they would be back before lunch. They walked toward the new wing under construction. Tom continued to talk.

"I hope you appreciate what I'm teaching you," he said. "I'm doing this because I want you to be successful. I told Gross that you could do the job. He was hesitant about going outside, but I told him we needed new blood, new thinking. So I don't want you to fuck up."

Ray was puzzled. When Emil Gross had contacted him at the business school, he had said he wanted marketing knowledge from outside the company. He told Ray that absolutely no one else at Amsaco knew what his plans were. It did not sound right that Chessman knew about that, much less talked Gross into it.

"You know, Procino was dead set against bringing you in," Tom went on. "Dennison too. They would just as soon leave things as they are, do just what we're doing now, just package it different. They're comfortable with what they're doing and very uneasy with something new. Procino would just as soon see you fade away."

This did not sound right to Ray either—it sounded like an exaggeration. After that morning meeting Ray had the feeling that Vince would be happy to see some new developments.

"Yeah, Procino is good enough at working out the details with our ad agency, but he doesn't have the creativity to conceive a program of his own. And he wants Dennison's job yet. Can't see that no how. No way he could run Marketing."

Ray was bothered by the uncalled-for attack on Vince. Tom seemed to want to sabotage Ray's relationship with his new boss. Ray decided he needed to say something.

"You said you couldn't tell if a manager could do the job until you dropped him in and let him sink," he ventured. "Maybe Vince would show a lot more if he was in a bigger position."

Tom glared at Ray without answering. Ray was not sure if the glare meant "What the hell are you talking about?" or "What are you, some kind of troublemaker?"

At that point they walked into the compressor room. Tom went over to a window looking out on the parking lot. There were about six men at work in the lot. One was tearing up the concrete with a jackhammer, while the others were carting away the pieces and preparing a new section.

Tom pointed to the man with the jackhammer and explained his experiment. "They've been tearing up that place for three days, and that guy on the jackhammer just keeps at it. He must have shaken out his brains by now, but I wanted to see if I could still train him. Now watch, I started this yesterday."

Tom walked over to a valve and started to screw it shut. As he neared the shut position, he looked out the window to see that the jackhammer was in operation. Then he closed the valve.

The hammer went dead. Tom watched as the worker shook it. After a few shakes, the man seemed to remember something and slowly started to point the hammer to the sky. When he had it almost over his head, Tom turned on the air. The man felt the power come back, lowered the hammer, shook his head, and started to work again.

Tom was very serious as he said, "No matter how much shaking or kicking he does, the thing doesn't work until he lifts it within 45 degrees of straight up. Here, let me show you again." Tom checked to see that the hammer was working and shut the valve.

The worker threw the jackhammer down in disgust. Then he picked it back up and started to raise it toward the sky, just as another man walked up to him. Ray figured it must be the foreman. He watched them argue, gesture, and point to the hammer. Just as the worker started to raise the hammer again to show his boss how it worked, the foreman looked toward the compressor room and started to walk toward them.

"Why don't we get out of here," said Ray.

Tom said nothing, but waited at the valve. When the worker had the hammer within 45 degrees of straight up, Tom opened the valve and said, "Let's go."

They hurried through the door and down the hall toward the office. "If I had turned the air back on before he got that thing up to 45 degrees, I would have ruined the whole thing. Now there isn't a damned thing that foreman can say to convince him that the way to unstick a jammed jackhammer isn't to point it in the air."

Ray just walked along looking down, shaking his head, saying nothing. Tom kept talking.

"I'll bet you don't teach anything like that in college, but that's the real world." Ray wasn't sure what deluding a jackhammer operator proved about the "real world," and the phrase irked him—after his discussions with Henry. "That's what you work with to get the job done," Tom continued. "You don't make a profit with theories or books but with simple basics. You sell your product for as much as you can, and you pay as little as you can for materials and labor, whether it's shop labor, or office, or executive. You want a salesman who can get his price, a purchasing agent who squeezes his suppliers, and a personnel man who gets his people to put out the work for minimum pay. That's how the company stays profitable."

This did not sound right to Ray, either. He felt the base of a company was in skillful marketing planning, financial controls, and proper implementation of major programs by the operating groups. Getting his price was part of any salesman's job, but making sure the customers felt they were getting "value" for their money was more important. Getting a good price was part of Purchasing's responsibility, but developing reliable suppliers was the real job. And getting people to work for minimum pay was exactly opposite of what Tom had said himself. He had just shown Ray the computer printouts to prove that managers were not paying enough and losing good people as a result.

As Ray was trying to decide what—if anything—to say, a rather good-looking young woman passed by in the hall. Tom turned to watch her go by and said, "Did you see the tits on that broad? I think she works for Hanson in Accounting. How the hell can he count straight with her around?"

Ray laughed and said, "Maybe counting is overrated. Besides, you have a pretty good-looking woman working for you. Doesn't she distract you?"

"Na," said Tom, "she's no sexpot. I think she's a lesbian."

This shook Ray again, and irritated him. It was not right for anyone to throw out a remark like that, whether or not it was true. It hadn't occurred to Ray that she might be a lesbian, but now as they came to the lunchroom, he found himself wondering if she was.

"Goddamn," Tom boomed, "look at all those broads in the lunchroom. They're ten minutes early for lunch and their goddamn supervisors don't even stop them. They're mostly from Lyons' Manufacturing Engineering group. C'mon, I'll put a stop to this."

Ray trailed along as Tom hurried back to his office. He rushed through to his desk and grabbed the phone. Ray walked slowly past Marge, who smiled calmly. She seemed to be used to her boss rushing past in one direction or another. Ray smiled back at Marge, with the feeling that his smile was stupid, while hers was knowing.

He noticed she was dressed, very attractively, in a red knit dress that was tight fitting but appropriate. She wore her honey-blonde hair shoulder length. He was sure she could not be a lesbian, no way.

Just then a voice came through the speakerphone, "Lyons here."

"Damn it Lyons," Tom started without bothering to say who he was. "Your department is hitting that lunchroom twenty minutes early. I want you to dock every gal a half hour's pay and tell them you'll fire the next one that leaves early."

"Hold on there, Tom. Wait a minute," Lyons said defensively. "We're following all the rules. Starting last week, the Personnel Department asked us to stagger the lunch hours to ease the load on the food lines. We're supposed to go to lunch ten minutes earlier, remember?"

Tom seemed to be taken by surprise by this reference to his own department's directive, but only temporarily.

"Well, your gals were in there twenty minutes early. We can't have them sneaking up this timing."

"OK, Tom, I'll check on it," Lyons said, sounding a little wary. "Actually, when I look around, most of my staff is still here. Are you sure it was my group? It could have been Production Planning in the next office. I don't see any of them around. Exactly who did you see?"

"No damn it, they were your gals, damn near a half hour early. You gotta manage your department."

"Well, I'll check into it," said Lyons, obviously hoping to end the conversation. "We follow the rules here. I'll check it out."

"The only way to make the point is to dock their pay. You can't always be a pal if you're gonna manage."

"OK, I'll check it out."

Tom pushed the button, cutting off the conversation. Turning to Ray, he said, "Those engineers always want to be a pal. They have no discipline."

Ray just listened, his smile frozen on his face, wondering what was next. He did not have to wait long, as Tom reached into his desk, pulled out a deck of cards and a score pad, and started toward the door. He did not indicate where they were going, but just said, "Let's go."

As they passed through the outer office, Marge smiled at Ray as she straightened out her desk, preparing to go to lunch.

They walked down the hall past each executive office, going higher and higher in rank, until they reached the corner office of Emil Gross. Tom walked right past the President's secretary into Gross's office. Betty did not seem surprised and nodded as Ray followed him.

Emil was on the phone and ignored Tom as they came in. Tom went over to his desk, put the cards and score pad down and started to clear off some space. Ray followed halfway through the door and waited. On the credenza behind Emil was a platter of sandwiches and a six-pack of Cokes. Ray wondered if he was supposed to have lunch there.

"OK, call me back tomorrow before noon," said Emil as he finished his conversation. "I want those figures exactly. No blue sky!" He hung up the phone without any good-bye and turned to Ray, still ignoring Tom.

"Well, what do you think of our operation so far?"

Ray could have spent the next hour just outlining his thoughts, but he figured this was not the time for serious analysis. "Very interesting," he said. "I've been learning quite a bit, especially this morning."

Tom shuffled the cards and started to deal. He said, "That god-damn Lyons is letting his office out early again, so they can beat the others to the lunch line. I'm going to put some pressure on him and the other softies too. We're gonna run this place like a business."

Emil was sorting his cards and said, without looking up, "You take care of it." Ray just stood there for a few seconds, waiting for the next question, but Emil just started playing cards. "Keep me up-to-date on what you see, Ray," he said.

Ray nodded, understanding that it was time for him to go. A courteous "Thanks Tom" was answered with a grunt as he left.

From the empty outer office, Ray heard Tom's voice. "He looks pretty good to me. Makes a lot of sense. We need his type of thinking to shake those sales guys up a little."

Emil said, "Gin."

Ray did not hear Emil's response. He knew he hadn't said anything to Tom that had made "a lot of sense." He'd scarcely had a chance to talk. He was relieved that Tom was giving a good report to the President, but there was no basis for it. Tom had no idea what he knew or what he thought, and that bothered Ray. He was uncomfortable with Tom's negative comments about everyone from Vince to Rizzo to his own secretary. And his claiming that he had had to persuade Emil to go "outside" for new blood. And with the way he kept switching track, leaving Ray disoriented and confused. There was something else that bothered him even more, and he couldn't put his finger on it.

As he walked down the hall, he remembered his conversation with Emil. "Tom knows everything that's going on, everywhere," Emil told him. "Whenever I want to know what's happening, I ask Tom."

Ray continued down the hall. His face still had a frozen, almost stunned, expression, but the smile was gone. What kind of operation had he gotten himself into?

6. The Professor's Barrel

That night, after the kids had gone to bed, he described his meeting with Chessman to Dorothy as they unpacked books in their family room. Dorothy laughed, commenting, "He must be a real character."

"Yeah," said Ray, shaking his head, "He's a character all right. Everyone sort of laughs at him, but they're also afraid of him. What bothers me is the influence he has with Emil Gross."

"But, he said nice things about you, didn't he?"

"Sure, but he had no reason to. I hardly said a word. Whenever I had a comment ready, he was off in another direction. I just followed him around like a puppy dog."

Ray stopped unpacking and looked at the half-filled bookcase and the unopened boxes. "Geez, I didn't realize we had so many books. Have we read them all?"

Dorothy looked quizzically at Ray. "Have *we* read them all?"

"I suppose most of them are mine," Ray agreed, as he viewed the accumulation of twenty years as a student and as a professor. "It's amazing, I actually have read most of these." He moved closer to the bookcase, looking over the titles of the books. "And I don't think there is one book here that can help me with Tom Chessman."

"Oh, stop worrying so much about Tom Chessman. He must like you or he wouldn't say good things about you to Emil. He probably was just showing off. You'll get along fine with him, like you do with everyone else. You'll do a good job, and that's what counts."

Ray smiled at his wife. "I hope you're right. I'm no good at playing gin with the boss." He walked across the room and kissed her lightly. "What about you and the kids? How was your day? Paul sounded excited about Little League."

"Glad you asked," she said a little sarcastically. "We're not doing much better than you are. Right now Paul's just moping around. I hope that once I get him on a team, he'll make friends. I'm not sure about Barbara. She's not that good at making friends. She just trails me around. Helped me take the laundry to the laundromat. Boy, I sure will be happy to get the washer hooked up. Then she kept me company at the Motor Vehicle Bureau and helped me empty about a thousand boxes."

"She's real helpful."

"Yes she is. But when I get all this stuff put away she'll be the one moping around. We should have moved while school was in session."

"They'll be all right," he said. "It just takes time. How about you? Meet any neighbors or anyone?"

"Haven't had time."

Later that night, as they got into bed, he said, "I know things are tough right now. When I came out of Emil's office, I was thinking how nice it would be to be back in Boston."

She laughed. "Me too. That's exactly what I've been thinking. Barbara said the same thing."

"What did you tell her?"

"To give it time. That after a while she'll like it here.... But I don't know if I believe that myself." She buried her face in his chest as a few tears began to form.

He stroked her hair and said consolingly, "It will be all right, hon. The kids will be just fine, and you'll have time to make new friends...and I'll come up with my own version of the American Barrel. It's kind of scary now...like going away to school, remember?"

"Yeah, I remember," she said. "I never felt so alone. I wanted to go home."

"We'll come out of it." He kissed her forehead softly. "Besides, we're not alone. We've got each other."

He looked into her eyes and she smiled back. Then he softly kissed her nose, her lips, her neck, and her breast.

"This isn't the same as when you went to school, is it?"

"No," she whispered as she slid her hand down between his legs. "This is different."

He fell asleep right after making love. She lay awake for a long time, looking into the darkness.

■ ■ ■

At the office the next morning Ray was enthusiastic and determined to develop some great ideas. The only trouble was he did not know where to begin.

Vince gave him the responsibility for the promotion programs, explaining, "If we were starting an American Barrel program, we would consider it a promotion, so why don't you take over our present programs and see where you can go from there."

The two main programs were the American Bucks for the Jobber and the American Trip for the Warehouse Distributor. The "Bucks" program gave out certificates, or "bucks," to the Jobber when he bought shocks from the Warehouse Distributor. When he accumulated enough "bucks" he could order premiums from a catalog. Different shocks earned more awards than others, so the Jobber could be directed to more profitable items or items that were being promoted. It was a simple plan, administered through a premium house in Chicago.

The "Trip" program sent the Warehouse Distributor and his wife on a vacation to places like the Bahamas or the Greek islands or Costa de Sol if he met a sales goal for the shocks. Emil or Dave Dennison would host ten to twelve customers each year. It was very expensive, but it developed loyalty with the Warehouse Distributor and his wife—especially his wife.

"It's expensive and the accountants hate it," Vince told Ray. "But it ties the distributor and his wife to Amsaco. I'd hate to be the distributor who had to tell his wife he just switched lines and they couldn't go to Monte Carlo. In fact, when we lost Automotive Distributors to Blackwell last year, part of the deal was they had to send Earl Cooper and his wife on a vacation to New Zealand for three weeks. I don't know what they'll do next year. One of these years, Donna Cooper is going to talk Earl into coming back to Amsaco, so she can go on our trips with her friends."

Ray took over the administration of these two programs and several other smaller ones, at the same time looking for new ones.

For a week he searched for ideas that would result in a major increase in sales for Amsaco, with no real breakthrough.

He expressed some frustration when he was having coffee with Vince and Al Goldman. "I don't know how I can come up with something great that our competitors can't copy. Didn't they copy Emil's American Barrel?"

"Sure they did," Al answered. "After a while. But that wasn't the beauty of Emil's barrel. The beauty was that making the consumer aware of his need for shocks increased the total market for everyone. We increased market share temporarily, but even when Blackwell got it back, we kept growing. Everyone did."

"So I'm supposed to come up with something to increase the whole shock market?"

Al laughed. "If that's what Emil wants."

"Emil wants market share," Vince pointed out. "And he doesn't want the same old crap, warmed over."

Al laughed again. "You sound kind of sensitive. But maybe you've been looking in the wrong place. There are lots of ways to increase market share besides some half-assed merchandising program. Isn't that right, professor?"

Ray was thinking. "Yeah, there sure are," he answered. "I've taught a lot of classes about market share changes. Let me think about this one, Vince."

When he got back to his desk, he did a lot of thinking, taking a much broader, objective view of the situation. He analyzed the key elements of Amsaco. What were its strengths and weaknesses? Who was the real competition? Where was the shock market going? Just as if it were an assignment to his class, Ray developed several business strategies and objectively analyzed and reanalyzed various courses of action. This was the way he knew how to operate. He began to enjoy himself for the first time since he had started at Amsaco.

While the various possible actions became very complicated, and there was much information not yet known to him, Ray did develop what seemed to be a direct, although difficult, approach toward improving Amsaco's position. The key was market share.

Blackwell Manufacturing was too big and powerful to compete with profitably. Blackwell had big advertising and promotion programs to help their customers maintain and improve their large sales volume. Amsaco had to work just as hard for their customers, but the resulting sales volume was much smaller; their marketing costs therefore were much higher as a percentage of sales. Blackwell had more salesmen in the field, a bigger and better advertising program, better promotions, and lower costs, proportionally.

The same was true in Operations. It took just as much engineering to develop and maintain Amsaco's product line as Blackwell's. Blackwell's engineering costs were half as much as Amsaco's, proportionally. Blackwell had manufacturing plants in Columbus, Indiana; Kinston, North Carolina; and Fullerton, California; and a distribution center in Los Angeles. They could serve their customers faster, had less freight cost, and still had more volume going through each plant than Amsaco.

Blackwell's accounting, legal, and other administrative costs were the same as Amsaco's, but half as much proportionally. While Amsaco struggled to be profitable, Blackwell made large profits. If Amsaco tried to use price to get more business, Blackwell could go lower. They were a tough competitor.

Ray saw this as a classical case, similar to many he had studied. When one company had the dominant market share, they were much more profitable and difficult to unseat. Developing a new and better product would be one way to go around their power, but Ray did not see any opportunities. Finding a new market for the product would also be effective, but Ray saw none. Ray saw no major opportunities to improve their share by attacking Blackwell.

Crane Automotive, however, was not that strong. Their one big plant in Dayton, Ohio, also manufactured their other products, including driveshafts, rear ends, front ends, and other hard parts. They were a strong manufacturing company and had a good after-market sales organization, but shocks were not their main product line. Their market share was small, except for the Sears account. Sears was the largest shock customer in the world and was growing steadily, which was increasing Crane's market share.

Ray came to the conclusion that the best opportunity for Amsaco was to take the Sears account from Crane. First of all, it was possible. With the right marketing package they could show a sales increase for Sears. And Amsaco could put together a better shock merchandising program than Crane and could improve the distribution system. Some product line improvements would also be welcomed by their buyers. Ray was sure he could put together a total program that Sears would seriously consider.

The second reason was Crane would not be likely to retaliate strongly. The loss of Sears would not create a problem in Dayton, because of the dominance of their other hard parts. Their sales force was selling their entire line, and would continue to do so. Only the Sears group would be laid off, and if the customer requested it, a few key people might be hired by Amsaco.

Ray was convinced that it was worthwhile to pursue this project. For the next three days he organized his facts and his logic and presented a full plan to his boss. Vince was amazed. He was not used to this type of organized report. Working with the field sales force and his advertising staff, he found it difficult to get an organized expense report, sales call summary, or proposed budget, much less a written marketing strategy.

"Holy shit, Ray," he said as he leafed through the report and the backup material. "You're not supposed to do this. It would take my whole staff two or three years to put something like this together. You did all this in three days?"

Ray smiled. "Just trying to earn my salary."

"Well, you just earned your first year's salary. Now slow down." Vince shook his head and took a few minutes to read sections of the report, including the executive summary.

When Vince looked up, Ray was smiling. "It's exciting to be part of the game, rather than discussing a case study after it's over."

Vince laughed. "I suppose it is. Trouble is, the game never ends." He paused. "As far as our game is concerned, Ray, let me give you some advice. I've just leafed through this thing so far, and you might have something real good. I don't know yet. This is big. Takes in the whole company. But you'll have to sell it. You'll be disturbing the status quo, asking people to approve something that may not work. You'll be asking them to take a risk. They may not want to do that."

"But people do that every day," Ray replied. "There is always something new coming up. It's part of the job."

"Yeah," said Vince, "But they're comfortable with the normal decisions. A Regional Manager might have to decide who should fill a new District Manager slot, or a field salesman might ask for an extra thirty days for a good prospect. But these are minor. They're not going to lose their job over them. You're talking about a major change, where a guy could lose his job. And his boss could too if it doesn't work out."

"But then, nothing can ever be changed," Ray responded. "We can never make a major change."

"To some extent that's true," said Vince. "Most new ideas die from lack of support, because no one wants to stick his neck out." He stood up and walked around his desk. "But sometimes it's more risky to do nothing. In this case, Emil wants you to produce something different. Therefore Dennison wants you to, and so do I." He turned toward Ray. "It would be more risky not to produce something different. The same is true for Burch or Chessman or Steele. They don't want to risk looking negative. You can probably sell them, if what you're selling is anywhere near reasonable." He laughed. "They have an additional incentive in that they can point to Dave and me and ask, 'Why didn't you think of that?' This thing just might fly."

Ray smiled. "Well, it's my American Barrel. I guess I have a selling job to do."

7. The Corporate String

Ray spent the next ten days refining his plan and going over it with Vince. He ended up with a proposal that covered everything from product line modifications to distribution service to merchandising to financial projections for both Sears and Amsaco. Vince was impressed. "This is good," he said. "Really good. Now the real work begins."

Selling the plan turned out to be a different matter. Each person had his own way of not listening to Ray's ideas. No one expressed violent disagreement, but no one encouraged him or joined him in his project. It was like pushing on a string. He met no resistance, but he could not apply any force.

Dick Wise in Accounting was a good example. Dick, a short, energetic, ambitious man, was forty-two years old. His round face was getting rounder and redder, as his previously thin body was getting heavier. He had always been small and had been intimidated by jocks all through high school and college. He took particular enjoyment in having many of these jocks working for him as he progressed through the business world. He went by the numbers and had no use for the dramatic "bullshit" from salesmen. He put the Sears plans in that category and wanted to talk about Ray's other assignments, mainly the merchandising programs.

"Giveaways, just plain giveaways," Dick declared when Ray visited his office. "The American Bucks program just gives the Jobber the premiums for nothing. He doesn't have to sell anything. He only has to buy. But we don't know what he returns to the distributor. We just give him the bucks. He can order and return the same merchandise five times and come up with enough American bucks to buy his bike or TV or whatever. And anybody can get the jackets."

The jackets Dick referred to were classy-looking racing jackets with an American shock over the breast pocket and an American flag on the sleeve. They were available as premiums, but they were also given away to any good customer because of the Amsaco identification. They also ended up with almost every Amsaco salesman, the marketing staff, and the families of many executives.

"Costs us $27 per jacket," Dick emphasized, "and we hardly sell any of them. We give 'em away."

"Oh, I don't know, Dick," Ray said, somewhat defensively. "They're a walking advertisement for Amsaco. The jackets have good identification."

"That's fine," Dick replied. "It's a good jacket. But they can be sold. We can get just as many in the field if we sold them. And then your marketing costs will go down and we could make some profit. But it's easier to just give 'em away. Our salesmen become nice guys to the customer. But they're supposed to be businessmen. Same thing with the "American Trip." The WD is supposed to meet goal in order to qualify for the trip. So our salesman sets the goal so low, he can't possibly miss."

Ray did not particularly like the program himself. Still, he defended it because he was on the marketing "team." "The trouble is we have to make our trip plans months in advance. We can't wait until the results are in, so we have to be pretty sure he'll make it."

"So change the dates," Dick responded. "Set the goal to end in June to qualify for the trip in January. It could be done. The trouble is you guys made that trip so fancy that you're afraid to tell the customer he can't go. The Greek Islands, Hawaii, Monte Carlo, for Christ's sake. The customer's wives plan to get together every year on our money. You've created a monster."

Ray said nothing. Dick was right, but that was not what Ray wanted to talk about.

"It's a bribe," Dick continued. "Plain and simple. Look, you think we ought to go after Sears. The way our salesmen work, the only way we'll get Sears is with price. And to beat Crane's price, we wouldn't have any profit left. You can make more money for the company by getting marketing costs under control than by getting Sears."

This was going too far. "No, Dick," Ray came back. "I don't

think we should use price to get Sears. I think we could show them better merchandising and advertising than Crane. And we can improve the ordering and delivery system. And I'll be after Engineering to cut down the number of part numbers they have to stock. I think we can show them a better return on their investment with Amsaco."

"All very fine and good," Dick replied, holding both hands up to stop Ray. "But when our sales guys get through with it, we'll be giving the stuff away. Cut costs! That's what you can do to help this company."

■ ■ ■

Ray did not do much better with Jim Steele or Bob Simpranian. He talked to them in Steele's office after the monthly product planning meeting.

Jim Steele was tall and slim. He would joke with friends about his increasing baldness, but he was frustrated because he could do nothing about it. He was over fifty and serious about keeping himself in good shape by running every morning and working out at the YMCA.

Jim had gained Emil's respect since being hired as Plant Manager of the Seward, Nebraska, plant in 1962, while Emil was running the Kansas City District. The plant had opened in 1960 with all sorts of problems. It took Jim less than a year to straighten things out, and when Emil took over the company, he soon brought Jim in to head Manufacturing.

Bob Simpranian was also concerned with staying in shape, and had lost even more hair than Steele. But Bob accepted the loss as a naturally occurring, scientifically predictable event. When he had turned forty, he had run into some mild heart problems, experiencing chest pains when he exerted himself. He did not panic, but in true engineering fashion decided to improve his body's operation to maximize its useful life. He followed the doctor's orders and stopped smoking, got into a regular exercise program, and watched his diet. He also increased his insurance. He was now forty-four, and his problems had not recurred. Loss of hair on his head had no functional effect, so it was of little concern.

Simpranian had no tolerance for politics and was never close to Emil's inner circle. He was well accepted by the other executives partly because he did his engineering job well, but mostly because he was not a threat to anyone.

Steele and Simpranian worked well together because they trusted each other. Both were basically honest and serious about doing their jobs. When Ray had outlined his thoughts on getting the Sears account, Jim Steele was the first to answer.

"I like some of what you're saying. Lord knows we could use more volume. And if you finally get Bob here to standardize the product some, you've really accomplished something." He paused as he and Simpranian exchanged knowing glances. "But, supplying each store separately is impossible. With all the different part numbers you guys create, we have them stacked all over the place, and it takes years to pick an order. I don't know how you guys can come up with so many variations on a simple shock absorber. The salesmen want one for every application and the engineers just copy what's out there instead of coming up with a simpler line. They just cover their own ass."

Simpranian smiled. He had heard this many times before. "There's a reason for every variation on the design," he countered. "It's got to fit, and it's got to last...and it's got to give the customer the ride he expects."

"Ah bullshit," Steele responded, reaching behind his desk for some sample shocks. He laid them on his desk and showed them to Ray. Simpranian looked away, apparently well aware of what would come next. "Look at these two shocks. They're identical, except for this little washer."

"That's a valve, Jim," Simpranian interrupted. "And it changes the ride."

"Yeah, yeah, I know...a valve. But I'll bet the customer can't tell the difference. And it adds a part number that we have to stock and keep separate in assembly and in the warehouse. A pain in the ass. You make this hole a little bigger, and you can use it in both, and eliminate a part number. We won't have to build it, won't have to stock it, and won't have to pick it...and we sell more of the other one."

"But it won't meet the heavy-duty specs if you do that."

"Yeah, I know. Your damn specs. You engineers always hide behind your specs. But this is even worse." He reached for another pair of shocks, one white and one black. "These two are exactly the same, except for the paint. But you salesmen sell it to two different customers, probably at two different prices, and you want it to look different."

Simpranian, glad to have Steele switch from engineers to salesmen, chimed in. "But it's the same shock. Either we're losing money on the cheaper shock, or we're gouging the customer on the expensive one."

"Maybe the price isn't based only on manufacturing costs." Ray responded. "Maybe it's based on marketing or distribution costs."

"Sure it is," Steele came in. "But if you didn't have so damn many parts, the distribution costs wouldn't be so damn high. If you want to do some good for the company, forget about adding expenses with the Sears business. Concentrate on simplifying the product line. Sell it in one color. And don't try to have a product for every application ever made."

Ray said nothing. He was somewhat confused as to how to respond since he was not responsible for the product line. Simpranian took that as an opportunity to join in.

"What bothers me about Sears is their quality. Their shocks are not really heavy duty. They're closer to our regular line than our heavy duty. It's a compromise line so they don't have to stock two lines, but they call them heavy duty. And they only carry the fast movers."

"Don't they have a low-priced line?" Ray asked.

"Not really. They have a few low-priced shocks for the smaller cars, so they can advertise a low price. Most of what they sell is their regular line...and it's not heavy duty."

"Sounds like they have the right idea," Steele said with a mischievous grin. "They satisfy their customers, but they don't need a million units in inventory. We ought to copy them."

This was an insult to Simpranian. His concept of a well-run engineering operation was to have others copy him. "No, Jim," he countered, "Their customers don't get as good a shock as ours. We give them a real heavy-duty shock. And sometimes the ride is better than they had with the original equipment shock."

"Yeah, but the customer doesn't know it. He can't tell the difference."

"If we told him what we're giving him, and had him look for it, he could tell the difference. That's what you can do, Ray. Set up your marketing plan to inform the customer what a good shock we're giving them."

"I'll go further than that," said Steele, with another grin. "Just set up a marketing plan, period. The stuff you guys put in your plan now is just useless garbage. I can't use it to plan anything. You come up with big schemes to concentrate on this channel and go after this customer. But hell, I need to know what you're gonna sell. And not just totals. What part numbers and how many...and when. You want to help this company, forget the Sears business. Concentrate on an accurate forecast for our present business."

■ ■ ■

Ray expected more support from his own Marketing Group, but even Dave Dennison was a disappointment. Dave was an aggressive, all business, professional salesman...a real "ball of fire." He had come up through the ranks with Emil and knew all the customers, the prospects, the competition, the field sales force, the home office support staff, the engineers, and anyone else who helped him make a sale. Sale of shock absorbers for Amsaco was his life. He could talk all night about business, then be up at 7:00, all neatly dressed, shoes shined, and ready to be at the customer's office at 8:00. He had little use for accountants, because he viewed them as a roadblock to sales.

Ray and Vince talked to Dennison in his elaborate office. Dennison had a fancier office than Emil's. He had redesigned Emil's old office with a special desk, plush carpet, comfortable couch, and other trimmings. He even had a special chair for himself that was higher than the visitor chairs. He did not like to look up to anyone who was taller than he was, which included almost everyone. His justification for spending so much on his office was that the top sales office should impress customers. Ray was certainly impressed.

"Look Ray," Dave explained. "You can't go around telling the accountants you're going to pick up a big chunk of business like Sears."

"Why not?"

"Because then they expect it. They want you to justify it and put it in the marketing plan."

"But I can do that," Ray responded, trying to hold back his frustration. "I can write plans. And I have the basics already worked out. You know, I'm Emil's college professor and I can do these things."

Dennison sighed, knowing that Emil would probably ask about "Singleton's" plans. Experience had taught Dennison never to predict any new account, much less one as big as Sears. If he kept his forecast low for new business, he could pick up some big accounts, surpass his forecast, and look like a hero. But, if he forecast getting a lot of new business, like Sears, and did not get them on board on schedule, he would be behind forecast and would be the reason Amsaco was not meeting profit objectives. And that would go on month after month, all year.... Still, Emil would want to know what Ray was coming up with.

"What have you got?" he asked, unenthusiastically.

"Well, I'm just getting into the details, but what I'm trying to put together is a total program, hitting them from several angles. First we need to improve the product line. We—"

"What's wrong with our product line?" Vince interrupted. Product planning was one of Vince's responsibilities.

"Nothing really wrong," Ray replied, trying not to embarrass Vince in front of his boss. "Our line is fine for the traditional Jobber. He has a whole bunch of products. He doesn't mind a lot of part numbers because he doesn't need to stock them all. He can send his truck over to the warehouse to pick up a part and then deliver it with other parts to the garage. The warehouse can afford to stock a lot of items, because he serves so many Jobbers. The system works. But the Sears store has no local warehouse backup. And every time they have to go to a local Jobber to get a part, they figure they're losing money. So they need maximum coverage with a minimum inventory. We need a compromise line, with just a few numbers, engineered to fit a wide range of applications."

"What do you mean by compromise?" Asked Vince.

"Well, in two areas. We need just one line, somewhere between our regular and heavy-duty lines. And it can't have too many numbers, so we might need extra brackets or adapters to make them fit. So the compromise is on quality and fit."

"Can that be done?" asked Dennison. "Have you talked with Simpranian?"

Ray smiled sheepishly. "Well, Bob doesn't like standardizing too much. And he doesn't like compromising either. But Jim Steele was all in favor."

"Yeah, Jim has been preaching that for a long time," Vince agreed. "So Steele likes your plan?"

"Well, he likes the standardization part." Ray could not be anything but honest. "But, he didn't go for the service part so good."

"What's that?" Dennison asked, pulling his chair closer. "What's the service part?"

"That's how we tie them into us, get their system tied into ours. And it gives them something they're not getting from Crane." Ray saw an interest growing in Dennison's eyes and elaborated. "We put in a couple of customer service girls to serve Sears exclusively. They set up a schedule and call each Sears store regularly, at a set time, to take their order. Each store knows that at a certain time, say every other Tuesday at four o'clock, they give their order. Then we ship each order on a schedule that's fixed. It evens out our shipping patterns and order picking."

"But we're shipping little orders to every store," Dennison countered. "I can see why Jim doesn't like it. That's expensive."

"I don't think it would be too bad. He can set up a system to pick several orders at the same time...one trip. And they will all go on the same truck in the same sequence. And it will be steady every day, no big end-of-the-month surge. I think it can be worked out."

Dennison sat back and thought for a few seconds. He looked at Vince, who was jotting a few notes, then at Ray. "No," he said slowly, "it has some appeal, but I don't think Simpranian will give you the line you're looking for. He'll insist on staying close to what we have now. Otherwise he'd be admitting our present line is wrong. And our Distribution Group?" He smiled at Vince. "They can't ship a full truckload to one customer without losing half of it. A Sears system would be a fiasco."

Ray, having no counterargument, just sat there. How could he authoritatively say they had the capability when he hardly knew the organization?

"What kind of advertising would you use?" Vince asked. "How would you increase their sales?"

"Quality," Ray responded, glad to get on to something else. "I'd emphasize quality. Let the consumer know that he gets the best quality heavy-duty shock at Sears. Sell that concept through television, and then use the newspapers for price specials—'buy three and get one free' type of thing. But first he should already know from television that Sears shocks are quality. That's why we need a good quality line."

Vince tapped his pen on the desk as he listened. Then he said slowly and deliberately, "Yes, Sears could sell that. They did it with batteries, they could do it with shocks, if they want to."

"Oh, they could do it all right," Dennison countered. "But why do it with our line? They could do it with Crane."

Ray answered, "But we're giving them a better product line and better service."

"Yeah, and it's costing us a bundle. How are you pricing this? Are we going to give them a better price too? We're giving them everything else."

"I don't think we have to be below Crane's prices," Ray responded, aware of the sarcasm in Dennison's remark. "The main thing is to show them a better margin—increase their selling price. I think we can show them how to make a lot of money on shocks."

"I'd like to see the pricing…and our costs."

"I'm putting the whole thing together, but it's not easy. Everyone has something more important."

"Not surprising. You're asking Distribution to do something they've never tried, and they're having trouble doing what they have tried. And you're asking Engineering to standardize, or compromise, or rationalize, whatever, and that's sacrilegious to an engineer. And then you want Sears to pay more for our shocks and change lines."

Dennison's face was getting red as he summarized. Ray knew it wouldn't be easy to push through change, but he expected some encouragement from somewhere.

"It makes more sense when you look at the total program," he explained, trying not to appear beaten or discouraged. "If successful, our distribution will be simpler and steadier. And our additional volume will reduce our overhead rate and lower costs. And the engineers might find a new way to simplify our entire product line. It's a lot of change, I know, but it could make things better."

Dennison looked at Ray, then at Vince, then exhaled slowly, as if to give in. "OK, put together a picture of the whole thing, especially the costs and pricing. I'll take a look, but I'll be damned if I'll back something that has so many chances to fail. Now, how's the 'American Trip' program going? Is anyone in trouble?"

■ ■ ■

Just getting an OK to write up his plan was not what Ray was after. He wanted somebody to agree with his approach, anybody. But no one seemed to understand the basic concept. No one seemed interested in making a major change, a major improvement. Getting Sears would set Amsaco solidly ahead of Crane as the second-biggest shock absorber company in the States. It would also give them the volume base to reduce unit costs and go after more business. If someone would come up with an argument that this was not true, or that it was not possible, then Ray could argue back. They could debate the issues and come to a conclusion. But they were saying that Ray's plan was possible, but he could help the company more by watching marketing costs, or putting together a better sales forecast, or standardizing the product line. These were all worthwhile goals, but they weren't even Ray's responsibilities. Besides, the company could work on them and a Sears strategy. It was frustrating for Ray.

As Ray worked on his plan, and the "American Bucks" and "American Trip" programs, he was unhappy. This was not what he expected. Emil Gross had talked to him about developing new strategies and new programs. Maybe it would be different when he got the plan together and could present it to Emil himself. If he could develop a good enough plan, eventually Emil and everyone would see the logic in his approach and give him their support.

Ray would not have been quite so unhappy if he was aware of several events that were taking place at the same time.

■ ■ ■

Ralph Burch continued to write down numbers on his extrawide analysis pad as Dick Wise told him about his conversation with Ray.

"I told him to forget that Sears thing," Wise said, "and concentrate on getting sales costs under control. Increasing market share is expensive."

"Yes," Burch agreed. "Especially when the market is down. Still, a one-shot deal like this might be doable. What's Crane going to do about it? Blackwell would pin our ears back. They'd be after every good distributor we have. It would be war, and we'd lose. But Crane?"

Wise was surprised. "You think so?" He thought for a moment. "I guess it's possible. But would it be worth it? I don't believe the sales numbers. Sears isn't that big."

"Where'd the Professor get his numbers?" Burch asked.

"He guessed at them, He thinks Sears could do a lot more than they're doing if they pushed shocks...like they do with batteries. He says customers like being able to drop off the car and go shop at the mall. And paying with the Sears credit card gives them a big advantage."

"He may be right," Burch agreed. "The credit card thing is a big deal. A lot of garages and service stations don't even take checks."

"Romano in Computing says pretty soon we'll all have cards that will let us charge things anywhere," Wise added. "There'll be no need for cash."

Burch dismissed the idea. "I'll believe it when I see it."

There was silence as they both thought about it. Then Burch said, "Let him run with this. See where it leads. The Professor might have something."

As Wise left, Burch started a new set of numbers on his analysis pad. He estimated sales, manufacturing costs, distribution costs, marketing expenses, and all the other factors, and tested this proforma using different assumptions. Ralph always analyzed each situation by himself, in the same way. He sat upright, writing neat numbers in columns, adding them on his calculator, methodically testing one variable after another.

A ghost of a smile appeared on his face. "This might not be so bad," he thought. "Let Emil absorb all the costs. It'll put me in a stronger position when I take over."

■ ■ ■

As Burch was contemplating his proforma, Tom Chessman burst into Jim Steele's office, asking, "What's this shit about the

Professor taking on some big account?" Chessman didn't like learning about things via rumors. Whatever the "shit" was, he wanted to be the first to know and the first to pass it on to Emil. "You keeping secrets from me?"

Steele laughed. "Tom, I could never keep secrets from you." He turned to his secretary, who was taking dictation. "Let's finish this later."

She smiled at Chessman and asked, "Would you like some coffee?"

"I don't have time." He sat down and stared at Steele.

She smiled again and left the office, closing the door.

Steele knew Chessman too well to be intimidated by his stare. "Yeah," he explained. "The Professor wants to go after the Sears account, and I think I just might be on his side."

"Why?"

"Because of this," Steele said as he reached behind him to his credenza and pulled out a bunch of papers. "This is an appropriation for automation equipment. Two million dollars worth of state-of-the-art machinery to bring us into the twentieth century. I've been trying to justify this for the past year, but I can't put together numbers that will get through the bean counters."

"Why not?" Chessman asked, adding sarcastically, "Aren't they reasonable professionals?"

Steele ignored the sarcasm. "Because I'm trying to justify it on the basis of cost reduction, and the only acceptable cost reduction I can use is direct labor, and that's not enough. There's no particular material savings that we can put in our standard cost. There'll be a reduction in scrap, but I can't use that because I'm not supposed to have scrap in the first place...or very little. And better quality or faster response time can only be measured by increased sales. But Marketing won't raise their sales forecast because we're supposed to have good quality and fast response time already. Its a 'Catch-22.' The same with reducing absenteeism. These machines don't get sick or take coffee breaks. But I can't quantify that for justification." He stopped to think. "I suppose I could take a saving from increased efficiency, but it's not enough. I know instinctively that it's in the best interest of the company to get this equipment, but I can't justify it. Meanwhile our operation is getting old and out of date."

"Sounds like you've got a problem," Chessman agreed.

"If we add Sears," Steele went on, "we increase sales and profit, which justifies some expenditures. But, in order to produce for Sears, we need more capacity...more equipment."

"But do you need all that *automated* equipment for Sears?"

"Damn right. The bean counters can't argue with me about what equipment. We're the professionals there. We choose the equipment."

Steele sat back in his chair and smiled. "Marketing will have to justify the Sears program based on profits from this new business. But that's Marketing's problem. Their Professor shouldn't have any problem with that."

Chessman thought about where he should place himself in this situation. It certainly could do no harm to be on the same side as Operations and Marketing. And the Professor was coming up with an idea, which was what Emil wanted. And he could hedge his opinion by saying that he hadn't seen the final numbers, but the idea was good.

"I'll mention it to Emil," he said. "Makes sense to me."

"Good."

When Chessman left, Steele looked at each item on the appropriation and imagined the new machinery in place, producing perfect shock absorbers, one after the other. Even the accountants would be happy with the improvement in profits. He imagined giving Emil and his staff a tour of the plant, explaining the operation of his modern manufacturing equipment.

■ ■ ■

As Jim Steele sat daydreaming, Bob Simpranian questioned Ted Lyons in his office. "What do you think, Ted? Are my product guys too fussy? Are they the only ones who can drive a car and tell if the shocks are regular or heavy duty?"

Ted Lyons was head of Manufacturing Engineering. Simpranian had worked closely with him on many projects and had a lot of respect for his opinion, even on a Product Engineering problem. Ted had come up through Manufacturing, from foreman to plant engineer, to the home office. He was tall and slender, with rough cowboy features and squinting eyes.

"Bob, you may not like my answer," Ted said, "but, yes, your guys are too fussy. But they want their product to be good. The trouble is they're too close to it. They understand every little thing that can go wrong. If the shock is perfect for everything but high-speed turns, they know that. A customer might be happy with the ride and could care less about high-speed turns, but your engineers can't accept that. It's their baby, and it's got to be perfect. If it takes a different valve and a new part number, so what? They can't let out a product that isn't exactly right."

Simpranian sighed. Ted was right. That was not what he wanted to hear. "But they know the most about the product. And they protect the customer. How else can we design, if we don't aim for the right product for the job?"

"Design it up to a point," Ted suggested. "Then let Manufacturing modify the product to make it easier to produce. If the Manufacturing guys go too far, then pull back. But get some Manufacturing thought into the design...and into your engineers too. The product design is too important to leave to the product engineers."

"Yeah, fine," Bob countered. "But you're a Manufacturing man. You've been trying to design the product for years. Maybe the Marketing guys would like to design the line themselves, so it does everything for everyone. And the accountants too. They'll make it out of plastic."

Ted laughed. "Well, let them all take a crack. You'll probably end up with a better product." He thought for a few seconds and added, "But don't let Personnel get in the act. I hate to think of what Chessman would do to a shock."

"What's Tom doing to you now?" Bob asked, grinning.

"Now he's on a degree kick. We need engineers with advanced degrees, master's and Ph.Ds and stuff. He has some research guy he wants me to hire. The last thing we need is some guy with a lot of fancy theories to dump on the guys in the plant. Our plants are having enough trouble just keeping things going. They need help, not more problems."

Simpranian, still grinning, said teasingly, "Yeah, I heard Tom telling Emil that the reason we don't have the best manufacturing process is because we have nondegree manufacturing engineers. And they don't have the creativity that a college graduate has."

"Bullshit," Ted said angrily, getting to his feet, "Give me the manpower and the capital budget and I'll give you the best operation in the country. I need budget. I don't need any goddamn Ph.Ds."

"Whoa, whoa," said Simpranian, "I'm on your side. Chessman is after me the same way." He paused as Ted sat down again. He smiled, "But he doesn't get after me the way he goes after you. What is it about you, anyway?"

"Just lucky, I guess. He's been that way ever since I made Manager. I think he's trying to prove that Jim made the wrong selection when he made me Manager. Maybe it's just politics, Chessman trying to make Steele look bad. I don't know. Tom never even knew I existed before that."

"Well Jim supports you. And he has no use for Ph.Ds either. He's already having enough trouble with our new Professor. Pendleton wants to get the Sears account by giving every Sears store personalized service. Scares the hell out of Jim. Actually, that's why I'm asking you about our product engineers. Pendleton thinks we can design a real simple line to give Sears coverage, quality, and price. And I guess you agree with him. You said we can—"

"It's a matter of degree," Ted interrupted. "I think you can relax some of your specs, make the product more standardized. But Marketing is always asking for more part numbers to satisfy customers. They never ask for a shorter line."

"Maybe they want another line, in addition to what we have now."

"Probably. I never heard of Marketing doing anything that helped us."

Simpranian replied with a smile, "I haven't either. But I don't know..." He stared up at the ceiling. "Maybe there's something here. If Sears only needs a short line, why does anyone else need so much more? Maybe our engineers—"

■ ■ ■

Dave Dennison was also thinking of Ray's project. He didn't believe Amsaco could take Sears away from Crane without a major battle, and he did not particularly like Ray's proposed individual service for each store. It would be too expensive and too complicated.

But, as a salesman, he could not ignore the possibility of nailing such a large account. It would certainly be a stepping stone to succeeding Emil as President. It could also be disaster for him if everyone expected Sears and then he failed. Dennison was too shrewd and too experienced to endorse Ray's plan publicly. But privately, he would probe this possibility a little further.

He was having a drink with Ed O'Brien, his National Accounts Sales Manager. "Ed, how strong is Crane in National Accounts?" he asked. "Are we in danger of losing any accounts to them?"

Ed O'Brien was a "good ol' boy" Irishman. His smiling face was known by all the important buyers in the automotive retail organizations. Even more important was the fact that he was well liked, and doors were always open for him. He loved a good drink, a good story, and a bad woman, in that order. His escapades with some adventuresome customers were well known in the company. Dennison did not particularly approve of Ed's methods, but he did approve of his results. Ed knew what was going on everywhere, and obtained business for Amsaco wherever it was available.

"No Dave," he answered with no doubt in his mind. "Crane is no danger to us. In fact, I was going to put this in next week's report. I think we might have a shot at one of their accounts. I had dinner with Jack Landaur at Penneys, and he's interested in our program."

"Any particular reason?"

"No, not that I know of. Jack and I have put away many a bottle together over the years." Ed thought for a second, smiled, and continued, "Maybe he's interested in our program because I'm the best salesman."

Dave returned the smile. "I sure wouldn't put up with you if you weren't." He paused. "Think you have any chance to sell Sears? Got any buddies over there?"

O'Brien came right back, "Yeah, I know the Sears group. In fact, Jim Purcell, who heads the Automotive Group is an old friend." He smiled, remembering. "We had some good times together when I was with Bestco. Why? You thinking of going after Sears? I don't know. We wouldn't have much of a chance if Crane is doing their job. Sears doesn't change easy."

"I know. No, I'm just probing, nothing solid." Dave sipped his drink and continued. "But, if you get a chance, just sniff around."

"Maybe I'll give Jim a call next week when I'm in Chicago." Then O'Brien grinned as he imagined the meeting. "Unless he's gotten old, we'll probably end up on Rush Street."

"Okay, but don't make a big thing of it. Just sniff around."

■ ■ ■

An even more important conversation was taking place in Dayton, Ohio, in the office of George Lorenzo, the newly appointed Executive Vice President of Crane Automotive, a very ambitious man.

Lorenzo was thin and short; his expression was usually serious. He had worked his way through the Crane organization rather quickly. After obtaining his MBA from Harvard, he moved in a short time from a position in Long-Range Planning. At thirty-nine, he was Executive Vice President of all Marketing and Sales, and in line for the top job at Crane.

His methods were basic. He would pinpoint what was keeping the operation from being the most profitable, assign the appropriate people to improve these areas, and replace those who did not. Everyone knew that when George Lorenzo gave you an assignment you either did what he asked or you were gone. It did not matter if his assignment was impossible. That only meant your successor would also fail. The result was many people working frantically, in fear for their jobs. Even though some employees were unfairly let go, the operation improved, at least temporarily. That was all Lorenzo wanted. He would be promoted to some other position well before the long-term effect of his style was felt.

In his new job he had analyzed all of Crane's product lines and profit margins. Although shocks had a fairly good profit margin, the shock sales to Sears had low margins. George had dealt with a similar situation with original equipment sales to the automobile companies. The companies had used their size to extract very low prices from all their suppliers. Since the car companies were having quality problems with some of Crane's competitors, Lorenzo gambled on raising prices. The increases were accepted, at least temporarily. This improved profitability immediately, without major programs or expenditures, and made Lorenzo a hero.

Now he was trying the same strategy with Sears. He was laying out the ground rules to Joe Markham, Vice President of Sales, and

Don Peterson, the National Accounts Sales Manager.

Markham, in his late fifties, was tall, slightly overweight, and never without a cigarette. Peterson was younger, smaller, and much more nervous than his boss.

"We can't continue to operate like this," Lorenzo said emphatically, just below a shout. "We have all this money tied up in Sears and the return is not there. We need close to a 20 percent price increase to make this business worthwhile."

Peterson was stunned. He knew Lorenzo's reputation, but he also knew that Sears would never stand for a price increase of 20 percent. "But George," he answered. "The Sears account is almost a cost-plus account. It always has been. We use their volume to keep our costs down on the rest of the business. They know that. It was part of our original supply agreement. We can't just unilaterally change that."

Lorenzo was irked. "I know all about our arrangement with Sears. What I'm telling you is that it's not acceptable anymore. I also know you can't just walk in and raise prices 20 percent. I'm not a dummy. But there are ways to improve our margin, like changing our expense structure, or—"

"You mean pad our expenses?" Peterson interrupted.

"Call it what you like. Change the product line, change the material, run promotions, use different manpower. Find some way to charge them more...or I'll find someone who will."

Peterson was surprised, scared, and angry. The tension was building when Joe Markham broke in. "We'll find something, George."

Markham did not have the slightest idea what to do, but he knew if he resisted, he would be replaced. He had been around a long time and had seen many "whiz kids" come and go. The way to survive was to go along with them until they made a fatal mistake, and then go along with the next one. This was obviously going to be Lorenzo's baby, and if it did not work, it would be Lorenzo's fault. If Lorenzo failed, that was all right with Markham. Maybe then they would consider him for the Exec position.

"Let Don and me mull it around a little," he proposed. "This is new, but I'm sure we can come up with something. Don here knows Sears better than anyone. If anyone can do it, he can."

Lorenzo opened his pocket calendar and started to write. "You have until the 23rd. Bring me your plan on the 23rd, at 8:00 A.M."

As they left the office, Lorenzo was thinking, "I guess I gave those bastards something to think about. If they just get 5 to 7 percent more, Sears will be a nice account."

Markham was thinking, "We may lose the account, but Lorenzo is going to get what he is asking for. I'll make sure everyone knows this is Lorenzo's idea, not mine."

Peterson was not thinking anything. His brain was numb.

■ ■ ■

Ray Pendleton was explaining his frustration to Dorothy. "It's like pushing on a string."

8. Sears, Scotch, and Gin

Ray's reaction to frustration was to work even harder. In addition to his normal marketing duties, he camped on the doorsteps of the product engineers, the manufacturing engineers, the Distribution Manager, several accountants, his own Market Forecasting Group, as well as the executives, Wise, Steele, Simpranian, and Dennison.

He surprised the product engineers by working with them on engineering drawings, trying to consolidate similar shocks into one unit that would fit many vehicles. Where a question of quality arose, he would road test the vehicles with the engineers, playing the part of the customer. One Saturday in late September he tested six different vehicles with the engineers. They were all quite pleased that they had consolidated four designs into one.

When he got home, before he could tell Dorothy, Paul ran out to tell him he had scored two touchdowns in their first game.

"The coach took me out the last quarter," he explained. "Because we were ahead 26 to 6."

When they got inside, Dorothy told him, "You missed a great game. Paul is a great running back and he's not bad as a safety on defense. He makes the zone work."

"Oh," Ray kidded. "You know the positions and the defenses?"

"I take him to practice every day," she replied. "By the end of the season I'll know more than you do. You really ought to get out to his games. He really wants to show you what he can do. He's good."

"I will," Ray responded. "Don't worry, I will. I'm trying to get this Sears thing together and sometimes we can only get the equipment on Saturdays. But I'll be there next week."

Ray missed the next Saturday's game to meet with Dave Dennison, who had been gone all week. In fact, over the next two months he managed to see only two games. Barbara and Dorothy went to every game, and almost every practice. They were the Pendleton family who enjoyed being with the other families. Ray felt like a stranger when he did attend. He was gaining the respect of the Amsaco engineers, but Paul's friends and their families did not know him.

The attitude of Ken Swanson, the Distribution Manager, changed from "I don't need any more problems" to "Hey, this thing might work." Ray worked with him and his staff on trucking schedules, warehouse layout, order-picking schemes, boxing of the small orders, and other distribution concerns. He brought home lists of Sears locations and developed shipping schedules to serve each one without overloading the order pickers.

He worked on his schedules in the kitchen, while Dorothy and the kids watched *Laverne and Shirley* or *The Bionic Woman*. At first, Dorothy would tell the kids to be quiet when they went into the kitchen, so they would not disturb Ray. But by the end of October she did not particularly care. She would scrub the kitchen floor while he worked, or yell in from the living room, "Hey Ray, c'mon in and watch this *One Day at a Time*. It's really good."

Ken Swanson got his staff together and told them to look for other ways to use some of the "Professor's" ideas with their present customers. "The guy knows what he's doing," he told Jim Steele.

But Barbara asked, "Dad, are you ever gonna be through with that Sears stuff?"

Dorothy really became irritated when Ray did not go to the PTA meeting in November. "You already missed the October meeting," she pointed out. "I think you just look for excuses not to go."

This was not far from the truth. He much preferred his work to the PTA meeting, but he would only say, "It's just temporary, honey. I'm almost finished with this and it's important that I do it right."

In the office, Ray was having trouble doing it right. His biggest problems were with the accountants and with Dennison. He could not get Dennison to approve a sales forecast for Sears, which included a large increase. He and Vince had developed an advertising program aimed at making Sears the leader in shock sales. They considered Sears a "sleeping giant" who could dominate the shock business with their program. Dennison, however, would only agree to a mild increase from Sears' present sales. This made it difficult to justify the cost of the Sears effort, especially with the costs of the new equipment. Accounting was adamant about only using numbers that would go into the sales forecast, and Dave Dennison insisted on taking this more conservative approach. Just thinking about taking on the Sears account made Dennison nervous.

The same thing was true with Manufacturing. Jim Steele had insisted that new equipment would be needed to handle the new volume. This new equipment was expensive and made the program less attractive. Ray knew from working with the manufacturing engineers that there were less expensive alternatives, including using existing equipment more efficiently. But Steele saw this as his opportunity to obtain the new equipment, and would not back down.

In addition, Dick Wise questioned whether there was enough capacity for the large volume Ray originally forecast. Steele went along with Wise. "You may be right," Steele said, smiling. "We may need a third plant." This third plant was another pet project of Steele's that he had been campaigning for quietly for some time. This raised the scope beyond what the Sears program could hope to justify. In the face of Dennison's hesitation and the talk of a third plant, Ray backed down to a lower forecast. This would result in poor justification numbers, but he felt he could show that the program would give other benefits, and he could convince Emil that the numbers would be better. Once under way, he was sure they would beat the numbers.

Ray put the whole program together in a document that included a three-page executive summary, a thirty-three page report, and an appendix with over one hundred pages of backup material. If any of his students had brought in a report like that, he would have given them an "A." Ray had looked at his project critically many times, pinpointed some weak areas, and done additional work to correct them. He objectively covered every aspect, producing a thorough, professional business strategy and plan of action. He had been with Amsaco for almost seven months and was confident with his project. He was ready to sell it.

■ ■ ■

Ray's chance came in December, when they were flying to the National Sales Conference in Miami. Dennison had invited Ray on the executive jet for the purpose of presenting the plan to Emil. Dennison wanted Burch to be in on the conversation, but he did not want a big formal meeting. The company plane atmosphere was perfect.

The Falcon was one of many owned by United Tire. Amsaco had the use of Number 629. They could use several others stationed in the Midwest, but primarily used 629. This Falcon was similar to other corporate jets, with plush seats, fold-down tables, provisions for hot meals, and most important, a fully stocked bar. It was designed to seat nine passengers, four up front and five in the rear. The four seats up front had two on each side of the aisle, facing each other. Emil always sat in the forward-facing seat on the right. As he got on, the copilot brought out the seat belt extension to allow Emil to strap himself in.

Dave Dennison sat in the forward-facing seat on the other side of the aisle. This was unofficially the second-ranked seat. Since this was a sales trip, Dave had organized everything and was second in command. Ralph Burch sat facing Dennison, and Dave motioned Ray to take the seat facing Emil. Jim Steele, Tom Chessman, Bob Simpranian, and Mike Evans, the Vice President of Sales, walked through to the back. The eight passengers were all Dennison wanted. Even Ray's boss, Vince Procino, flew down "commercial."

This was the first trip on the Falcon for Ray, and he was impressed. Before they even took off, Mike Evans was serving drinks. Mike was fairly tall, with a round, friendly face. He was approaching retirement age and had a great relationship with most all of the Warehouse Distributors and many Jobbers. He was 100 percent salesman, like Dennison.

"Hey, Professor," Mike asked. "How 'bout a scotch?" Scotch seemed to be most popular with the others, and Ray went along with a scotch and soda. Although he was no connoisseur of fine liquor, he did notice the scotch was Chivas Regal, a pretty expensive one. Burch just had a Coke.

After they were up in the air, Evans brought out the platters of sandwiches and vegetables with dip. The sandwiches were put on the table between Ray and Emil, and the vegetables across the aisle with Dennison and Burch. Two other platters went in the rear. The sandwiches were ham, turkey, roast beef, and tuna salad, cut diagonally into quarters. Ray was sampling each and enjoying his drink when Emil opened the subject.

"What's with your Sears project?"

Ray swallowed his roast beef and answered enthusiastically, "I think we have a good program here. I think we can get the Sears business from Crane and keep it. And it can be profitable." He was skipping the theory of improved market share and the effect on profitability, assuming Emil was well aware of that, which he was. Ray reached behind his seat to get his report from his briefcase. He noticed Emil had the three-page executive summary.

"I have the plan in pretty good detail here. Let me just go through the basics."

As Ray went through some of the details, Emil listened but turned away repeatedly to get some carrots or tomatoes with dip, or to ask if there were any more ham-on-white on the tray in the back, or to ask Evans for another drink. Once Ray stopped talking as Emil yelled toward the back, "Hey, you guys got any peanuts back there?" Then, annoyed that Ray had stopped, "Go on, I'm listening." Dennison half-smiled at Ray; Burch sat expressionless. Ray continued.

When Ray was in the middle of explaining the need for the shortened product line, Emil interrupted, "Let's play gin."

Ray was not ready for that and just stopped with a surprised look. "You want me to switch seats with Tom?"

"No, no." Emil seemed annoyed again. "I want to hear about this Sears shit. You play gin, don't you?"

"Yeah, sure," Ray responded. He knew how to play gin rummy, but he had not played that much. He preferred bridge.

"Good! I need someone else's money besides Chessman's."

The others helped clear away the food as Emil pulled out the cards and the score pad and laid them on the table between them. He grabbed three more little sandwiches as they were taken away. "Have another drink," he said, with a sly smile.

Evans brought Ray his third scotch and soda, and Ray continued talking about the product line. Emil shuffled and started to deal the cards. Dennison had a grin on his face, and Burch was still expressionless, sipping his Coke.

Ray sorted his cards, continuing to explain the salability of the shortened line. As he put the cards in logical order, he noticed Emil was already waiting for him to throw a card. He picked out an eight of spades, which did not seem to fit anything in his hand, and laid it down. Emil smiled as he picked it up. "Looks like I'm going to enjoy this game."

Ray finished the product portion of his plan after they had played five cards. His hand was beginning to take shape. Emil discarded and turned toward Dennison. "What do you think, Dave? Can a short line do the job?"

Dennison sipped his drink and replied slowly. "I think so. I think this would appeal to Sears. They would have a heavier duty shock with fewer numbers to stock. I think Ray did a good job with the engineers."

Emil nodded, then smiled as he picked the right card and laid down his hand. "I got two."

Ray counted up his points. "I have twenty-four. You get twenty-two."

Emil wrote the score down as Ray continued with the distribution plan. He was interrupted twice as Emil won two consecutive hands. This did not bother him, as he was concentrating on his plan.

"The beauty of the ordering system is that it makes them order to fit our schedule. It doesn't really cost us more because it just smooths out our workload."

Emil was taking a handful of peanuts. He asked Burch, "Can we do that? Sounds like it would be expensive."

Burch responded matter-of-factly, "It could be done. I don't know if we could be that sophisticated, but it's possible."

Ray added, "When I first hit Distribution with this, they were negative. Figured it would louse up their present operation. But as we got into it, they agreed that by daily rescheduling during peak periods—"

"Gin," Emil interrupted, laying down his hand. "And spades, double."

Ray counted up his points, and Emil gleefully added up the score. "I'm out in the first game. On a blitz." Looking at Ray he added, "Sounds like you've done your homework on your Sears program. How are you gonna merchandise it?"

Ray started to describe the merchandising plan, but his mind wandered back to the gin game. He had not yet won a hand and they were playing for money.

"How much are we playing for?" he asked.

"Aw, we'll just keep it friendly," Emil answered. "Penny a point."

Ray made a quick calculation and figured he had lost about $7 in the first leg of the first game. He was pleased the way the conversation was going, but he thought maybe he had better pay some attention to the gin game, keep track of what cards were played and what Emil picked up. It was hard to do this when he was trying to concentrate on selling his Sears program.

Mike Evans was pouring Ray's fourth scotch and soda. "Make it kind of weak," Ray directed.

"Make it strong," Emil bellowed as he sorted his cards. "The man here is doing just fine."

Dennison was smiling. Burch was expressionless. Tom Chessman walked over to stand behind Ray to watch him play his cards.

Ray salvaged only one hand out of the first game. It avoided a triple blitz and irritated Emil.

"Lucky son of a bitch," Emil murmured. Then, pointing to the executive summary, he asked, "Why the 6.8 year payback?"

Ray started to answer, but saw that Emil was looking toward Ralph Burch.

"That's what it looks like," Burch replied. "With the two million in new equipment, we don't generate enough sales quick enough to get the payback."

Seeing this as a critical issue, Ray interjected, "I think we can generate substantially more sales than we show. Sears has the potential to do a much bigger job."

Emil turned toward Dave Dennison. "Well, what about it Dave? Can we do better? I don't want to try and sell a 6.8 payback to United."

"Sears is a big operation, Emil," Dennison responded, talking slowly and emphasizing each point. "I agree with Ray that they have potential, but they also have inertia. It's hard to change their system and their way of thinking. We have a 2 percent yearly increase in that forecast. I wouldn't want to bet on more than that."

Ray was pleased to hear Emil respond, "Two percent? Sounds like sandbagging to me." He was not pleased to hear Emil continue with, "Gin."

Dennison did not like to be called a sandbagger, especially when it was close to the truth. "If Sears were our only customer, we could do a lot of things that might make them grow faster," he countered. "But, we have to consider our present customers. I'd hate to have to tell Ed Brown that his sales were down because we're taking care of Sears."

Dennison knew how to get Emil's attention. Ed Brown was a big Warehouse Distributor customer in Pennsylvania. He was very close to Emil, the two having caroused together many times. Ed would have no trouble chewing Emil out if he thought Amsaco was favoring Sears over him. He might even threaten to change lines. By mentioning Ed Brown, Dennison was really bringing up the problem with all of Amsaco's traditional customers.

Amsaco viewed the automotive aftermarket as "traditional" and "nontraditional." The traditional customers were the Warehouse Distributors, or "WDs," who stocked a large inventory of automotive replacement parts and sold them to the auto parts stores, or "Jobbers." The Jobbers, in turn, supplied the service stations and garages in their area.

The nontraditional customers were just about everyone else, and included mass merchandisers such as Sears and Penneys, automotive parts store chains such as Western Auto, and specialty stores like muffler shops.These customers bought direct from the manufacturers, by-passing the WDs.

The WDs did not like to see manufacturers sell directly to other customers, who could pass their savings to consumers. However, Amsaco could not ignore the nontraditional channels of distribution because they sold so many parts.

Emil and Dave Dennison had been brought up in the traditional channel. Emil knew just about every Warehouse Distributor owner in the business, including the Blackwell customers. He had grown with these customers through credit problems, family problems, bad times and good times. Emil was an important man in this group, holding top offices in the industry organizations, giving talks at industry conventions, and privately counseling with most everyone in the industry. He was one of the "family."

Emil knew that the manufacturers could not continue to protect their WDs from the growing market strength of the nontraditional customers. But to lead the change would not be enjoyable or easy. Emil could explain the business reasons for taking on Sears, since his customers and friends were businessmen who would understand. But they would also resist as best they could, demanding other concessions from Amsaco under the guise of competing with Sears. Sooner or later this would have to be done, but Emil was not anxious to do it.

Dave Dennison knew this also, and his reference to Ed Brown was designed to bring the point home to Emil.

As they were discussing the effect on their traditional customers, Ray's hand took shape quickly, and on the fifth card he announced gleefully, "Gin."

Emil scowled. "Goddamned no brainer," he muttered as he counted up his points and wrote in a big total for Ray. Ray just smiled and shuffled the cards.

"How about it, Dave?" Emil asked. "How much trouble would we have with our WDs?"

Dennison knew this would be a key question and was ready. He answered in two stages.

"First of all," he started, looking at Emil and then at Burch. "We have to decide this ourselves. We can't let a few key customers make this decision for us. We have to listen to their concerns and come up with something to offset them. But we have to make the proper business decision for Amsaco. If taking on the Sears account makes good business sense, then that's what we should do. And it's our job to handle our current accounts."

This preamble was necessary to show that Dave was a good businessman. This adherence to the proper business terms such as "good business sense," or "profitability," and "return on investment" was what separated run-of-the-mill salesmen from Management executives. It had served Dave well, and he was using it now for Emil's benefit, and in case this subject went further, for Emil's boss at United Tire. This made little impression on Ralph Burch, who thought anyone without an accounting background did not really understand business anyway. Tom Chessman recognized the preamble for just what it was. Tom himself would have said something similar, and he thought Dennison did it very well.

"Be that as it may," Dave continued. "We'll have a hard time. If I were in Blackwell's shoes, I would welcome this. I would be in to every Amsaco customer, asking them if Sears was any competition. I'd ask them if they got the same price as Sears. I'd ask if they liked the Sears short line, and whether they got the opportunity to buy the same product line from Amsaco."

Emil was listening to this carefully and imagining himself in the same position. Emil himself would have to face these customers sometime. He imagined the American Warehouse Distributors meeting in Las Vegas, where they met with every customer for an hour in their suite. He usually enjoyed AWDA, the gambling and taking the customers to shows and dinners. With the Sears program to explain, all the fun would be gone. It would be work…hard work.

As Emil was thinking these depressing thoughts, Ray picked up the perfect card and knocked, beating Emil with another "no brainer." Emil, who was ahead about $50, saw the momentum changing.

Dennison continued, "We can talk with our customers and show them they would be no worse off with us supplying Sears than with Crane. In fact, we could keep things under control better than Crane. And we could even tie some fill-in sales for our Jobbers if they are near a Sears store. But it would be rough. We would be forced into some price concessions…and we would probably lose some business."

Emil scowled and Dennison added, "But we can handle it. That's our job. We'll have a rough six months, maybe a year. But we're not being paid to have fun. This will test how good we are."

Emil found little consolation in this thought. "What bothers me is that we don't gain anything from all this trouble. The whole program has a lousy payback. Even after going through all this shit, we don't make any money."

Ray jumped in at. "The numbers don't reflect the real possibilities," he argued. "With the Sears volume our manufacturing operation should improve...we should produce at lower costs. And I'm sure we can improve on the sales numbers. Sears is capable of selling much more than we forecast. I'd say these numbers are ultraconservative."

In that short statement, Ray had disagreed with Jim Steele, Dave Dennison, and Ralph Burch, the three highest-level executives behind Emil. He had said to Emil that Steele could produce at a lower cost than agreed to in the report, that Dennison could sell more than shown, and Burch had agreed to "ultraconservative" numbers. He was not sure if the drinks had anything to do with it, but he immediately wished he had been a little more diplomatic.

The effect was not lost on Tom Chessman, who asked with a little too much innocence, "Ralph, you think these guys are bein' ultraconservative?"

Burch was too experienced to criticize the numbers of the other executives when the numbers were all estimated anyway. There would be plenty of time to criticize when the numbers were proven wrong. And they always were, one way or another.

"The numbers speak for themselves," he answered. "I have no reason to believe Dave's forecast is conservative." This identified the forecast as Dave's. "And as far as production costs," he continued, "Jim had Ted Lyons spend a lot of time costing the new equipment. With this equipment, Jim will lower our production costs. But that's built into the figures." This statement identified the production costs as Jim's and informed Emil that the new equipment was an important part of the low payback. It also mentioned Ted Lyons, which was aimed at irritating Chessman.

This worked, as Chessman added, "Lyons is a sandbagger."

"Maybe so," Burch replied, "But Jim depends on him. I'm sure Jim has gone over everything in the plan. Let's ask Jim."

"Nah," Emil said as he held up his hand. He knew what Jim would say. Right then he was debating which card to throw from his hand. He selected the four of diamonds.

Ray grabbed the card, placed it correctly among his cards and pronounced, "Gin!"

"Shit," said Emil as he added up the score. He wasn't pleased that Ray could win three hands in a row.

Everyone stopped talking momentarily as Ray shuffled and dealt. Emil reached for another sandwich and thought about trying to sell this to Ed Brown or the other WDs. He saw no problem selling the program to United Tire. He knew that when they put an appropriation together to get the funds from United, his people could redo the numbers to show less investment, more cost savings, and more sales. Less investment was easy. Every request for manufacturing equipment that Emil had ever seen was for the best and the most. If Jim were told to do the job for 50 percent of what he asked for, he would do it. And they could show an improvement in efficiencies to give significant cost savings. This, together with a slight increase in the Sears sales projection, would change the numbers enough to show an acceptable payback.

He also knew that United would never be able to audit the project to see if Amsaco ever made their projections. Everything would be scrambled in with the rest of the operation, and the Sears numbers would not be available as they now appeared. The profits on the Sears business would be shown eventually, but Burch could make that come out any way he wanted. There would be no problem with United. They would probably like the idea.

But the WDs would be a problem. There would be some who would really feel betrayed. And they would make this personal with Emil. He could think of fifteen or twenty customers he would personally have to meet and console…and not just at the AWDA meetings. He knew of others who would use Sears as an excuse to weasel some price concessions from him. Dennison understood the situation. It meant trouble, and Emil did not want trouble. He was having enough trouble just trying to beat this "patsy" in gin rummy.

"No, I don't think so," Emil announced suddenly. "It's not good business. We spend too much money, get our customers pissed off, and then we add volume and headaches without any big profits. No, I don't think it's worthwhile."

Ray was sipping his fifth scotch and soda as Emil talked, and he sat up suddenly, almost spilling it.

"But Emil," he argued, "It will be worth it in the long run. We use the reduced production costs to increase our sales in other areas than Sears. And we can do better than—"

"Nah," said Emil shaking his head, "that market share theory is a bunch of crap. It'll cost us through the nose with all of our customers. Sears ain't worth it."

Ray threw an eight of diamonds and immediately saw that it fit his hand and he should not have thrown it. A few cards later, Emil was smiling as he laid down his hand.

"Gin!"

Ray's mind was spinning. He was just getting started—how could it be all over? He had overcome the apathy of the organization. Now that they had a feasible program laid out, Emil would be receptive. Emil would understand the benefits from increasing market share, the logic of the plan, the practicality of targeting Crane. The plan made sense. The only major hurdle would be convincing Sears to change suppliers. But if they ran into a stone wall at Sears, they would not spend any of the funds and would lose nothing. Handling present traditional WDs was a minor problem—Dennison himself said they could handle it. And Emil would see that the numbers underestimated the payback on the investment. Emil would see that these numbers were ultraconservative.

Dave Dennison lit up a cigar and moved to the back to talk with Mike Evans. Chessman poured refills for Ray and Emil, and took Dennison's seat. Even Ralph Burch sat back and drank a glass of white wine, a good German Mosel.

Emil would not let Ray stop playing cards. The momentum had changed and Emil was winning hand after hand.

"You play an interesting game," commented Chessman. "We ought to play sometime."

Ray, in a daze, rambled on about his plan, but no one was listening.

Ray had lost track of how many drinks he'd had, but he knew it was too many.

As Emil kept winning, he became happier. "I like the job you did on the product line," he told Ray. "Do you think we could offer that to our Jobbers? Maybe you ought to work on that. Our traditional customers would want a low inventory line. This might be just what they need."

"Maybe as a second line," Ray responded cautiously, trying to get his thoughts together. "There are still a lot of holes in the line. The

Jobber still wants to have coverage for every car on the road. But if we cut some costs, maybe we could develop a second line, a price line."

"Sounds good to me. Work on it." Emil was adding up the points he had just won. "And another thing," he added, "the ordering system could also work for our WDs. We can call them up regularly to take orders. The muffler people have the whole thing on the computer. They actually manage the WD's inventory. Your system could be modified to do that. What do you think?"

Ray again answered cautiously, "I'm sure there is something there. The problem would come when our WD also carried competitor lines. They don't do that with mufflers, because of the space the pipes take up. They only carry one line, so the muffler people can control the whole inventory. But maybe we can use a program like that to push our competitors out. We could offer them the service for nothing if it will push our competition out."

"Good," said Emil, smiling. "I like the way you think. Do it."

As the plane approached Miami, Emil took pity on Ray and ended the gin game. As he added up the totals he stated emphatically, "You did a real good job on this, Ray. First class!"

"Yeah, but you turned it down."

"Don't worry about that. You can't always get what you want in the real business world."

Emil finished up the tally "It comes to $91.56. Just make it $90 even."

Ray pulled out his wallet and started to count out the $90. Luckily, he had cashed a check for $150 just before he left. He did not think he would need much money because Vince told him everything was paid for as a group. He felt the others were laughing at him as he paid, but no one even smiled.

As Emil was putting the money in his wallet, he continued, "No Ray, don't worry. I think you did a fine job, just what we need. You looked at the overall picture and came up with a sound strategy. What's more, you worked out the details, the stuff that makes the strategy work. And now we have some ideas you can apply, even if we don't go after Sears. This is just what we brought you in here for."

Chessman was smiling and Burch nodded as the plane came in for a landing. Ray's thoughts were confused. He had never been turned down so nicely before.

Two limousines were at the plane to take them to the hotel. Ray felt somewhat woozy as they walked to the men's room before getting in the limos.

Tom Chessman walked back with Ray, congratulating him. "That was a great session. Best business meeting I've been to in a long time. You did a good job."

"What do you mean?" asked Ray,

"Well, you heard Emil. He really thought highly of your work. I'm glad we brought you in. We would never get that type of a job from the other sales yo-yos."

"But Emil rejected my plan. He turned me down." Ray thought for a moment. "And it cost me $90."

"Don't worry so much. You did just fine."

Then, as they approached the limo, Tom put his arm over Ray's shoulder. "Just relax and enjoy the meeting. They have a great golf course here, and the food is first class. Maybe we could play some gin tonight after the speeches."

9. Up the Proverbial Ladder

At the sales meeting reception, Ray explained to his boss what had happened on the plane. Sipping on club soda, Ray described the arguments leading to Emil's rejection. Procino laughed when Ray told of his disastrous gin game, but seeing Ray's unhappiness, took a more consoling tone.

"Don't take it too hard Ray. You did a good job. And apparently Emil recognized that, or he wouldn't have said all those nice things. Emil isn't known for saying nice things."

"Well, I know I did a good job," Ray responded emphatically. "I worked on this for six months, and it wasn't easy. And you know! I could have dropped it right in the beginning when everyone was against it. But the program made sense. That's why it kept going, because it was right. And it still is."

"Hold on Ray," Vince interrupted. "Have some patience. Don't try to make everyone go faster than they want to. It looks to me that Emil just wasn't ready for such a big step. Or Dennison or Burch either. Believe me, Dave can get what he wants from Emil, but not *when* he wants. He has to wait for the right moment."

"You mean Dave knew this was the wrong time? Was this trip a setup?" Ray was showing a little anger.

"No, no, nothing like that," Vince said defensively. "Dave couldn't know how Emil would respond. It might depend on what mood he was in, or how good the food was, or—"

"Well, he must have been pleased with how the gin game was going," Ray said bitterly, not remembering that when Emil rejected the plan, Ray had won three straight hands. He sighed gloomily. "I don't know, Vince, it's discouraging. Maybe this job isn't for me." Maybe after all he was just a Professor with theories that looked good on paper. Ray shuddered as he imagined Henry saying, "I told you so." Ray stood sipping his club soda with a morose expression.

"Quit feeling sorry for yourself," Vince said, poking Ray in the arm. "You're doing just fine. I'm your boss and I say you're doing fine. Let's meet some of the sales force. That's what we're here for."

All around them Amsaco field salesmen and home office personnel were loudly greeting each other. Stories of exploits with customers were being told and plans were being made for carousing later that night.

Vince led Ray across the room. "I want you to meet Casey Brown, our District Manager in Alabama. He's a real character, but I swear he sells more shocks in his little southern district than there are cars. Find out how he does that and we'll have a worthwhile trip....Hey Casey, I have a Professor here who I want you to give some selling lessons to."

Ray followed Vince and met Casey Brown and many others. He did not learn anything about selling, but he did learn not to play poker with Brown. The game lasted until 3:00 A.M. and cost Ray another $40. By the time the first seminar started at 9:00, Ray was tired, slightly hungover, and quite a bit poorer than when the trip had started.

■ ■ ■

When Ray got home, he filled Dorothy in on the details of his meeting with Emil and the rejection of his Sears plan. He expected her to console him, tell him he was really very good and not to worry. Everything would be all right.

He was surprised at her reaction. "Why don't you tell them to shove it?" she said angrily. "If they weren't interested, why didn't they stop you sooner?"

"Well they did, actually," Ray responded. "Or at least they tried to. But each reason they gave that I should stop, I came back with a solution—"

"And you were right. If they didn't want to do anything different, why did they hire you to come up with something different?"

Dorothy was angry at Emil's rejection. But she knew it was more than that. The move to Michigan had left her lonely and frustrated. After the family was settled, Dorothy gradually was left alone.

Paul signed up for Little League, and soon he found two other boys from the league who lived in their neighborhood. He spent his days playing baseball or basketball, swimming, or doing nothing at all at a friend's house. By the time school started, Paul had all but forgotten his old New England friends. Barbara made new friends when school started and became busy as well.

Dorothy was alone during school hours and sometimes after. She was alone at night when Ray was on a trip. She was even alone sometimes when Ray was home but working on his Amsaco business. Worse than being alone, Dorothy felt alone.

Back home in New England, she had enjoyed her time alone. Friends, neighbors, and school acquaintances were always nearby if she wanted company. There was always something to do, someone to talk to, never enough time. When she was alone, it was a relief, a chance to get something done.

Dorothy had not "clicked" with any of the Amsaco wives, and Ray made no effort to socialize from work. The Grosses and the Dennisons were part of the country club set, a different social strata. Dorothy had met some of the neighbors and some of the school parents, but hadn't become better acquainted, except with her neighbor Mary Kelly. But an occasional cup of coffee with Mary was not a social life.

She could have tolerated loneliness if at least Ray's job were going well. But to bear the loneliness and hard work of getting her home and family settled and to still see Ray unhappy made the move to Michigan seem worse than useless. While the additional money was nice, the main reason for moving was to give Ray a chance with a real company. It was infuriating to go through all this and have Ray ignored. "Why don't you just quit," she said angrily. "The money isn't worth it."

Ray looked at his wife, surprised and a little anxious. He couldn't understand why she was overreacting. She was usually so sensible.

"I can't quit just because of that," he said, putting his arm around her shoulders. "I have to stick it out some more. This is just one idea. There'll be more. I promise you I'll keep fighting. Things will get better.

■ ■ ■

Ray did not have to wait long. The following Wednesday, Vince was waiting at Ray's desk when he arrived. He had a knowing grin on his face.

"Ralph Burch wants to see you."

"What about?"

"Can't say. Ralph will fill you in."

Ray wondered what Burch could want from him, since the Sears deal was dead.

Burch greeted Ray, asked him to sit down, forced a little smile, and came right to the point. "Ray, Emil is modifying our organization somewhat, reducing the number of people reporting directly to him. Right now he has twelve. With the growth of Amsaco, this arrangement is no longer workable. In order to give proper attention to his business associates and to give proper direction to all parts of our organization, he has made some modifications to our organization."

Ray heard what was said, but thought he heard something more. "Is there anything wrong with Emil, with his health?"

Burch appeared annoyed at the interruption of his official explanation. " Emil's health is fine. This is strictly a move to distribute management responsibilities better. That's all! It's good business policy in a growing organization."

Ray did not completely buy this. For one thing, they were not growing that much. But Burch's tone discouraged any further questions.

Burch continued, "As part of this reorganization, I would like you to join my department as Director of Long-Range Planning. The promotion from Manager to Director is significant, and it includes a salary increase to $46,000 per year."

Burch let this sink in for a few seconds. "As a member of my staff," he went on, "you would also be eligible for our Management Bonus Program, which, depending on our earnings, could generate up to 50 percent of your salary in a year-end bonus. Two-thirds would be paid before Christmas, based on projected earnings, and one-third in March, after earnings are confirmed."

Ralph went on, speaking in a flat, unemotional tone, "Of course, you should not count on a 50 percent bonus. Over the past five years we have averaged 12.8 percent, with a high of 22.3 percent in 1973, and a low of 5.1 percent last year. It depends strictly on company earnings."

Ray was stunned. The last thing he expected was to be promoted.

His main efforts had gone into the Sears program, and that had been rejected. And why a promotion to Finance? Ralph had not said ten words to Ray since he had come to Amsaco. Why Long-Range Planning? This was Elmer Wilde's area and mainly concerned financial data showing projected performance over the next five years. "What about Wilde?" he asked.

"Yes, I should have mentioned that first. Elmer is going down to Dallas, to the United Tire Business Planning Department. His knowledge of our operation should be very useful to United. You'll be working with him in your new position."

"Well, it certainly is a surprise," Ray said.

Ralph nodded. He said no more, so Ray asked, "Why did you pick me? I'm not complaining," he added quickly, "but what would you expect of me?"

"In the Long-Range Planning position we need someone with a good overview of our business, both by itself and in comparison with other businesses. We need someone to assess what changes are needed and how we can get those changes, and to help present these plans internally and in Dallas. We need someone with a knowledge of business strategies who can put together a creative plan. And a practical one." Burch paused. "You're clearly the right man for the job."

Burch had been impressed with Ray's analysis of their business position, which had led to the Sears plan. And he was even more impressed with the thoroughness of Ray's work with Engineering, Distribution, Manufacturing, and the other disciplines. Ray would give him good business programs that would build Burch's credit with United Tire. He could use Ray's talents.

What Ralph did not tell Ray was that he was too good a businessman to leave under Dennison—not that the Marketing people would ruin Ray, but Ray might make better businessmen out of the Marketing Group. Dennison was Burch's main competition for Emil's job, and he did not want him looking good to Max Simpson and United Tire. If the Sears plan had gone to Dallas, it would have been Dennison's presentation. Burch intended to be the only one to present good plans to Dallas.

Ray thought over what Ralph had told him. Ray had always concentrated on marketing strategies, but these were always based on what marketing had to do to support the overall business strategy. Even his Sears plan had started as a basic business plan showing a need for an increased market share. In fact, had he been able to tie in the long-range benefits the whole organization would have received, he might have been more successful. It made sense for him to work on overall business planning. Burch wouldn't be the most congenial of men to work with, but he was clearheaded on the business issues—and the opportunity had great possibilities.

"The more I think about it, the more I like it," Ray said. "I've always been oriented to marketing, but within the context of total business planning."

"Exactly," Burch agreed. "That's why I want you in Long-Range Planning."

"But what about the reorganization? What other changes have been made?"

Ralph pulled out the new organization chart.

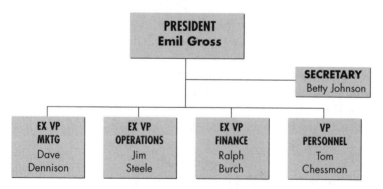

"It's not really complicated," Ralph explained. "Emil will now have five people reporting to him. Jim Steele is now Executive Vice President of Operations, handling Engineering and Distribution as well as Manufacturing. Ken Swanson and Bob Simpranian will report to him, as well as Ted Lyons and the Plant Managers."

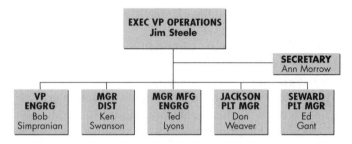

"Dave Dennison will have all Marketing and Sales, with Dick Dorsey and the International Operation reporting to him."

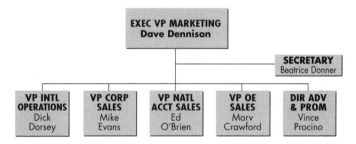

Ray sensed some irritation in Ralph's voice when he described Dennison's international responsibilities. He wondered if Burch thought the assignment was undeserved, that Dennison could not handle it.

Burch continued. "My responsibilities will now include administration as well as finance. I will have legal responsibility, with Jack Rule reporting to me. Pete Stark and Public Relations will report to me. And of course, Long-Range Planning."

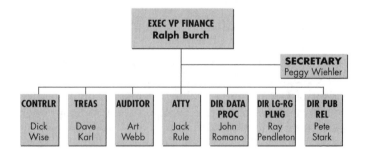

"And Chessman?" Ray asked.

"Tom will continue to report to Emil. And of course, Betty Johnson makes five."

Ray was trying to digest all the implications of the changes. The strongest executives on Emil's old staff were the only ones left on his new staff. Dave Dennison was getting the International Operation, which included Manufacturing as well as Marketing. It meant more responsibility, and it was good training for the top job. Jim Steele was getting Product Control in addition to Manufacturing and Distribution. He would have 80 percent of the company's employees reporting to him, as well as 90 percent of the company's assets. Ralph Burch would have control of all the communication between Amsaco and United Tire. Tom Chessman would still be playing gin with Emil.

Ray was smiling as he thought of Chessman. Burch leaned back in his chair and asked, "What do you think? Does this position sound interesting? I need your answer as soon as possible. We'll be announcing this on Friday."

Ray thought for a moment. "It sounds great," he said. "The more I think about it, the more it seems to fit. Business planning is really my expertise. I might be a little weak in the financial area."

"I agree," Burch said. "You would have help from Al Goldman. He will be given the assignment to work with you on the financial implications of the plan."

This impressed Ray. Burch had recognized not only Ray's strengths but also his weakness. "Yes, that would work out well. Al and I could work together. He's one of the few accountants I can understand."

Burch did not laugh at his joke. He smiled, faintly. "Then it's settled?"

"Well, I should talk this over with my wife first. We usually discuss things like this."

"What for?"

Ray thought for a moment, noticing that Burch seemed a little annoyed. "Dorothy and I always talk over any changes that affect the family." Burch's expression was getting more serious, his eyes narrowing as Ray talked. "I'm not asking for her approval. We just talk over any important move."

Burch sat back in his chair, staring coldly at Ray, saying nothing. Feeling the tension building, Ray kept talking. "Of course, this doesn't really change anything for the family. We don't have to move or anything. It's just a better job, a promotion."

"Exactly."

"OK then. I accept." Ray stood up to shake Burch's hand. "When do I start, boss?"

Burch's faint cold smile reappeared. "My secretary, Peggy, will get you situated in your new office. Elmer should be out early next week. I suggest you get in touch with him and he will bring you up-to-date on our present plan. Don't say anything to the others until the announcement on Friday."

Ray fully intended to keep this information confidential and tell no one except Dorothy. On the way back to his office, however, he was congratulated twice on his promotion, once by a product planning supervisor and once by his secretary. When he walked into Vince Procino's office, Vince was smiling broadly and stood up to shake his hand.

"Congratulations, Professor."

"You son of a gun," Ray said. "Why didn't you tell me? I've never been so surprised in my life."

"Sorry, I just couldn't. The job offer is made by the new boss. That's the way the system works. I'm real happy for you. Looks like a good opportunity, and well deserved. We'll miss you here though."

"Will you be replacing me?"

"Not exactly. I'll move the promotion programs around. The marketing planning I'll handle myself."

"Then, we'll still be working together."

"In a different ball game, yes."

"You know, Vince," Ray went on, "we have had a different relationship than I expected in a big corporation. Even though you've been the boss, we work more like friends. You've helped me in lots of ways. And you've backed me and been a real friend. And I want you to know I appreciate it."

Vince grasped Ray's hand. "Well, let's see if we can continue to be friends now you're an accountant." He laughed. "That's a stiff test. It's hard to be friends with an accountant. Just don't forget your humble beginnings in Marketing."

■ ■ ■

Ray called Dorothy with the news and told her to get the kids some fast food and get ready to go out to a fancy restaurant to celebrate. They drove over to Win Schuler's in Marshall. He thought she would be miffed that he had accepted the job without talking it over with her, but that did not seem to bother her at all. He thought that she would be overjoyed with the raise, but she showed surprising reserve.

"I'm happy about the new responsibilities and the promotion," she told him as he dug into the little meatballs on the appetizer tray. "And the money and all that. But, there's something about this that makes me uneasy."

"What's that?"

"I don't know exactly." She sipped her drink slowly. "Something just doesn't add up. If they thought so much of your work, it had to be based on the Sears plan. That was all Gross or Burch saw of your work. And if they were so impressed, why didn't they buy it? You said yourself that Burch didn't do anything to help you on the plane. It doesn't add up."

"Well, they had their own reasons for not going along with the Sears plan," Ray responded. He found himself defending Gross and Burch, when he really had the same doubts as Dorothy. "That doesn't mean they didn't see the logic in the plan. Or the fact that I did a good job. I thought they missed that, but apparently they didn't." Ray was getting a little annoyed.

Dorothy picked this up and smiled. "Here you get this nice promotion and I'm just looking at the gloomy side. I'm sorry."

"Apology accepted. Here, try these meatballs. They're delicious."

Ray dove into the relish tray as Dorothy tried the meatballs.

"Go over the money part again," she said, smiling. "That sounds OK."

"Salary of $46,000. That's an increase of 15 percent. And at the Director level, the bonus could be up to 50 percent of my salary. But Burch said they've never gotten that much. It averages about 12 percent."

"The best we ever got from the university was a $25 gift certificate."

"And if we take the basic salary of $46,000 and we add the 12 percent, that's $51,500. Twice what I was making at Harvard." He smiled broadly as the waiter set down Dorothy's filet mignon and his New York steak. "With that kind of money, we can eat this way all the time."

"I could learn to live like this," Dorothy agreed. "What's this meal going to cost us? Two steaks, a bottle of wine...$20? For one night out? I can remember when we held our groceries to $20 a week." She thought a moment as she sipped her wine. "I just get nervous when I think that everything depends on Gross and Burch...and Chessman."

"Well...me too. But I guess we'll have to get used to it. Look, six months ago, I didn't know if I could make it in this company. But they like my work, and now I'm a Director in line for a bonus."

"You're right," Dorothy said emphatically. "I'm just being gloomy. We might as well enjoy it. This steak is delicious, by the way, and I love this restaurant. The kids are doing great and you're doing great and I'm glad they really appreciate you." She paused and frowned thoughtfully. "It's just your new boss, Burch. He seems like such a...creep."

10. The Creep

Vince and Ray had always discussed ideas and talked about other employees, about Amsaco and industry legends, about marketing theory, industry politics, and their own experiences. By the time Ray had something formal to present, Vince already knew all the facts because they had already discussed it many times.

Ray did not expect the same level of rapport with Burch, but he would need some solid discussions to help him understand the complexities of planning for Amsaco. When Ray first considered a change in the planning schedule, he stopped by Burch's office to discuss the idea. Burch was working at his desk calculator as Ray entered. As he finished a calculation, he looked up at Ray, saying nothing.

After an uncomfortable silence, Ray figured he was supposed to speak. He smiled. "Well, I finally got Elmer Wilde on his way down to Texas, and it wasn't easy. I don't think he wanted to leave the friendly confines of Jackson, Michigan, and Amsaco for the big city of Dallas and United Tire." Ray wanted to break the ice with a little light conversation.

Ralph looked at him stonily. "It's a good opportunity," he said.

Again, uncomfortable silence. Apparently small talk was unacceptable. Ray came to the point. "One of the last things Elmer and I discussed was the planning schedule. Elmer had it set up to get preliminary plans from all groups at the same time. While this works out well for our schedule, it gives Manufacturing and Engineering some real problems."

He paused, but Burch said nothing. Ray continued. "I would like to get the marketing plan out first, so that Operations will know exactly what they have to produce when they make out their plan. It extends the schedule somewhat, but there will be less re-hashing and changing."

Jim Steele had asked him, "Why should Manufacturing have to guess at next year's production requirements, and Engineering guess at the product line requirements, only to find out Marketing is pushing a different product or product line? Why not make Marketing submit their plan first, at least a preliminary plan?" This made sense to Ray. But Elmer Wilde was skeptical that Marketing could get a plan together on schedule. Ray wanted to bounce this off Burch to see if there was something he was missing. Burch listened but showed zero reaction and offered no comments, helpful or otherwise. Ray saw why Dorothy might consider him a creep.

Ray continued. "I think we can push Marketing to get their rough forecast and product plans put together first. Even if the promotion programs and other internal plans are not complete, they can get enough information over to Operations so they don't have to guess at the figures. Our schedule will be a little tighter, but reasonable."

Burch replied, "Let me see the schedule before you send it out."

This was not an approval, but it was not an objection either. More of a dismissal. Burch was not going to give him any guidance, but he did not want Ray to go ahead without his approval. Ray might as well not have bothered him until he had a finished schedule. Ray saw that it was time for him to leave. He stood up and walked toward the door, a little embarrassed that he had wasted Burch's time. "OK, I'll get it to you," he said.

Burch grunted as he turned back to his calculations.

Ray told Al Goldman of the meeting. Al just smiled and said, "That's his MBA training...MBA 101. 'Let a Manager do his own work, but better check it before it goes out.'"

"I didn't want him to do my work," Ray said, feeling a little defensive. "I just wanted to get his thoughts before I went too far, so I didn't go off on a tangent...different from what he wants."

Al kept smiling. "He'll tell you if you went off on a tangent when you bring in the schedule."

"But it would be a hell of a lot less work if I knew what he wanted in the first place."

"Less work for you, not for him. It's his MBA horseshit. He's much more comfortable with a piece of paper, summarizing the situation, than with conversations or meetings. This way, he only has to think about it once. When you put the schedule in front of him, you'll get his opinion."

■ ■ ■

Ray attended the first of the obligatory staff meetings Burch held every Monday morning in order to be ready for Emil's staff meeting in the afternoon. Dick Wise started going over "the numbers," the financial results of the previous week. This was interesting at first, but as he went on to cover each line item for every department, Ray gradually tuned out.

Wise reported, "The efficiency at Jackson is down 1.4 percent, but only down 0.7 percent at Seward."

"Why is that?" Burch asked.

"Mainly volume. Steele switched some volume from Jackson to Seward. No sense using high-cost union labor in Jackson when we have empty capacity in Seward."

"Good," Burch said, then asked, "Are we full then in Seward?"

"No," Wise answered with a slight smile. "Nowhere near full. Steele wants to take it slow so we don't start any trouble with the UAW." Burch just nodded his understanding and wrote down some notes.

Wise droned on: "—Production Planning is 22.6 percent over their data processing budget. They're running some kind of simulation.

"—Corporate Sales salaries are 2.3 percent under budget, but only because they have six open reqs. When they fill them, they'll be over budget, and way over last year.

"—Manufacturing Engineering supplies are 6.8 percent over. They bought some fancy calculator."

Ray looked at his watch. Wise had been at it for forty minutes. Ray was impressed at how Accounting seemed to know everything that was going on, but he did not see why he and the others at the table had to sit through this conversation between Burch and Wise. Wise could just as well have given Burch the report. Ray started to get a little sleepy.

Finally Wise finished and Burch called on Dave Karl, the Treasurer; then Art Webb, the Auditor; Jack Rule, the Attorney; and John Romano, the Director of Data Processing. Only Romano took more than two minutes, as he explained that they were running into some problems with the new Honeywell computer system, but it should be operational in three weeks.

When it was Ray's turn, all he could report was that he was thinking of changing the Long-Range Planning schedule so that Marketing would come up with their requirements first.

"Let me see that schedule," Burch said, and Ray was done.

The only hint of excitement came during Pete Stark's Public Relations presentation. He had two requests, one for an executive to join the Jackson Chamber of Commerce Board of Directors, and the other to give a speech at the Seward Lion's Club luncheon.

Burch looked annoyed. "We don't need to waste our time with the Chamber of Commerce. What do they do for us?"

"But we're one of the biggest employers in town," Stark protested. "They're asking us for someone to be a Director so we'll be represented—so we'll have a say in what goes on."

"Then you do it. That's your job." Burch paused and looked around the table. "Anyone here got nothing to do? Want to be a Director? How about you, Ray?"

Everyone but Ray and Pete Stark laughed hysterically at the boss's joke at Ray's and Pete's expense. Ray would have liked to be on the Chamber Board, but not under these conditions. He just shook his head.

Burch looked at Stark and said, "You do it."

Stark nodded, then asked, "What about the Lion's Club in Seward?"

"Let the Seward plant handle it."

"But our Plant Manager's the one who asked me. He told them he would get someone from the home office. He wants someone who will say how important Seward is to Amsaco."

Burch thought for a moment. "Ask Dennison," he concluded. "He always has someone on the road. He, or one of his vice presidents, could tell them how important Seward's shipments are to sales."

With that, the meeting was over. Without saying a word, everyone left the room. Ray was not happy about the meeting. Nothing had been accomplished, and he had been the butt of a not-so-funny joke. Outside in the hallway, Pete Stark commented ironically to Ray, "Those accountants sure are a wild bunch."

■ ■ ■

The trouble with Burch's joke was that it was too close to the truth. It was not that Ray had "nothing to do," but he did not have very much. The long-range plan and the next year's business plan did not require a lot of time. On the other hand, long-range planning was a full-time job.

Ray approached planning the way he would teach it at Harvard. He analyzed the key elements of the company. What were Amsaco's strengths and weaknesses? Who was the real competition? What were the strengths and weaknesses of the competition? Where was the total shock market going? Where should Amsaco go? Where could Amsaco go? These and many other detailed questions pointed to a corporate goal and a strategy to get there. The long-range plan would be the way to implement this strategy.

But whenever Ray tried to discuss long-range goals and strategies, Burch was dismissive. "Your job is the plan. Just get the plan out on time, with accurate numbers that everyone agrees on."

"But how can we write a plan without a strategy for the plan to implement?" Ray asked with some frustration. "And how can we have a strategy if we don't have a goal?"

"We have a goal," Burch answered, impatiently. "I don't know what kind of goals they teach at Harvard, but our goal is to be profitable. And everyone knows that goal. Now, if a good acquisition comes up, fine. We'll take a look at it. And if a marketing opportunity comes along—fine. We'll look at that. But they don't go in the plan. You understand?"

"Yes, I understand. But isn't looking for these opportunities part of my job?"

Burch threw up his hands in frustration. "Fine, look for opportunities. Do whatever you want in your spare time, but make sure the plan is done accurately and on time."

Ray left Burch's office confused. If all they needed was to coordinate each department's plan, any accountant could have done that—and better than Ray. He had seen his promotion to Director of Long-Range Planning as an agreement between Emil and Burch to put him in a better position to develop and direct company strategy. "What other reason would they have?" he asked Al Goldman.

Goldman laughed. "You're assuming they had a reason."

Ray shook his head. "I don't like working for an accountant."

Goldman laughed louder.

■ ■ ■

Ray would have been less confused, but more worried, if he had heard a private conversation between Burch and Dick Wise. To Burch and Wise the corporate world consisted of the financial people versus everyone else. Wise viewed his job as providing Burch with all the information he needed to fight the other executives on Emil's staff—and Emil too, for that matter. This was not just an idle thought. Once Burch had told Wise, "When we take over this company, I'm going to have a financial man in every key position. Then watch costs go down."

"What's the Professor doing with next year's plan?" Burch asked Wise after one of his staff meetings. "He seems to be taking a lot of time, and I want—"

He was interrupted by his secretary, who said, "Mr. Tracy's office is on the line. Do you want to take the call?"

"Yes, of course."

Alan Tracy was the Chief Financial Officer at United Tire, reporting directly to Dave Torres, the Chairman of the Board. While Burch technically reported to Emil, Tracy had a direct line to the top financial man at every United company. This irritated Emil and his boss, Max Simpson. Simpson did not like anyone at the home office to know what was happening at his companies unless he told them. But this was one of the checks and balances in Torres' organization.

Burch picked up the phone.

"This is Ralph Burch."

"Hold on, Mr. Burch," said Tracy's secretary. "I'll put Mr. Tracy on."

"Morning, Ralph. How's it going?"

"Morning, Alan. Not so good, really…not so good."

"What's the problem?"

"Same as usual, no improvement in sales and no reduction in costs."

"Damn it," Tracy muttered. "I thought it was clear to Emil that if sales didn't pick up he had to get his costs in line."

"Yeah, that's what I heard," Burch answered. "But you know

Emil. He's always been a spender—and a dreamer. He figures things will pick up any day now."

"I know, I know. He's a salesman. But I need some accurate numbers. What will your quarterly report show?"

"It'll show no improvement, but we'll show next quarter getting better."

"Like you always do."

"I'm sorry, Alan, but I don't run this company."

There was silence for a moment. Then Tracy asked, "Could you send me down some accurate numbers? Let me know what you'll officially send down, and then send me what you think you'll hit year end, realistically."

"I'll get it out today."

"Good. That's all I need right now."

"Say, Alan, there's something I wanted to touch base with you on. A little personal."

"Go on."

"It's not much. It's about my daughter. She's finishing up her first year at Washtenaw in accounting."

"Your daughter's in accounting?"

"Yeah. I don't know why. I don't know where she thinks she's going with it. But she thinks she can go anywhere a man can."

Tracy laughed. "Yeah, this women's lib shit."

"I guess so. My son will be in accounting. But he can work his way up to the top. Of course, he's only in ninth grade now, but he can become a Manager. My daughter says she can too. Can you imagine girls at our management meeting?"

Tracy laughed again. "It's coming. Our political people say it's coming. They say those lesbians in Washington are going to get it done. Anyway, why do you bring it up?"

"She's looking for a job for summer, and I don't think she should work here. I was wondering if there was somewhere else in the company, like Berringer. But I didn't want to start anything before running it by you." Burch knew it would not have been a problem to handle this himself, but he also knew Tracy enjoyed using his influence whenever he could.

"I don't see any problem," Tracy said after pausing to think. "I'll give Lynch a call and tell him you'll be calling."

"Great, she'll love Chicago. Thanks."

After hanging up, Burch went right back to where he and Wise had left off. "OK, so what's the Professor doing? I want to know what the plan will look like so I can get it down to Tracy."

"He's spending a lot of time with Procino," Wise answered. "Trying to get Marketing to commit to an early estimate to help Operations."

"I told him to show me his schedule," Burch said, somewhat annoyed, "before he runs with it."

"He will. He's just trying to nail down some realistic dates before he shows it to you." Wise paused, then added, "It's not next year's plan that worries me. It's his long-range plan."

"Why is that?"

"Well, next year's plan is not that much different than this year's. I mean we'll take our estimate for year end and add 2 percent or 3 percent. No problem. But then the long-range plan starts from there, and the Professor is looking at making big changes—increase our market share and all that."

"Damn it. I thought he understood not to do that," Burch said. "I'm not putting through any pie-in-the-sky plan—a bunch of goals we can't achieve."

Wise shrugged his shoulders. "He thinks Emil wants a change —a major sales increase."

"Of course he wants it. He wants another American Barrel, too, but he's not going to get it." Burch thought for a moment. "I should let them go ahead. It would be another nail in Emil's coffin."

Wise smiled. "Sounds like you been doing some nailing?"

Burch did not smile. "I've put in a nail or two. But Tracy already knows about Emil. Sometimes I think Emil's his own worst enemy. I don't know why he doesn't lose some weight."

"Does his weight bother them down there?" Wise asked. "I can see with the spending and missing forecast and stuff. But weight?"

"Oh yeah. Tracy doesn't particularly care about Emil's weight. But Torres does. I was speaking to Ed Morgan, and he said Emil doesn't have the right corporate image. Torres wants 'lean and mean,' and that sure doesn't describe Emil."

"Sounds like you've been busy in Dallas."

"I've planted a few seeds," Burch said with a cold grin. "But I want you to watch the Professor. He's pretty smart and I don't want him upsetting things. His Sears plan was good—very good. He's capable of doing something we can't ignore."

"Should I make him stop this market share thing? Make him stick to just the plan?"

Burch paused to think. "No. Let him do whatever he's going to do. But keep me up-to-date. If he comes up with something good, I'll be the one to present it to Dallas. Don't worry, I can handle the Professor. We can stop him any time."

■ ■ ■

Ray explained his frustration to Dorothy as they had coffee after dinner. "When Emil told me to come up with another American Barrel, he was asking me to do something that I probably couldn't do. But it was fun trying."

Dorothy laughed. "You didn't sound like you were having fun after your gin game with Emil."

"Well, at least I was doing something. With Burch it's just the opposite. All I have to do is put together the plans. Then I can sit around and do nothing and still get my paycheck—and a bonus. But I'll die from boredom, especially if I have to sit through his staff meetings."

"You didn't know this when you took the job?"

"No. I thought Burch and Emil wanted me to direct the company strategy. You know, decide where we were going and how we were going to get there."

"Then do it."

"But that's not what Burch wants me to do."

"Do it anyway. Why listen to that creep if you know better?"

Ray thought for a moment, then smiled at his wife. The obvious answer was, "Because he's my boss." But Dorothy was not going by the organization chart. She was being logical. Someone in the company should be directing the planning, and Ray was probably the best man in the company to do it. In addition, he was in the job where he could do it, even if he had to do it in his "spare time."

He reached over and kissed her. "You're right, hon. That's what I will do. What's the creep gonna do, fire me?"

11. The Foreign Plan

Ray came up with a new idea and wanted Al Goldman's opinion. Goldman did not fit the pattern for accountants—his friendly smile and occasional emotional outbursts gave him away. He knew the language and all the rules, and he was technically competent, but he did not have the narrow vision the pattern required. His colleagues saw the world of business as profit and loss, return on assets, and net worth. Al understood this very well, but also saw the human side.

He saw the MBA craze as humorous. Burch had gotten his several years earlier, and Al's boss, Dick Wise, was attending classes at night to get his. Neither of them knew any more than Al as a result of the classes, but it looked good on their resumes and would probably help them get ahead. Al knew this, but he was not about to waste his time on it.

He was a perfect guide for Ray in the world of accountants. The only area he did not know well was the individual customer operations. Direct customer contact was jealously guarded by Dennison and the Sales executives. They did not want anyone, especially an accountant, to know the content of their conversations with the customers. Still, when Marketing needed help, they came to Al Goldman, with the result that Al knew more about the marketing operations than anyone else in Accounting.

Not only did Al know more, but he was willing to discuss everything with Ray. Although Ray was now in the Financial Group, he was still considered a Marketing man and consequently the "enemy." He was received politely, but coldly. His questions were answered, but no help was offered. If he did not ask the right questions, no one but Al Goldman would steer him to the right ones. Al gave this help to Ray partly because he liked Ray. But Al would usually be helpful and brutally honest with associates. As a result he was liked and respected by the Marketing and Operations groups, but not quite trusted by the Accounting fraternity. He was like a magician who told the audience the other magicians' secrets.

Tom Chessman had confided in Ray that he would always check out new ideas on personnel policies with Al before discussing them with Emil. Several times, Al had saved Tom from proposing policies that sounded good at first, but would have been disastrous financially. Ralph Burch or Dick Wise would have enjoyed embarrassing Chessman, so Tom had Goldman screen new proposals.

It was with this thought in mind that Ray first discussed his foreign car plan with Al. The major item that influenced company strategy was always the market forecast, which started with the seemingly boring projected count of cars on the road. The number of older cars on the road was directly proportional to replacement shock sales. When he saw the projection of the number of foreign cars five years in the future, Ray got an idea.

"It's a future need," he explained to Al. "Just look at the figures. The foreign cars are pouring into the market. Beetles all over the place, but now the Japanese are starting to come in faster than the VWs. In ten years, a third of the cars on the road will be foreign. And we only cover a few fast-moving parts."

Goldman countered. "But foreign car owners go back to the foreign car dealer for this service; our gas station mechanics don't have the know-how or the tools to work on foreign cars. The foreign car dealer has the equipment, and he gets his parts from the factory."

"Sure, he does now. But wait until he gets more competition. There are garages now that specialize in foreign car work, and there will be more,...and they're gonna need parts."

"So, when they need them, we'll make them. What's the big deal?"

"The problem is volume."

"Volume?"

"Yeah. It's partly the nature of foreign cars, and partly our own system. First of all, with a whole bunch of different cars, there's no standardization. So the total number of each shock required is small. And our system doesn't trigger a new shock for our line at those low volumes."

"Our system is based on making a profit when we add a new number," Al explained. "Are you saying we should add it anyway... even if there aren't enough parts required to do it profitably?"

Ray smiled and replied carefully, "No, not necessarily. I'm not sure. I'd like to have Engineering look at what they could do to standardize designs or consolidate part numbers. And I'd like to see if Manufacturing can come up with a way to build smaller volumes profitably. Maybe there's a way we could get this under control."

"Even so, even if we could, what's the big advantage?" Al was not criticizing, just probing. "Why not wait until the market is big enough?"

"Well, this is just a feeling, Al. I'm sort of thinking out loud."

"Sure, bounce it off me."

"There's two things, really. One is that I don't think the volume on foreign car shocks will ever be high enough. I mean, there will never be enough volume on any one part number. If we're gonna be competitive, we have to profitably produce smaller volumes than we're used to."

Al just nodded and Ray continued. "The other key is competitive advantage. We need something more than our competitors... even if it's not much. I used to tell the story in my class about the Professor who was trying to decide between two offers to teach, one at M.I.T. and one at Harvard. He had gone through all the advantages of one versus the other, from salary to medical care to prestige to work satisfaction, and so on. He was telling his friend that the two offers were absolutely equal. His friend said that if that were true, he should go to Harvard. 'Why Harvard?' he asked. 'Because it has better parking,' was the reply. 'Better parking? I should make a decision as important as this based on better parking?' The friend said, 'Sure! If you really believe that everything else is really equal, then parking is Harvard's competitive advantage. It makes their offer better.' If we have something better than our competitors, the customers will choose us."

Al looked quizzically at Ray and said, "If that's what you taught in college, I'm glad I'm not wasting my time getting an MBA."

Ray laughed. "It sounded much more profound in my class. But I do want to pursue this further. I have a gut feeling that this could be important."

"Well, go ahead," Al said, somewhat encouragingly. "I guess if this is going to be one-third of the market, we certainly should see if we can get our share. That turns into big numbers."

■ ■ ■

Ray wanted to cover every possibility that could occur and have solutions to every problem before he presented anything to Ralph Burch. He carefully considered how the others would view his new idea. It would mean more work for anyone who got involved, so he would expect resistance. But he also would rely on their professionalism, their desire to do a good job.

The engineers would tend to resist a program where they were not making significant "technical" advances. A program to consolidate many part numbers into a few did not have "technical appeal" —it did nothing to improve technology. The engineers would not feel their technical expertise was needed to look under the cars and see how one design could be modified to do the job of three or four designs. A technician could handle that task, and indeed, most standardization and consolidation was handled by technicians and draftsmen. In some cases, even the salesmen knew more about the specific applications, and this really irritated some of the engineers. Ray knew it would be hard to convince the engineers.

He also expected resistance from the manufacturing engineers. Even if some consolidation was obtained, the net result would still be more changeovers. Manufacturing liked to get their production system operating smoothly and automatically, and let it run and run. Changing over from one part to another meant increasing downtime and increasing scrap as they overcame problems with the new part. Then, just as the new part started running well, production would stop and they would have to switch to a different part with more problems. No doubt, Manufacturing would be a real problem.

On the other hand, Ray expected a favorable reception from Marketing. Salesmen were always looking for something new to promote their line. Many times, if nothing worthwhile was coming from the home office, they would invent their own "new developments." A bona fide change like additional foreign car coverage would fit perfectly with their needs.

As far as the accountants were concerned, Ray knew it would come down to return on investment. How much would it cost and what profits would result? If he could show a return of over 15 percent, he would have a good chance. The problem was that Ray was not sure yet what the numbers would be. He also knew now, after the Sears program, that the numbers could change drastically, depending on what the involved parties wanted them to show.

The first step was to find out more facts. Ray was not sure of this program. He was not sure the sales would be there; he was not sure if a consolidated line could be developed; and he was not sure if it would be financially worthwhile even if it worked out technically.

After his preliminary discussion with Al Goldman, he went to Vince Procino. As expected, Vince gave Ray his honest appraisal. Surprisingly though, Vince was not very encouraging.

"Just off the top of my head, Ray, it doesn't sound that good. I mean it's good all right, just not that important. At least not now."

"What do you mean, 'not now'?" Ray asked, trying to understand exactly what Vince was thinking.

"Well, according to your numbers, the real need won't be for five or ten years, in the eighties."

"But, there's a need now, right now. It's not that big, but it's growing every day. In the eighties it will be very big, but there's a need right now too."

"Sure," Vince said, smiling. "I'm not shooting it down. Our men can use it in the field, but we're not going to sell that many. If our customers put it in their inventory, they're going to want to sell a lot of them."

"And if we promote this as a big program," Ray interjected as he followed Vince's train of thought, "they're going to be disappointed." Vince had brought up an important point that Ray had not even considered.

"Right. They'll start showing us part numbers that they put in stock that haven't sold for a year. And that's bound to happen with some parts with some customers. Different foreign cars sell differently around the country. It's not an even market." Vince paused, thinking about the problem, then continued. "You know, Ray, maybe we could handle this with a special classification. It might be workable."

"What do you mean?"

"Well, I'm just thinking out loud on this, but follow me. The foreign car market is spotty. You see big concentrations of certain cars in certain areas. Like Datsuns are all over the West Coast, but you don't see them in Alabama or Wisconsin, and so on. So, we put a small inventory in all our warehouse distributors and find out with our field force what sells in their area. Then we load them accordingly, and take back what doesn't sell in their area... and send it to the area that needs them. But, we don't load all our Jobbers with all the products."

Ray was smiling. "Sure. That's the way."

"But it's not that easy. Our system isn't designed that way. We would have to modify the system and someone would have to watch it closely...probably our field sales force. Even then, Ray, you know just having the stuff in stock won't sell it. They have to go to the foreign car specialists and let them know we have the foreign parts. And the customers will have to be sold that American-made parts will fit their cars. It's a long, tough job...a lot of training for our men."

"But it gives us something no one else has," Ray countered. "A competitive advantage. It has to bring us new customers, even if the sales increase is slow for our present customers. We get both, a good selling-tool for new business and a sales increase for our present customers. And it will continue to increase from year to year. And we'll be trained to handle the big market when it comes. We'll be known as the foreign car shock specialists as that market grows."

Ray was getting more and more enthusiastic. Vince laughed. "OK, let's see where this goes."

■ ■ ■

Jim Steele's reaction was surprisingly positive. When Ray briefed him on the subject, he immediately called in Bob Simpranian and Ted Lyons.

"The Professor here has another 'opportunity' for us," Jim explained, rather sarcastically. "He thinks we can gain a major competitive advantage by introducing an expanded line of foreign shocks, stuff that our normal customers don't carry."

"They carry foreign stuff," Ray corrected. "But only a few fast-moving items. Most foreign cars have to go back to the dealer."

"Anyway," Jim continued. "Ray wants us to design and build a consolidated line of foreign shocks."

"I don't know if you can consolidate the foreign shocks," Simpranian interjected. "We're having enough trouble trying to consolidate our American shocks."

Steele sat back, allowing a smug smile to come across his face. This was one of his pet programs, consolidating the seemingly endless number of parts, so that Manufacturing could have longer production runs and better efficiency. "Well," he answered, "That's what you have to become expert at. That's where your engineers can contribute...earn their big salaries."

Simpranian winced. Ever since Steele had become his boss, he had been pounding the same theme. "Consolidate! Standardize! Stop wasting time with sophisticated new stuff that no one wants anyway. Help us make some money with our present stuff." It was not that Simpranian did not want to do that. Engineering always had an ongoing effort at consolidation, but he defined Engineering's primary job as developing new products and improving present ones. He felt he was being pushed too far in the manufacturing direction. He had protested several times to his new boss. Steele would listen and be temporarily convinced that Simpranian had a balanced program. But then he would come back to the same theme again and again.

"What do you think?" Steele asked Ted Lyons, who was now Manager of Manufacturing Engineering and Steele's liaison with the plant engineers.

"I'd love to see some standardization or consolidation," Lyons answered quickly. Then he added, "Anything that would reduce indirect labor. Chessman has been making my life miserable over indirect labor."

Steele laughed. "What the hell is Chessman talking to you about indirect labor for? And what the hell does he know about indirect labor anyway?"

"He doesn't know anything about it, but that never stops him,"

Lyons answered, shaking his head.

Ray and Simpranian had to laugh also. From Ray's first day at Amsaco, Chessman had been after Lyons about something.

"Some of the accountants attended a seminar or something," Lyons continued, "and they were bending Tom's ear about indirect costs...overhead and inventory and the cost of money and all. Tom heard some of the key words and ran to Emil. One of them was 'indirect labor.' Then he hit me at the Management meeting, with all the Plant Management people around, at the bar one night... Said the reason we weren't making money was because of our indirect to direct ratio. He said that Manufacturing Engineering should come up with ways to reduce that ratio....Gave me a hard time in front of everyone. And he keeps hitting me with it every time I see him. 'You've got to help the plants reduce their indirect to direct ratio,' he says. 'That's where all our profits are going.' He drives me nuts."

Steele laughed but offered to help. "I'll talk to him." Then, as if he was thinking out loud, he added, "But damned if I know what to say. I mean...indirect to direct ratio. Maybe I should start by explaining to Tom what a ratio is."

They all laughed and Steele continued. "If I can plant a few ideas in Tom's head, maybe he'll get off your back and start on someone else. But let's face it. Chessman is dumb like a fox. I have to have something credible to tell him." Then with a mischievous grin he turned toward Simpranian and said slowly, "Something like 'Lyons and Simpranian have come up with a real good plan to reduce indirect labor. They have come up with a standardization of the product line and a quick changeover manufacturing system that will enable us to run lower volumes and still reduce change-over costs. Not only that, but this will lead to a reduced finished goods inventory... And not only that, but this will give the Professor his foreign car coverage, which will significantly increase sales.' My God, Chessman will have an orgasm. He'll make Ted here a hero. The company will make millions. Ray will get his competitive advantage. And it all depends on you, Bob. Get us that standardization."

Simpranian groaned as he sat with his head in his hands. "OK, OK! Let me see what I can do."

■ ■ ■

Ray was pleased with the positive responses—just the fact that no one appeared to be against the plan was more than he expected. He was absolutely amazed as the program gathered more and more momentum. He had tossed a few pebbles and they were cascading and growing into an avalanche.

Ted Lyons took the manufacturing task on himself. First, Lyons had engineer Ed Coombs lay out a representative sample of all the various foreign shocks they wanted to produce. It was truly amazing that this simple shock absorber could be put together in so many ways and require so many different connections, while doing the exact same function on the car. Each vehicle called for a different way to mount the shocks and different space requirements to make room for the other vehicle components. In addition, there were internal differences in shocks, which gave different performance.

When Ray saw the display, he was ready to give up on his consolidated foreign line.

But Coombs and Lyons saw it as a challenge. At first, they put extra holes in existing brackets and welded on extra brackets so they could mount on more than one application. The big change came when Lyons convinced Coombs to try a smaller shock where a larger one was normally used. Lab tests showed a definite difference, but it was hard to tell any difference in the ride. Coombs tried twenty-five vehicles and only two really showed a poor ride. Four others were questionable, but Lyons and Coombs agreed that it took a trained engineer to notice that difference. At that point, the "Standard Core" concept was born.

The concept was simple. Use one small basic core for about 80 percent of Amsaco's shocks and attach different brackets for the various applications. In this way, all the expensive, high-speed automatic equipment could keep running without stopping for changeovers. Only at the end would the attachment brackets call for a low volume, manual type operation. It gave the manufacturing plants what they needed, drastic reduction in changeovers, while still giving Sales all the various applications they needed. It was simple...exactly what Jim Steele had wanted. All it had really needed was Product Engineering to agree that it was technically acceptable.

When Bob Simpranian reviewed the results, he had to agree it made sense. It made him nervous with some of the small shocks taking the place of larger ones. But Coombs and Lyons had proven their case by demonstrating many vehicles. They had proven Steele's theory.

The only change required was to add a separate larger-diameter "core" for heavy-duty shocks. This was at Marketing's request, so they would have a low price and a heavy-duty line to offer, allowing the jobber the opportunity to advertise the low price, and then "sell up" to the heavy duty. The volume would still come mainly from the cheaper "standard core" units, and the heavy-duty units would be produced on standard equipment already in production. The plan would work.

It would take a great deal of engineering to change the product and some major changes in the manufacturing system to take advantage of the simplified new product, but it would be worth it. There were big savings to be generated.

When Lyons and Simpranian presented their preliminary findings to Jim Steele, he was pleased. Actually, he was more than pleased; he sensed an opportunity. Lyons was planning to rearrange existing machinery at relatively low cost, but Steele saw an opportunity to justify the new equipment he had been after. He attacked directly.

"I think we need new equipment for this program."

"No, Jim," Lyons responded. "That's the beauty of it. We can modify our present assembly just by—"

"Ted," Steele interrupted. "Listen to me. I don't want to scrounge around half-assed. I don't want to interrupt our present operation. I want to use this to improve our operation. Do you understand?"

Ted nodded, as did Simpranian.

"Good! Now listen to the ground rules. A new production line will be built for the new product line. The present lines will continue to operate. Once we have the new line running...and running well, you can fool around and modify our present manufacturing." Steele thought for a moment and continued, "And I want these savings to justify that new Schumag Cold Drawing Machine. And a high-frequency mill. And maybe—"

"Whoa, wait a minute, Jim," Ted had to interrupt. "Where we gonna put all this stuff? We're all scrunched up now. We have no extra room. With what you're talking about, we'd need a new addition...or a new plant."

"A new plant?" Steele smiled. "Like at Harrisonburg?"

Simpranian smiled also. Steele had been after a new plant in Virginia for years.

"There's some beautiful country down there, Bob. The Chamber of Commerce people from Harrisonburg showed me some proposed plant sites we could have for practically nothing. And they would finance the building on good terms...excellent terms. The town is in the right place, with good highways, close to our biggest market. We would save shipping costs. Good labor! And it's just beautiful, right in the Shenandoah Valley...beautiful country."

"I hate to interrupt these beautiful dreams," said Lyons, good-naturedly. "But I don't think this consolidation can justify a new plant. There's just not enough savings."

Steele thought a moment and replied, "That's true, Ted. It needs more. But let's look at the whole picture. The consolidation is the right move, right?"

Simpranian and Lyons nodded in agreement.

"And to do the job right, we need new equipment. Right?"

Lyons started to object, when Steele injected, emphatically, "Right?" Lyons nodded in agreement.

"Now, the new equipment will generate savings in itself, right? Right!" Steele was continuing now, not waiting for agreement. "But we need a new plant for this new equipment. So, what we have is savings from consolidation, savings from the new equipment, savings from the new location, and costs of the new plant and equipment. What we still need is additional sales—enough to justify new capacity. The Foreign Car Program has to generate the additional sales. Then we can justify the expenditure on our cost savings plus additional sales. This thing can work—it can fly."

Simpranian was not used to Steele getting so excited. Lyons was also a little surprised, and somewhat amused.

Steele continued. "Bob, I want you to run with this. Get hold of the Professor and get him started on a good forecasted sales increase. Explain to him that we can support his program in every way—increased foreign car coverage, improved delivery, lower inventory. Make sure you include all that in your projected savings. And especially in your return on investment....Tell you what, get Pendleton in here after lunch and I'll tell him. If he can get a sizable sales increase out of this, it can fly."

Lyons added, with a grin, "And it will improve our indirect to direct ratio."

■ ■ ■

Ray was excited after his meeting with Steele. Everything seemed to be fitting together perfectly. Engineering had done a terrific job. Manufacturing had also been a surprise. Steele had seen the low-volume trend of the future, in American as well as foreign shocks. He knew they had to be able to handle the low volumes efficiently. The emergence of the new plant and new equipment was just a bonus. There did not appear to be any problem with Marketing or Finance either. The increased sales forecast might be resisted, but Marketing would get a good selling tool, a "competitive advantage." And the financial numbers should be good. It looked like a "no-lose" situation.

Ray's went into Al Goldman's office. Al was packing books into a carton when Ray came in and excitedly brought him up to date. "I tell you Al, it's all fitting together, the foreign car line, the consolidation, the automation, the expansion. Everything looks good. It's a no-lose situation."

Goldman stopped packing and grinned at Ray. "I've never heard of a 'no-lose' situation."

Ray asked impatiently "How can we possibly lose on this one?"

"Simple," Goldman responded. "Just don't hit the numbers. If Engineering doesn't consolidate as much as they expect to. Or the automatic machines don't get the output they predict. Or the maintenance cost doubles because of problems with the new equipment. Or the inventory doesn't get smaller. Or, and this is the big one, your sales don't increase."

"Aw, c'mon Al."

"No, I'm serious. Engineering is the only group that ever meets their numbers. That's because they're so damn cautious—it's just about a sure thing before they take a chance. But Manufacturing and Sales? They never hit their numbers. Especially Sales. The only thing going for you is you're not predicting any big increase for a few years. By then, everyone will have forgotten." He paused, then added, smiling again, "Come to think of it, this probably will fly. Everyone gets what they want, and it will be years before anyone can say it didn't work. Yeah, it will probably be approved."

"But not by you, Al?"

"Doesn't make any difference. I won't be involved." Goldman pointed to the cartons around his office, some half-filled with his books and belongings.

For the first time, Ray noticed what Goldman was doing. "I'm sorry, Al. I'm so absorbed in my project, I don't see anything. What's happening? Something good?"

"I think so. It's the international job. I'm the new Director of International Operations, under Dennison." Before Ray could ask, Goldman continued, "Dick Dorsey will stay, but he will only be involved in sales. I think I can help. I can contribute."

Ray smiled broadly. "Well, congratulations. You bet you can contribute. Sounds like Dennison is smarter than we thought."

This was what they both were thinking. To get control of a complicated international operation required someone with an accountant's objective viewpoint, as well as some good practical experience—and some smarts besides. Goldman was the perfect choice. With him controlling the operation, they could be successful. Ray wondered how Ralph Burch liked the idea.

What neither of them were aware of was that Burch strongly opposed the move, saying he needed Goldman in the Financial Group. However, since he had no better position for Goldman, Dennison won out. Emil had intervened, telling Burch he had to "consider the good of the company more than your own personal needs."

■ ■ ■

With Goldman gone, Ray was handling the long-range planning job by himself—with no "advisor." Actually, he had no trouble. He discussed it with Burch, who seemed annoyed that he had to be bothered by the effects of Goldman's leaving. They agreed that Ray could handle the job alone and go to Dick Wise for financial advice. But there was not that much detailed financial work to do. Except for the Foreign Car Program, all he was really doing was collecting the other groups' plans and putting them together. He was spending most of his time with Simpranian, Lyons, and Coombs on the foreign car details.

Ray wanted to be sure he was thoroughly prepared when he presented the plan to Burch. First of all, the return on investment had to be at least 15 percent after taxes. Anything less than 15 percent would make it necessary for Burch and Emil to defend the program before United Tire—a negative position. Above 15 percent would make them look like heroes. He had to hit 15 percent.

Jim Steele guaranteed Ray that if Marketing could forecast a 10 percent increase in sales each year for five years, then the ROI would exceed 15 percent. Ray pleaded and bargained with Vince Procino and Dave Dennison to agree to the sales increase. They had been stung before with high sales forecasts. Dennison knew that whatever he agreed to for this appropriation would have to be included in his next year's forecast. He was not planning on anywhere near a 10 percent increase.

After several meetings and much paper shuffling, Dennison finally agreed to "consider" a graduated sales increase, starting at 4 percent and working up to 10 percent in five years. His logic was that it would probably take a year to get the program in gear, and filling the pipeline the next year would give them the 4 percent. After that everything would get blurry. As Goldman had pointed out to Ray, no one would be able to measure their performance. In the meantime, Jim Steele would have more capacity and there would be fewer back orders. Besides, by then Dennison hoped to have succeeded Emil to the presidency, and the question would be moot.

Ray took the graduated sales increase to Jim Steele somewhat apologetically. Steele's reaction as he reviewed the sales figures was to turn to Ray and say, grinning, "This is enough."

"But we didn't get the 10 percent yearly increase."

"This is enough," Steele repeated, then explained. "We have plenty of cost savings to justify the expenditure. The savings from the new equipment could almost justify the expenditure by itself. When we added the savings from the standardized core, we went over the top. In almost every case we reduced the size of the stock, which gives us tremendous material savings." He laughed. "Like Chessman's indirect costs, that just adds icing to the cake. The additional profits from your increased sales will make it just so much better."

"Then why did you need the sales increase so badly?"

"For capacity requirements. Capacity! Without your sales increase, we wouldn't need the new plant. We could make it a cost reduction appropriation."

"But is our little increase enough?"

"Oh, it's enough." Steele grinned even more. "I would rather have the 10 percent increase next year. It would make it that much less critical. But the total increase is, let's see, 4 percent the first year. Then 5 percent, 6, 8, and 10. That's a 33 percent increase. Need a new plant!"

Ray looked as if he was not quite buying Steele's logic. Steele moved closer to explain.

"Look Ray, if there were no other reasons, and I needed the 33 percent increase, I could squeeze it out of the existing facilities. A third shift, some new equipment, even this standardization will increase capacity. But that isn't the real story. You can't just squeeze by in manufacturing. Sooner or later we get pushed for more than we can make. The accountants don't understand this. They say use the minimum amount of assets. Maximize return on investment. It's all numbers. But that's not right. There's more, and you can't put it all in numbers. For example, Chessman will love the idea of a new plant. Why? It makes the union less powerful. If we have two plants and one goes out on strike, we really hurt. With three plants, the other two can pick up the slack. We'll talk about "indirect costs" to the accountants, but Chessman knows the real advantage of a third plant. And so does Dennison. He doesn't want to lose a sale. And it happens sometimes if we're close to capacity. He's gonna sell more than we can make sometimes, and then we're gonna ship late and ship incomplete. Our service level goes to hell for a week, or a month, or several months. He has to take the guff from the customers, and we end up with a bad reputation for delivery. And in the long run, that loses sales.

"Understand this, Ray…Professor, this is the right move for the company. Your Foreign Car Program is the official reason for the need for the expansion. It gives us the numbers we need. So let's use it and run."

When the appropriation was complete, Ray could see the power of the numbers. The ROI had turned out to be 22 percent. The company was spending a lot of money to open a new plant, put in new equipment, and run a major engineering redesign on most products. This would all be paid for by profits from:

—direct labor savings from the improved efficiency of the new equipment,

—more direct labor savings from the lower wage rates in Virginia,

—material savings from the new smaller product design,

—inventory reduction from the standardized product,

—freight savings from the new location, and

—profits from the increased sales of foreign car shocks.

Further benefits from the program included the shutdown insurance of a third plant and improved service levels to the customers because of the additional capacity. In addition, Marketing was implementing Vince Procino's "regional stocking plan" to enable customers to stock just those items with strong sales in their areas. The whole program was falling into place better than Ray had ever dreamed.

Engineering, Manufacturing, Personnel, and Marketing were enthusiastically behind the program, although for different reasons. On Emil's staff, Jim Steele was the main supporter, dreaming of his new equipment, located in a new plant in the Shenandoah Valley. Tom Chessman had already told Emil of his support to reduce "indirect labor," and was looking forward to the improved labor relations strength. Dave Dennison was feeling better and better about the program as he thought about introducing the Foreign Car Program at the next year's sales meeting. He was not concerned about the 4 percent sales increase needed in two years. Actually, he thought the improved service level would result in a larger increase than that, but he was not saying that to anyone but Procino. Al Goldman might have questioned the need for the new plant, but he was on his way to Europe.

There did not seem to be anyone opposed to the plan. Ray was covering every base as he prepared to present the program to Ralph Burch. He did not want to repeat his embarrassing first meeting with his boss, when Burch sent him back to finish the job. He also did not want to present the program to Emil on a flight down to Florida, drinking scotch and playing gin. He planned to get Burch's verbal agreement and then send the appropriation through the system to obtain the executive signatures. They would then make a formal presentation to Emil.

He took an extra week to gather all the necessary materials. The revised five-year marketing plan showed the gradual increase in sales as a result of the foreign car coverage. The regional stocking plan was written up to demonstrate how the additional coverage could gradually go into the right customer's inventory. An example of the new standardized shock was assembled and compared to the existing shocks. A list was made to show all the parts that would no longer have to be built. The new equipment was listed, along with pictures, and a summary of the direct labor savings and other benefits associated with each piece of equipment. A map demonstrated the freight savings available from the new location. This was all summarized in the capital appropriation, with the financial calculations showing a 22 percent ROI.

The package presented an overwhelming argument for approval. Emil and Burch would look very good explaining to United Tire how Amsaco was preparing for the future, which looked very bright. Ray could not imagine anyone rejecting the plan. He did not figure Ralph Burch correctly.

■ ■ ■

Burch was aware of the plan and the numbers with the big ROI. Ray had told him he was working on the "Foreign Car Plan," and had given periodic reports at Burch's staff meetings, but they did not really give much information. However, Dick Wise had helped Ray put the numbers together and had filled Burch in on all the details.

"I don't like the total program," Burch told Wise. "I like the product standardization and I guess we should be adding some foreign car coverage. However, these cost very little and provide all of the sales appeal and most of the savings. What I don't like is Steele's addition of new automatic equipment and a new plant. I can see through all his merged calculations. But the standardization and foreign car coverage can be put into effect within existing facilities and with very little additional equipment."

"You think Steele's trying to sneak in his new equipment?" asked Wise, with a grin.

"I'm sure he is," Burch answered. "But I'm not really opposed to his new equipment. Steele knows what he's doing. But this is not the right time. The market's not strong enough. There's been no growth in the shock market or the whole automotive market for the past three years. I don't see why that will change. There's just as much chance of a drop as there is for a rise. Not only that, but there's an overcapacity in the industry. Blackwell and Crane have more capacity than they need, so the industry doesn't need more capacity at Amsaco. That would only lead to price cutting and profit deterioration."

"I agree," said Wise. "That sales forecast comes out of the blue. They might fill the pipeline, but they're not getting an increase of 4 percent from foreign car sales."

"That's right. I can see us spending a lot of money building a new plant, putting in expensive new equipment, and adding a staff of people, without any more sales than the two present plants are handling now. It's not a good business decision. When the Professor brings it to me, he'll get it right back. He can write an appropriation for the cost reductions only...no expansion."

Two days later, when Ray was ready to present it, Ralph Burch was gone.

12. The Keeper

The departure of Ralph Burch was a complete surprise to Ray and to most others. Ray was called in to the boardroom on Monday morning by Betty Johnson, Emil's secretary. He asked her what the meeting was about so he could prepare, but was told, "Mr. Gross will explain."

When Ray arrived, Steele, Chessman, and Dennison were just leaving. Steele and Dennison looked serious, but Chessman had a silly grin. He winked at Ray as they passed.

Inside, Dick Wise and the rest of Burch's staff came in and took seats around the big boardroom table. No one sat at the head of the table. That was reserved for Emil. No one sat in the two chairs next to the head either, as that would be interpreted as "ass kissing." Ray had learned this from Tom Chessman after he had inadvertently sat there during a meeting with Emil. Whoever was supposed to sit there would be designated by Emil.

Everyone sat down, looked at each other, and said nothing. The door to Emil's office opened, and Emil entered along with a tall, slim, neatly dressed man, who took the designated seat next to Emil. He had a strong, weathered face and appeared to be in his early forties. His high forehead showed the start of balding and some greying showed at his temples.

Emil wasted no time. "Ralph Burch has left Amsaco," he stated bluntly. "I'm not sure exactly what he will be doing. He might be moving to another United Tire operation."

Ray was stunned. While he was somewhat uncomfortable with Burch, he felt that at the Executive Vice President level, Burch was a permanent fixture. It was only a few months before that the company was reorganized, giving Burch more responsibility. He looked around the table, and everyone except Dick Wise looked surprised.

Emil continued. "I'd like you to meet Dan McCormick, who is our new Vice President of Finance and Administration." He gestured toward McCormick, who nodded with only a faint trace of a smile. "Dan comes to us from United's Chemical Division, where he held a similar post. Some of you may know him. Dick, you've met Dan, haven't you?"

Dick Wise smiled at McCormick, who nodded in return. Jack Rule reached over to shake hands, saying, "Dan, we've met at the United Management meetings."

McCormick acknowledged this with a slight smile and said, "Good to see you, Jack."

"Things will continue as they are now," Emil explained. "No organizational changes. You will all report to Dan. At least until Dan sees how he wants to run his area." He paused, breathed heavily through his mouth, as if tired from this short speech. "You want to say anything, Dan?"

"Just a few words, Emil," he answered with a slight Texas drawl. "I've been with United Chemical for fourteen years, the last six as Chief Financial Officer. Before that I was with United Tire in Dallas for eight years, starting with them after graduating from Southern Methodist. I've been through the financial numbers with Emil, and I was somewhat familiar with them as part of United. You men have a good record, and I hope I can help maintain it and maybe improve it. I'll need a little help learning the automotive industry, and I'll depend on your support."

"Thanks, Dan," said Emil. He looked at the others around the table. "Don't be fooled by Dan's good ol' boy manner. Dan did a terrific job at Chemicals and can be pretty tough when necessary."

McCormick turned toward the others. "Emil and I have gone over the operation pretty thoroughly, but I'd like to meet with each of you and go over your area. So please put together a brief but thorough report on your operation. I especially want to know of programs that will need my approval in the near future. I don't want to hold anything up, but I don't rubber-stamp either."

"You see?" Emil said, smiling. "Any questions?"

Ray wanted to know what had happened to Burch, and so did the others. No one said anything, however, and the meeting ended.

When Ray left the meeting, he decided to go over to Tom

Chessman's office. He was not sure what kind of wild story he might get from Tom, but he had the feeling that Tom knew what had happened. Certainly his gin games with Emil at lunch would give Tom some insight. When Ray looked inside Tom's office, he was surprised to see Al Goldman talking with Tom. They greeted Ray warmly and told him to come in.

"Looks like you have a new boss," Al said, grinning.

"Yeah. I was just breaking my old boss in," Ray said. "I've been here less than a year, and I've had three bosses."

"Standard procedure," Chessman said. "To keep up, just leave instructions with your secretary, 'If my boss calls, get his name.'"

They all laughed.

Ray turned and shook Goldman's hand. "Good to see you Al. I didn't even know you were in town."

"I'm just in for a few days. I go back on Thursday. Actually, I was in to go over next year's budget with Burch. I hope McCormick has time."

"Do you know this guy?" Ray asked. "Have you met him?"

Goldman started to answer when Chessman interrupted. "Yeah, we know him. I'll tell you, Professor, he's a tough cookie. I got the lowdown on him from Garrison, the Personnel man at Chemicals. He's a strict one. Goes by the book—weekly reports, ROI, P&L, all that crap. You better get your act together."

Ray smiled and asked Goldman. "Is he really that tough?"

Goldman was also grinning. "I don't know. If Tom says so… whatever Tom says!"

"Go ahead—don't believe me," Chessman replied as he looked through a stack of papers. "But don't say I didn't warn you. I'm telling you the guy is a tough cookie. And that's my business, knowing how guys tick, knowing what's going on. Just like I told you a year ago, Al. About Burch. I told you a year ago he had to leave, didn't I? A year ago?"

"Yeah, Tom, you said that." Goldman replied. "But you also said Dennison would be gone, and Steele. And you also said that about me, and the Professor too. The only one you never said that about was your secretary, Marge."

"Yeah," Tom agreed. "She's built pretty good. But I could see Burch had to go. He was undermining Emil. He was criticizing his cost controls, his failure to cut back overhead, his failure to gain market share, everything."

Ray shook his head. "That's hard to believe. I never heard anything like that."

"Well, of course not. He was talking to Dallas, mostly the financial people. Burch wasn't about to knock heads with Emil. With his connections at United, he could throw in some barbs about Emil's performance. Whatever didn't work out, it was Emil's fault. Even your Sears program."

"They talked about my Sears program at United?"

"Only after Emil turned it down. Then a few innuendoes about Emil not trying to increase market share; just being satisfied with the status quo. It wasn't blatant, but it spread around. And Burch was the source. I know because my contacts fill me in. That's my job. I know what's going on."

Chessman paused, looking at Ray and Goldman. Ray just shook his head slowly. Goldman sat with a knowing smile.

"The thing that blew it was his criticism of Emil's weight," Chessman continued, "Emil always suspected Burch because of the constant criticism from the Financial Group in Dallas. But that could have been just financial. Accounting didn't understand the automotive business, especially accountants in Texas. So bickering with them was standard procedure. But the weight thing was personal. That came back through Emil's boss, Max Simpson. Simpson asked Emil if he thought his weight was hurting his performance, or hurting the morale of his management team. That had to come from Burch, and it did. Ed Morgan asked me about that one."

Tom explained Ed Morgan's position to Ray. "Ed's the Senior Vice President of Personnel at United, and this morale thing brought him in. We talked for an hour over cocktails at the last Management meeting. He really was concerned. I told him it was just bullshit and asked where it came from. He didn't want to say, but it was Burch. I got it out of him. I can handle Morgan. Emil sure was pissed. He never had much use for Burch, but he put up with him. He thought you had to have a Financial man around, and Burch was no worse than any other one. But this really got him mad. It didn't take him long to find McCormick."

It registered with Ray that Emil must have found out about

Burch's activities from Chessman. He did not think he should mention this, and asked instead, "What's Burch going to do?"

"I think he'll latch on to another United company, actually. He's got some friends in Dallas, so I don't think he'll be too bad off. It'll be a little chilly though, when he and Emil get together at Management meetings."

Ray just kept shaking his head slowly, saying, "It's hard to imagine. I mean all this subterfuge. I thought Ralph Burch was just an iceberg, doing everything according to the book.... What's right for Amsaco? What is the right business decision? It's hard to imagine him doing all that."

"Believe it," Goldman interjected. "Burch can be ruthless to get what he wants. He's very ambitious. They probably don't teach that sort of thing in college, but Emil was in Burch's way to the top."

"Yeah," said Chessman. "But he underestimated Emil's strength. Emil *is* Amsaco. And Emil's no dummy. Ralph should have just waited. He was too impatient."

"Maybe impatience is part of it," said Goldman. "But it's more... well...just understand the accountant's mentality. To the accountant, everything comes down to the numbers. You can talk about getting accounts from your competitor, or putting in a new automatic machine, or changing prices, or adding dental insurance, anything. To the accountant, the only question is how does it affect the numbers. And when you give him the projected numbers, he is suspicious."

Ray laughed. "Not suspicious, hostile."

"Right, and with good reason," Goldman went on. "They've heard so many times how sales are going to increase, or efficiency will go up, or sales will decrease if we raise prices...or all sorts of estimates that never pan out. So, they make their own estimates, and they are usually right. They can make a better prediction on how the numbers will turn out than any Marketing or Manufacturing guy can, because they're not emotionally involved. Not only that, but some salesmen or engineer will promote an idea that, even if it turns out, can have a negative effect on the numbers. The accountants learn not to trust nonfinancial people. They make their own estimates based on past performance. If sales are going down, they will continue to go down. If our market share is increasing, it will continue to increase. Whatever the trend, it will continue. And they have a better batting average than anyone else."

"But sometimes trends change," Ray reasoned. "Sales that were going down will go up."

"That's true, but not very often. Most of time the salesman is wrong. And even if a change does take place, it's usually for some other reason that the salesman hadn't even thought of. No, the accountant's view is the most accurate. No emotion, just numbers."

Chessman just sat and smiled as Ray kept shaking his head, saying, "It just doesn't seem right. What about the guy or the idea that will change things?"

"That's exactly the type of guy Emil is," Goldman replied energetically. "Emil thinks in terms of changing things. Take his American Barrel Program. That was as effective a program as this industry has ever seen, and so simple. Just get the mechanic and the customer to play with the shocks, a bad one and ours. And everyone likes to push a handle. The shocks sit on top of the barrel and—"

"I know," Ray interrupted. "I know about the American Barrel. That's all I've heard since I got here."

"OK, but understand this—Emil was the only one to recognize how powerful it could be," Al continued. "He used it, improved it, and refined it. He put the barrels in all over his territory and then got the Jobbers to carry our shocks to service these accounts. Everything multiplied. He tripled the sales in his territory, and when it went national, it put Amsaco on the map. Not only that, but it educated the public to the need for shock absorbers, so that the total market increased…not only our share. It was beautiful."

Goldman paused and looked at Ray and Tom. He continued thoughtfully. "The trouble is Emil is still looking for another 'American Barrel,' something that will shoot us past Blackwell. And that stuff doesn't come along very often. But Emil wants to accomplish something significant, and he doesn't have any 'Emils' working for him to come up with a new barrel program. Meanwhile, Burch thinks Emil's a dreamer. Burch wants to control costs to get the profits up with existing business. United Tire wants us to do that too, and Emil knows that. So, that's what he does. But it's frustrating for him. It's not what he likes to do…not what he's good at. And Burch thinks he can do a better job than Emil. So impatience is part of it, I guess. But it's more that accountants just think that accountants should run the company. They think they actually are running the company. I guess that's what Burch was thinking, and he probably got encouragement from the Finance people at United. Emil just reminded him who was actually running the company. Emil!"

Ray left Chessman's office a little dazed. It was his first exposure to the politics of corporate life. He was not so naive as to think there was no such thing as politics in the business world—in fact he had tried to prepare his students to deal with this reality. But his own first encounter was somehow shocking. For someone as straight and conservative as Ralph Burch to be so blatantly involved in politics was hard for Ray to accept. He still did not buy Chessman's version 100 percent. In fact, Chessman appeared to be the leader in playing politics. Nevertheless, it certainly appeared that Burch's demise had nothing to do with job performance. It was politics, pure politics.

These thoughts dominated Ray's thinking as he prepared for his meeting with Dan McCormick. How would McCormick react to Ray's Foreign Car Program? Ray had not evaluated how the program would impact politically. Would McCormick have a "no spend" attitude to give United an impression of toughness? Would he be against whatever present management was doing in order to show United that he was going to "clean up this mess"? Was he an egotist, more intent on showing his strength than in doing what was right for Amsaco? Was he really an Amsaco employee, or was he sent in as a United "spy"?

■ ■ ■

"C'mon in, Professor," McCormick drawled as Ray entered his office. "Emil's been telling me about you and I've been looking forward to meeting with you. How have the Captains of Industry been treating you?"

Ray was a little surprised at this sociable greeting, after the grunts he customarily received from Ralph Burch. "I'm afraid I'm still going around in circles," he answered. "I have trouble just remembering who my boss is."

McCormick laughed. "I guess you might. But I hear differently. I hear you're a pretty smart fella. Full of good ideas."

"Well, I'm glad that's what you hear," Ray answered, smiling hesitantly. "I have a lot of ideas, but you be the judge about how good they are."

"I will, believe me. But first, let me tell you how I operate and what I expect from you. Just sit here. Care for some coffee?"

Ray was getting less nervous. "Yeah, please. Just black."

McCormick used the intercom. "Peggy, please bring us a couple of black coffees." He waited a few seconds until his secretary came in with the coffees. Ray watched as Peggy brought in the two mugs. He did not know her very well. She had been Ralph Burch's secretary for a long time, and Ray wondered how she felt about these events. She still had the same job, but what was she thinking? She gave no hint about that as she smiled at Ray and left.

McCormick continued. "First, I want to know what you are working on and what you want to accomplish. And I'll tell you the same. If we're working towards the same goal, we're half-way there." He paused to let the thought sink in, then continued. "If we're not, then I'll give you a chance to change your direction."

Ray was surprised to hear himself say, "What if you're the one going in the wrong direction?"

McCormick did a double take and then laughed, slapping his knee. "I don't know. No one ever asked me that before."

"Well, I didn't mean…I mean it's just my logical brain…it's a possibility—"

"Don't apologize. You're right. I might be wrong—but don't count on it." He laughed again. "But let's get back on track. The way we make sure we're going in the right direction is honest communication. First of all we talk. Not a lot. But we have to get together often enough, whenever necessary. The other way is by flash report. I want a short report on my desk every Thursday morning. Not in the afternoon, in the morning. If you're out of town, dictate it to your secretary, or to Peggy. She'll be glad to help. Then I make my flash in the afternoon and it will be on Emil's desk Friday morning."

"Fine. No problem."

"Good. Now most of my flash report will be accounting numbers; month-to-date and year-to-date results, plus estimated month end and year ends. But your report is important also, even if I don't include it in Emil's."

"No problem. It'll be on your desk on Thursday morning."

"OK." McCormick sat back in his chair. "Now let's talk about what's gonna be in it. What are you working on?"

Ray opened his briefcase and took out his long-range planning file. "Well, two things mainly. I'm putting together the long-range plan, for submission to United by September. I'm trying something a little different this year. Rather than every group submitting their plans at the same time, I'm pushing for Sales to come up with their forecast, or at least a preliminary forecast, for Operations to use as a guide for their plan."

"Makes sense."

Ray was waiting for more, but that was all McCormick said, so he continued. "Sales doesn't like the idea. They say they don't know what this year's sales will be, so they don't know where to start for next year. But I figure we can take a look this summer, when we have better numbers, and then—"

"I imagine we'll modify those numbers anyway," McCormick interrupted, "when we see the whole picture forming. The final plan will be determined by Emil—by what he wants to present to United. We'll make the numbers fit what Emil wants. That's the way it is."

"OK then, I'll keep pushing for a sales forecast."

"Good! Now what's the other project?"

Ray was surprised. He had gotten approval in about two minutes. McCormick had listened to what he had said, agreed with the idea, added some insight, and agreed with his course of action. Then he had remembered there were two things, and invited Ray to continue. Ray continued.

"The other project is really an offshoot of the plan. When we look ahead, a large part of the market will be foreign shocks, and we don't have much of that market."

"Who does?"

"The car dealers, their service departments. They get their parts from Japan or Germany, wherever they're already tooled. There are so many different shocks, that the volume of each is very low, not enough for us to tool up for and put in our line. But the total volume will be significant in five years or so. They must be in our long-range plans."

"So, we have to find a way to handle these foreign shocks—profitably," McCormick stated, almost like a question.

"Exactly!" Ray paused. He had a whole bunch of arguments on why the foreign shocks must be put in the line. The arguments were not needed, however, because McCormick apparently understood. Ray skipped ahead. "What we're doing, what Engineering is doing is changing the design so that we can consolidate into a few basic shocks that can fit many applications. They're calling it a 'standard core,' one basic shock, a small one, that can fit many applications by attaching different mounting brackets. The shocks are different from OE and they give a different ride, but Engineering—"

"What do you mean by a 'different' ride?" McCormick interrupted.

"Well, the car handles different. When you turn the wheel at different speeds, go around corners, or go over bumps. The engineers have terms for all that. But basically the engineers say there is not much difference. They can tell and the car factory engineers can tell, but the average driver can't. They gave me a demonstration ride and I couldn't see any difference. We can set up a demonstration ride for you too."

"Not necessary, but tell me, if we can do that, why can't the Japanese engineers? Why can't they standardize?"

Ray smiled. "I asked that too. Got a lot of answers. First of all, the different manufacturers don't talk to each other. Even the design groups within one company don't necessarily communicate. And then they don't design the car around the shock. They fit the shock in wherever there's room. Our Marketing people feel that they do that deliberately, so that we can't afford to tool up for all their different designs. They become the only source and control the replacement market."

"I believe that," said McCormick. "They're very clever. But you think our engineers have designed around that?"

"It looks that way."

"Great. That'll show those little bastards something about American ingenuity. Sounds like a good project." McCormick started to get up.

"But, there's more." Ray did not want to stop while he was on a roll. "This has led to a number of other things."

McCormick said "Oh?" as he sat back down.

"Yes. You see, the need for the new shocks created a capacity problem. But the new design was perfect for some automation equipment. And the new equipment plus the smaller design has led to substantial cost reductions...proposed cost reductions."

"Are you putting through an appropriation?"

"Just about. We're ready to start. But there's more."

McCormick nodded. "Go on."

"Well the additional foreign car sales over the next five years means we need to expand. And Jim, Jim Steele, has tied this in to our need for a distribution point in the east, our biggest market. We are looking for an existing plant, probably in Virginia someplace. The new location should generate good freight savings, not to mention the cheaper labor, and—"

"What about the inventory for the new plant?" McCormick interrupted again. "And the additional overhead." He was well aware of the negative aspects of opening a new plant.

Ray answered with confidence. "With the standardization and consolidation we show a net reduction in finished goods, and a major reduction in in-process inventory, companywide. The additional overhead at the new plant is minimal, because we'll direct most of the operation from here. There are some additional overhead costs, but they are small compared to the savings. The project has good numbers."

"How good? What's the ROI?"

Ray responded deliberately, "22 percent."

McCormick's eyes opened wider.

"After tax," Ray concluded, grinning.

McCormick sat thinking, swiveled in his chair so his back was to Ray. After a few seconds, which seemed longer to Ray, he swung around toward Ray and asked, "Where do you stand on this?"

"Well, most everything is ready for the appropriation. I thought I would get everything together informally and present it to you. Then we could use your input and write the appropriation, and send it through the system for signatures. Then we could make a formal presentation to Emil."

"How long will that take?"

"Give me a week to put this together. I have to work with Jim

Steele. It's really his appropriation. And then, after we show it to you, we can write the final appropriation in about a month. From what I understand, we will need at least a month to get the signatures....We should be ready to present it to Emil by the end of June."

McCormick thought for a moment, pulled out his appointment book and said, "Today is April 8th. Emil and I are going to Dallas on June 4th to meet with United. I want to present this program to them at that meeting. You get that appropriation written and signed and ready to present to Emil by...May 23rd. I'll set up the meeting and prepare Emil."

"Don't you want us to present it to you first?"

"What for? You've got a program that will prepare us for the upcoming foreign car demand. You're generating additional profits by simplifying the product line, automating the manufacturing, using less materials, reducing labor costs, and relocating to better serve our customers and save freight costs, right?"

"And increasing sales with a corresponding increase in profits," Ray added, smiling broadly.

"And you generate a 22 percent ROI," McCormick added. "What else do I have to know? No, you better get moving. We'll meet with Emil on May 23rd unless you hear differently. Have the appropriation ready for my signature on the 18th. Anything else?"

"No," said Ray as he stood up, gathering his papers. "I guess I'd better get moving."

■ ■ ■

Ray went directly to Jim Steele's office with the positive news. Steele was ecstatic as he pictured his new plant in the Shenandoah Valley coming closer to reality. He called in Lyons and Simpranian right away. The four of them decided right there on a plan to get the appropriation through the system by the May 18th date. And they carefully probed for any hidden problems. If this was really going to fly, they had to be sure it was right.

Ray was excited as he drove home that night. He was really impressed with the way his new boss had handled himself at their first meeting. He had been friendly, but firm. He had listened carefully to what Ray had said, questioned him, added his comments, and then made his decision...followed by a specific plan of action. Ray had almost become accustomed to a negative first response to any of his ideas. McCormick's positive response was a vote of confidence for Ray. It had said, essentially, that Ray and the others knew their jobs and had come up with something worthwhile for the company.

This confidence also put some pressure on Ray. He had better be sure that every detail was covered and there were no hidden problems. Emil and McCormick must not be embarrassed in Dallas. This was more like what Ray had envisioned in big business when he had decided to come to Amsaco. He could not wait to get home and tell Dorothy.

"Dot," he called as he came into the house. "I have to tell you what happened today."

"And I have something to tell you too," she answered from the kitchen.

They were both smiling as he came into the kitchen and gave her an enthusiastic kiss.

"Well," she said. "Looks like it's something good, anyway."

"Yes it is. But you look pretty happy yourself. What's your news? What did you buy?"

"I didn't buy anything," she said. Her smile turned to a scowl. "What makes you think I don't do anything but buy things? Is that your picture of—"

"Whoa, wait a minute. Honey, that was just a joke. I'm just kidding around."

"I know. But joking is just one way of saying what's really on your mind. I don't like to be ridiculed like that. I'm not just a silly housewife—who doesn't do anything useful all day." She turned her back and said, a little more calmly, "Anyway, that has to do with my news. But now you've spoiled it. I don't know if I want to talk about it now."

Ray did not know what to say. He had apparently made a bad joke. But he hadn't meant to. And it was such a minor remark. He had to fix this. He certainly could not tell her of his good news at this moment.

"I'm sorry, honey," he apologized. "Really. The last thing I would do is ridicule you. I just made a bad joke."

He stepped toward her and put his hands on her shoulders.

She spoke, without turning. "I took a job today." Then she turned and looked directly at him. His eyebrows raised, but he said nothing. This made her smile and say cynically, "Weren't ready for that, were you?"

"No, I sure wasn't. What happened? What job? Why?"

She looked straight at him as she explained, "I got the lead from Barbara's friend's mother. She works in Ann Arbor at the U of M, in Admissions. She said they were swamped trying to handle all the scholarship evaluations and paperwork. I told her I had some experience in that at Harvard. She said I should go over and talk to Dean Clarke, and I did...and they hired me...and I start Monday."

"Why...that's great," said Ray. "If that's what you want. I just had no idea. I just—"

"I've been thinking about it for months. Ever since we got here, actually." She moved closer to Ray and put her arms around him and her head on his chest. "Ray, I've been so lonely."

He hugged her close to him, still confused, but glad to be hugging her. "Why would you be so lonely?" he asked. "I know this is a new place and we don't know a lot of people, but I'm still here... and the kids."

She looked up at him, still hugging him. There were tears on her cheeks, "That's just it. You're not still here, and neither are the kids. They're growing up. They have their own friends, their own lives. And you're at Amsaco, even when you come home. You know who you are and the kids know who they are. But, I'm here all day long. I'm done cleaning before noon. I can shop for whatever we need in a couple of hours every three days. What else should I do, watch the soaps? Join the club? Go out and buy things?"

"I suppose this wasn't the best time to joke about shopping."

"The timing couldn't have been worse," she said, half crying, half laughing. "You poor sap. You really walked into that one." She sat down at the kitchen table, took out some tissues from her purse, and dabbed at her tears.

"Why didn't you say something?" he asked. "I just didn't dream you were so unhappy."

"I did say something, but you didn't hear me. You were so busy with your Amsaco, you didn't hear what I was saying."

He thought for a moment, but could not remember her saying

anything. "I'm sorry, Dot," he said truthfully. "I just don't remember you saying anything. I missed it completely. I must be getting old."

She looked at his sad expression and smiled. "You know, for a professor and a big time executive, you really are a dummy." She walked over and kissed his cheek. "I guess I never actually said the words—but I said it in a lot of other ways. You should have known."

"I'm sorry," he said, not wanting to argue.

"No, you're not, really. You just want to get off the subject. OK, what's your good news?"

He really was happy to change to a less emotional subject. "I met with McCormick today," he started, enthusiastically. "And it's like I died and went to heaven."

He told her the details of the meeting, how McCormick had listened carefully, questioned him, added insight, and then taken action, how he had also shared Ray's humor and acted friendly; most importantly, how he had respected what Ray and the others had done and had assumed they were all qualified professionals who knew their area. What a change from Burch.

"Sounds too good to be true," Dorothy said happily.

"Yeah, it does," Ray agreed. "But there's a flip side too. If he is going to accept our plan, it had better be right. We had better perform like qualified professionals."

"I'm not worried about that," she responded. "You know what you're doing." She smiled wryly. "At least in the business world."

He smiled back at her. "Well, you're the professor at home. You'll just have to teach me. But I'll tell you what. Why don't we celebrate? My new boss and your new job. Put this stuff in the refrigerator for tomorrow, get a sitter, and let's go to Schuler's."

"Sounds good to me. But I'm going to need to bring home a paycheck if we keep celebrating at Schuler's."

As they walked into their room to get ready to go out, Dorothy smiled. "Sounds like you've got a good boss this time. Why don't you keep him?"

13. The All-Star Game

Ray had the appropriation on McCormick's desk on May 17th. It took some pushing to get it through the system, especially with Accounting and Dick Wise. Accounting questioned all sorts of details and sent Ray back to Simpranian, Lyons, and Procino to get more backup for their figures. Next, it was debated at McCormick's staff meeting. Wise and Ray had been arguing over the credibility of the sales forecast. Wise did not believe they would hit the numbers, while Ray defended them.

Finally, McCormick broke in. "I don't know whether the figures are right, and," looking at both of them, "neither do you. But I want that appropriation on my desk on May 18th. You fellows resolve your differences and get that appropriation moving."

After that, it was easier. Wise still insisted on some changes, but they were reasonable and Ray had no problem. The ROI went down to 21 percent, but Jim Steele was still smiling as he signed it.

Dave Dennison signed rather reluctantly. "You had better be right," he said as he signed. "We have to live with this addition to the sales forecast."

Ray did not know what to expect when he presented the appropriation to McCormick. He found out the next day when his boss called him in.

"This is an excellent presentation, Ray," McCormick said. "You have backup to answer almost any questions. It's all logical and practical. The only questionable area is the sales forecast."

Ray grinned. "Yeah. You noticed my discussion with Dick."

McCormick also smiled. "I'd have to be deaf and stupid not to. But that's OK. You were both doing your job."

"The trouble is," Ray broke in, "I can't prove the sales will be there. I can prove the cars will be on the road. But I can't prove we'll get the sales."

"Of course," said McCormick. "No one can ever prove a sales forecast." He picked up the appropriation and handed it to Ray. "But what we can do is see what our risk will be. Before I sign, I want to know what the ROI will be if you only get half of your sales increase." He noticed Ray's grin disappear. "But it could also go the other way. What would the ROI be if the increase was 50 percent higher?"

Ray's grin returned. Of course, sensitivity! He had taught sensitivity in his classes. He should have had that information already. "I'll have a sensitivity analysis ready for you tomorrow morning," he said, adding, "I should have done that already."

McCormick smiled. "Sensitivity analysis? Is that what it's called?"

"Nine o'clock! Tomorrow morning," Ray said enthusiastically, as he left.

■ ■ ■

Ray was not surprised with the low and high figures. The ROI was mainly the result of the cost reductions, not the sales increase. So the ROI dropped only to 18 percent with half the sales increase. On the other hand, with 50 percent more of a sales increase, the ROI rose to 27 percent. The profits from the additional sales came with very little additional cost.

McCormick was smiling as he signed the appropriation. "I can propose this to Emil now with no reservations. The new equipment is justifiable. The addition of foreign car coverage is preparing for the future. The only risk is that we will build a new plant when we don't need it. But eventually we will need it anyway. And if things turn out better than forecast, we will definitely need it." He paused, thinking to himself. "Yes. It's a good business decision."

Ray was invited to present the program to Emil at Emil's weekly staff meeting. Besides the numbers, he had samples of the consolidated shocks, graphs showing how the car population would change, pictures of the new equipment and more. The presentation went much better than his Sears presentation, mainly because McCormick had prepared Emil by explaining how well this would be received in Dallas.

Of course, Steele gave enthusiastic support. Dennison was

more reserved, but he had signed it, so he had to support it. Even Chessman supported it with the comment, "Sounds like this will improve our indirect to direct ratio."

The surprise came when Emil concluded the meeting. "Looks like we have a winner," he said. "Dan, we can present this to United when we're down there next week. Simpson has been on my case about looking to the future and all that crap. This sure fits that bill. Maybe we ought to have the Professor here make the presentation. Show them how our new blood fits right in."

"Sounds like a good idea, Emil," said McCormick. "Ray could repeat this presentation and field questions better than we could."

"OK, but I want to be up-to-date on some of the details. And I want to go over exactly what we're going to say. We'll go over it on the plane." Turning to Ray, he said, "That's June 4th. Wheels up at 7:00 A.M."

■ ■ ■

On this trip Emil was like a different person—all business. Emil sat in his same seat, facing forward. The seat facing him was empty. McCormick sat across the aisle, facing forward. Ray sat facing McCormick, flying backward. With a 7:00 A.M. takeoff, and with no Sales personnel aboard, there was no booze served, just coffee. A tray of tiny sweet rolls was placed on the table in front of Emil. Ray particularly liked the ones with cheese and commented, "These are great cheese danish."

Emil looked at him quizzically. "What cheese danish? These are sweet rolls. What country are you from?"

That was the extent of the levity. Emil then took out a copy of the appropriation and began asking questions from the United Tire point of view, from: "What is the state of the automotive replacement business?" to "Why not open your plant here in Texas?" to "What help do you need in Washington?"

Some of the questions seemed a little silly to Ray, but Emil assured him they were not. United was a conglomerate, and thought differently than Amsaco, or any other automotive manufacturer.

"Dan, why don't you fill him in on United's background. He should know who he's talking to."

"Yes, good idea. United Tire has an interesting history. I don't know how much you know."

"Some, not a lot," said Ray, seeing the chance to get the real story from someone who knew. He had actually used the United Tire takeover by Alfred Sands as a case study, but he had always felt there was a lot he did not know. "I've read their annual reports."

"Well, OK, you know some of today's players. But let me start from the beginning. The original company was the Dallas Oil Company, run by Alfred Sands, who was a real entrepreneur. He built the company into a fair-sized operation during the war, mainly in oil distribution. But he also got into oil exploration and gas transmission, which required land. After the war, they had accumulated property in Texas, Louisiana, and Oklahoma. The property was on their books for practically nothing, but was increasing in value rapidly. That made them a prime acquisition candidate, and United Tire came after them. United figured they could pay for most of the acquisition cost with their own stock, pay off the rest by selling some of the land, and essentially pick up Dallas Oil for nothing.

"But Alfred Sands—you didn't call him Al—was too sharp for them. He had such tight control of the Dallas Oil stock, that after the acquisition, he only needed a few stockholders from United to take over control. He did, kicked out the old United management, and moved the home office to Dallas."

"It's like the little fish ate the shark," said Ray. "He must have been very clever."

"Yes, he was. And hard-working too. After that he kept building up the company. He acquired oil companies, land companies, gas companies, went international. And with United Tire as a base, expanded into other manufacturing companies like Amsaco, Commerce Yards, and Berringer Paper. He built quite an empire; he died in 1973."

McCormick paused, as if in memory of Alfred Sands, and then continued. "Stan McCall was his second-in-command and took over after Sands. He held things together for a few years, but then retired. Dave Torres took over and runs the place now as Chairman. He's very strong. Came up through the oil company. Knows everybody. Big in Washington. Also in Texas politics. Has quite a 'good ol' boy' network. Torres will be at our meeting. He'll sit at the head of the table, but he won't say much, at least at first. He'll leave that to Max Simpson, our boss, who's the Group Vice President for Manufacturing. Max has Amsaco, Berringer Paper—where he came from—United Tire, Commerce Yards, and a few others. He came up through Sales at Berringer. He ran Sales for many years, got his MBA, and was made President. He did pretty well, putting on some real good accounts, and moved up to Dallas. His replacement, Charlie London, is an engineer and is up to his ears with the paper company's environmental problems. Max is so glad to be in Dallas." McCormick exchanged a knowing glance with Emil.

"Let's see, also in our meeting will be Stan Moore, the President. Here, let me show you the organization." He took out a piece of paper and drew a rough organization chart.

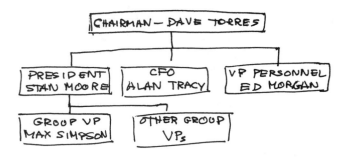

"Stan's also from the oil company, and has worked with Torres for many years. He's heir apparent to Dave, but Dave's pretty young. Besides, Alan Tracy, the Chief Financial Officer, is well thought of by the board. They brought him in from GE and he's very smart. I've worked with him for two years and he has my respect. He'll be in the meeting with his new Vice President of Long-Range Planning." A mischievous smile came over McCormick's face. "You might know him. Ralph Burch."

Ray's eyes opened wide. Emil gave an annoyed grunt.

"We just heard this yesterday," said Emil. "Tracy called me. There's this loyalty shit, I guess. Damn accountants stick together." McCormick just smiled at the thrust at accountants.

Ray wondered what this meant. Burch's new position, even though it was at corporate headquarters, had to be a demotion compared to being the Chief Financial Officer of a major operation like Amsaco. Emil seemed annoyed that Burch had gotten even that. And how would Burch feel in a meeting with McCormick, who now held Burch's old job, at a higher level than his? Not to mention being in a meeting with Emil. And now, Ray would be reporting to Burch in his Long-Range Planning job! And what about Tracy and United's top management? Did they find a home for Burch at Emil's request, or did they do that in spite of Emil? It was all very confusing, but all he said was, "I can't keep up with all these moves."

"Don't even try," said Emil. "Now let's go over the reasoning for the new plant again. Why can't we expand—"

■ ■ ■

Ray was extremely nervous about making the presentation. He understood his program and was thoroughly prepared for the technical side of the meeting. But discussing his ideas with these major executives was something else. Dave Torres was a top industry figure, on the boards of several big corporations, friendly with top politicians in Washington, and even had dinners at the White House. The others were also big time. When Alan Tracy was hired from GE, it generated a front page article in the *Wall Street Journal.*

Ray had felt his move to Amsaco was like joining the major leagues. He was proud that he was doing fairly well and deserved major league status. But very few of his fellow major leaguers ever came to Dallas to meet with Dave Torres. This was like going to the All-Star Game. He understood that he would be the lowest-ranking person at the meeting, but it was still exciting.

At the airport in Dallas, they taxied right into the United Tire hangar, where a limo was waiting. A tall black man with greying hair met them. He was wearing a dark blue chauffeur's uniform and greeted them as he took their briefcases and Ray's box of samples.

"Mr. Gross, Mr. McCormick, welcome to Dallas," he said with a warm smile.

"Thank you, Robert," said McCormick. "This is Ray Pendleton."

Robert shook hands with Ray and then held the door for them as they got into the limo. Ray looked around before getting in, and noticed two other Falcons and two bigger planes in the hangar, with room for several more. In the limo there were two big, comfortable leather seats, one facing forward and one facing rear. While there was room for three people in each seat, it was more comfortable, because of Emil, for Ray to take the rear-facing seat, across from the others. He looked around, noting a small bar, a television set, a telephone, and a temperature control panel, all nicely packaged into the doors and sides.

"This is pretty nice," he said.

"Oh yeah," said Emil as he looked around. "They live first class around here."

The limo took them downtown to the United Tire building, where Robert parked right in front of the main entrance. He held open the door as they got out and told Emil he would bring their packages up to Mr. Torres' conference room.

As they passed the guard's desk in the lobby, the guard smiled at them and said, "Good morning, Mr. Gross." The elevator operator said the same thing, as did the two secretaries outside Mr. Torres' office. The elder of the two showed them into the conference room. Dan told Ray she was Mr. Torres' secretary, who had a secretary of her own.

Inside, Max Simpson and Stan Moore were standing next to a long credenza, sipping coffee. Coffee, tea, and Coke were on the credenza, with another array of sweet rolls. The conference table and twelve chairs as well as the credenza all looked very expensive to Ray.

Ray was introduced and the greetings were cordial. He was sampling another cheese danish when Dave Torres came in through his office door, along with Alan Tracy and Ralph Burch. Again Ray was introduced with warm greetings from Torres and Tracy, and a slight grunt from Burch.

The seating proceeded carefully. Torres sat at the head of the table, with Moore taking a seat on his right and Tracy on his left. Simpson then sat next to Moore, and Burch next to Tracy. Emil sat next to Simpson, and McCormick next to Emil. Emil signaled Ray to sit next to McCormick, and Ray realized everyone was next to his boss in a perfect chain of command.

Torres got right down to business as he asked Tracy to update everyone on the year-to-date results for United. Tracy covered many key figures, emphasizing that United, in total, was slightly ahead of budget, but that Amsaco was behind. Ray thought it was interesting that McCormick, not Emil, answered, outlining Amsaco's position. Apparently, the official word came from

Accounting. McCormick explained that profits were below budget because sales were behind forecast. This was because the whole automotive replacement industry was down. However, it was expected to turn up during the second half of the year. Amsaco expected to make budgeted sales and profits.

Max Simpson commented, looking at Emil, "I've been hearing that every quarter for the past two years, but it hasn't turned up. Why do you think it will in the second half of this year?"

Emil had to answer. "You're right, Max. And to be perfectly honest, we're not that confident. But the signs are there. Our Market Research guys say there are more cars coming on the road in the five-to-ten-year-old range. They're our market and we'll get our share. Actually, our market share has not dropped. The soft market is an industry thing."

Simpson could not argue with this. The cars on the road and market share figures were generated by Amsaco's Market Research Department, which made it sound very official and objective. But he knew the figures could be manipulated because that was exactly what he had done at Berringer. "Let's hope you're right" was all he could say. But Ray noticed he exchanged glances with Tracy. The feeling in the room was not comfortable.

Torres changed that. "Well, we'll see as the year progresses," he said, ending the subject. "Now, what have you got for us today?"

Glad to be changing the subject, Emil answered, "I think we have something good here. While we are somewhat at the mercy of industry and national business cycles, one thing we can do something about is getting our share of what is out there. And we can control our costs to make sure what we do get is profitable."

He stopped, waiting for a sign of agreement. At his own staff meetings, everyone would be nodding their approval at such a patriotic statement. At this meeting, however, while Ray nodded, the others just stared at Emil and said nothing.

Emil continued. "Well, Ray here has put together a program that does both. He's identified a growing market segment that will be significant in the future. Then, while working with our operations people to prepare for this market, he put together a major cost reduction plan. But Ray can explain the program best. Ray, why don't you fill us in."

Ray was on. Starting off slowly, he covered the need to be ready for the future foreign car market. This did not sit well with Torres. He did not like the idea of the Japanese and Germans being successful in the American market. If GM and Ford would do their jobs, there wouldn't be any foreign car market. Ray did not know what to say. He was not about to defend GM and Ford. Luckily, Max Simpson broke in to say that the foreign car problem was a fact that Amsaco had to recognize. Alan Tracy added that recognizing a trend was good marketing, whether you liked the trend or not. Torres did not like it, but he accepted that logic reluctantly. Strangely, however, this put Simpson and Tracy on Ray's team.

When Ray went through the engineering problems of covering all the different Japanese designs, Torres was scowling. Ray then brought out the samples and showed what a great job the Amsaco engineers did to overcome the problems. Torres started to smile. When McCormick said, "This will teach those little bastards about American ingenuity," everyone was on board.

Ray covered the cost reductions from the new equipment, the freight savings and better customer service from the new location, the profits from additional sales, and the customer satisfaction from the new stocking plan, but they were just icing on the cake. The engineers' "standard core concept" that outsmarted the Japanese was the center of attention. Ray's samples were passed around the conference table.

"There are a few people in Washington that I would like to show this to," said Torres. "Any problem?"

"No problem if you can trust them," Emil answered. "When we come out with our designs, it will be new in the industry, and eventually our competitors will copy us. Just like they did with the 'American Barrel.'" Emil always liked to remind everyone of his big success. "But we should have two or three years on them, and that's enough."

Ray thought of commenting that it really was no problem because Engineering was already working on the new designs and the first models would come out in January with the 1978 line. They were also using the "standard core" concept on the domestic shocks and some of them would appear next year also. Then it dawned on Ray that for a good portion of the appropriation they were asking for approval for something they were already doing. He said nothing, but noticed Burch whispering something to Tracy.

"Good," said Torres, turning toward Moore. "I think Anderson would really like to hear this story."

Moore smiled. "Yeah. He could sure use some good news." Turning to the Amsaco people, he added, "Anderson is an Undersecretary in the Commerce Department and a good friend. He's getting killed by the Japs."

Torres looked at his watch and said, rather abruptly, "Well, we have to get prepared for tomorrow's Board meeting. Is there anything else?"

Emil answered, "No, that's about it. We wanted you to hear first-hand about this program. We think it's a good one."

"I agree," said Torres. "The appropriation should have no trouble going through our system." He looked at Tracy. "Should take about two weeks." Tracy nodded.

Torres stood up to leave, then looked at Ray. "I must say, this is the most comprehensive program I've seen in some time. You've taken a serious problem, used your experience and ingenuity, and turned it to your advantage—to our advantage. I'm glad you're on our team."

Ray answered hesitatingly, "Well, it wasn't just me. Our engineers came up with the technical solutions."

Emil interrupted. "He's just being modest, Dave. Ray has a knack for analyzing a situation and getting people moving in the right direction." Emil had no problem giving Ray the credit. After all, he had brought Ray into the company.

"I can see that," said Torres as he shook Ray's hand. "Max, are you taking care of lunch for these guys?"

"We're all set upstairs," said Simpson, referring to the Executive Dining Room.

■ ■ ■

Ray just floated through the rest of the day. The Executive Dining Room on the 32nd floor was a new world for him. They looked out on the Dallas skyline like a royal family gazing out upon their kingdom. Down below, people were scurrying around doing all sorts of jobs, while they sat in luxury, being served by old black waiters with friendliness, care, and the utmost respect. Ray wondered if these waiters really hated these rich white men, but put on this act as part of their job. He could not detect any sign of animosity. They must have been paid very well.

The food was delicious. Ray tried the red snapper, which he could barely finish after two hard rolls and the black bean soup, not to mention all the cheese danish before that. A French red wine was served. Ray could not see the label as the waiter poured, but it tasted expensive. No one had more than one glass. There were no prices on the menu, and no one even signed anything. The head waiter knew everyone, and Ray figured someone at each table would have the bill charged to his budget. Or maybe it was just run as a free perk. He did not know how they did things at this level... but he was impressed.

On the plane ride home Emil was relaxed and insisted that Ray play gin. Ray did, reluctantly, but was careful to drink just one scotch and to pay attention to the cards. He did pretty well, losing only $11.

He could not wait to get home to tell Dorothy of his day. He had not only gone to the All-Star game, but he had won the Most Valuable Player award. Dave Torres, who had dinners with presidents, now knew Ray and had been impressed with his work.

As he entered the house, his daughter Barbara ran up to kiss him, saying, "Mom said they were having a late meeting to go over some applications or something. She said you should take us out for pizza."

"OK," he said. "Where do you want to go?"

"Chucky Cheese?"

"Chucky Cheese it is."

As Ray sat with Paul and Barbara over pizza he realized how little attention he'd been giving them. When Dorothy was with them, he monopolized the conversation telling her all about Amsaco. When the kids would interrupt, he would courteously tell them to wait until he was finished. But he rarely got back to them. The silence at the table this evening was tense.

Ray asked, "Paul, how's your team gonna do this year?"

Paul stared at the piece of pizza on his plate. "All right."

"Do you have a good pitcher?"

"Jonas is OK."

"Are you playing third again?"

"Yeah. But they may move me to center."

"How come?"

Paul looked up."Well, we have a pretty good infield, but we're weak in the outfield. But Ernie can come in from left and play second and move Justin to third. Then I go to center and Phil goes to left. I've got a good arm, and that's what coach Watkins wants in center."

"Yeah," Ray agreed. "You need strength down the middle: catcher, pitcher, short, second, and center. That's good defense. Can you guys hit?"

"You bet." Paul then proceeded to go right down the batting order until Barbara interrupted.

"I'm going to be in Mrs. Cutler's piano recital this year."

Battling for his attention, Paul and Barbara brought him up to date on their baseball, piano, school work, friends, and other activities. It was as if the dam had burst. Tears came to Ray's eyes—how could he have ignored such wonderful kids? He promised he would come to Paul's next game and listen to Barbara's new piece when they got home.

While Ray finished his pizza and sipped his beer, the kids were playing the electronic games. A robot dressed like Elvis was on stage singing "I Want To Hold Your Hand," and an employee in a Chucky Cheese outfit was handing out balloons at a birthday party a couple of tables over. Ray sighed contently, figuring he was the only executive from that day's meeting who was having dinner at Chucky Cheese.

■ ■ ■

When they got home, Dorothy was eating some leftovers in the kitchen. The kids grabbed her attention, and it was not until they were getting to bed that Ray could fill her in on his day. She listened politely as he told her about the hangar full of jets, Robert and the limousine, Torres' secretary who had a secretary, and everything else. Best of all, he told her of the compliments Torres had given him.

"That was the icing on the cake," he said while she was brushing her teeth. "It's like I went to the All-Star Game. Working at the top level at Amsaco is like being in the majors, but only a few go down to Dallas to meet with Torres."

With one hand holding the toothbrush in her mouth, she bowed toward him.

"I'm not bragging," he explained. "I'm just trying to tell you what happened...put it in perspective."

She got a chance to talk while he was brushing his teeth. "You know, you haven't even asked me why *I* was staying late."

He mumbled something unintelligible with the toothbrush in his mouth.

"Well," she continued. "Emmett wanted to go over a few difficult applications, and he asked just Shirley and me, because he values our opinions."

Ray took the toothbrush out of his mouth, "Emmett?"

"Dean Clarke. I can't keep calling him Dean Clarke if we're working together."

"Oh?"

"Anyway, Shirley had to leave at 6:00, so Emmett and I handled over twenty-five different applications in less than two hours. He was very pleased. He said I could see beyond the obvious."

"Just you and Emmett?"

"Yes," she answered, a little annoyed. "Just me and Emmett." As she pulled the covers back to get into bed she added sarcastically, "We thought about having a sexual encounter, but I wanted to be back before you and the kids went to bed."

He went along with her joke, even if it was sarcastic. "Good," he said as he got into bed. "The kids wanted to see you."

She scowled as she watched him get into bed. Her scowl slowly turned to a smile. She kicked the covers off with her feet as she laid back, putting her arms back over her head. She said, "But he did get me sort of turned on."

Ray pulled the covers back over him. "The strangest thing," he said, looking straight ahead, "was seeing Burch at the meeting."

She groaned. Straddling him, she pulled up her nightgown. "Shut up," she said sternly. He shut up.

14. Qualifications

Dave Dennison was concerned. It was only three months since the foreign car appropriation had been signed and they were already talking about introducing foreign shocks at the sales meeting in December. This was a full year before he had figured. He discussed this with Mike Evans, as they drank coffee in Dennison's office. Evans puffed on a cigarette, while Dennison smoked his expensive cigar.

"This thing's moving too fast. We weren't supposed to have a new manufacturing facility until the beginning of next year, but Steele's going to have it ready by the end of this year, and he'll be able to build some in Seward before then. Even worse, Engineering's already got about twenty foreign shocks in the line for next year. I didn't figure we'd have to sell those damn things until 1979."

Mike said, "I've never seen anything move through so fast."

"Me either...never. The appropriation just sailed through here—and Dallas, and that son of a bitch Steele just couldn't wait to get his damn Harrisonburg plant in Virginia. He started his engineers before the appropriation was even signed. And now it's only October and Vince is putting together a stocking plan and a promotion to introduce at this year's meeting. So we'll be selling all that shit in 1978. And there's no way I can stop it. We're gonna have to sell those foreign shocks, and our Jobbers and Distributors don't know how."

Evans thought for a moment. "I don't see any problem getting them into the WDs' inventory," he said. "But they're gonna be there for a long time. The Jobbers would have to sell them to the foreign car dealers, and they're no good at that. They don't even know those guys."

"I know," said Dennison sadly. "I never should have signed that damn thing."

They both sat quietly for a moment. Then Evans grinned slightly and said, "Sounds like you got a problem."

"What do you mean, I've got a problem?" Dennison responded, a little annoyed.

"Well, the way I see it, it will be a year before the shit hits the fan. By then, I plan to be sunning myself in Florida."

Dennison had forgotten that his right-hand man was planning to retire. Evans had been around so long that it was hard to imagine the company without him.

"You sure you don't want to reconsider?" Dennison said, "I could keep you on until the shit hits the fan. And then I would have someone to fire. And then you could get severance pay."

Evans smiled. "Sounds tempting. But it would be just my luck that they'd fire you, and I'd be left with the mess. No thanks."

"OK, it was worth a try." Dennison thought for a moment, then continued. "Any idea who should take your place? One of your 'Three Musketeers?'" Evans' three Regional Managers could hardly be described as musketeers. They were all very different, would rarely talk to each other, and did not like each other at all.

Al Donaldson was an old friend of Evans and had followed him in the Regional Manager's job when Evans became Vice President. He was tall, white haired, and good looking, not smart, but 100 percent salesman. Some of his escapades, especially with customers, had become folklore within the sales group. His wife had divorced him fifteen years before, with good reason. They were still friends, however—it was hard to stay angry with Al Donaldson.

Sam Kemper was smart. His IQ had impressed Tom Chessman, who pressured Evans into selecting him. But Kemper lacked the warm personality necessary to win over customers. Some longtime customers had complained to Evans. Not vehemently, because Kemper took care that each customer was served well. He just did not personally cater to their individual needs or idiosyncrasies.

Just the opposite was Walt Morris. Walt was a real dynamo, drumming up business, creating deals, and telling everyone what they wanted to hear, not only customers but also Evans, Dennison, and even Emil. Emil thought he was executive material, but Evans did not really trust him.

He said to Dennison, "Walt is probably the top candidate, but I never know if he's telling me the truth. Al will always tell me the truth...if he knows what it is. He'd be honest with you, too. But he really doesn't know that much. He's the world's greatest salesman, but as a home office executive...?" Evans squinted and shook his head. "I don't know."

"What about Kemper?"

"He's a good technician, but not much with customers. If he came in as Al's assistant, maybe. Let Al tour the circuit with customers and Sam keep everything in order."

"I don't want two guys to do one guy's job," Dennison retorted. "But while we're on the subject..." He reached over and dialed his phone. "Tom...Dave. Mike's in here and we're talking about his retiring, and potential replacements. Like to have your input. Do you have a minute?"

Chessman came right over to Dennison's office. If there was going to be a change of personnel at the executive level, he wanted to know what was happening. Emil was sure to ask his opinion. He walked in and sat on the couch, not wanting to sit across the big desk, looking up at Dennison. He greeted Evans with, "You son of a bitch. You mean you're actually gonna retire before we fire you?"

Evans went along. "Not 'til my anniversary date next April. You still have time."

"We can't afford the severance, Tom," said Dennison. "Mike's been here a hundred years."

"Yeah. That's the problem in Sales. Everyone's been here too long. You're paying them too much."

Evans was not going to fall into that trap. "It isn't the pay that keeps them with us, Tom. It's our warm personnel policies—the insurance, the pension, the moving allowance. Everyone in Sales just loves Tom Chessman and his Personnel Department."

Chessman was stopped. He had no retort, so he changed the subject. "Kemper's your man to replace Mike," he said to Dennison. "The bastard's got a 142 IQ. I don't know how the hell he ever got into sales."

"We've been talking about Kemper," said Dennison. "Only Mike has real concerns about how he gets along with customers."

"Yeah, Dave," Evans broke in. "I haven't had a chance to tell you yet, but we're worried about Bob Goodman and Jobber's Supply in Flint. Kemper's never gotten along real well with Goodman. And now Blackwell's making a run at him. God knows they have enough of the Michigan market with Automotive Supply; four big warehouses around the state. But they must feel they have a chance with Goodman. I'm going to see him tomorrow."

Dennison put his hands to his head and groaned. "More good news." Then, he turned to Chessman to explain. "When the whole industry is down, we're all scrambling to fill our plants. And Blackwell's got the most plants to fill up. Now they're coming right into our backyard." He turned to Evans. "If Blackwell's decided to be aggressive, then we're in trouble. They have the money to buy some of our key customers. We're in deep shit."

Chessman grinned mischievously. "You can fight them with your Foreign Car Program."

Dennison was not in the mood for jokes. "That's how this whole conversation started," he said seriously to Chessman. "The damn Foreign Car Program is moving so fast, just so Jim can get his damn Harrisonburg plant. And we're not gonna sell that many. We'll get our pipeline fill, but then nothing much. I was hoping it would go slower, the way it always does. Then the foreign car sales would be lost in our normal sales increases. But if Blackwell is getting aggressive, we'll have to fight like hell just to keep even. We'll never make the sales figures in that foreign car appropriation. I never should have let that damn Professor talk me into that thing." He turned to Evans. "Whoever takes your place is gonna be in a hell of a lot of trouble. The shit is about to hit the fan."

They sat quietly for a moment, digesting the situation. Then a smile slowly started to form on Chessman's face. "You sales guys got tunnel vision," he said. "I know who should be the next VP of Sales."

He stopped to let his statement sink in. The other two said nothing, but just stared at him.

"The Professor!" he said, smiling broadly.

Dennison scowled. "Blow it out your ass. I've got a real problem here."

Chessman, however, kept smiling.

"You're serious!" said Dennison. "My God, what the hell kind of qualifications does the Professor have?"

"He's smart," Chessman answered. "And he knows marketing."

"But he doesn't know how to sell."

"He sold his Foreign Car Program."

Dennison groaned again. Evans laughed. "It may not be as bad as it sounds, Dave. A marketing guy that doesn't know sales may not be any worse than a sales guy who doesn't know marketing... and we have plenty of those. Our customers might look at him as someone who knows what he's talking about. Make them feel smarter when they tell him their marketing strategy. And our other sales guys, and you, and Emil can still stroke the customers and wine and dine 'em."

"And besides," Chessman added. "He's just going to be there until the shit hits the fan."

Dennison thought for a moment, smiled, and said, "And if anyone should get fired over this foreign car shit, it certainly should be the Professor."

"You see, he's qualified," Chessman added, triumphantly. "You can't be more qualified than that."

■ ■ ■

Everyone but his wife and the three Regional Managers were glad to see Ray get the Vice President of Corporate Sales position. Emil liked the idea because it made him look good in Dallas. Dave Torres had been impressed with Ray's presentation and knew that Emil had brought Ray into the organization. It showed that Emil was open to new ideas and new people. He would put capable people into key positions, not cronies. This would be perceived as a modern, businesslike decision.

Before agreeing, however, he checked it out with Tom Chessman, who told him, "Dennison seems to think the customers will love him."

McCormick and Steele liked the change because it put a businessman into the Sales Department. Ray would have an understanding of finance and manufacturing. He would take any outlandish sales scheme and modify or change it to make it practical, before presenting it and wasting their time. In fact, Jim Steele had several of his own ideas to present to Ray that would simplify the manufacturing tasks.

Actually, Vince Procino had the job of coordinating the Marketing and Operations systems. But he had felt lonely trying to keep the Sales people realistic. Dennison and the Sales VPs were all salesman, and many times Vince found himself all alone, representing reality.

The problem was that the salesman's job was to keep his customers satisfied. He was supposed to do this within company policy so that the company could make money. However, almost all of the salesman's time was spent with customers who could care less about Amsaco making money. The company policies became rules to get around instead of guidelines for profitable operation. Once a year, at the National Sales Meeting, the home office would scold the sales force for bending the rules, lay out the programs for the next year, and explain the rules that must be followed. The salesmen would then immediately start to figure out ways to circumvent the new rules.

Vince Procino was glad to see Ray in his new position. He did not expect too much from Ray because of Ray's naivete. But it would be nice to have an ally, and eventually Ray would learn. Besides, they were friends.

The Regional Managers were not that happy. Al Donaldson was not too concerned. He was perfectly happy to serve out his last four years in his present post. He would have preferred to report to his buddy, Mike Evans. But if that could not be, he would rather have Ray, whom he could control, than Kemper or Morris, who would have their own agendas. Evans had already instructed him to use Ray's business background to impress customers, but "don't tell him too much about what's was going on."

Sam Kemper was disappointed and somewhat confused at Ray's appointment. Sure, Ray Pendleton was smart, but so was he. In addition, he had the field experience and the knowledge of the customers and the industry. Kemper had no idea that his poor relationship with some customers had kept him from the promotion. He had good relationships with some customers and was not aware that others did not like him. He was aware that he had disagreements with them, but usually he was defending company policy. He did not "give away the store" like some others in the field and felt this posture was necessary to become a home office executive. Actually, if the Accounting Department had been making the decision, he would have been the new Vice President.

Also disappointed was Walt Morris. Walt had done a good job in the West. He had added new accounts and was getting more sales out of existing accounts. The only thing keeping him from getting attention was the poor condition of the entire automotive replacement market. While he was increasing his market share in the West, he was only keeping even in dollar sales. He was objective, however, and considered Ray's appointment as a temporary setback. He started planning how to use Ray in his region and how to become his replacement when Ray moved on. And he started thinking of several ways he could hasten that move.

Dorothy was happy to hear the news, at first. Ray called her at the university as soon as he left Dennison's office. He was the new Vice President of Corporate Sales, with a salary of $55,000 per year, plus a bonus, which would be bigger than he would get as Director of Long-Range Planning. Mike Evans would stay on as Vice President of Industry Relations to help Ray ease into the new position, introducing him around the industry, especially to customers.

"That sounds wonderful, honey," was her first response. "Wait a second. Let me transfer this over to my desk." Then after a few seconds, "There. I have more privacy here. So…a Vice President. How about that. What will they say back at Harvard?" She giggled. "What will Henry say? I suppose this means another dinner at Win Schuler's."

"Absolutely. What time should I make the reservation?"

"Well, I haven't seen much of the kids lately. I'd like to make them supper. What about 8:00 o'clock? Too late?"

"No, that's fine. I think that's the time Vice Presidents are supposed to eat, anyway."

As they drove to Marshall, they talked about the kids and some things that happened to Dorothy at her office. When they were seated at Schuler's, Dorothy said, "So. You lost another boss, did you?"

Ray grinned. "I guess so. A good one too."

"Yeah. I told you to keep that one."

Ray paused. "You know, honey…of course I can't turn down a vice presidency, but I don't think I'll have that good a relationship with Dave Dennison. He was nice to me today, offering the job. But we've tangled in the past. I always got the feeling that when we were discussing something, he had something on his mind he wasn't telling me. With McCormick, we would lay out the problem, the facts, the possible solutions. Then we would discuss it. Everything was out on the table and we were both looking for the best solution. With Dennison, there always seemed to be something in the background, something I didn't know. And if I don't know, how can we discuss things intelligently? How can I contribute if he's holding something back?"

"Maybe it will be different when you're working together, when you're part of his team."

"I hope so."

They looked at the menu, and Ray studied the wine list. "What about a good French red wine?"

"Oh, I don't know. Red or white? I'm not sure. And we don't need an expensive French one. California would be fine."

"Yeah," he answered, still looking at the wine list. "But I had a real good French red when I was down in Dallas. Maybe they have one like it. And we ought to celebrate."

"Fine. Red would be fine."

Ray ordered the filet mignon, while Dorothy ordered the trout. They started into the hors d'oeuvres tray when Dorothy asked, "What's involved in the Sales Vice President's job? What do you do?"

Ray smiled and answered, "I'm not sure. I guess finding out is my first assignment." Then he thought a bit and answered more seriously, "I'm basically responsible for corporate brand sales—everything with the Amsaco label. Corporate brand sales account for two-thirds of Amsaco's sales…our domestic sales."

"But what do you do? Like who reports to you? What groups do you boss?"

"There are four people reporting to me—Al Donaldson in the East, Sam Kemper in the Midwest, and Walt Morris in the West. They're our Regional Managers. Plus Harry Fitzimmons, the Sales Manager for Universal Auto Parts, a national outfit and our biggest customer. The RMs have District Managers reporting to them, and the DMs have Territory Managers and Sales Reps. And Harry has about fifteen in his group. All together, I have about ninety people reporting to me." He shook his head, almost in disbelief.

Dorothy just nodded as she spread cheese on a special Schuler cracker, so Ray continued. "My job is to see that all these guys are well armed and well informed when they go out to sell and service our customers. Most of the information comes from Vince's department; all the programs and the advertising, even the training."

"Are there just guys?" Dorothy interrupted. "No females?"

"Actually, there is. Pete Fowler, our District Manager in Southern California, hired a female Sales Rep last year. Some of the guys were joking about it at the National Sales Meeting last year."

"What's so damn funny?"

Ray looked at Dorothy's belligerent expression. "Hey, I don't know. Just the usual bad jokes. Men stuff." He grinned at her. "Hey, I don't want to fight about it."

Dorothy did not smile. "It's just unfair," she said, poking her toothpick into a tiny meatball. "I mean, she's probably real serious about doing her job, and all she gets is a bunch of jokes behind her back."

"Well, that's the way it is. She's a pioneer in the automotive replacement business, and she gets the pioneer's reward."

"What's the pioneer's reward?"

"An ass full of arrows."

Dorothy laughed just a little. "It's still not fair." She paused for a moment, then added, "Maybe you could add a few more women … if you're the boss over ninety people."

"You bet I can. And maybe some blacks. I can do some good." He stopped, thinking for a moment. "You know, this is a new experience. I've never had more than my secretary reporting to me. Everything I've gotten done, I've basically done it myself. Now my job is to sell millions of shocks and I won't do any of it myself. The guys reporting to me do the selling."

They said nothing as the waiter brought them their salads and refilled their wine glasses. Dorothy was thoughtful as she stirred the dressing into the salad. "If Vince puts together all the programs and trains the salesmen, and then they go out and sell, what do you do? Sit around your office?"

Ray laughed. "I doubt it. I've got to see that they're doing it right, and come up with better ways, better than our competitors. Like Emil did with his American Barrel program. I've told you about that haven't I?"

"Oh, yes," Dorothy said, holding up both hands. "I've heard the American Barrel story many times—from Emil, from Vince, from you. Is Amsaco still using it?"

"Sure," Ray replied. "We even give American Bucks to Jobbers who get garages to use them."

"So the Jobber sells to the garage."

"Right."

"And you sell to the Jobber?"

"No, actually we don't." Ray smiled as he realized how complicated the automotive replacement market really was. "We sell to the Warehouse Distributor, the WD."

They talked about this complicated market until the waiter came with their main course. He set their plates down, poured the rest of the bottle of wine and asked if they would like another.

"Sure," said Ray, while Dorothy just raised her eyebrows.

"I'm feeling the wine already," she said. "I'll be under the table."

"We're celebrating," said Ray.

"OK, but I will not be responsible for my behavior."

"Good."

They stopped talking momentarily, as they started to eat. The waiter came back and opened the second bottle of wine, giving Ray a new glass for tasting. It was excellent, just like his filet mignon. Dorothy looked pleased with her trout. They ate quietly for a while. Ray felt relaxed and happy. Dorothy was apparently deep in thought.

Ray broke the silence by jokingly commenting, "We might have to get used to this type of living."

"Why?" asked Dorothy warily.

"Well, good living's part of the sales job too," he explained. "We have to meet with customers and prospective customers, and their wives—"

"We have to meet with customers?" she interrupted. She looked at him doubtfully.

"Sometimes. But at real nice places. First class. Look, honey, I'll be doing most of the travel to customers and sales meetings, but you'll be invited to special trips and industry meetings, and—"

"What are those?"

"The industry meetings?"

"Yes."

Ray thought for a moment. "I'm not exactly sure myself," he said carefully. The tone of the conversation was not going the way he wanted. "There's this big ASIA show every year for the whole aftermarket industry. I don't know exactly what goes on, but I know everyone gets involved for about two weeks, right up to Emil. And another one is AWDA out in Las Vegas. I don't think everyone is involved in that one, but I know Emil and Dave Dennison and Mike Evans were gone for over a week last spring. And they have something called Distributor's Institute that Dennison was—"

"It sounds like you're going to be away an awful lot," Dorothy interrupted again. "How much travel is involved?"

"I'm not sure," he answered. "Not until I get into it myself. But Dennison said I should plan to go somewhere every week, or at least a few days each week."

"Every week?" Dorothy had a pained expression. She put down her fork and sipped her wine, thinking over the situation. "I don't know if I like this job. This could put another roadblock between us."

"Roadblock?'

"Maybe that's not the right word. But something's been coming between us ever since we came to Amsaco. It's not the same as it was. We don't seem to get a chance to talk. We're leading separate lives."

Ray was shocked. "Where's this coming from? I thought things were going fine since you got your job. I know I'm busy. We're both busy. But that doesn't mean we're—"

"It's been fine for you, not for me." She looked away. "It's been bearable. But with all that travel, I'll never see you." She reached over and poured herself some wine. He started to say something, but she continued. "And it's not just me. You're becoming a stranger to Paul and Barbara, too."

"Oh c'mon, Dot. The kids are growing up. They're starting to lead their own lives."

"Sure they are. But they still need you. Maybe more at their age. You told Paul you'd come to his games, but you didn't. And you hardly ever talk with Barbara." She sipped some wine and continued, "I know you're there if they have a problem. It's not that. It's more like a feeling. We're not a tight family anymore. We don't do things together. Everything revolves around Amsaco."

She breathed deeply and sat back in her chair. "Even tonight. We finally get to go out, just you and me, but we're talking about your job, about Amsaco."

"But we're celebrating my promotion. That's why we came." Ray was having trouble with her logic. "What is it? Is it more time for the kids? Or more time for you and me? What's the problem?"

"Oh, I don't know. It's everything." Tears started to form in her eyes as she looked straight at him, started to say something, then stopped. Slowly she reached over to touch Ray's hand and said softly, but firmly, "Ray, when was the last time we made love?"

He was not ready for that question. He was not ready for any of these questions, but especially that one. "I don't remember exactly," he stammered. "Last Sunday, wasn't it?"

"That's about it," she said. "Every once in a while on Sunday mornings. And even then, we just go through the motions. We fuck, we don't make love."

Ray was stunned. She had never talked like that. Maybe it was the wine. It must be the wine. But he saw real tears in her eyes, and it hurt him to see her hurting. He loved this woman. She was his mate, his companion. They had gone through so much together, they were like one. He wanted to say, "I love you." He wanted to ease her pain…to make her smile again.

"It's not the same, Dot. We're getting older. It's just natural to have less sex. We still make love when we want to. It's just less frequent."

"It's not because we're getting older, Ray. We're not as close. We don't do things together. We're not partners in the adventure. You didn't even talk to me first, before you took this job."

"But what could I do?" Ray was confused. This celebration was turning into a disaster. "Should I have turned down the vice presidency? And the salary and the perks? Besides, I thought this would be great for us, that you would be thrilled. We'd have more money to do things and we'd go on the company plane together to some of the fancy hotels and restaurants. I thought you would—"

"What hotels and restaurants?" Dorothy was getting louder. "I don't want to fly on the company plane."

"But you've never been on the company plane. Or gone to a fancy resort or restaurant." Ray was almost in tears himself. "I've had just a touch of the stuff, and I want you to have it too. I want to share it with you. And now you'll get in on some of the good times."

Dorothy sat back in her chair and asked, sternly, "What role do I have in this new job?"

"Just some of the industry things. The good stuff. We entertain customers and their wives at some of the industry functions. It means the best resorts and restaurants. Places we would never get to ourselves. Certainly not on a Professor's salary."

"What about my job?"

Ray had not even considered Dorothy's job. That was just one more question he was not ready for. He answered rather weakly, "It's not that much, really. Most of the travel I'll do myself. It's just a few times a year. And it should be great. Like a vacation, almost. You can get the time off, can't you?"

"Maybe. Depends on when it is. We're real busy at certain times of the year."

Ray did not know what to say. Dorothy's job was part-time and would bring in maybe $4,000 a year. Should he be expected to turn down the vice presidency because of that? He knew he should not ask that question.

"What can I do?" he asked. "There's hundreds of guys in the company that would give their eyeteeth to get this job. And their wives would give even more. I never dreamed that you would be against it. Let's try it. It should be great for—for both of us."

Dorothy gulped down her wine, stared away from Ray, and said simply, "I'll see."

15. Conversations Over Lunch

Ray was enthusiastic about taking on his new responsibilities. Up until now, he had always been involved in plans, either making new plans or analyzing old ones. Now he would be responsible for carrying out the plans. He would be measured by results. He had a lot to learn and it would be an adventure.

He understood Dorothy's reluctance. Dorothy was smart. She did not blindly accept everything; and she was frightened about how this new job might change their lives. That was only natural. But Ray knew this was a good move, not only for his career but for the whole family. He was sure she would come around.

Ray never thought of failure, only the excitement of finding new ways to succeed, as he had always done. He was not aware of four conversations going on around the country.

■ ■ ■

Walt Morris was taking advantage of Emil's quick trip to Los Angeles by meeting him for lunch at the Beverly Hills Hotel. Walt chose the Beverly Hills because it had good food and the Hollywood atmosphere that he figured would appeal to Emil. Many celebrities would have lunch there, as well as celebrities to be. The hotel still used an old-fashioned paging system—a uniformed bellhop would walk through the lobby and restaurant, loudly calling someone to the phone. Many of the good looking young men at the bar would have themselves paged just to get noticed by important people. Walt thought Emil would get a kick out of that.

As they sipped their martinis, Walt informed Emil that he was behind the latest move. "I just wanted you to know that I think it's a great idea to get new blood into the organization."

Walt was a good-looking young man, serious about selling. He was always neatly dressed, with shoes shined, ready to "go out and sell." He had a talent for telling people what they wanted to hear, and in the process, getting his own message across. Whether what he said was the truth was not important as long as it accomplished his objective. "I talked to Pendleton last year at the sales meeting and he's pretty sharp...lots of good ideas."

"Good," Emil agreed. "That's why I brought him into the company."

"Well, I'm glad you did. Some of the guys don't see the big picture. They complain he doesn't know anything."

Emil laughed. "I asked Dennison exactly that question before I approved the move. And Dave said 'He'll be all right. He doesn't know anything, but he knows he doesn't know anything.' How's that for a recommendation?"

"That's right," Walt said seriously. "We can handle the customers as long as he doesn't shake them up too bad. It might add some work to introduce the professor around, but that's what we get paid for. But the important thing is we'll get some fresh ideas. If our customers have any objections, it's our job to set them straight."

"I appreciate that attitude," Emil replied. "I hope the others feel the same way."

"My guys will. I don't know about Kemper. His nose is probably out of joint because you went out of our sales group. He wanted Mike's job."

"That's our decision. Guess he'll have to live with it."

"Right. We each have our own job to do. I'm not going to worry—"

Just then the bellhop was walking through the restaurant calling, "Walt Morris...Walt Morris. Paging Walt Morris."

"Sorry, Emil," Walt apologized. "I left word where I would be. But I told 'em I was with you and not to call unless it was important." He did not mention who 'em was.

He took the message from the bellhop, handed him a dollar, and followed him back out to the lobby. The studs at the bar watched as Walt walked past. They didn't see him as much competition, but they wondered if the fat guy at the table might be some important producer or something.

When Walt got back the waiter was serving their food. "Am I imagining things?" Emil asked. "Or are those pretty guys at the bar watchin' us?"

"Maybe they're just evaluating the competition."

"Yeah, sure."

Walt laughed. "Everyone here looks at everyone else. There's all sorts of important Hollywood people here. When I walked out, I passed the table where Sissy Spacek was sitting."

"Who's that?" Emil asked.

"Sissy Spacek...from the movie *Carrie*. She's a new star. Pretty famous."

Emil shrugged. "I don't go to movies."

Walt wondered if this really was the best place to have taken Emil. Actually he had paged himself and had planned on joking about it with Emil—maybe even have Emil paged. Better change the plan. "That was Jim Carney," he said. "He's been complaining about returns. Says he has a bunch of our stuff he wants to return for credit. I think he just can't pay."

This did not surprise Emil. "That's what happens when business is slow—everyone wants to pay with returns. Stay with him," Emil instructed. "He's been with us a long time. And don't count his returns too closely. He probably needs a little help."

Walt winked. "I'll take care of it."

"Is there a lot of this going on?"

Walt nodded. "Yeah, it's tough. But we can handle it. It sure would be nice though if you started the professor out with Kemper or Donaldson. Donaldson's got plenty of time."

"OK," Emil said. "Talk to Evans."

■ ■ ■

In Ann Arbor, Dorothy was nervous as she walked into the restaurant with Emmett. It had been a long time since she had been out to lunch alone with a man other than Ray. Emmett had talked about going over work plans, particularly her schedule, but she wondered. They could have eaten at school, but he had chosen a fairly nice restaurant specializing in all sorts of fancy fish dishes.

She ordered a salad and turned down his offer of a drink.

After Emmett finished speaking about the upcoming schedule, he was quiet for a long moment. He turned his fork around in his fingers, looking down at his plate.

Dorothy sat silently, not wanting to hear what he was going to say.

"Dorothy, I have to be honest with you," he said, looking up at her. "Putting together our schedule was not really why I asked you to have lunch."

She remained silent, but looked straight at him. He was not a bad-looking man. His thin face and wire frame glasses seemed to fit with his baldness and gave him an honest, mild appearance. She could not help thinking that he looked a little like Ray.

"I...I wanted to talk to you...personally," He continued. "I know you are married, and I think I know I'm divorced. And if you don't want me to say...if I say something I shouldn't, just tell me and I'll stop. But I wanted you to know I...I'm very fond of you and—"

"Emmett," She interrupted. "Maybe you should stop. I mean, I am married."

"Yes, yes I know. But lately when we talk...or when I hear you talk to others, I get the feeling that you're...not happy...in your marriage." Before she could answer he spoke quickly. "I know I shouldn't say things like this...and I have no right to ask you about these things. But I didn't want this opportunity to pass by. I can be a friend...and more than a friend. And if I didn't say anything you might not even—might never know."

"Emmett—"

"I'm not suggesting anything sordid or improper, but I—"

"Emmett," she interrupted a little louder. "I understand. I understand what you're saying. And I'm kind of flattered." Then more quietly, "Emmett you're a very nice man. And yes, I have been having troubles. But that's all they are—troubles. And they're personal. And my husband and I will handle them."

"I'm sorry," he apologized. "I'm sorry. I understand." He looked away. "I shouldn't have said anything."

They were both quiet for a moment. He started talking again, looking down at his fork. "I don't know if you know what it's like being divorced. Of course you don't. And really, I hope you never do. It's lonely. But you can't let on. You have to put up a front about how you have everything under control and you're really enjoying the freedom. But after you accept the fact that you're really divorced—and that takes a few years, then you start looking at every woman, and I mean every woman that goes by, and ask, 'Is she the one that's going to cure me of my loneliness? Is she going to be my mate?' But then you don't say anything because she probably has someone else…or won't like you even if she doesn't. And then you never know."

He looked up. "But as I got to know you more and more, I thought, 'Don't pass this one up. She's special. Take the chance.' So I took the chance."

"I'm sorry, Emmett," she said softly. "Maybe if things were different…But I'm sure you'll find someone…your mate. You're a fine person."

"Yeah," he said with a little laugh. "I hear that a lot."

They were silent as their food was served.

"I hope this won't ruin everything," he said as they started to eat. "I hope this won't make you quit your job or anything. Everyone likes you, and you're really very good at your job. And I promise I won't bring this up again."

Dorothy kept eating. She knew what he had done was wrong. Even if he thought her marriage was in trouble, he should never have said anything. She should end it by leaving her job and breaking off all contact. But then, he was just being honest. He really just asked if there were any chance, and accepted the fact that there wasn't. And he promised this would be the end of it. He looked like a scolded puppy.

"No, I won't quit," she said quietly. "If this doesn't happen again, I'll stay on." She reached over and touched his arm. "Like I said, you really are a nice man. So as long as you keep your promise, I think we can be friends."

His face lit up. "Good. I'd like to be your friend."

A little while later he said, "You know, your husband is a very lucky man. Very lucky."

"Hah." she laughed. "Tell him."

■ ■ ■

In Dallas Alan Tracy and Max Simpson were having lunch together in the company dining room. This was not unusual. This time, however, Tracy had asked Simpson not to bring anyone with him.

Tracy sipped on a glass of white wine as Simpson lit up a cigarette and exhaled slowly, waiting for Tracy to start. Both men were wearing expensive suits, but Tracy's was buttoned and very neat, while Simpson's was open and showed a wrinkled shirt, and there was a small stain on his tie.

"I wanted to talk to you about Amsaco," Tracy began. "They're spending a lot of money on the Professor's program, but they're still not going anywhere."

"But the foreign car sales aren't supposed to come until next year," Simpson answered defensively. It bothered him that Tracy was telling him about his own company.

"Yeah, but the foreign car sales don't amount to a hill of beans anyway." Tracy explained. "Their appropriation was based on capacity. They needed more capacity because of total sales, which were supposed to pick up. But the total sales are not increasing."

"I know that."

"Of course. You said yourself that Emil predicts every quarter that it's going to pick up next quarter."

"Yeah. I know. And it's beginning to burn my ass a little."

"So the bottom line is that they're adding capacity when the market's going down," Tracy concluded. "And Burch tells me that in Jackson, they're beginning to call the new plant 'Emil's White Elephant.'"

"Burch still keeps in touch with Jackson, eh?"

"It's part of his job."

Simpson thought about the situation. Expanding during a decreasing market was a cardinal sin. It encouraged more competition and price wars. He had approved the Professor's appropriation only because of the prediction of increased sales, and Torres' fascination with the engineers' feat in outsmarting the Japanese with standardized shocks. But if things went badly, Simpson was sure Torres would forget the engineering job and remember the cardinal sin. Tracy would see to that. While it was Amsaco's responsibility because they had made the sales prediction, Simpson would share the guilt unless he took action and punished someone at Amsaco.

"I'm well aware of the situation, Alan," he answered. "And I've got a few ideas. We have to change something at Amsaco. If the market's not going up, we have to cut costs."

"Right. Either we do or Emil does," Tracy reasoned. "And putting his Professor in charge of sales isn't going to do it. That just added costs. He promoted the Professor, but kept Evans. They don't need both of them. Emil never cuts costs. He still uses the yacht as much as ever, and he still finds reasons to stop in Las Vegas. He's a spender."

Simpson could see Tracy had done a lot of work to prepare for this conversation. And he was sure he had spoken to others at the top—maybe even Torres. They would be watching to see what Simpson would do. And doing nothing was the worst alternative.

"I appreciate your input, Alan," he said in a friendly tone. "I'm well aware of what's going on at Amsaco. I've been holding back a little to give Emil a chance to turn things around. But he hasn't done it and now it's time for strong action, and I know how to do that. I hope you'll back me when I go to Torres."

"You can count on it. I just wanted to fill you in on what I heard from Burch and the others. Thought it could help."

"It does, and I appreciate you coming straight to me."

■ ■ ■

An important meeting was taking place at the country club in Columbus, Indiana, the home office of Blackwell Manufacturing Company. Alan Tracy was not the only executive who thought there was overcapacity in the shock absorber industry. Andrew Wilson, the distinguished, white-haired, well-dressed President of Blackwell had gone to Harvard Business School and knew all about what overcapacity did to a market. He was explaining that exact theory to his Senior Vice President of Sales, David Brown, as Morgan Farnsworth, his Chief Financial Officer, listened. Brown was a volatile, overweight, red-faced, sloppily dressed salesman; Farnsworth a neat, conservative accountant, with perfect posture and emotional control.

"Brownie, you've got to understand, the problem's not getting more business," Wilson was saying. "It's not market share. It's over-capacity. The whole industry is down. Our plants are at 60 percent of capacity, and Amsaco and Crane have got to be hurting also. No one is making money. What's it look like for year end, Morgan?"

"Profits will be down more than 30 percent," said Farnsworth crisply. "Mainly due to sales."

"And we've got over 40 percent of the market," Wilson added. "Amsaco and Crane have got to be doing even worse."

"But I can get us more business," argued Brown. "I think Jobber's Supply in Flint is vulnerable. Marge and I had dinner with Bob Goodman and his wife, Doris, last week, and he's not too happy with Amsaco. I think if we send them on a nice trip to Hawaii or something, and if we lift their inventory, I think he's ready to change."

"Brownie, you're missing the big picture," Wilson countered. "That will cost us an arm and a leg. And then, what's Amsaco gonna do? They can't afford to lose an account like Goodman. They have to get that business back somehow. And it doesn't matter if they come back at us or at Crane. 'Cause then Crane has to react. Pretty soon we're all taking business from each other, our costs go soaring, and in the end nobody picks up any more business."

Farnsworth was nodding in agreement. "That's right," he said. "When business is bad, you cut costs. You don't start wars."

"But we can get Goodman," said Brown. "We've been after—"

"Forget it," Wilson interrupted. "I'm not going into a Board meeting and tell them the market's gone to hell and we're starting a war. You just pull back. Cut down on travel. Don't give raises. And don't replace anyone who leaves. Cut costs! You hear me?"

Brown knew his part of the meeting was over. "I got to get back to the office," he said as he got up to leave. "I hear you loud and clear. It really bugs me, but I hear you."

"Good...Morgan, you stay here."

When Brown had left, muttering to himself, Wilson continued. "Brownie's good, but he's never gonna cut costs. I never knew a salesman who could. Besides, the big costs are in Operations. We're gonna have to make major cuts in our operations. I'm thinking of closing a plant."

Farnsworth was not surprised. He had planted the seed himself, raising that possibility at several of Wilson's staff meetings. "It makes sense," he said. "At 60 percent of capacity, we won't miss one plant. Except the North Carolina plant. They're turning out 40 percent of our total production right now. And costs in Kinston are low."

"I know," Wilson agreed. "North Carolina and Mississippi have the lowest costs. They're nonunion. Simple as that. So is California, but they're not big enough to save much. No, it may cause some fireworks, but our most expensive plant is right here in Columbus. This is the one that's got to go."

Farnsworth smiled and shook his head. "The UAW is not going to like this."

"They brought it on themselves. They're making too much money and all they ever do is ask for more, more, more. They've got to be competitive too."

"How about the Board?" Farnsworth asked. "Will they go along?"

"I think so." Wilson smiled. "I talked to Anderson and McCloud last night. They both reacted positively. McCloud said he was glad someone finally had the balls to stand up to the UAW."

"Me too."

16. Teaching the Professor

Ray spent most of his time with Vince Procino and Mike Evans preparing for the National Sales Meeting. Ray wanted to be ready when he met the field force at the Doral Country Club in Miami in December.

Ray had thought of Mike Evans as a hand-shaking, hard-drinking, story-telling, good ol' boy salesman, always joking around and never serious. But as they worked together on the 1978 plans, Ray was more and more impressed with Evans' knowledge. He knew the personalities and capabilities of each of the Regional Managers and District Managers, and even some of the Sales Reps. He understood the internal politics at the home office and what could be realistically expected from the 1978 programs. Evans seemed to know all the customers personally and how they would react to new programs, as well as how these programs might be abused by certain members of the field force.

"You can't give a lifetime guarantee in this market," he explained when they met in Ray's new office to consider such a program. "The muffler shops can do it because they use it as a come-on. If a customer comes in to get his free muffler, you can bet he'll still pay plenty for the muffler pipes plus the hangers and flanges and clamps. They're trained on how to use the guarantee. It's a marketing program. Besides, they tie the guarantee into the owner-ship, and usually the car changes hands or the guarantee gets lost before the muffler wears out. I'll bet less than 25 percent of the guarantees are collected. It's a well-controlled marketing program."

"Why can't we do that?" asked Ray.

"Because in the traditional market we sell to the WD, who sells to the Jobber, who sells to the garage or service station, who sells to the consumer. And we have no control over the garage mechanic, our final salesman. If someone comes in for a replacement shock, he'll replace it at no charge. Then he returns it to the Jobber and it goes back through the system and ends with us. But we don't even know if it was a bad shock."

"Supposing we tried it anyway," Evans continued. "How do we prevent fraud?"

"Fraud?"

"Yeah, at any level. How do we know if the garage really replaced a shock? How do we police it? The Jobber doesn't want to police his customer."

"We could demand to see the shock," Ray answered. "Or the guarantee."

"Who would do that?" Evans replied. "Our field men? They'd be spending all their time checking bad shocks. Even then, they couldn't cover all the service stations and garages."

"Couldn't we collect the shocks at the Jobber level, or even at the WD?" Ray asked.

"We might." Evans smiled as he looked at Vince and Ray. "But our customers are not going to use space for collecting scrap. Even if they did, how do we know they're our shocks?"

"What would really happen," Evans went on, "is the Jobber or the WD would demand credit for a bunch of worn shocks when our man came in, regardless of guarantees or policies or any of that crap. And most of our field guys would cave right in and write up a credit."

"And there's no way we could police it from here," Vince added. "We'd be swamped."

"Right," said Evans, sitting back in his chair. "And someone like Willie Schaum in Santa Ana would be out buying scrap shocks and essentially selling them back to us at new shock prices. Hell, we'd probably end up paying for a bunch of Blackwell and Crane scrap too."

"But couldn't Walt Morris police something like that?" asked Ray. "It's his region."

Evans looked at Vince and winked. "Walt would be the one that would explain the whole scheme to Willie."

Vince laughed and said to Ray, "You just got your first lesson in the real automotive replacement world."

Ray shook his head and sighed "I could never teach this in school."

■ ■ ■

Not surprisingly, the final program was not much different from the previous year's. It continued the "American Bucks" for the Jobbers and the "American Trip" for the WDs. Both plans contained requirements to stock the new foreign car shocks, and the advertising program emphasized the Amsaco foreign car coverage. They used the same advertising agency and trade magazines, with similar ads featuring the American flag. Most of the automotive aftermarket people were fairly conservative, tired of the "hippies" running the country. The American flag was effective.

Ray thought the agency was pretty clever, tying in the American flag with foreign car coverage and the slogan "No shocks are foreign to Amsaco."

Evans and Procino were happy with the ad program, but Vince warned Ray, "Emil won't be thrilled. Every year he calls this, 'The same old crap, warmed over.' In fact, it was during one of our advertising meetings when he first mentioned bringing in someone from the outside. Someone who could put together a total marketing plan."

"But that's just what we did," said Ray. "The Foreign Car Program just gives us a small competitive advantage. And we've added your new stocking plan, and we've redesigned the product line to—"

"It's not an 'American Barrel,'" Vince said. He and Evans laughed.

"But maybe," Vince went on, "when Dave and I go to get Emil's approval for the ad campaign, you can come with us. You can sell the 'total program' idea. It might help."

"Maybe we should get more input before we go to Emil," Ray said warily. "Maybe someone from the field."

Evans thought for a moment. "Good idea. Why don't we get the Regional Managers in to critique the whole plan. They're good at that."

Vince agreed. "Yeah, they're always telling me what we should have done."

Evans added, "We could all present the plan to Emil, and he's more likely to go along. He likes to talk with the RMs. He might even take us out to lunch."

■ ■ ■

Like true professionals, all three RMs congratulated Ray on his promotion and welcomed him as their new boss when they met in the conference room on Saturday. Their concerns and jealousies never came near the surface. They each invited Ray to meet important customers. Al Donaldson had "real interesting" distributors for Ray to meet. Sam Kemper had a couple of "problem" accounts where Ray might be of help. Walt Morris had some "prospects" to cultivate.

Walt was enthusiastic. "Foreign cars are big out West," he said. And we haven't had much to offer our customers. All I hear is 'Blackwell has Datsun. Blackwell has Toyota. When is Amsaco gonna wake up?' We've needed this." He looked over the list of cars that would be covered. "Yeah, but we still need more. For those little Jap trucks."

"Engineering is working on a bunch more for next year," said Ray. "They've done a great job."

"We've got a great bunch of engineers," Walt said. "But they've just been sitting on their ass—or working on shit we don't need, like improved ride or long life. You've done a real service to this company, directing them to stuff that helps sales. Sales is what keeps this company going."

Evans was smiling as he said to Ray, "That's Walt's ongoing sermon. The company revolves around sales."

"Well, it's true," said Walt. "Nothing happens 'till we sell something. Emil agrees."

"Sure," answered Evans. "He's a salesman. You haven't done that well convincing Accounting."

"You mean the Sales Prevention Department?" Walt said.

Evans laughed. "What about you, Al? This program gonna help you in the East?"

"We don't have as many foreign cars as Walt sees in California," Donaldson said. "It'll give us something to talk about, but it won't be a big deal."

"We have even fewer foreign cars in the Midwest," Sam Kemper added. "I see some problems loading my customers with foreign shocks."

"Oh?" asked Ray. "What problems?"

"Well, I don't want to sound negative," answered Kemper. "But right now, most of my customers want to reduce inventory, not add new parts...unless there's a real demand. But I don't see—"

Walt interrupted, "It's our job to see that the WDs carry everything, like they're supposed to. So when the market develops, they're ready. That's their function."

"I know that," Kemper answered, somewhat annoyed. "But new things always happen in California first. You've probably got so many foreign cars on the road out there that the foreign car dealers can't service them all. So independent garages get a share of the market. But we're four or five years behind California, and our WDs don't want to inventory those parts."

"That's where Vince's new stocking plan comes in," said Ray. "They only stock what's going to move in their area. The WD will have a very small inventory of everything, but he'll only have quantity on what moves."

"That part sounds good," said Kemper, realizing that he was alone in his objection. "But we have to emphasize the idea that it's only a small investment, very small." He thought for a moment and added, "We could pitch it as an inexpensive way to be ready to meet future demand."

That approach sounded good to everyone, but Morris just shrugged his shoulders, as if to say "I don't need that."

As Evans predicted, Emil had the whole group out to lunch at the country club and approved Vince's programs before dessert. Dennison was pleased that he did not have to go through Emil's "same old crap, warmed over" routine. He told Ray in the parking lot that the meeting was a good idea. "Having the RMs come in showed unity," he said. "Showed the field guys think the program's practical."

"It wasn't unanimous," said Ray, grinning. "Kemper wasn't too enthusiastic."

Dennison only said, "Kemper's smart."

■ ■ ■

In Ray's view of the corporate world, white-collar workers and blue-collar workers were "classes." On the other hand, executives were "individuals." The fate of corporations depended on the personalities and capabilities of executives. Case studies discussed decisions made by these executives and what resulted. The cases never discussed machine operators or secretaries, or programmers or engineers, or any of the individuals who made the corporation function. Ray was aware that they had to do their jobs, but so did a typewriter or a drill press. His views were academic. Madge Larson gave him a friendly lesson on the real world.

Madge was a nice-looking woman in her early fifties, who had worked as Mike Evans' secretary for twelve years. Mike suggested that she work for the Ray and him until he retired. "She knows what's going on around here. Probably better than I do. And she knows the salesmen. Madge can help you a lot."

This was fine with Ray. He had usually shared a secretary, anyway. He wrote out his own letters and reports, never dictating, and handled his own travel arrangements and personal schedule. He used secretaries to type letters and reports, to answer the phone, schedule meetings, and make coffee. He treated the secretaries respectfully and always got along well with them, but they never became a real part of his working world—or his personal world.

While preparing for the National Sales Meeting, Ray was trying to develop his understanding of sales cycles. How did seasonality affect sales? How did advertising plans or promotions affect sales? In what regions or districts? What about vacations or plant shipping capacity? How could the sales force plan their efforts most efficiently?

To get started he wanted to see the monthly sales for each district. He called John Romero, the Data Processing Manager, and explained what he wanted.

"You need monthly sales by district? Gross or net?"

"Both," Ray answered.

"That shouldn't be too hard," Romero said optimistically. "I'll check with Robinson and see when we can get it in the schedule. I'll call you back."

He called back about an hour later and told Ray, "If we can give it an "A" priority we should be able to get on it in about four weeks. It should only take a couple of weeks to write the program and run it."

"But I need the info now," Ray said. The National Sales Meeting was coming up in three weeks.

There was silence for a moment, and then Romero said, "I

understand, Ray, but everyone needs their info now. And we're swamped. McCormick's on my back to get our payroll glitches straightened out, and we're still trying to get the new Honeywell unit debugged. I'll tell you what. Get your RFD over to me as soon as you can, and I'll see what I can do."

"What's an RFD?"

"A Request For Data. Your secretary can pick one up from Shirley."

Ray complained to Madge, "The data has to be sitting there. It shouldn't be so much trouble. Can you get me an RFD? Do you know who Shirley is?"

"Shirley Francone," said Madge. "She's in charge of RFDs. But I don't think it will do much good. RFDs are also known as 'Reasons for Delays.' It'll take a week just to get in line."

"But Romero said he would see what he could do."

Madge smiled. "He really doesn't make those decisions."

"But he's the head of the whole department."

Madge kept smiling. "What is it you need? Write it out for me and let me see what I can do."

Ray was about to ask what she thought she could do, not even being in the department. But he saw her smiling calmly, as if she knew something he did not. He wrote out the information. Madge took it and left. It was 2:00 P.M.

The next morning a computer printout was sitting on his desk: the monthly sales, by district—not for the past three years, but for the past five—plus sales by each Territory Manager in the district, and even more valuable, sales by each customer.

Madge came in while he was studying the printout. "They ran it last night," she said simply.

"But how—"

"Patricia Stacey is Mr. Robinson's secretary. She's very nice. We worked together on the women's Christmas party. She asked one of the programmers, who works at night. It's not so hectic at night."

"But what about...I hope no one gets in trouble."

"No one else even knows about it. Please don't tell anyone."

Ray smiled. "Not a soul."

Two days later, John Romano called to ask if Ray had sent in his RFD.

"No," said Ray. "It's not that important. I can use other figures. But—uh—thanks for your effort."

■ ■ ■

Ray had gone to great lengths to prepare for the National Sales Meeting in Doral, but it was not really necessary. His only assignment was to give a short speech when Mike Evans turned over the leadership at the end of the meeting.

Mike still ran the meeting. Ray watched carefully, because he would have to do it next year. Evans opened the meeting on Wednesday morning in the small ballroom, all decorated with Amsaco promotional material featuring the American flag. Mike had told the Manager of Advertising, "Let them know why we're here and what we're selling."

Evans gave a short welcome, introduced the Amsaco senior executives. He did not spend too much time reviewing last year's results, because they had not made forecast. Emil did not want to hear about it any more than he had to, and neither did anyone else. Evans turned the meeting over to Vince Procino.

Vince and his staff spent the rest of the morning going over the 1978 programs: the product line—including the "standard core," the advertising program, the American Bucks program, and a new training program for all Territory Managers.

Ray observed that no one seemed too interested in the presentations. Some people perked up a little when Vince went through the Foreign Car Program, but most of the time the salesmen were talking to each other about golf plans or card games or going out to the restroom. The energy level picked up at coffee break, but subsided again until lunch.

The afternoon seminars were more lively. Each of the morning's presenters had a breakout room to go over their subjects with smaller groups of salesmen. The smaller sessions proved much more productive, with a great deal of good-natured arguing. Ray made a point of sitting in on each seminar, as did Dan McCormick. The other home office people seemed to disappear.

They reappeared that night at dinner, when the sales force had a "roast" for Mike Evans. Emil spoke first, followed by Dave Dennison and Walt Morris. They made some derogatory remarks about Mike that Ray did not think were very funny. Every insult got a good laugh, however. Ray joined in halfheartedly just to be sociable.

Al Donaldson got up to tell a story. "Remember that hot night in Albany?" he said, grinning at Evans. He explained to the audience, "It was the hottest night in the year, and we had to give a presentation to Herb Dryden's Jobbers. We had just changed Herb's Capital Distributors operation to Amsaco, and we had to get his Jobbers to change, or at least stock our line. He had us booked into a little room in this downtown hotel, and it was hot in there.

"I was sweating before we ever started. Luckily, Herb had plenty of beer and everybody had two or three before they sat down to listen to something they really didn't want to hear...Some of you young guys don't remember hotels or motels without air conditioning...hell, some of you don't even remember hotels."

Everyone laughed with Al. It was true. Most of the sales force had never been exposed to anything but air-conditioned motels. Only the old-timers remembered when motels were scarce and the only choice in most was an old local hotel. An older salesman turned to Ray. "Yeah, I remember," he said. "Those old hotels could sure get hot."

"Mike was Regional Manager," Al continued, "and I was his TR. We were wearing suits and ties and sweating like crazy. Mike gets up to start his pitch, then stops and says, 'Hell, I don't need this.' And takes off his jacket. Herb says, 'Hey, that's a good idea,' and takes off his. So I do too, and so do the few Jobbers that were wearing one.

"And Mike starts his presentation. Well, he wasn't two minutes into it when he says. 'I don't need this either.' And he takes off his tie. So do we. But it's still hot as hell, and humid. The sweat's pouring off. Mike's shirt is soaked through. He stops, goes over and pours another beer and says, 'Hey, you guys don't mind, do you?' And takes off his shirt. Herb says, 'good idea' and takes off his. And so do all the rest of us.

"Well, Mike drinks some of his beer, walks over to the front of the room, as if to start again, but then stops and says, 'Shit, it's too damn hot,' and he takes off his pants. So, Mike's standing there in the front of the room in his shorts and his undershirt and his long black socks and garters, and one of the Jobbers stands up and says, 'you got the right idea,' and takes off his pants.

"Well another Jobber does the same thing, and Herb, and me, and pretty soon we're all sitting there in our underwear, drinking beer, still sweating, but feeling much better. And Mike, he doesn't even crack a smile, but picks right up on his presentation, telling them about our great products and programs, and what a great company Amsaco is…and they're all listening, asking questions.

"You got to imagine the picture," Al said. "This whole room full of guys in their underwear…" He looked toward the back of the room. "Carla, maybe you shouldn't imagine it."

Carla Grant, the only woman on the field force, was laughing. She yelled back, "I'm picturing it right now, and it's making me kind of sick."

Ray joined in the laughter as Al continued. "The most amazing thing is that afterwards, we got every one of those accounts for Herb. The next day I started calling on each one of them, and every single one signed up. Every one! I'd just walk in to their shop, and they'd come out from behind the counter smiling and telling me what a great presentation that was, and that Mike was the best factory man in the business. To this day, when I get to Albany, I call on Herb and have lunch with one of those guys, and we still laugh."

Al stopped and everyone started to applaud. He reached under the table, pulled out a small box, and held up his hand for silence. "I consider that one of the great selling jobs in the automotive industry. A Hall of Fame performance. In memory of that, and in case Mike wants to repeat it sometime, we've gotten him something special."

He opened the box and pulled out a pair of white boxer shorts, dotted with red hearts. He presented them to Evans. Someone took pictures of the two of them holding up the shorts.

Ray was really enjoying himself. He was not yet part of this friendly new world of comraderie, but he was ready to join it. Each sales person he met was friendly and had a good word about Ray's promotion. He realized of course, that he was their new boss, which would certainly influence their behavior. But still, most of them seemed genuinely friendly, welcoming him to their team. He was determined to earn his position.

After dinner, he was invited into a poker game with Casey

Brown, the District Manager from Alabama, and some others he had played last year. He had been mourning over the rejection of his Sears plan and quickly lost $40. He was much happier this time, but he still lost $25.

He noticed a crowd around the table where Emil, Jim Steele, Tom Chessman, Walt Morris, and two District Managers were also playing poker. "Stay away from that one," said Elgin Cramer, the Sales Rep in Ray's game. "They'll build up to a pot limit in that one. You could lose a few hundred in one hand."

There were three poker games going on in the room, plus bridge and a few gin games. Other people just hung around drinking and socializing and watching the games. There were a lot of oohs and aahs from around the big poker game.

At midnight the room was closed and the games had to break up. Ray and most of the others went up to their rooms. But Ray noticed some of the men going into the lounge. Also, Emil, Walt Morris, and the two DMs from their game were leaving through the lobby. Elgin drawled, "Those boys are gonna have big heads tomorrow morning."

Ray was tired, but felt good. He enjoyed being with these guys. It was strange to be their new leader, who would show them how to improve their performance, yet feel they were the real pros who knew more than he did. But Ray was confident. In time, he would prove his worth and be a real member of the team.

When he got to his room, he thought of calling Dorothy, but decided it was too late. He did not have time in the morning, as he had a breakfast meeting with Evans and the RMs to go over the quotas for next year. He attended the seminars for the rest of the morning.

Thursday afternoon was open to play golf, lounge around the pool, go sightseeing, or anything else. Ray went back to his room to catch up on some paperwork and go over his speech. He called home, but Dorothy was out.

Thursday night was the banquet, where awards, bonuses, and quotas were given. To a round of applause, Emil gave the President's Award for the outstanding District Manager of the year. Ray was asked to give out the outstanding Territory Manager award to Stan Bronski from New Jersey.

There was less enthusiasm when it cam time to give out bonuses. They were based on how much each district exceeded quota and sometimes ran up to 50 percent of the salesman's salary. But 1977 had not been a good year. There was even more gloom when 1978 quotas were given out because the increased sales forecast made higher quotas necessary. The depression passed quickly, however. Most groups rallied, agreed it was tough, but said they could do it. Ray was impressed. It seemed like a good group. He was even more determined to get them big bonuses next year.

The banquet ran late, and Ray skipped the card games to go up to his room to call Dorothy.

He was full of enthusiasm. "They're a real bunch of pros," he said. "I never saw a bunch of men so confident. And Carla Grant, the female rep, her too."

"That's nice," said Dorothy. "Look, I signed Paul up for the boy's basketball league at the recreation center. They have practice Saturday. Can you take him?"

That was not what Ray wanted to discuss, at least not yet. "What time?" he asked. "Dave called a meeting for Saturday morning to go over a bunch of things from the sales meeting. I'm free in the afternoon."

"No," Dorothy said abruptly. "It's at 10:00 o'clock. I'll take him."

"I'm sorry, Dot," he apologized. "I'll take him next week. They really keep me busy here. I tried to call you before. It was too late to call you last night, and I missed you this afternoon. I don't like being away like this. I—"

"That's all right," Dorothy said. "It's not much different than when you're here."

■ ■ ■

Ray missed almost every Saturday morning practice, as well as the games. Something always came up—he was either out of town or meeting with Dennison or Evans or Emil. Once, he left the office for an hour to catch part of a game. He was proud to see Paul score two baskets while he was there, but he had to leave before the game was over.

His travel increased significantly. Each Regional Manager took him around to meet key customers and see their operations. Ray was impressed with the variety of ways WDs ran their businesses. At school, Ray would analyze the industry, and all Warehouse Distributors would fit into one group. They were assumed to react the same way to the various industry events. In reality, the relationship with each WD was very personal, and each operation was unique. Some were well off financially, others scrambling to get by. Some had large inventories, some hardly any. The building might be new, on the outskirts of town, or it might be an old dilapidated warehouse in the middle of the city. Deliveries to Jobbers were once a week for some operations, daily for others, and "on demand" for some. The owner might be a Harvard Business School graduate who inherited the business from his father, or a hard-working tough guy, who built the business up from a scrap yard to a parts store to a warehouse.

Interestingly, none of these characteristics correlated to success or failure in the business. Each owner had his own methods. A good example was Paul Bloom in Detroit. Bloom was a short, stocky man who always had a cigar in his mouth. He had an old, three-story warehouse in a tough area of the city. He maintained a large, neatly arranged inventory, and an efficiently run counter and loading dock. Three young black men loaded the trucks coming in for a pickup, unloaded the deliveries, directed the traffic, and guarded the cars parked in the street.

Bloom told Ray, "They let the neighborhood know that we're all right, that there's a bunch of jobs here for blacks, but if there's a lot of trouble, we would have to move. And we're good neighbors. We sponsor Little League and bowling and other local projects. We have a neighborhood picnic every year. We co-op with several kids in the vocational school, two girls in the office, and three men in the warehouse. Right now, this is probably the safest place in the city. You could leave your car in the street, with the keys in the ignition and your wallet on the seat, and no one will touch it." Still, Ray kept his wallet in his pocket.

Bloom's father had started with an auto junkyard and eventually opened an auto parts store. Bloom, still in high school, took over when his father died. He built it into a four-store operation, opened a warehouse to supply his own stores, and then expanded to supply other auto parts stores all over Detroit. His son Carl had graduated from the University of Michigan and was learning the business.

Ray brought Dorothy with him to Detroit to have dinner with Sam Kemper and Mr. and Mrs. Bloom. They ate at Carl's Chop House, the best steak restaurant in Detroit, according to Bloom. Sam wanted to try out the idea of hiring a black Sales Rep for the Detroit area. He and Ray had agreed that it was the right time, and Detroit was the right place. Sam had already interviewed a young graduate from the University of Detroit, who looked good.

"You mean you don't have any blacks in your sales force?" asked Helen Bloom, Paul's wife. "Not one?" Helen was taller than her husband. Dorothy could see that she must have been a real beauty when she was younger, and was still attractive.

"Not yet," Kemper answered.

"Why not? Don't tell me Amsaco's prejudiced." She had a sort of twinkle in her eye, and Ray did not know if she was a liberal, or if she was just teasing them, or both.

"No, Helen," he said, "I don't think Amsaco is prejudiced. We have many minorities within our own operation, at the home office and at the plants." He did not mention that they all walked in at low-level positions. There were no minority supervisors. "But in the field force, we have to take into account our customers' feelings."

"Your customers? Like us? We're not prejudiced. We have many fine minority employees...and customers."

"We know that," said Kemper. "That's why we're talking about putting on a black Sales Rep in your district. But we don't want to just barge ahead if it will cause any trouble with your customers."

"It won't cause any trouble with our customers," said Helen, somewhat angrily.

"It will with some," Paul broke in, looking at his wife. "You know Frank McManus is always referring to 'those damn niggers.'"

"His big mouth is going to get him in trouble," said Helen.

"Yes," Paul agreed. "And you know Gert Weinstein is always after Mel to sell the store in the city and open a new one in Troy, to get away from the blacks. And we have a few others that may find it hard to be taken out to lunch by a black guy."

"That's their problem," said Helen, looking straight at her husband.

Paul smiled and relit his cigar. "Yes, it is," he said. He turned to Kemper, "We appreciate your concern, but we'll handle our customers—even if we lose a few."

Helen smiled at her husband.

"Most of our customers will have no problem," Bloom continued. "If your guy is capable, he'll be welcome here. You just get us a good man."

"We will," said Kemper. "And I'll train him myself."

■ ■ ■

With Mike Evans and Al Donaldson, Ray next visited Ed Lambert's operation in Pittsburgh. The warehouse was nice enough, with plenty of room, located on Forbes Avenue away from downtown. The problem was there did not seem to be any activity in the place. Lambert commented that they did most of their shipping in the morning, but Ray observed there was not much inventory.

Lambert invited them into his office, where he lit a cigarette and pulled out a bottle of Jack Daniels from his desk. He took a swig, and passed it around to Evans, Donaldson, and Ray. Ray did not know whether to drink or not, but after everyone else did, he took a small swig.

"That's right," said Lambert, taking off his metal framed glasses and rubbing his eyes. "I don't trust a man that doesn't drink." Then, turning to Donaldson and grinning, he added, "Anyone who's sober is fighting against me."

Everyone laughed, but Ray wondered what type of businessman would drink in the afternoon in his office. Evans explained later that Lambert had gone into business with an uncle who ran the operation. Lambert handled sales. They had done very well, but when his uncle died, Lambert never really tried to take his place. The operation became sloppy. Lambert kept a few good accounts, enough to pay the bills and buy Lambert's booze. Lambert's divorced wife had long since remarried and his kids were grown, so his expenses were low.

When they went out to dinner, Ray expected a pizza or hamburger at a strip joint. Instead, they ate at Lambert's club, the Duquesne, *the* private club in Pittsburgh. The club was in an old building with many rooms and high ceilings. Paintings of famous industrialists were hung everywhere. Their table was near an enormous portrait of Andrew Carnegie.

Waiters in tuxedos moved smoothly across the carpeted floors. Lambert was greeted warmly. The others ordered their drinks, but Lambert did not have to. His double Jack Daniels was served quickly, followed by another as soon as he downed the first one. After the third, he was laughing with Al Donaldson about some old adventures.

"Yeah, I remember Betsie," said Al, smiling and shaking his head. "How could I forget?"

Lambert turned to Ray. "We were having a party up at the old Boswick Hotel, just four of us. Al here had called earlier and I told him to meet us there. He comes a little late and the party was well under way. There's a knock on the door and I figure it's Al, so I say, 'Betsie, why don't you answer it?' You got to understand, by that time Betsie's only wearing panties. But as she goes to the door, she stops to take *them* off."

He paused to let the picture sink in. Evans and Donaldson were laughing. Ray had a smile frozen on his face.

"Well, she goes right to the door and opens it wide. And you should have seen the look on Al's face. I thought his jaw was gonna drop and hit him on his pecker, which was rising up anyway. I tell ya, I couldn't stop laughing."

"That was before I really knew you," said Donaldson. "I'm not surprised so easily now. If I know you're involved, the sight of a naked girl doesn't make my jaw drop any more."

"Or your pecker rise," Lambert added, laughing loudly.

The rest of the evening went along the same way. Several times Lambert started a story and then stopped, saying, "Maybe we better not talk about this one."

Everyone would laugh, but Ray could not imagine what could be worse than the ones he was already telling. He was glad Dorothy was not at this dinner.

The evening was long. It took an hour and a half of drinking before they even ordered. Ray noticed there were no prices on the menu and he asked Evans about that. Evans whispered that only the host member had prices, and only members could pay the bill. Later he would pay Lambert cash and put it on his own expense account.

The atmosphere of the Duquesne Club was calm and elegant, except when Lambert laughed too loudly. Ray could not help but compare this with the Executive Dining Room at United Tire. This was even classier. Ray found it odd to see this crude, alcoholic womanizer treated with the same respect as the big industry executives at United.

■ ■ ■

Ray was recovering from jet lag in Los Angeles when he received a call from Emil. It was 5:30 in the morning. "Ray, I heard you were out in L.A. This might work out pretty good. I'm flying out there this afternoon with McCormick and Simpranian. We have a meeting tomorrow with Gold Electronics in La Mirada. They have some kind of adjustable shock where you can control it from the dashboard. Simpranian says it works, and we're looking into buying the company. You can help us evaluate if we should buy it or just negotiate for patent rights or manufacturing rights. We're scheduled to tour their operation in the morning and then to meet the rest of the day, if necessary. Can you go with us?"

"Sure," said Ray. "As he gradually came fully awake, he recalled the day's scheduled appointments. "We're going in to see Jim Carney this afternoon, but I think Walt can postpone it for a day."

"Great. You're at the Airport Marriott, right? We'll have dinner there about 7:00 and fill you in. And Ray, don't let anyone know who we're meeting with, not even Walt. The last thing we need is that big mouth Carney spouting off. We'd have six companies in there bidding against us."

"I won't say a word."

The Amsaco plane arrived late and they did not sit down to eat until 8:30. It was 11:00 before they finished. Ray was ready to go back to his room and get ready for the next day.

"Nah, it's too early," Emil said. "How's the Foreign Car Program going?"

"You guys go over that," said McCormick. "I want to review the flash reports. I'll see you in the morning."

"I need to go over Gold's R&D reports," said Simpranian.

In the next instant they were gone, leaving Ray with Emil. "C'mon," said Emil. Ray followed Emil through the lobby, outside, where they got into a cab. Emil directed the cab back to the private air terminal. The two pilots were in the lounge waiting for Emil. They boarded the plane. Less than an hour later they were in a cab in Las Vegas.

The rest of the night was a blur to Ray. He had never been to Las Vegas before, and he spent most of his time watching others gamble. Emil liked Caesar's Palace, where they held their AWDA meetings. He knew several of the blackjack dealers. He told Ray to look around and get familiar with the place because they would be back in April, entertaining customers. That, apparently, was the business purpose of this trip to Vegas. Then Emil sat down at the $25 blackjack table and Ray was on his own.

As Emil had instructed him, he walked around the hotel to get acquainted with the restaurants and the general layout. Caesar's had a couple of normally priced restaurants, a fancy Roman-style expensive one, an even more expensive exclusive one, as well as their big name nightclub. There were several smaller bars, a beautiful outside pool, some very expensive shops, slot machines everywhere. He had to go through the casino to get almost anywhere. A person staying there would never need to leave the hotel.

He was amazed at the number of people gambling on a week night, after midnight. He could only guess at the time because he did not wear a watch and there were no clocks anywhere. Another onlooker told him that was no accident. The casinos did not want gamblers knowing what time it was when they were spending money. The tables were open 24-hours-a-day, every day. The outside world hardly seemed to exist.

Ray was also amazed at the amount of money changing hands, and the speed. At first it seemed like fun. The chips were thrown around like toys. When he found out how much the various chips were worth, however, he watched with more respect. Eventually, his curiosity won out and he tried the blackjack table, the $2 table. He lost $20 in about five minutes, and that ended his gambling.

He had no idea how long they would stay there. He stopped to watch Emil several times and asked what the plans were. Emil would only grunt, play his cards, and mutter something like, "Don't worry. Just enjoy yourself." Ray would leave and roam around some more. Somewhere around 5:00 A.M. when he went by Emil again.

"Don't bother me," said Emil. "I'm losing 400 bucks. Why don't you get yourself a drink and relax." He pointed to the bar nearby. There was nothing much else to do unless he went back to the tables, so Ray sat down at the bar and ordered a beer.

He was still amazed at the number of people scurrying around at 5:00 A.M. on a weekday. The place was not crowded, but there were still several hundred people gambling, drinking, or working. He was watching people, imagining what they did when they were not there, when a pretty, young redhead sat down next to him.

"You look lonely," she said.

Ray was startled and just mumbled, "Er, no. I'm just relaxing."

"Well you look lonely to me," she said, smiling at him. "Buy me a drink and I'll see what I can do about it."

Ray just nodded. "Sure."

She motioned to the bartender, who quickly came over with a glass of something. She did not touch it, but reached down and rubbed Ray's thigh, showing quite a bit of cleavage in the process.

"My name's Monica."

"Uh...I'm Ray."

"Hi Ray. Do you need some company?"

Ray was startled, but he could think straight enough to understand Monica was a hooker, making a pass. He had never been approached by a hooker.

"No...thank you, but no," he stammered. Then, looking at the sad expression on her pretty face, he added, "I appreciate...I mean I...I just have to leave pretty soon. My boss is right over there."

He looked toward Emil and saw Emil looking back at him and laughing. He looked back at Monica and she was laughing too.

"I know that," she said. "He's the one who said you were lonely." Then with her smile changing to a pout she asked, "Are you guys just teasing me?"

Ray looked anxiously at Emil, who was still laughing as he played his cards, and then at Monica, who looked as if she were going to cry.

"No, no," he stammered again. "I...didn't know. I wouldn't...no, I think it's just a mistake."

"Well, if you don't want company," she said calmly, as she sat back. "I certainly won't force you. But I don't want to waste my time. My time is worth something."

A light went on in Ray's head. He reached for his wallet, took out a twenty, and handed it to her. She just looked at the twenty and looked back at Ray. He handed her another twenty.

She smiled and said, "Thanks. Look me up sometime when you are lonely. You'll find it's worth it."

Ray watched her walk slowly away, then gave the bartender a twenty to pay for his beer and her drink. The bartender was laughing as he gave Ray $12 change. Ray left $2 for the bartender and got up to leave. Out of curiosity he reached over to taste her untouched drink. Ginger ale.

Later, Emil asked him how much he had given her.

"Forty dollars."

Emil laughed. "That's the easiest $90 she ever made."

They did not get back to the hotel until 8:00 P.M. Emil slept soundly on the plane ride back, but his loud snoring kept Ray from getting any sleep. He had time to shower and shave before they met McCormick and Simpranian for breakfast. No one said anything about the night before.

Ray was all right during the tour of the Gold operation, but after lunch he could hardly keep his eyes open. Emil however, seemed to feel no ill effects. He negotiated, then conferred with his staff, then negotiated some more, until agreement was reached around 6:00 P.M. Emil would propose to United Tire that they acquire the Gold operation as part of Amsaco.

The Gold President dropped Ray off at the hotel after taking the others to the plane. Ray went up to his room, lay down on his bed, and did not wake up until Walt Morris called from the lobby at 7:00 A.M. Ray would remember the lesson of this trip—Try to steer clear of Emil after work is over.

17. The Good Life

For Ray, Emil's interruption of Walt Morris' schedule meant another difficult long-distance explanation. He waited while Dorothy said good-bye to the kids. When she came back to the phone, he said anxiously, "I'm sorry...but Jim Carney just couldn't see us until Monday, and Walt's got us scheduled all day Saturday. And I thought it wouldn't make sense to catch the red-eye Saturday night just to come back here on Sunday night."

"No, that wouldn't make sense," she agreed. She laughed. "And that settles it."

"Settles what?" Ray asked, beginning to be worried.

"I've been thinking of taking the kids for a quick trip to Boston. It's the perfect time. We'll take a long weekend and fly back."

Ray was relieved. Not only was Dorothy not mad at him, but now he would not have to go back and spend a weekend with his mother-in-law and Henry. "That's a great idea," he agreed.

She laughed again. "Yes, but we're still going back East on vacation this summer. You're not getting out of that."

■ ■ ■

Saturday night after the kids had gone to bed, Dorothy was sitting with her mother in her kitchen. "Mom," she said, "everything I was afraid would happen is happening."

"What do you mean?" Her mother asked, genuinely surprised. "I thought things were going so well. Ray is a Vice President, isn't he?"

"Oh yes."

"And that's a very good job? With good pay? And a good future?"

"Yes, yes. Things are going very well for Ray. And financially we're doing great—"

"How great?"

"Pretty good. Ray's making a lot more than he did at Harvard."

"How much more?"

Dorothy smiled. "Well, if you must know, his salary is over twice what he was making, and he's eligible for a bonus for a lot more."

"And *that's* what you were afraid would happen?"

"Don't be sarcastic, Mom. Just listen...please."

"OK, talk. I'll listen."

Dorothy took a deep breath. "On the outside things look fine. We've got a lot more money. The kids are doing well in school and have new friends. And even I like my new job at the University. I know you must be wondering what I'm complaining about—"

"I certainly am."

"Mom! Just listen. I'm not really complaining. It's just that things are so different at home...between Ray and me. And between Ray and the kids." She paused trying to find the right words. Finally she threw up her hands and blurted out, "It's the company. It's Amsaco. That's the whole problem. At Harvard Ray would work hard at school and then come home. He would enjoy his work, but then leave it at the office. When he came home we were a family. We would think family and do family things. Yes, he had papers to correct and reading and research, but not *all the time.* At Amsaco his work *always* comes home with him. His mind is always at the office. And now, with this promotion, there's much more traveling and entertainment...and we'll never be a family again. It's like he left us."

"But he does come home," her mother argued. "Almost every night and almost every weekend. He—"

"No, Mom," she interrupted. "I'm not talking about his physical body. Yes, that comes home. But his mind is all Amsaco, all the time. It's like he left us...like we got a divorce. Sure he brings home a lot of money, but it feels almost like alimony or child support. Because I'm alone. The kids and I are alone."

They were silent for a moment. Then her mother started talking slowly and quietly. "Listen, Dorothy, listen carefully. I can't solve your problem, but I think I can put it into a better perspective. You are not alone. Ray may be paying too much attention to his job, but you are *not* alone."

She stopped to emphasize what she was going to say. "I'll tell you what alone is. When your father died, I was alone. That's alone. All the responsibility for you kids and for myself was mine. No one else's…only mine. I was *never* going to see my husband again. I couldn't ask him to do anything. I couldn't ask him what *I* should do." Tears started to form. "Sometimes I wished I could just ask him for advice…or have him hold me or make love to me… or just speak to me. But he was never going to do that. Jim and Sarah Spivak had become just Sarah Spivak." She took a deep breath. "That's what alone is."

Dorothy also had tears in her eyes. "I'm sorry, Mom," she apologized. "I didn't mean to compare—"

"Listen, Dorothy, I'm not saying Ray is right and you're wrong. He's paying more attention to Amsaco than to you and the kids. You're playing second fiddle, and maybe you should do something about it. But be glad it's Amsaco and not another woman…or that he's not sick and getting ready to leave you forever. Put it in perspective."

"You're right, Mom. You're right, of course. I do love Ray, and I'm lucky to have him…even when he's an asshole." Then Dorothy smiled and asked, "But what can I do to get him away from Amsaco…from that 'other woman?'"

"Wait. Just wait. In the long run you have much more to offer him than that company. Meanwhile, save your money."

Dorothy could not accept everything her mother said, but it helped her to hear it and—yes—put her own problem in perspective. She could not compare her mother's situation with her own. At the same time, her mother had never experienced what *she* was going through. Dorothy lay awake that night in the bedroom she had slept in as a child. She wondered, "And if I wait and wait until he comes back…will there be anything left?"

Dorothy felt a little more cheerful the next day when the family came over. Sarah could not resist bragging to Ray's parents and Henry. "Yes, the kids are doing very well," she informed them. "Besides being a Vice President, Ray is bringing home two or three times what he did at Harvard."

"Mother," Dorothy protested.

"Well, we're all family and we're happy for you. Tell them about the other things, the hotels and all that."

"Oh, it's not that much," Dorothy said, trying to downplay it. "Ray says we'll be doing a lot of entertaining. Attending industry events and taking customers to nice places."

"Like where?" Ray's father asked.

"Oh, to restaurants and resorts. They take their distributors and their wives once a year to places like the Bahamas, or Monte Carlo...nice places."

"No kidding," Henry said, beginning to become more interested.

Dorothy liked the idea of impressing her brother. "Yes, and I understand we'll use the company plane and maybe even the yacht."

"The yacht?" Henry whistled. "I didn't think old Ray had it in him. Looks like he's going to give you a taste of the good life."

■ ■ ■

The good life started for Dorothy at the ASIA show, a week-long industry event in Chicago for Jobbers, WDs, and manufacturers. Almost all the automotive parts manufacturers in the country showed their products at McCormick Place from Monday through Thursday. The events started the previous Saturday, with award dinners, seminars, society meetings. Entertainment went on all week long.

Emil had made it a tradition for Amsaco to include wives to entertain important WD customers. The company plane took Dorothy and Ray, Ann and Dave Dennison, Irene and Mike Evans, and Emil and his wife Marilyn to Chicago on Saturday. They scheduled dinners from Saturday to Tuesday night; the women would be flown back on Wednesday morning. Wednesday night was the Academy Dinner, an all-male event for the top executives in the industry.

Ray could see that Dorothy was a little miffed about the seating arrangements on the plane. The four men sat in the front, with the women in the back. He explained to her that they had to firm up plans for the week—who was taking out which customer on which night. "Yeah, sure," was all she said.

One of his goals was to make her understand that they were now among the elite in the industry. Only four from Amsaco flew in on the company Falcon with their wives, had suites at the Drake, were going to expensive restaurants with important customers, and sat at the Amsaco table at the banquet on Sunday.

The restaurants were impressive. Saturday night, with the Dennisons, they took Les and Lori Richards of Atlanta to the Empire Room at the Palmer House, where Carol Channing was the headliner. The Richards kept up a steady stream of snobbish complaints, finding flaws in the service, the food, even the show. Ray exchanged glances with Dorothy several times. He was concerned that she was not enjoying her company role. The evening dragged on.

Ray was more hopeful after Monday's dinner with the Blooms and Mike and Irene Evans. They ate at Eli's, where the atmosphere was more relaxed and the steak was the best he had ever eaten. Dorothy also seemed to enjoy herself. The Blooms were the only customers Dorothy knew amid all the new people they were meeting, and she and Helen Bloom planned to meet again for lunch back in Michigan.

Tuesday night's dinner at the Ritz-Carlton was a disaster. Their dinner companions were Sid and Elaine Berman from Connecticut, their son Ron and his fiancée Gina, and Emil and Marilyn. The dining room at the Ritz-Carlton was very fancy, and the expensive china and silver, the beautiful furnishings, and the snooty waiters were intimidating. A roving violin trio played classical music. The prices added even more to the pretentious atmosphere. Emil and the Bermans, who had been all over the world together on "American Trips" and other industry events, seemed completely at ease. They handled luxury with grace.

Not so their son Ron. When Sid and Elaine left early to attend a WD committee meeting, Ron became the center of attention. He puffed himself up as soon as his parents were out of sight. He ordered the most expensive soufflé for dessert, messed it around on his plate, and called the waiter back. "This tastes like shit," he said and waved it away, making the waiter take it back to the kitchen. Ron stared after him. "Faggot," he said.

Ray and Dorothy looked at each other. Ron hadn't even tasted the soufflé.

When Marilyn and Gina went to the ladies room, Ron leaned over and confided to Ray that Gina was "not that smart, but she gives the best blow job in the country."

Ray had no answer. He looked around to see if anyone else had heard. Ron chuckled.

Over after-dinner drinks Ron told Ray and Dorothy how he got the Tower suite at the Chicago Hilton. "When they brought us up to this other suite, I told him he could do better. 'Oh no, Mr. Berman,' he said. 'This is our finest suite.' 'Don't give me that bullshit,' I said, and I pulled out a buck and gave it to him. He had something better. Up in the Tower." Ron looked at Ray smugly. "You know, a 'buck'—that's a hundred."

Ray nodded as if he had known that. Dorothy just stared.

Ron also touched on the shock business. He told Ray what a bad idea the Foreign Car Program was. "Whoever thought that one up is in dreamland. There's no way that junk is going into my inventory." Ray exchanged glances with Emil, but did not argue. He wondered if Ron knew that the Foreign Car Program was his creation.

It was a relief when Ron said, "We have to go," though he spoke rather rudely. "Our limo driver's waiting to take us to a party. He's got some top grade pot. I'll do a few lines of coke." He smiled. "Want to come?"

Dorothy and Ray just looked at him with their mouths half open.

"Some other time," Emil answered. Ron laughed, and they left.

As Emil ordered another round of drinks, Ray asked, "Is that guy for real?"

Before he could answer, Dorothy asked, "How can she stand him?"

Marilyn said, "He has a lot of money. And Gina was a stewardess for ten years with Piedmont. That gets old after awhile and Ron's not too bad looking—"

"But he's so obnoxious," said Dorothy.

"He was just showing off," Marilyn answered. "In the ladies room, Gina told me he's not always like that. She's no dummy."

"You bet she's not," said Emil. "I'll bet once she's married, Ron will calm down quite a bit. If not, she'll walk off with a good chunk of his money. That's what Sid is worried about." Turning to Ray, Emil grinned. "You let me know what happens on that."

"What do you mean?" asked Ray warily.

"Over the years, Marilyn and I have built up a good relationship with the Bermans. We've gone on American Trips with them to the Greek Islands, and Hawaii, and…and…"

"Italy," Marilyn injected.

"Yeah, Italy. And we've visited them at their summer place on the lake, their 'camp' they call it. And on—"

"And on the United yacht," added Marilyn.

Emil seemed annoyed at the interruption. "And we see them every year at Distributor's Institute. They've become our friends… and our loyal customer. A big customer. And we're their loyal supplier. Not that it keeps him from jewing us down on prices or demanding super service. That's business. Crane comes in every year, and Sid just listens to their offer, thanks them, and then lets us know what they said."

Emil paused. He grinned and continued, "But Sid's getting old. Within the next five years he's going to turn the business over to Ron. Marilyn and I won't be cultivating that relationship. That's your job."

Dorothy was shocked. She just stared at Emil and then at Ray.

Ray understood Dorothy's shock. The thought of spending time with Ron was repulsive. Making it a career-long project was frightening. But Ray also perceived a subtle logic that Dorothy did not. Emil was passing the baton. He could have passed it to Donaldson or especially Dennison. But no, Emil was designating Ray as the key Amsaco man for the future.

"I hope Gina makes him clean up his act," he said, trying to avoid Dorothy's stare.

Dorothy was quiet that night back at the hotel. Ray could see what was on her mind. He tried to help her sort things out.

"I guess customers are like anyone else," he said. "Some of them are nice, some aren't."

"I didn't particularly like the Richards," she said. "But Ron Berman was just obnoxious…on purpose—doing everything he could to be offensive."

"Yeah, he's not exactly someone we would choose as a friend. But the Blooms are nice. You seemed to hit it off pretty well with Helen."

"Yes, I like her. We're having lunch next Tuesday at the Red Fox in Birmingham. She lives near there."

"Oh, good. You see, you're turning into a salesman."

"I'm not selling Helen Amsaco or anything else. I'm having

lunch with her because we like each other. I couldn't be friends with Gina, or Lori Richards, or anyone else I didn't like."

"I know, honey, I know. It looks like that's going to be my job. But let's enjoy the good parts. What about ordering a room service breakfast tomorrow? You don't have to get to the airport until 10:00."

"Fine," Dorothy agreed. "Maybe the women can sit it in the front of the plane if you guys aren't there."

Ray ordered room service breakfast and then went into the bathroom to wash up. When he came to bed, Dorothy appeared to be already sleeping. There was no lovemaking that night.

The next morning, after breakfast, Ray got ready to leave for the show. "Just call the bellhop when you're ready to leave," he instructed. "Tell him to take the luggage to the Amsaco limo. Then give him a couple of bucks."

"I think I can handle that. I'm a big girl."

■ ■ ■

On the flight back, the women sat in the front of the plane, the best place for four people to hold a conversation. It was a relief for Dorothy to sit back and drink coffee without dealing with customers. The others felt the same way.

They talked about their families, places they had lived, restaurants in Jackson and Ann Arbor—anything except Amsaco business.

Dorothy asked the others a question: "Has it been difficult to have your husbands travel so much?"

"Oh, you get used to it." Irene Evans replied. "Mike's been traveling ever since we were married, so I guess I've never known anything else."

"It was harder when we were first married," Ann Dennison said. "It was just the two of us with a baby. And the company kept moving us around. We lived in apartments and I was always alone in strange places. But usually there were other women in the apartments who were in the same position, so I had friends."

"That sounds rough," Dorothy said.

"Oh, it wasn't so bad. We didn't know anything else, so we had no complaint. And it got better as Dave moved up. We got to stay in one place for a few years, so we could buy a house and the kids could go to one school for awhile."

"But even then," Dorothy asked. "Dave would still be traveling most of the time, wouldn't he? Your husband would still be gone."

"That's the best part," Marilyn Gross said, getting a laugh from them all. "But seriously, you just have to accept that. That's the way we make our living. The men go out selling, and we have to take care of things at home."

The others nodded in agreement, but Dorothy shook her head. "I don't know if I want to do that."

"The system has its perks," Irene said. "We get to run our own house with no interference."

Ann added, "And then we get to go to all sorts of nice places. It's like taking vacations all the time. I love coming to these conferences or shows, and eating out at all these expensive restaurants. And the trips. You haven't been on those yet. A chartered jet, nicest hotels, and we go places we'd never go without Amsaco. Like Monte Carlo, and the Greek Islands, and Hawaii. And I don't mind if Dave travels. It gives me a rest."

"But, this was *work*," Dorothy argued. "We had to be nice to some real jerks."

"Some jerks," Marilyn answered, "but some nice people too. Some of them have become good friends. Didn't you have jerks at Harvard? It can't be that different. We have nice people and we have jerks." Then she smiled. "But I guess you don't have to be nice to the jerks at Harvard."

"I'll bet you do," Ann said, "if you want your husband to get ahead."

"I suppose that's true," Dorothy agreed. "But Ray never was into getting ahead that way at Harvard. He just wanted to be a good teacher—and get tenure."

"At Harvard, he wasn't in sales or management," Marilyn pointed out. "I'll bet there are top people at Harvard who are very nice to some rich alumni...who are jerks."

Dorothy had to agree. "Yes, I'll bet there are. Ray just wasn't in that game at Harvard."

"But he is at Amsaco," Marilyn said, smiling at Dorothy. "And your problem is that apparently he's good at it. And what's even worse is that, just like our husbands, he probably likes it."

"You think so?" Dorothy said thoughtfully. "You think so?"

■ ■ ■

Ray felt pretty good after he kissed Dorothy good-bye that morning. She seemed to fit in pretty well with the other women, and except for Ron Berman, maybe even enjoyed the trip. And she had a much better idea of the new world he was entering as a marketing executive. He got a little better idea himself that evening at the Academy dinner.

Only the top industry people were invited, Mike Evans had told him. "What does the Academy do?" asked Ray.

"We have this dinner. When you get the invitation you just send in a check and tell them you will or won't attend. If you don't, you don't get invited back."

"Just a dinner? Is there any business?"

"You'll see."

■ ■ ■

The dinner at the Ambassador East was first class—good food, good drinks, good hors d'oeuvres, plenty of room, good service, and comfortable surroundings. "We pay a lot to get the best," Emil told Ray. "But we don't waste it on fringes. You won't find any flowers on the tables."

Evans spent a lot of time introducing Ray around, impressing Ray with the warm receptions he received, not only from WD customers but from the other manufacturers—even competitors.

When they were talking with Andy Wilson and Dave Brown of Blackwell, Brown joked with Evans. "Sounds like you're getting out at the right time. I was about to tear you up in a couple of places, but Andy wouldn't let me. Says I have to wait."

"It's not the time to start wars," Wilson said to Evans. "No point destroying each other. But tell Emil when things pick up, I'm gonna let Brownie loose on you guys."

"We'll be ready," said Evans. "Or rather, the Professor here will be ready."

When they walked away, Mike said to Ray, "That's good news. They must be pulling back from Jobber's Supply. That'll give you a chance to repair relations with Bob Goodman. Make sure he wins an American Trip."

Ray also met their other big competitors, George Lorenzo and Joe Markham from Crane. They shook hands and exchanged greetings. Ray felt Lorenzo was sizing him up in a cold, downright hostile fashion.

Afterward Mike said, "Lorenzo's a cold fish. Accounting type. But Markham's one of the best. Don't underestimate him. Don't trust him either, but don't underestimate him."

When they sat down to dinner, Harry Liscio, a WD from Kansas City, and Wayne Timpanelli from Fram Filters walked up to the lectern. "All right you guys," said Harry. "Pipe down. It's time for our meeting."

(Applause!)

"First of all, I'll read our by-laws."

(Applause!)

"Answer your god damn invitations and send in your money or you won't get invited back next year."

(More applause!)

"Now Wayne's got the financial report."

(Applause!)

Wayne Timpanelli took out a sheet of paper about three inches square, put on his glasses, and reported, "You guys sent in a shit load of money for this dinner."

"Yeah!" "Damn right!" came shouts from around the room.

"Well, you're in the process of drinking it all up, and next year it's gonna cost you more."

(Even more applause as Timpanelli sat down.)

Liscio came back to the lectern. "Now, some special business."

(Applause!)

"We want to give out the award to the outstanding Academy member of the year."

Everyone listened, somewhat surprised, not knowing what to expect.

"We want to give it out, but there ain't no outstanding member, so fuck it. Meeting adjourned."

With that there was a standing ovation. Ray was standing and applauding along with everyone else at the table, except Emil, who sat laughing. "Harry's a great guy," said Emil. Then, looking at Dennison, he added, "I don't know why he's not our account."

Dennison just rolled his eyes. "We can't sell everyone."

"Why not, we do," joked Paul Breen, Sales VP for Champion

Spark Plugs. That was true. But with small items that moved fast, like spark plugs, the WDs would usually stock several brands, and just about everyone carried Champion.

"Thanks, Paul. You're a big help," said Dennison.

"Anytime."

As they ate their delicious prime rib dinner, Emil swapped old automotive stories with Rich Kittrell, President of Champion, and Charlie Torsone, Purolator's Executive VP. Ray just enjoyed listening.

Just before dessert, Max Wechsler, an old-time WD from Philadelphia came over to their table and announced he was going to do a magic trick for them.

"I'm going to turn this napkin into a peach," he said, looking around as if to see if anyone at the table wanted to argue. He sat down and took a large cloth napkin, gripped it in the middle, and slowly pulled it through a circle made with his thumb and forefinger. When it was through, he carefully molded it so that it stayed upright, but bulged out at the top. Then he held it on his lap, making it look like an eighteen-inch erection, covered by the napkin.

He looked back and forth, proudly smiling at the others. "Ain't that a peach?" Then, as they laughed, he walked away with his napkin to entertain another table.

Ray noticed that everyone seemed to know everyone else and what was going on at each company. He was surprised at the amount of information that was passed around. Like Andy Wilson letting them know that Blackwell was not going after Jobber's Supply. The message suggested a temporary truce. Ray wondered about the legality of sending messages like that. But of course, nothing was spelled out in words.

He thought also about Sid Berman telling Emil about Crane's offers. George Lorenzo had to be aware that Sid and Emil were friends and that any information about Crane's prices and other incentives revealed to Sid would get to Amsaco. Apparently it was an accepted way to let a competitor know what you would and would not offer. Crane and Blackwell probably had similar arrangements with their special accounts. And this was only at the highest level. There were many more contacts at lower levels, so that everyone probably knew what everyone else was offering... or at least what they wanted others to know. The exchange of information was as effective as a meeting of competitors to discuss their pricing...which would be illegal. This was not something he had known about—much less covered—in his classes at Harvard.

He bounced this thought off Mike Evans.

"You're catching on," Mike said. "Blackwell's source is Harry Liscio. Dave and I go into Harry's place almost every year and make him an offer to change over. I'm sure it all gets back to Andy Wilson. And it happens even more at the lower levels. If you want to know what's happening in the industry price-wise, ask Vince. All the information gets fed back to him. He has Paul Sudarsky on that stuff almost full time. And Paul has counterparts at the other companies who keep each other up-to-date, so they all look smart."

Mike paused as he looked past Ray. "You're learning fast. But it looks like you still have one more lesson to learn tonight. I gotta get back to the hotel. Bye."

Before Ray could ask him what he meant, he was gone. Ray turned to see what made him leave so suddenly. Coming toward him was Emil, along with Max Wechsler. It was too late to escape. Ray spent the rest of the evening at various strip joints on Rush Street, and did not get to bed until 3:00 A.M.

■ ■ ■

Ray managed to be showered, dressed, packed, and in the lobby at 6:00 A.M. to get to the airport in time for the takeoff at 7:00. He was drained. Emil, however, with only two hours' sleep, looked awake and as sharp as ever. He was going over the sales figures for the year so far.

"Things don't look so good," Emil said, as the four of them looked at their copies of the sales analysis for March and year-to-date.

"I don't think we're doing so bad," Dennison countered. "We're not quite up to budget, but we're 2 percent ahead of last year."

"The only thing holding you up there are the foreign car sales," said Emil. Ray started to smile, but then Emil added, "You've loaded everyone up, but are they reordering?"

No one could answer that. Dennison said the sales were following the normal new product pattern. Evans said Walt Morris was expecting strong reorders. But no one really knew.

Ray made a mental note to find out. When he got back to the office, he asked Madge if she could get that information. The next day it was on his desk, and it did not look good. Except for some small reorders from the West Coast, there was almost nothing.

He talked it over with Evans, who was somewhat vague. "We still don't know," he explained. "There has to be a lull after the pipeline fill. Once the WD has it in stock, he can work with our guys to convince the Jobber to go after that business. It gives our advertising a chance to let the Jobbers know they have an opportunity. But then they have to find out how to sell the stuff, and that takes some time. There might be some enthusiasm out there, but there has to be a lull in our sales. We'll find out how they feel at AWDA."

■ ■ ■

The AWDA meetings were held at Caesar's Palace in Las Vegas at the end of April. All the major WDs came to Caesar's for three days of gambling, nightclubs, and meetings with manufacturers. The manufacturers hosted the WDs at the dinners and shows at night, and also at the work meetings during the day in their rooms or suites. Wives did not go to Las Vegas. "It would be like bringing a sandwich to a banquet," Mike told Ray.

The meetings only lasted about forty-five minutes, and when things were going well, they might be nothing more than a friendly chat between top executives. When Ed Lambert came in, it was only necessary to serve Jack Daniels. But when things were not going well, the WDs came in looking for solutions from the manufacturers.

Most of Amsaco's customers did not look on the Foreign Car Shock Program as a solution, at least not to *their* problems.

"Sure," said Jack Maluk from Cleveland Supply. "You guys sell the damn things and get paid. But we sit with the stuff on our shelves."

Old Doug Wilmot from Montgomery, Alabama, made his point in a slow southern drawl. "When thangs er slow, y'awl have to fahnd ways to save us money. This here foreign shock boondoggle *costs* us money."

"But the total program will save you money," Ray argued. "There will be pockets of foreign cars popping up, and this is an inexpensive way to be ready. The consolidation will mean you stock fewer parts and still get the coverage. The foreign car coverage is just part of the whole program."

"Ah ain't seen no savings, son."

"Not yet," said Ray. "You still have the old units in stock. But when you reorder those units, you're gonna get more coverage with fewer parts."

Wilmot looked quizzically at Ray. "Mebbee you're raht, sonny. Y'awl sound pretty smart. But all ah know now is ah'm spending more money and selling less. And ah don't see any of them little Jap cars drivin' roun' in Alabama."

Joe Beluga from Automotive Warehouse in Louisiana told Ray, "Whoever thought up this program should be fired. Is this one of Kemper's ideas?" Beluga looked on Kemper as a Yankee with crazy new ideas, like hiring black salesmen. Kemper's predecessor, Jack Caldwell, had been a southerner with a good ol' boy manner. Caldwell spent a lot of time with Beluga, not only at the bars and restaurants but on the golf course and at Beluga's hunting lodge. Kemper was all business.

"Amsaco's changing," Beluga went on. "Used to be a friendlier company."

Ray talked to Emil later, at the blackjack tables. Emil was playing two hands. This not only gave him a challenge and allowed him to gamble twice as much, but it gave him more room, since the chair in front of his second hand remained empty. He was playing both hands perfectly, as he discussed the negative meetings.

Emil was surprisingly calm. "Don't worry too much about these guys," he consoled Ray. "Things are bad everywhere and you have to expect them to bitch and complain. All the manufacturers are hearing this."

"Yeah, maybe," said Ray. "But they sure sound angry to me. Joe Beluga sounded like he was going to change lines."

"Of course, you've got to take them seriously," Emil replied. "You've got to...shit," he swore, as the dealer drew twenty-one and beat both of Emil's hands. "You've got to treat each one separately, and look between the lines. Like Beluga. He hasn't been getting the attention he used to get with Caldwell. So he blames Kemper and takes it out on anything that Kemper sells. This time it's the Foreign Car Program. Beluga just needs stroking. Maybe you ought to develop a relationship. Maybe you should take him on the yacht. He's getting big enough."

"What's the deal on the yacht?" asked Ray. "Mike mentioned that we ought to take the Goodmans on the yacht."

"Good idea. The yacht is a place to cement a relationship. Mainly with the wives. It's United's yacht, a seventy-five-footer."

"How do we arrange it?" asked Ray. "What do we do?"

"You get the Falcon and pick them up. Pick up the Goodmans in Flint. Then fly down to Baton Rouge for the Belugas. Then to Nassau. Reuben will pick you up at the airport. He's the captain. We're docked at Lyford Cay, a real classy place…for international millionaires. You can use most of the facilities, but probably you'll just want to cruise around for the three days. Reuben will tell you where. And Donald does the cooking, a first-class chef. He's as good as any at the fancy restaurants. You just go and have a good time. Make believe you're rich. The wives love it and they make sure their husbands treat us right so they can come back."

Ray hesitated. "I don't know. Three days with the Goodmans and the Belugas. Dorothy and I don't even know them. And how will they get along with each other?"

"Don't worry," said Emil. "You'll all love each other by the time you leave. You'll be lifelong friends. I'd go myself, but these are the guys *you* have to develop a relationship with. Let me check first to see if there are any open dates in May."

■ ■ ■

Dorothy did not want to go. The only date open was for the middle of the week and she was busy at work.

Ray could not understand. "It's a trip to the Bahamas," he argued. "We fly down on our private jet. We cruise around the Bahamas on a seventy-five-foot yacht, eat gourmet meals, get treated like royalty…Most people would give their right arm for a chance like this. How can you not want to go?"

"I have important work," she replied. "This is a very busy time."

"But it's only a part-time job," he said with frustration. "I know it's important to you, but it's only twenty-five hours a week. Make up the time next week."

"It doesn't work that way," Dorothy said, somewhat offended. "I'm part of a team. When Emmett calls us together, we discuss these borderline applications. I don't set the schedules."

"But, I don't really set my schedules either," Ray explained. "These are 'borderline' customers that we have to do something with right now. I mean, I'm on the job only a few months and we're in danger of losing some customers…because of *my* Foreign Car Program. And the yacht is only available now. I have to make this trip…and it includes wives. You're part of my job, too. And that's the job that gives us our income."

"I'm bringing home a paycheck too."

"For what? A hundred a week? Big deal. Should I give up my job so we don't disturb Emmett's schedule?"

"You don't have to get sarcastic," she said sadly. "I suppose I have no choice." She paused and they both took deep breaths. "Who are we taking? Not Ron Berman, I hope."

"No, two couples. Joe Beluga and his wife Nancy. They're from Baton Rouge. He was pretty tough on us at AWDA. And Bob and Doris Goodman from Flint. I don't know him very well, but apparently Blackwell's been making overtures to him. Of course, I don't know either of the wives. Emil says we'll all love each other by the time we go home."

■ ■ ■

Ray could see almost immediately that Emil was wrong.

When they picked the Goodmans up in Flint, Doris was arguing with her husband about getting on the plane. Flying down to Baton Rouge, she could not drink the coffee because of the caffeine and she did not like the canned orange juice. She would not eat the sandwiches on the flight to Nassau, the conch chowder or the grilled grouper prepared by Donald on the boat, or even the steak at the fancy Martinique on Paradise Island. She was afraid of being seasick and had to be persuaded just to get on the boat, even while it was docked. On the first day, they cruised around the mainland over to Paradise Island. Doris had the first mate drive her through Nassau, over the bridge, to meet them.

Joe Beluga was irritated. "Why the hell does she come on a boat, if she won't go out on the water?" he asked Ray.

Joe was also irritated about the stateroom he and Nancy were given. While persuading Doris to get on the boat, the captain had suggested the Goodmans take the larger stateroom because, being in the middle, it would roll the least. So the Belugas and the Pendletons were left with the smaller ones.

After drinking scotch on the plane, Joe continued to sample rums and exotic liquors when they got on board. He was feeling pretty loose as they went in to eat around 8:00 P.M. He put his arm around Ray and asked, "Yer a smart feller. What's black and tan and looks good on a nigger?"

Ray looked up, surprised.

"A Doberman pinscher," said Joe, laughing.

Ray looked around. Dorothy and Nancy were right behind them and heard Joe's joke. No one laughed, except Joe, who added, "Tell that one to Kemper."

Joe was as irritated with Bob as Bob was irritated with him. Ray wondered what Emil was thinking when he paired up this northern Jew with a southern redneck. Privately, each had already complained to Ray about the other. Joe could not understand how Bob could let Doris whine and moan all the time. The man had no control over his wife. On the other side, Bob did not understand why Joe did nothing whatsoever but make obnoxious remarks and drink. Beluga was not even interested in gambling at the Paradise Island casino. The only two things they agreed on were how much they did not like Sam Kemper or the Foreign Car Program. The two of them teamed up to give Ray this message every chance they got.

For Ray, the most enjoyable part of the trip was a tour on motor scooters in Nassau with Nancy Beluga and Dorothy. Nancy was delightful. She never said much while her husband was around, but as they sipped drinks at a small bar looking out on the water, she talked freely and thanked Dorothy and Ray for hosting them on this wonderful trip. They talked about life in Baton Rouge, life in a college atmosphere, life in Nassau, and stayed away from life in the automotive industry. They all felt a little sad when it was time to go back to the boat.

The captain had suggested they cruise over to the eastern end of the island on the final day, to some coves where they could swim and snorkle. Ray swore to Doris that if she took Dramamine and stayed on deck where she could see the horizon, she would not get seasick. She reluctantly agreed, if they promised to come in to land immediately if she did feel sick.

The trip took almost two hours. On the top deck, Ray and Dorothy attended Doris, who sat motionless in her chair, gripping the arms. Captain Reuben kept the boat in calm waters, and after a while, Doris saw that she was not going to be sick and relaxed a little. It did not stop her demands, however.

Ray had to go below to get her sunglasses and suntan lotion. He made a second trip for her wide-brimmed hat. Dorothy sat listening to Doris complain about her husband spending too much time with the business, her teenage kids not listening to her, and how difficult it was to get domestic help these days. When Ray finally got through with his errands, he sat listening to Doris for a few minutes and then volunteered to go below again and get gin and tonics. Dorothy gave him a dirty look. When he came back up, Dorothy excused herself to go to the bathroom and did not come back for a half hour.

When they got to the cove, Dorothy and Ray went snorkling with the Belugas, while the Goodmans waded around the rocky beach looking for shells and some shade to protect their sunburns. Dorothy did not really want to snorkel, but anything was better than listening to Doris Goodman. She actually enjoyed herself, however, once she became comfortable with breathing through the mask.

"It's absolutely beautiful," she told Ray when she surfaced. "Amazing colors. And the water is so clear."

"Just keep your eye out for sharks," Joe said. He was joking, but Ray could feel that he had spoiled it for her.

A few minutes later Dorothy was back on shore.

■ ■ ■

The trip back to Lyford Cay was calm. Ray stayed with Doris on the top deck, while Dorothy escaped with the others to play bridge near the bar.

Ray listened attentively to Doris's litany until she wore herself out and dozed off in her chair. He lay back and watched the sky and the water and gratefully breathed the sea air. It felt like the first time he had relaxed in months.

Dinner brought him back with a jolt. The fine meal Donald had prepared for them that last night was spoiled by Ray's customer-guests.

Bob Goodman did not want to miss a last chance to scold him.

"That Foreign Car Program, at this particular time, is a dumb idea," he said as he cut a tender piece of filet mignon. "Was that Kemper's idea?" He apparently had picked up that suspicion from Beluga.

Ray exchanged glances with Dorothy before answering, "No. Sam just implements the programs." He avoided Dorothy's eyes as he added, "The programs are developed in the home office."

"Well damn it," Goodman said while chewing, "Right now interest rates are sky high and business is slow. The inventory stays in our stock for a long time, and we're paying through the nose for it. And then you guys come up with a plan to add even more. You know what you should do?"

"What?" Ray asked, with apprehension.

"You should give us twenty-four months to pay for these foreign shocks. That's how long it's gonna take us to sell 'em."

"You should give us more time on all the inventory," Beluga added. "Or a better discount so we could pay the high interest rate. Amsaco's got plenty of money...or anyway United Tire has."

Ray had no answers. He had no confidence in the pitch he had prepared about putting in only a small inventory of foreign shocks as an inexpensive way to be ready for the pockets of sales that would show up. Goodman and Beluga took turns berating him. Finally, Nancy broke in saying, "Leave the poor boy alone. How can we enjoy our meal with all this business talk?"

They let the subject drop. Ray was thankful to Nancy.

Later, Goodman pulled Ray aside to him, "We were seriously considering changing lines. And we still are. So you give Emil our message. You guys have to do something."

On the flight back Ray's customers resumed their complaints. They sat in the front with Ray and bombarded him. Goodman even describing some of the details of the offer he had received from Blackwell. Beluga listened attentively, obviously planning to use this information to his advantage. Ray thought that was going too far. He wanted to say, "If you like Blackwell so much, just switch over. Then we can take someone on this trip who appreciates it." But how would he explain to Emil that he wined and dined these two important customers on the United yacht and still managed to lose them? He said nothing except to promise that Emil would get their message.

On the flight back to Baton Rouge, Nancy made a point of thanking Dorothy and Amsaco for a wonderful three days. She never thought she would be yachting in the Bahamas, with a crew of three harkening to her every wish. Of course, neither did Dorothy. They laughed together about getting used to the "good life."

After they dropped off the Belugas, Dorothy had to listen to Doris for three more hours. She would have been furious at Ray for not coming back to help her out, but she could see that Ray was not exactly enjoying himself with Bob. It was a relief to drop them off in Flint. At that point they got some belated smiles and a thank you from the Goodmans.

Dorothy and Ray were quiet on the short flight back to Jackson. The trip had been anything but relaxing, and they recognized that they had not enjoyed themselves very much. With the constant worry about the customers, it had been mostly work. At some future time they might reminisce about the blue waters or the scooter trip around the island or Donald's wonderful meals, but right now they were exhausted.

As they drove home, Ray said he would have to run into the office to pick up his messages for the past three days. "Things pile up," he said. "And it will help me tomorrow if I just get organized this afternoon."

"You're out of your mind," Dorothy said tiredly. "Fine. I'll unpack and take Mrs. Proctor home and cook supper."

"Maybe we should eat out with the kids. Chucky Cheese maybe."

Dorothy put her hand to her forehead, closed her eyes, and shook her head. "There's no way that I could take Chucky Cheese. Just bring home some Chinese."

He started to say something, but she cut him off. "I don't want to argue. Go back to your goddamn office. I'll take care of things here. Just bring back some Chinese food."

Ray felt depressed and dull as he drove to the office. Dorothy always seemed to be angry with him, and everything was going wrong with his job. It looked like the Foreign Car Program was a flop. It came across loud and clear that the customers did not like it. And company sales were down and getting worse. In his new position, Ray was responsible for a good portion of the company sales.

United Tire couldn't be happy with this continuing slide in sales...and profit. Ray thought of the recognition and praise he had received for his Foreign Car Program—and now look at what was happening. How long would United put up with that? How long would Emil put up with it?

"My God," he thought. "If things don't get better, I can get fired. I can actually get fired." This job was not fun.

And his life was on a slide at home. Even when he was in town, he stayed in the office until 7:00 or 8:00 most nights, and worked Saturdays—he never seemed to spend time with the kids. On Sunday he was exhausted...if he was in town at all. He and Dorothy were always arguing and drifting farther and farther apart. Ray thought back. It was at least a month since they had made love.

■ ■ ■

The building was quiet. Almost everyone had gone home. Even Madge, who always stayed an extra half hour or so, had left. There was a pile of mail on his desk. He picked up a note from Mike Evans, which was sitting on top.

"Ray, had to leave for Atlanta. Looks like Les Richards has changed to Crane. I have to see what we can salvage. I'll call you when I know what's going on.

Mike"

Ray sat slumped at his desk. Things were not going well at all.

■ ■ ■

In Dallas, Max Simpson, Alan Tracy, and Stan Moore were having a serious discussion with Dave Torres.

"It's not changing," Simpson said to Torres. "That foreign car plan was supposed to help, but it hasn't."

"And now," Tracy added, "they've got this new plant with nothing to put in it. Burch says they're calling it a 'white elephant,' even in Jackson. Emil's always been a spender, but this may be too much."

"He just doesn't listen," said Moore. "He hasn't cut any costs... no headcount reductions. He still takes questionable flights...to Vegas. And their use of the yacht has even gone up."

"He may be trying to increase sales," Torres argued.

"But they just take existing customers on the boat," Simpson countered. "You don't increase sales that way."

The others were silent as Torres thought over what they had said. He figured correctly that part of what was going on was politics, pure and simple. But politics were part of the job at the executive level. These were his key people and he had to listen to them. He was most concerned with how this change would affect United's stock. He figured the reaction would be positive. Replacing an old-timer with a young financial executive would be viewed as a sign of fiscal competence, of looking unemotionally at the bottom line.

Simpson was also thinking. He was not that negative about Emil. After all, if someone were fired every time there was a slump in sales, he would not have gotten to his present position. But to get further, he had to show executive strength. He had to make the difficult decisions. To back Emil while Tracy was demanding a change would be a sign of weakness. Simpson had to be tough. "He sure doesn't fit your lean and mean image," he pointed out.

"No, I guess not," Torres agreed. "And he's had plenty of time to do something about that. I guess we have to make a change. OK, but make sure he gets a generous termination package."

■ ■ ■

Dick Wise was called out of a meeting to answer a call from Ralph Burch. Burch's message was simple.

"I got 'im!"

18. "No Changes"

Madge came into Ray's office while he and Mike were talking about the loss of Richards in Atlanta. "Can you boys take some bad news?" she asked with a very serious face.

"We're not exactly talking good news right now," said Mike. "A little more won't hurt."

"Well, this is more than a little more." She came in, sat down, and came right to the point. "The rumor going around is that Emil is fired, and Ralph Burch is coming in to take his place."

The two men stared at her in surprise. "That can't be," said Ray.

"No," said Mike. "He's not gone. He's flyin' to Chicago this morning with O'Brien. Madge, see if Ed's still here."

Madge went over to the phone, and Mike said to Ray, "I suppose it's possible that Emil could be in trouble, but Burch coming in to replace him—never."

Madge handed the phone to Mike. "Ed," Mike said softly, "aren't you going over to Chicago with Emil this morning?...No?...He cancelled?...Oh, just some rumors...I'll call you back." He turned back to Ray and Madge. "Emil cancelled. Didn't give a reason."

"It couldn't be," Ray said in disbelief. "Emil *is* Amsaco." He thought back to when Chessman had said the same thing.

"He always has been," Mike agreed. "But things change. And Madge is usually right."

"I'm always right."

The next morning, Max Simpson and Ralph Burch walked into the President's office. They called a meeting of Emil's staff to announce that he was "retiring" and Burch was the new President. The only other changes were that Pete Stark, the Public

Relations man would report directly to Burch, and Peggy Wiehler, Burch's old secretary, would switch with Betty Johnson, who would become Dan McCormick's secretary. Simpson gave Stark a press release for the public, and Burch told him to get an internal bulletin to the employees within two hours. That was not necessary. The whole organization knew within fifteen minutes. It was the most efficient communication ever to go through Amsaco.

A lot of time was wasted that day. Everyone was going from office to office, speculating on what had happened and what was going to happen. Ray called Tom Chessman to see if he knew the inside story. For once he did not.

"I don't know," Tom said honestly. "I guess we weren't making enough money. Or Emil was spending too much. Or maybe it was his weight. We'll never know. But apparently Burch convinced them he could do better, the prick. I guess I'm going to become fiscally responsible."

Ray laughed. "Do you know what that means?"

"Hell no! But I'm going to spend some time with Al Goldman when he gets back in the country." He paused. "I guess I should look at the bright side. This is like a pay raise for me."

"What do you mean?"

"Burch can't beat me in gin."

Manufacturing and Engineering were not too concerned with the change. They figured no matter who had the corner office, Amsaco still needed shock absorbers to be designed and manufactured.

Sales was a little more concerned. They were losing an industry legend as their leader, and worst of all, he had been replaced by a "bean counter." Dennison told Mike Evans, "Now, not only do I have the Professor to chaperon, but I have Howdy Doody to introduce around. And you're planning to leave one of these days. Please, stay and help me."

Evans smiled. "I wouldn't leave now. I don't want to miss all the fun."

Ray felt guilty and more worried than ever. He wondered if his Foreign Car Program had caused Emil's downfall. If so, would he be the next to go?

The rank and file did not feel much affected. Sales were picking up a little, and when things were busy, their jobs were secure. The UAW, however, were more concerned. They knew there was talk about a plant closing at Blackwell. They also knew that financial-type Managers like Burch often closed plants for the sake of the bottom line. They had had their battles with Emil and Chessman, but at least they were automotive men. During the four-week strike at Jackson a few years back, Chessman had been their bitter enemy. But he had given them the use of a little building on the property to keep the strikers warm, and even stopped to bring them donuts. One time he had actually walked the picket line with a "Management Is Unfair" sign. Chessman and the union knew and respected each other. Burch was viewed as United Tire's man, and Dallas did not really know the UAW.

It was hard for Amsaco's competitors to imagine the company without Emil—or his replacement by Ralph Burch. Emil was not only the President of a major shock absorber company, he was an industry pioneer, instrumental in the development of the whole after-market shock absorber industry. This action by United Tire merely confirmed what the automotive replacement industry suspected: that big conglomerates knew nothing about their industry.

The accountants were celebrating. As far as they were concerned, they now had control of the company. "We're running the show now," Dick Wise told Ray. "You'd better check with me if you think up another Foreign Car Plan."

Actually, many Amsaco employees had reason to be uneasy. Ralph Burch had thought out his plan in detail, and it was not good news for Amsaco employees. His first goal had been to become President of Amsaco and sit in the corner office. Now everyone in the organization reported to him. He had absolute power. He would use that power to carry out the final stage of his plan, which was to go back to Dallas as President and then Chairman of United Tire.

To do this Burch had to perform. He was certain that this was no problem. He would cut costs and expenditures. Emil had concentrated on company growth to increase profits and ROI; Burch would not. In his view, growth depended on too many factors: the state of the industry, or the performance of Amsaco salesmen, or Engineering coming up with a superior product or—even more uncontrollable—the moves of his competitors. While he had very little control over all that, he could control costs. If he decided to freeze hiring, or to close a plant, or to cut bonuses, or to slash budgets, then costs would come down. He could sit in his office and say, "Costs will come down by 20 percent," and they would. He could not sit there and increase sales.

Dick Wise was sitting in front of his desk. Dick already knew what Burch's approach would be. Burch said, "I've got just the guy to get costs down. Carl Buzzard."

"Don't know him."

"We got our MBAs together at Michigan. He's a tough son of a bitch. Believes all companies have too much fat, especially in middle management. Makes his living as a consultant, cutting costs. He comes in and heads roll and costs go down. Then he goes somewhere else."

"You want him to come here as a consultant?"

"No," Burch said thoughtfully. "Our guys are too entrenched. They'd fight him. No, I plan to bring him in to run Operations."

"To replace Steele?" asked Wise. "I thought Steele was OK."

"He is. But he could never make major cuts. It would be like dismembering the organization that he built himself. We need someone ruthless, like Buzzard. The only problem is he needs someone to follow him around to implement the firings and personnel moves, and that's not Chessman. I don't trust Chessman."

"Tom's a good politician," Wise pointed out. "He knows his way around in Dallas."

"I know," Burch agreed. "He has connections in Dallas. He's cozy with the UAW. I just don't trust him. He could be a real pain in the ass."

"Who would replace him?"

"I'm thinking about Art Webb."

Wise laughed. "Art Webb, an auditor with a financial background to run Personnel?"

"That might be perfect for working with Buzzard. He's used to being hated. And he'll have a staff to do the actual personnel work. And he'll be able to figure out what all those fancy Personnel policies really cost, and figure out how to cut them back. He'll be all right."

Wise sipped his coffee. "That takes care of Steele and Chessman. What about Dennison? There's a lot of costs in Marketing."

"We'll have to wait on that. Dennison knows the industry. I'll need him for awhile. We only have Evans and Dennison who really know the customers. And I think I'd have trouble with Max Simpson if I tried to get rid of Dennison at this time. I'd rather explain how we're taking care of our customers without Emil. Cost reductions in Marketing will have to wait. But you can watch Dennison closely as Chief Financial Officer."

Wise opened his eyes wide. "Oh?"

Burch smiled. "The position's yours. But I have to find some way to get rid of McCormick. He's well thought of in Dallas. Tracy likes him, and I can't just let him go. But the job's yours as soon as I figure out something."

"I can wait."

"Good," Burch concluded. "It's settled then. Dennison will stay temporarily, but Steele, Chessman, and McCormick will be replaced by Buzzard, Webb, and you."

At his first staff meeting, Burch told McCormick, Steele, Chessman, and Dennison, "At this time I don't plan any major personnel changes."

■ ■ ■

From Ray's vantage point, nothing much had changed. Things just went on as if nothing had happened. There was not even a farewell party or lunch. Emil just disappeared.

Ray asked his boss about that, and Dennison told him, " It's different at this level. Our boss is Burch, and it's dangerous to appear as if our loyalty is still with Emil. Besides, Emil must be embarrassed. I don't imagine he wants to see anybody."

"Haven't you seen him?"

"Nah. I haven't even seen him at the club. I don't think he wants to see anybody."

This amazed Ray. Emil and Dennison had been working closely together for over twenty years. They had been Sales Reps in the field together. They had entertained customers together with their wives. They belonged to the same country club. Now there was *nothing* between them?

Ray told this to Dorothy, who just shook her head. "I don't understand these people," she said. "I can't be like that. I just have to give Marilyn a call."

It was not that Dorothy felt sorry for Emil or Marilyn. Her first reaction to the news of Emil's demise had been, "I'll bet Marilyn's happy." And it was not that they were close friends either. Their whole social life together had consisted of a few dinners and a couple of flights on the company plane. But that was enough to make them "teammates" and to make Marilyn her friend. Dorothy did not like the idea of dropping them because it was politically "dangerous." No one in Dallas should be able to decide who her friends would be. Maybe Ray had to play that game, but she did not.

Dorothy called Marilyn, who sounded surprised, but glad to hear from her. "It's strange," Marilyn said. "We haven't heard from anyone at Amsaco except Betty Johnson. And that was about personal things that Emil left at the office. It's nice of you to call."

They spoke for awhile on unimportant subjects, until Dorothy asked how things were going with Emil being home.

"I thought it would be great," said Marilyn. "I really thought we could get off this merry-go-round, maybe do things together, travel together...with no customers to entertain. Just the two of us." There was a pause. Dorothy was going to say something when Marilyn continued, somewhat sadly, "But, you can't go back. Emil is not looking at this as retirement. He's still just as busy. On the phone all the time. Planning all kinds of deals. But he's always home and he's driving me nuts."

Dorothy laughed. "I thought your biggest complaint was that Emil was never home."

"That's true enough," Marilyn responded, thinking back. "With Emil gone all the time, I had to build my separate life. First it was just raising the children. That was a hell of a job all by myself. But as they left, it was like I was a widow." She laughed. "Half the friends I have are widows. But it was like two different lives. Some of the time I was going on Amsaco junkets and entertaining customers. The rest of the time, I was a widow. I didn't like it, but I had no other choice. Emil wasn't going to change."

There was another pause and Marilyn started to chuckle again. "Now that I've got Emil home all the time, I think I prefer being a widow." Marilyn laughed, but Dorothy shuddered. Was this the path she and Ray were taking?

"I'm tired," Marilyn continued. "All he talks about is getting back on his feet, or getting back at Ralph or Max, or starting his own business. Even though he's here, he's still in the office. I wish some of his old buddies would take him out to eat or something… and give me a break."

"I don't think Ray would do that," Dorothy said. "Ray still sees Emil as being his boss's boss. But maybe the four of us could go out to dinner or something. It would give the men some time to talk, and us too."

"I think Emil would enjoy that. He always liked the Professor. Our schedule right now is…let me see…free…seven nights a week."

Emil did like the idea, but he insisted on eating at the club. If he was paying the check, then he was still "top dawg." In addition, he had some information that Ray did not, and that was another "one up" on Ray. Not that he had a reason for wanting to be "one up" on Ray. It was just that this was an opportunity that he had not had for a while.

Ray was a little nervous about the dinner. He was always nervous with Emil. He always felt he was defending himself when they were together. And he worried that his Foreign Car Program had been the reason Emil was fired. He also worried about meeting Dave Dennison at the club—it would look as if he were ignoring his boss's advice. If Dennison was at the club, Ray planned on telling him the wives had made the dinner plans. It was not necessary, however, since the Dennisons were not there and there was no one else that Ray knew at the club.

Actually, Ray enjoyed the evening. Emil was obviously pleased at the respect being shown by the Pendletons. He acted more friendly than he had before. At first they talked about everything except the recent events. They laughed about the Bahamas trip with the Goodmans and the Belugas. They even laughed about Ray's assignment to take care of Ron Berman. Emil told similar stories of adventures with customers, with Marilyn breaking in to correct some of the details. Marilyn yawned as Emil retold his "American Barrel" stories, but the Pendletons paid attention. Marilyn asked Dorothy about her job, and Emil was surprisingly attentive as she described the admission procedures and some of the people working there. Ray learned a few things he had not known.

They were being served dessert when Ray asked Emil what he planned to do now. Emil said nothing for a moment, as he looked at Marilyn and then down at his chocolate sundae. "I don't know," he said slowly. "I'm good at running Amsaco. I never planned on doing anything else."

There was silence for a moment. Emil looked around at the others looking at him and added, "And maybe I will again. This is a crazy business." He laughed at the surprised expressions of the others. "Nah, just kidding. I still have a few connections though, some irons in the fire. Might even buy an auto parts store and put my son Eddie into it. Maybe another one for my son-in-law. Let him get his hands into something besides my daughter." Marilyn gave him a dirty look. "Maybe even a WD operation. Then I could buy the Amsaco line and you could take me out on the yacht."

"I like that idea," Marilyn broke in. "That's the one thing about the job I'm going to miss. And you can bet I'll be a lot nicer than Doris Goodman. Can't speak for Emil though."

"Depends on how the shocks are selling," said Emil, winking at Dorothy.

Dorothy smiled back. "What are you going to miss, Emil?" she asked.

Marilyn broke in again. "Las Vegas! Emil just loves the tables."

Emil winced. "I don't *love* the tables. When I'm there, I play some blackjack, but—"

"Ha," Marilyn interrupted. "Well you sure know a lot of dealers."

Ignoring his wife, Emil continued. "The one thing I'll miss is the company plane. That's the only way to fly. It's ready when you want to go; it takes you directly where you're going; it's comfortable; and it's fast. I hate going commercial…even first class."

Ray could identify with that. Walking through the crowd of businessmen to your "own" plane, and acting like it was nothing special, just an everyday occurrence, gave Ray that "one up" feeling. He was not just a salesman or an engineer, he was an executive. "Yeah," said Ray. "It sure is easy to get spoiled by the company plane."

"You men get spoiled by everything," Marilyn said. "Your secretaries wait on you hand and foot. You get such a lavish expense account that you don't even look at the prices on the menu. You play golf at the fanciest resorts and country clubs." She looked straight at Emil. "It takes something like...like this to get you back to reality."

Emil said nothing, and there was an awkward silence. To break the silence, Ray said jokingly, "Guess I'm not up to that level. I still look at the prices on the menu."

"Be thankful you do," said Emil seriously. "Your new leader is going to watch everyone's expense accounts. His idea of managing is not to spend any money. Dave is gonna have a hell of a time."

Something in Emil's voice made Ray ask. "Is Dennison in trouble?"

"No more than anyone else. But he makes a lot of money...and he spends a lot, too. Ralph is not going to let anyone spend much money."

Ray thought for a moment. "I'm spending a lot of money," he said, seriously. "You have to with customers. I mean the planes, and the dinners...much less the yacht. Will I be in trouble with Burch?"

"Sure you will," said Emil. "Ralph will judge you on how many dollars you *don't* spend. You'll find out come budget time. Dick Wise will go through marketing like a blitzkrieg. You understand what I'm saying?"

"I sure do," Ray answered. "Dick has been after me to get rid of 'American Bucks' and 'American Trip' since I first came to Amsaco. But is he going to be that powerful? Won't McCormick have a say in all of this?"

"Dan won't be there," Emil said slowly and dramatically. "He's on his way to the Yard." Emil grinned at the three surprised faces. "I still have some connections. United is going to save Dan. He's too strong to work for Burch. Actually, it's gonna be quite a nice move. Dan will be President and Chief Operating Officer. They'll kick Beaumont upstairs to Chairman and Chief Executive Officer." He turned to explain to Dorothy, "Everett Beaumont III is the last of the Beaumont family to run Commerce Yards. He's a nice guy, a real gentleman." Then turning back to Ray, he added abruptly, "But he hasn't got the balls to run the Yard. Dan will really be running things. His job will be to get the Yard to make some money...no easy task."

"Well that's just great for Dan," said Ray. "I suppose Wise will take McCormick's place?"

"Absolutely. I didn't hear that for a fact, but I know Ralph. Wise does exactly what Ralph wants. Been doing that for years. And Ralph wants to send a message that if you do want he wants, you get ahead."

Ray and Dorothy exchanged worried glances.

"I always thought Ralph was kind of a creep," Dorothy said, mainly to Marilyn.

"He is," said Marilyn.

"But he's in charge now," added Emil. "You'd better play his game."

"I'm not against cost-cutting," said Ray. "And I'm sure there's a lot of waste in my area. But there's much more to business than watching pennies."

"You'd better watch 'em," Emil advised.

"But not at the expense of sales." Ray countered. "The most important thing to Amsaco, right now, is to build sales. Now would be the worst time to sabotage our marketing programs."

"That's assuming the marketing programs have anything to do with sales," said Emil, who was enjoying his role as an outside expert, rather than having to defend his own actions.

"You mean the programs don't have an effect on sales?" asked Dorothy.

"Sure they do," Emil answered, "but only in the long run. Things like the 'American Trip' are aimed at developing customer loyalty...building market share. We do the same stuff every year. Our customers expect it and we give it to them."

"The same old crap, warmed over," said Ray, smiling.

Emil was surprised. "You bet your ass." Then he laughed. "At least somebody was listening to me." Turning to Dorothy, he continued. "But that doesn't determine how many shocks we're going to sell this month, or this year. That depends on how business is going in the whole automotive aftermarket...and God knows how that works. I've been trying to figure that out for thirty years."

"That's right," Ray agreed quickly. "New accounts can put us one or two percent higher or lower for the year, but the state of the market can vary up or down by 20 percent, or more."

"And things can't get much worse than they are now," said Emil. "So no matter what you do right now, sales won't go down."

"Actually," said Ray. "The last couple of weeks have been all right. The first time I've seen us hit forecast. I know two weeks is no trend, but it's the first time I've seen any good numbers."

"Just Burch's luck," said Emil, disgustedly. "Sales will probably turn around now, and the bastard will look like a genius… and I'll look like an idiot."

■ ■ ■

The key people at Amsaco's competitor companies were not planning on improved sales. They were financial men. George Lorenzo at Crane and Andy Wilson at Blackwell wanted immediate profit growth, regardless of the business cycle. They were putting their plans into action.

Lorenzo's formula was to get higher prices from the customer. These price increases went right to the bottom line—pure profit. In most cases, customers would accept larger price increases than the salesmen thought possible. The salesmen were always trying to get Management to lower prices or to minimize increases. Lorenzo knew this and never believed his salesmen.

"Of course he's going to bitch and complain," Lorenzo was telling Joe Markham, referring to Jim Purcell of Sears. "That's his job."

"But he's not just bitching," said Joe. "He's threatening to change lines."

"Ah, bullshit," Lorenzo responded disgustedly. "It would cost him an arm and a leg to change. And it's your job to make him understand that. He's still making good money with our shocks, and that's the bottom line."

"Well, we're playing a dangerous game."

"And we're finally making some money on that goddamn account. Welcome to the big leagues."

Markham said nothing more. He was sure Jim Purcell was not bluffing. He knew Jim well, and it worried him. He would have been even more worried if he knew Purcell was having dinner that night with Ed O'Brien of Amsaco.

■ ■ ■

Andy Wilson's formula for maximizing profits was to reduce costs. Blackwell already had the largest market share, so Wilson did not think too much about increasing that. He and Morgan Farnsworth put most of their efforts into making their large market share more profitable by reducing headcount, both direct labor and overhead. This had been difficult when they were busy, especially with the UAW work rules. Now, however, with sales down, cuts were being made. The biggest was the closing of their Columbus, Indiana, plant, which had just been announced.

No one at Amsaco knew this yet, except Jim Steele, who was looking over a resume from the Plant Manager of Blackwell's Columbus plant. Steele was looking for a permanent Plant Manager for the Harrisonburg plant. Ted Lyons was running it temporarily.

Ted had the luxury of getting things started slowly. He had been involved in startups before, but they had always been under pressure conditions. Production had been needed the moment a machine was running, regardless of new manpower requirements, debugging problems, and all the problems associated with startup.

This time, the other plants could handle all the volume without Harrisonburg. This was not the plan, but the lack of sales was making for an efficient startup. Ted could get things running right, before putting machinery into the production schedule. He told Steele he needed about two more months and they could be up to full speed.

Steele's worry was the lack of sales, which so far had made the new plant unnecessary. Jim did not want a "white elephant" on his hands, and he had heard that term around the office. As he read the resume and realized Blackwell's biggest plant was closing, he began to smile.

■ ■ ■

Things did start to pick up during the summer, slowly at first, in certain areas. New England at first. Then into New York and Pennsylvania. The West Coast was also doing well. Nothing spectacular, but up to forecast. The South and the Midwest remained slow.

Overall, sales were still behind forecast, but they were not falling any further behind. Since Richards had changed to Crane, no other customers had left. In fact, even the Richards loss was no disaster. A major effort by Mike Evans, Al Donaldson, and the Georgia District Manager had kept Amsaco shocks on the shelves of many of Richards' jobbers. Amsaco's losses were minimal.

Foreign car sales were almost nothing, except for the West Coast. Ray watched the numbers closely and talked with the

Regional and District Managers, as well as some key customers, about going after the foreign car shock business. He still felt that the potential was there, if customers wanted that business and knew how to go after it. He asked Vince Procino to develop a teaching program on how to get into the foreign car shock market. The plan was to feature this at the National Sales Meeting in New Orleans. Then they would choose a few likely districts and send extra help to get some Jobbers into the foreign car garages. He wanted a few success stories, just to break the ice.

Ray was encouraged when Wise accepted Dennison's 1979 sales forecast with only a few small changes. As Emil had predicted, Dick Wise replaced McCormick, who went to Commerce Yards as their new President. With the power of Burch behind him, Ray expected Wise to be extremely tough on the sales forecast.

Wise did not want an overly-optimistic forecast. A high forecast was all right to set high sales goals, so the salesmen would make smaller bonuses. But it also gave the other departments an excuse for increasing their budgets. Not that they would *get* the increased budget, but they would have justification and could argue with Wise. Ray had put in the system of sharing information between departments when he was in charge of Planning, and it was an irritation to Wise. He would rather have each department be unaware of how much the other departments were asking for.

What Ray did not know was that Wise had already made his own forecast, and it was higher than Dennison's. Wise had taken the last three months' sales, adjusted them for seasonality, and then extrapolated to a full year. His only question to Dennison was, "Do you see the last two months as a fluke, or as something that will continue?"

"I like the way it looks," Dennison answered. "Trends always start in the Northeast, Dick. Then they spread across the Midwest and down through the South. I think things are finally turning around."

Wise understood the logic. The probability was they would hit Dennison's numbers at a minimum, and do even better. He had seen it happen before. The scenario was perfect. They could forecast sales and profits only slightly higher than this year's and then beat those numbers. If Emil had done that, Wise would have said he was "sandbagging." Now, however, the goal was to make Burch look good in Dallas.

■ ■ ■

For some reason, Ray was feeling good when he and his boss walked out of Wise's office with an approved forecast. He tried to figure out why. His Foreign Car Program had been an embarrassment, showing little sales and causing problems with some customers. His record as a Sales Vice President was dismal. His contact with customers was nothing to write home about. Most of his time was spent listening to their complaints. They had lost Richards, a major account in the South. The man who brought the "Professor" into the company—his "patron,"—was gone. And yet, he was still here. Maybe that was why he was feeling good. If he could last through all of that, things had to get better.

And they did. Third-quarter sales beat budgeted forecast.

■ ■ ■

In September at the Distributor's Institute meeting at the Homestead in Virginia, the customers seemed a little friendlier. Ray golfed with Sid Berman, who told him sales were not too bad in Connecticut. Ernie Green, a big Blackwell account from Virginia, added that he was very busy, to the point where Blackwell was even back ordering some items.

Dorothy was a little more at ease also. Distributor's Institute was a meeting of a select group of WDs who met to discuss industry issues. The manufacturers were invited, partly to discuss these issues, but mainly to entertain and socialize. From Dorothy's view, Distributor's Institute was a three-day vacation at a beautiful resort hotel. The men had their meetings and their golf, and the ladies only had to listen to business talk at dinner.

The Homestead was a beautiful old resort in the Shenandoah Mountains of Virginia. Dorothy found two chances to take a long walk on the mountain trails, once by herself, and once with a new friend, Janice Lorenzo. The two of them laughed when they found out their husbands were competitors.

"This place is absolutely beautiful," Dorothy said as she breathed deeply. "Why can't the men take the time to enjoy this?"

"Because they're playing against each other and they're each trying to win."

"Win *what*, exactly?"

"I've never been able to figure that out," Janice said, laughing. "But it sure keeps them going. If the two of them were taking this walk, they would be all tensed up, trying to find out something that would give them an advantage. They'd never even notice the birds or the trees or the smell of the flowers."

"You're right," Dorothy agreed. "But why? Isn't there enough business for both companies? Isn't there plenty of money for all the executives?"

"It's a game," Janice answered. "They enjoy playing the game more than smelling the flowers."

They walked along in silence for awhile, thinking. Then Dorothy asked, "Do they enjoy playing the game more than they enjoy their families?"

Janice stopped and looked seriously at Dorothy. "I don't know. I really don't know. And I don't think I want to know."

"Neither do I," Dorothy said, adding, "Those bastards."

"Fuck 'em," said Janice. They both laughed and continued their walk.

■ ■ ■

Ray was feeling pretty good after dinner, sipping a French cognac, enjoying the balmy September evening in Virginia, when Dave Dennison pulled him away to a private spot in the lobby.

Dennison excitedly told Ray, "I just spoke to O'Brien. We've got a shot at Sears."

Sears—Ray's first major proposal that had been turned down almost two years ago. He had put it out of his mind, finally.

"Ed had dinner tonight with Jim Purcell, who heads up the Automotive Group at Sears," Dennison said. "Jim told him they were dissatisfied with Crane, especially since Lorenzo took over. If we can offer them a good package—stock lift, price, delivery, promotion, all that—they'll consider changing lines in time for their '79 promotions. We can be in their '79 catalog." He paused to let the idea sink in.

"Terrific," was all Ray could think to say.

"But we don't have much time," Dennison went on. "Ed remembered your Sears program and told Jim we were already prepared. Told him he'd be back tomorrow afternoon with our proposal. Purcell was impressed. Said that if we could do that, he would change lines…if the price was right."

"But how…how can Ed put it all together for tomorrow afternoon?"

"He's gonna use your old proposal. You had all sorts of details worked out…with Steele and Swanson. And isn't a lot of the product stuff the same as the foreign car shit?"

"Yeah," Ray agreed. "But we're not going back for a couple of days, and I can't—"

"You're going back tonight. I already spoke with Burch and the plane will take you back to Jackson tonight and bring you back here whenever you're done. Now, who do you need?"

Ray thought for a moment. "I'll work with Ed tonight. In the morning we'll need Swanson for the distribution details. And Simpranian and whoever he needs for the product line. And Vince when we put the presentation together."

"Good. I'll tell Steele to have those guys ready. If Wise agrees with the numbers, then Ed can go ahead. Just let me know what you come up with. A car will be in front to take you to the airport in about fifteen minutes. What are you waiting for?"

Ray smiled. "I think I'd better say something to Dorothy."

As he walked back to the table, Ray was all excited. This was what he had fantasized: two companies competing for a big account like Sears; using strategies developed at secret meetings; implementing their plans through the use of their weapons of engineering or distribution or marketing—just like a battle in a war. And Ray was an important general.

It was his basic strategy that made this possible, and he was the key man for successful implementation. The top company executives were informing their subordinates to be ready when he needed them. The company jet was at his disposal. No one was paying any attention to sleeping or eating schedules. Right now he was the most important guy in the company.

Dorothy did not see it that way. Her reaction was disbelief. "You're leaving right now?" she said. "Flying back to Michigan? Working all night? You're out of your mind."

"I'll be back for dinner tomorrow night."

"And what should I do?" she asked. And then answered before

he could, "Oh, don't worry. I'll take care of myself. I have a few friends. But this is ridiculous."

Ray did not have time to explain the situation to Dorothy. And if he had explained, it probably would not have made any difference. She turned her head away when he tried to kiss her good-bye.

The only person more annoyed than Dorothy was the pilot, who had a golf reservation the following morning. Now he would be waiting around the Jackson airport instead of golfing in the Shenandoah Mountains. He irritably told Ray to buckle up because they were going through some rough weather. Ray spent most of the flight planning how to put together a Sears proposal very quickly. The trip was not rough at all, except for a fast, bumpy descent into Jackson.

Ray got to the office a little before midnight and found Ed O'Brien in the conference room, working with Vince Procino, Paul Sudarsky, and Joe Gregario. Joe was going through the 1979 product line, choosing the fast-moving items with good coverage, in order to give Sears the maximum sales with the minimum inventory. Paul was pricing the items, trying to keep Amsaco competitive but profitable, while making the line attractive to Sears and to their customers. Vince and Ed were working on promotion ideas to increase shock sales for Sears.

"It sure took you long enough," O'Brien kidded. "We're almost finished."

"I didn't think you'd start until I got here and pulled out my old Sears plan," Ray responded.

Vince picked up a copy of Ray's plan and tossed it over to him. "If you remember, big shot, I was your boss when you wrote it."

"Maybe I'd better read it," said Ray. "And find out what I said."

"Well, let us know when you catch up." said O'Brien. "We can make some changes in the morning, but not many." He pointed to a stack of paper, a computer printout, at the end of the table. "There's a printout of every Sears store in North America, along with their total automotive sales for 1977. We don't have shock sales for every store, but you can estimate that from the total shock sales."

Ray looked through the printout. "Wow!" he exclaimed. "I'm impressed. Where did you get this?"

"Ed Purcell wants us to give a good presentation," O'Brien answered with a wink.

"Purcell gave you this?"

"Hell no. But he pointed me in the right direction. We both want the same thing. Our job is to make him look good."

"OK," said Ray, making a place for himself at the table. "Let's make him look good."

With the five men working separately and then together, the entire proposal was put together that night. It closely followed Ray's original plan. The product line was even better than originally planned because of the consolidation work already done on the Foreign Car Program. They would use exact copies of their present shocks, except they would be painted white.

Ray worked out a shipping schedule to balance the load for the three plants, with each day of the week reserved for a specific geographical area in a plant's territory. The big Sears stores would be shipped every week, the smaller ones every other week.

The promotions would use TV to sell quality, emphasizing the "heavy-duty" shocks. Price specials, such as "buy three and get one free," would appear in the newspapers. These were proposals only, since Sears would run their own advertising program. O'Brien just wanted Amsaco to look like the professionals in marketing shock absorbers.

Pricing was a little problem. O'Brien knew what Purcell wanted because Purcell had told him...pretty much. He wanted a price structure better than Crane's. However, the price information that he let O'Brien find out was the structure before Crane had raised prices—which precipitated Purcell's search for another supplier. Ed was suspicious that there had to be some reason that Purcell was so receptive, so he figured that matching Crane's numbers would do it.

When they went over the pricing the next morning with Dick Wise, Dick did not like the margins. He insisted they increase the proposed prices, which they did. But Sudarsky changed the estimated product mix to make the total look close to Crane's prices. Ray felt a little guilty at this subterfuge, but Purcell saw exactly what they had done. Even with the increase, Amsaco was still well below Crane's new prices.

Wise and Steele had conversations with Ralph Burch, and Ray and O'Brien spoke with Dennison. By noon, everything was approved. The presentation was ready by 2:00 P.M. when Tom Chessman walked in and asked if there was anything he could do to help.

After freshening up a little, Ray and O'Brien took off in the Falcon, dropping O'Brien off in downtown Chicago, at Meigs Field. He was making his presentation to Purcell by 4:00 P.M. On the flight back to Virginia, Ray poured himself a large scotch on the rocks, and fell asleep before drinking it. Back at the Homestead, he had time to shave, change clothes, and meet Dorothy, the Dennison's, and the Bermans for dinner at 7:30.

Sid asked him, "Did you get that slice straightened out today?"

"I'm working on it."

There was no late entertaining for the Pendletons that night. By 10:00 they were in their room and two minutes later Ray was sound asleep.

Dorothy washed up, put on her nightgown and sat in the lounge chair watching TV, with very little interest. She thought about how much her life had changed from what it had been at Harvard. Everything seemed to be better. Her mother had no doubts it was better. They no longer had any financial worries. Ray's salary was twice what he was making as a Professor. And with his "obscene" bonus, they could pay all bills and put a sizable amount into savings.

And she certainly was not bored. The new sales position was opening up new adventures she had not dreamed of at Harvard. The Homestead . . . the Drake . . . Lyford Cay . . . the yacht. Back at Harvard, a weekend at the Holiday Inn had been quite a treat, even with the kids. And the people she was meeting—there were many she did not like, but many she did, like Helen Bloom and Nancy Beluga. Even the ones she did not care for, like Ron Berman, were interesting. She laughed. Yes, Ron Berman was interesting.

Then why did she feel so unhappy? So lonely. Was it just that things were different? Was she just uncomfortable with change? She looked over at Ray, sleeping soundly, snoring occasionally. He was not uncomfortable. He seemed to be enjoying the change. And why not? To him, this was an opportunity, a challenge to show what he could do, a game. And he was winning. If they visited their old friends at Harvard, he could take a victory lap. The Professor who made it big in the big time. He was a hero. He was…he was… he…he!

Maybe that was the problem. Everything was he, he, he. She was nothing in this new world. Women were not important, except to keep things in order at home. Even at these big industry events, the women were there just for socializing, for window dressing. The men had the important task of business. And Ray had deserted her to join this fraternity of automotive executives. Amsaco had replaced her as Ray's number-one priority.

She stared at Ray for several minutes. Was this the man she had been sharing her life with the past fifteen years? Her lover? Who laughed with her and cried with her? Who shared her bed? Was this the serious young teacher with the goal of starting a family with her and raising kids with good values? Who shared dreams of some day working together in their retirement?

No, this was some corporate executive who took her along to dinners, and slept in her bed, and gave her the money to run the house. She looked again at the man in bed, with his mouth open, snoring quietly. She stood up and walked over to him, looking closely at his face. Who was this man?

■ ■ ■

Jim Purcell was very happy with the Amsaco proposal. Not only was he getting a better price, but he would be able to get by with a smaller inventory, backed by a network of Amsaco Jobbers and Warehouse Distributors. That was worth real money. The proposed system of getting calls from Amsaco's Customer Service Department he looked on basically as a gimmick. Sears was capable of keeping track of their inventory and ordering when needed. Still, it was worth trying. It might make it easier for Amsaco to ship regularly, and they had nothing to lose. The proposed advertising program was interesting, but again, Sears could handle their own advertising program.

The only thing Purcell requested was that Amsaco hire Don Peterson from Crane, and assign him the Sears account. He knew Peterson would lose his job when Crane lost Sears. O'Brien knew Peterson, and liked him well enough, but he had reservations. They were both National Account Sales Managers and were at about the same level. With the other Crane products at Sears, Peterson might even have a higher salary than O'Brien. He did not relish the idea of having someone around whose qualifications were as good or better than his. Actually, he had planned on giving the account to Mike Lagano, his top Salesman, and then hiring a new replacement. On the other hand, hiring Peterson for Sears and leaving Lagano with his current customers would mean experienced Salesmen in both positions and no hazardous breaking-in periods. It probably would mean a smoother transition and be best for the company.

In addition, he understood the underlying thought behind Purcell's idea, which was to look out for each other. The Factory Salesmen and the Customer Buyers for Sears, Penneys, Western Auto, and all the national accounts were almost like a fraternity. They all knew each other and helped each other as they moved up the ladder or changed companies. O'Brien knew that he could easily be in Peterson's position, and so could Purcell. When another buyer, Charlie MacGregor, recently got in trouble at Montgomery Ward, Paul Breen had given him a good job at Champion.

O'Brien promised Purcell that he would make Peterson as good an offer as he could. Purcell understood and shook O'Brien's hand. "This is a done deal," he said. "It will take a couple of weeks to get everything approved, but you guys can start working out the details. I want to do this geographically, from the West Coast to the East. No screwups."

"Don't worry, Jim," said O'Brien, smiling. "We'll make you look good."

It took longer than two weeks, and O'Brien had some anxious moments. But within a month, Purcell called to say it was approved. O'Brien and Dennison both went into Burch's office with the good news.

"It's official, Ralph," said Dennison, smiling broadly. "We start in California on December 17th."

"Then work our way east," added O'Brien.

Burch did not crack a smile. He frowned and looked toward the ceiling. "When will the change be complete?" he asked.

"By the middle of March," Dennison answered. "Maybe into April. They're going to ship the lifted inventories to their eastern stores as we go along. We want to give them time to sell as much of the old stuff as they can. We'll sell some of the rest of it ourselves, but what's left will go to Saul Palder."

Dennison would just as soon have pulled all the inventory out of the Sears system and replaced it with Amsaco shocks. But doing it slowly meant less cost to Amsaco, and he knew Burch would be concerned with the costs. So he had Procino work out this efficient scheme with the Sears personnel. He was proud of how this was being handled and expected some approval from his new boss, but none came.

Burch nodded his head and said, "Keep Wise informed on just what you're doing."

That ended the conversation and the two salesmen looked at each other and left Burch's office. Out in the hall, O'Brien commented, "He sure is a cold fish."

"Yeah," Dennison agreed. "You'd think he'd congratulate us or something. We saved him money."

"Yeah. We should at least get an 'attaboy.'"

■ ■ ■

Back in his office, Burch had Dick Wise on the phone. "The Sears thing is approved. Watch those guys closely. They're playing with a lot of money."

"Don't worry, I'm watchin' them. You can't trust those guys with a big appropriation. Steele will control the Operations costs, but those Sales guys…they go first class. Like the guy they're hiring to handle the Sears account. Did you know he'll be making almost what O'Brien's making?"

"No. I didn't know. How come I didn't have to approve it?"

"Well, you did, sort of. You approved the appropriation, which called for the addition of one head."

"Yeah, but not at O'Brien's level. Who is this guy?"

"I think he's the guy who had the Sears account with Crane. He must have been part of the deal."

Burch was getting angry. "No one told me he was part of the deal. Did Chessman know about this?"

"I imagine so. The employee requisition requires two signatures, plus Personnel. That would be O'Brien, Dennison, and Chessman, or one of his people. But none of his people would sign without

Tom knowing about it." Wise had no love for any of those three. "Do you want me to check it out?"

"No, don't do anything," said Burch, adding, "Don't say anything to anybody. I'll take care of this. Just forget it, for now. Look, I want to see what this Sears stuff is going to make next year's P&L look like."

"It's going to be big," Wise answered. "The Sears business is all addition to forecast. And the aftermarket in general is starting to move. We're gonna be way over forecast and favorable to budget."

"I know," said Burch matter-of-factly. "Put together a proforma on what you think '79 will look like."

"Sure. I'll have it to you tomorrow."

As he hung up the phone, Burch sat back in his big chair to think things out. He was angry with O'Brien and Dennison for hiring Crane's salesman...mainly with Dennison, who must have approved the decision. It was a bad decision because it set a bad precedent and was not really necessary. If Sears liked the Amsaco proposal, it was because it was financially attractive. And if it was, they would have accepted it without the hiring of the Crane man. This was just buddy-buddy stuff between salesmen. He could understand O'Brien, who was caught in the middle, but Dennison should not have approved.

Even more important was the fact that Dennison had done this without consulting Burch. He must have felt Burch would not have approved, which was accurate, so he went ahead and did it without asking. He probably hoped Burch would not find out, but if he did, Dennison undoubtedly had some justification other than "it was part of the deal." This was typical of salesmen. Get the sale, and talk your way out of the repercussions later. This was exactly opposite to the way Burch wanted to work. Maybe Dennison had not really accepted the fact that Burch was running the show. Dennison had been an Executive Vice President while Burch was coming up through Accounting. He might still be looking at Burch as just an Accounting pain-in-the-ass, trying to keep him from doing his job. If so, that had to change...fast.

Burch stood up and began pacing around his big office. Getting Dennison to accept Burch as his boss was one problem, but a much bigger one was forming: Dennison was going to look very good the following year. Between the additional Sears business and the recovery of the aftermarket in general, Burch knew that Wise's figures would show a substantial increase over budgeted sales and profits. And Dennison would get most of the credit, enough to make it difficult to get him to follow Burch's directions. He might even be a threat to replace Burch.

Burch thought for a few moments, digesting this logic, and then concluded that the solution to this problem was to get rid of Dennison quickly, before the big sales increases showed up. Rising sales meant changing plans. For one thing, he did not want to bring Carl Buzzard in just yet and possibly cause production problems when sales were going up. That would have to wait. But Dennison would have to go...soon.

He thought about handling the customers without Dennison. One possibility would be to put Mike Evans into Dennison's job. Then he, Evans, and Pendleton could do the job that Emil, Dennison, and Evans had done before. He would have to spend more time with customers than he wanted, but sooner or later he had to do that. He and his wife, Jeanette, had to be more visible and sociable at the head of the company.

He didn't really want Evans in charge of all of the Sales and Marketing activities. As far as he was concerned, Evans was a good ol' boy salesman and nothing else. Evans knew a lot of people, but they were all in the traditional aftermarket. He probably did not know any of O'Brien's contacts, and he definitely did not know anyone in OE. Working with the car companies required a businessman, not a salesman. Their purchasing people would be too tough on Evans. He would give away the store. And the thought of Evans trying to control Advertising and Promotion really scared Burch. Plus, Evans was ready to retire anyway. It made him too independent for Burch's liking. No, Evans was not right.

Maybe then, he should look outside the company. Anyone he brought in would have the capabilities he was looking for, and would certainly owe his allegiance to Burch. It would cause some bad feelings within the Marketing organization, but that did not bother Burch. That group could use a little shaking up...unless it caused Evans to retire early. Then it would be Burch, the new man, and Pendleton handling the customers. That would be too much of a change, too quickly. Evans had to stay for at least a year. He was needed to ease the way for Burch's introduction into the aftermarket social structure.

Then what about Pendleton as Dennison's replacement? Pendleton was more of a businessman than anyone else in Marketing. He could handle the advertising and promotion programs, and the OE end of the business. And he would know enough to leave Evans and O'Brien alone. Pendleton had some crazy ideas, but Burch could control him. If Evans could work for Pendleton, then Evans could just ease back into his old job, which he had not really left.

And most importantly, Pendleton would be easy to sell to Max Simpson and United. It would be a positive move, getting Pendleton on his staff to breath new life into Marketing at Amsaco. That was better than just tearing Dennison down.

Mentally, Burch presented his logic to Max Simpson: "If we're going to grow, the most important area of the company is Sales." Simpson would not argue with that. "And we need someone who's not afraid of change. Emil and Dennison were so afraid of hurting the feelings of our traditional customers that they killed Pendleton's Sears plan two years ago. When O'Brien came in to tell us the Sears thing was still alive, I told Dennison to get the Professor in on it, quick. In less than an hour, Pendleton was flying back to Jackson to work all night with O'Brien and the Operations people. And now we have Sears. You'll see the results by the middle of the year. And the Professor's Foreign Car Program is beginning to show promise." That might be bending the truth a little bit, but if the aftermarket sales keep rising, how would Simpson know the cause?

No doubt about it. The Professor was salable…and controllable, and maybe even capable. But only if Evans would stay on to run Corporate Brand Sales. Burch thought for a moment and almost smiled. The key to keeping Evans was money. Simple as that. Evans' retirement pay was based on his average salary for the last five years he worked and the total years employed by Amsaco. By offering Evans a substantial raise, plus a few more years of employment, his pension would increase considerably, maybe even double if the raise was big enough. And that was no trouble, because even with another raise for Pendleton, they were eliminating Dennison's big salary and the company would still save money. Perfect!

OK, that was it. Dennison replaced by Pendleton, as long as Evans stayed. He would have to speak to Evans immediately after Dennison was let go, before anyone else knew, even Pendleton. But he was confident the money would convince Evans. It would work.

Now the only ones getting credit for next year's profits would be Burch and Pendleton. And he was not worried about the Professor.

19. Whores

The last thing on Ray's mind was replacing his boss as Executive Vice President. Besides not being so ambitious or aggressive, he was too busy doing his present job. He was still meeting customers with Mike Evans and the Regional Managers.

Ray travelled all over the country, meeting new customers and visiting ones that he had already met. It seemed there was always some fire that had to be put out. In addition, he had to plan the upcoming National Sales Meeting, approve the advertising program for the next year, prepare the budgets for the next year, and handle numerous other administrative duties.

But the immediate problem was how to introduce the Sears program without causing problems with their old customers. Evans and Ray were in Ray's office working on a "party line" to tell the traditional customers.

"We can push the idea that their Jobbers will get the fill-in business from Sears," said Ray. "Business that they didn't have before, when Crane was in there. So this move will help increase their business."

"We can sell that," Evans said. "As long as sales hold up. But there's no place for logic if sales are down. They're gonna be pissed, really pissed, if we sell Sears and their sales go down."

"Sales are going up," said Ray. "It's a certainty, or Wise wouldn't have approved our forecast."

They were laughing when Madge came in and said Mr. Dennison wanted Ray in his office right away.

As Ray came into Dennison's plush office, Dave was sitting behind his enormous desk. He came right to the point. "You're invited to the United Tire Management meeting. Or maybe I should say the Untico Management meeting. They're modernizing the name and 'Grow With Untico' is the theme of the meeting."

Ray just stood there for a moment, then asked, "How come? What's the United Ti...Untico Management meeting?"

"It's a two-day meeting of all the...Untico companies. Two days of presentations and financial reports...and socializing. For the top echelon, usually the Presidents and their staffs.

"Burch wants you to give a talk on our Foreign Car Program. Peggy will get you all the info on the meeting. All you have to do is put together the presentation in two weeks. One week actually. Then you can present it at Burch's staff meeting next week, and we can make the necessary changes."

■ ■ ■

While Ray was nervous about making the presentation before all of Untico's top executives, he had no trouble putting it together. He used the story he had presented to Torres and his staff and had the slides made more professionally.

"You do good work," Tom Chessman told him as they were flying down to Dallas. Ray was sitting in the back of the plane with Chessman and Dick Wise. "You convert the marketing plans into numbers and show what it does to the bottom line. Emil could never do that."

Wise perked up. "If you can't turn it into numbers," he said, "it isn't real."

"I know," Chessman agreed. "I've been trying to get that across to these guys for years."

Ray had to laugh. He had never heard Chessman say anything like that. But most of the time there was no correlation between what Chessman said and what really happened. Now with Burch in charge Chessman had picked up all the new key words—like "bottom line" and "justifiable" and "return on investment."

Chessman gave Ray a dirty look. "What are you laughing about? You think your Sales guys care anything about fiscal results? They get an idea that sounds good, and they have no idea of the financial impact. I told Emil that he should teach the field guys something about the financials, but he said it would spoil their enthusiasm."

"The only enthusiasm they have," said Wise, "is to spend money."

Ray had to argue. "They may not be so good with financial numbers, but I've seen some of them figure the cost of a promotion faster than I can. And I've seen them say no to a customer when they have to." He saw the look of disbelief on Wise's face. "Sure, sometimes they have to be a little flexible with a customer, but—"

"You call it flexible," Wise interrupted. "We call it 'caving in,' and it's gotta change."

"And with Burch in charge," Chessman added, looking straight at Ray, "it's gonna change. I gotta give Ralph credit; he's not married to the old ways."

Wise nodded in agreement.

■ ■ ■

The meeting was held at the Pines, a luxury-home development of Untico's. Beautiful homes lined every fairway of the two golf courses. The home owners had automatic membership at the country club, which included a central recreation complex containing indoor and outdoor swimming pools, hard surface and clay tennis courts, a fully equipped conference center, and an excellent restaurant.

Ray shared a room with Tony Agnos, a Vice President in Stan Moore's Administration Group in the Dallas home office. Tony knew all the dirt about Untico. While they were getting dressed for dinner, he filled Ray in on what he should know about the meeting:

There were about 150 attendees at the meeting—the presidents of all the Untico companies and their staffs, plus about thirty from the home office.

Torres and his staff, the Board Members, plus the Company Presidents, had private rooms. Everyone else shared rooms.

This was the second year the meeting was being held at the Pines. Previously it had been at fancy resorts from Bermuda to Palm Springs. But the Pines was not doing that well, and Torres was making the point that this was a good place for corporate meetings…and for those who lived near Dallas to buy a home.

The agenda included a welcoming dinner with a Washington economist as guest speaker, morning meetings with presentations, a golf tournament, and a home office presentation with financial results from Alan Tracy and a summary from Dave Torres.

The concept of "Untico" was Alan Tracy's idea, aimed at pleasing Wall Street.

Everyone at the meeting was under surveillance by someone, and the worst offense was getting drunk.

A good deal of politicking would take place.

Anyone who scored too well in the golf tournament was suspected of spending too much time on the links and not enough time working for Untico.

There was a definite hierarchy in the social arrangements, from the selection of golf foursomes to the various card games at night.

The big card game was Torres' team gin game, with four top executives teaming up against another four.

It was all right to watch any game, but you only played when invited.

After dinner, Ray just toured the room, watching the various card games and talking to the few people he knew.

He was surprised that all of the Amsaco people were busily talking to someone. Dick Wise was talking to Alan Tracy and two others, probably Financial men. Jim Steele was in a poker game, but Ray did not recognize any of the other players. Dennison and Burch were at a table with Max Simpson and two others from Berringer Paper, Simpson's old company. Ray was not invited into any of these conversations.

He spotted Tom Chessman talking to Dan McCormick and went over to greet his old boss. While his reception was warm enough, it was obvious that he was interrupting something, and he left quickly.

He decided to go back to his room and go over his presentation for the following morning. He was somewhat nervous, but confident that the presentation would be well received. After all, he was emphasizing how American ingenuity would overcome the Japanese plans to control the American automotive aftermarket. It was received exactly as planned.

Dan McCormick was the first to present in the morning, and he painted a dreary picture of Commerce Yards. Over years of weak family management, the unions had taken over. High wages, obscene benefits, and featherbedding had made the Yard noncompetitive and unprofitable. McCormick intended to turn this around, but first he wanted everyone to know how difficult this was going to be. He had to be careful how he worded this, because some of the old family was in the audience. But everyone got his message. After his talk, Dave Torres expressed his confidence that Dan could do the job.

Charlie London was up next and showed a more profitable picture for Berringer Paper. But he then concentrated on the environmental problems that were going to make it difficult to maintain their profit level. The EPA was after the whole paper industry to stop polluting the rivers. Solutions to the problems were going to be expensive, very expensive. Berringer would not be a major source of profit for Untico over the next few years.

When Ray got up and started to explain the problems the Japanese car manufacturers were giving the U.S. aftermarket, everyone groaned, expecting another pessimistic presentation. But when he started to show the slides of the Amsaco engineers' solution to the Japanese consolidation problems, he actually received a round of applause, right in the middle of the presentation. From there, everything got better as he showed the expected improvement in profits as they added sales. Enthusiastic applause followed him off the platform. He was glad Ron Berman or Joe Beluga were not there... or old Doug Wilmot saying, "Sonny, ah don't see any of them little Jap cars drivin' roun' in Alabama."

Everyone he spoke to that day had some compliment for Ray. Dave Torres thanked him for turning an otherwise gloomy morning into an upbeat session. "I'm going to use this example of American ingenuity in my talk tomorrow," Torres said. "The whole idea of 'Untico' is to promote a modern, positive attitude throughout the company."

That afternoon Ray golfed with Huntington Forbes, Director of Research at Commerce Yards; Bob Vernon, Vice President of Governmental Affairs from Washington; and David Carroll, a Vice President from Dallas with some sort of real estate duties. They all congratulated Ray on a great presentation.

Bob Vernon was the most enthusiastic. "I'm going to tell a bunch of people in Washington about this. Tell them to get off their asses and stop complaining."

That evening, the praise continued. It was hard for Ray to believe that these high-ranking executives were so impressed. It was amazing that they even knew who he was, much less thought so well of him...especially for the Foreign Car Program. No one except the Amsaco people knew that the program, so far, was unsuccessful, and they were not about to let reality intrude on this pleasant situation.

Ray was just enjoying himself, talking a little with many people. It was much different than the night before. When he moved over behind the "big" gin game, Ed Huggins, a board member, looked up from his cards and said, "Good presentation!" The others grunted their approval, and went back to their game.

Ray recognized most of the players. On one side sat Dave Torres, Stan Moore, Ed Huggins, and Charlie London, the Berringer President. The other team was Max Simpson; Phil Voight, another board member; Ed Morgan, the Senior Vice President of Personnel; and one other, whom Ray did not know. The scoring was simple. Each player would play his hand against a player from the other team. The four scores would be combined to see which team came out ahead that round. If two players won and two lost, there might not be many points, but if all four won, it could add up substantially. Tony Agnos, who was watching along with about six others, told Ray that Emil Gross had started this team gin game, and it had become a tradition.

They were coming toward the end of a game when Torres' team won all four hands. Torres, Huggins, and London had each won their hands, and when Moore declared, "Gin!" a big cowboy "Yahoo" came from the other three.

Phil Voight stood up and said, "That's enough for me."

"Aw c'mon," said Huggins. "We can still take some more money from you."

"Nah. I'm playing on margin now. Find someone to take my place."

Torres was not ready to call it a night. Looking around for a replacement, he spotted Ray. "Come on in," he said enthusiastically. "If you're from Amsaco, you have to know how to play gin."

Ray was stunned. He had never dreamed of playing in the "big" game. The players in this game were the top of top management. To Ray they were "Mr." Torres and "Mr." Huggins and "Mr." Moore. And the stakes! He did not know how much they were playing for, but it must have been a lot.

"Oh, I don't know," he stammered. "I...er...I mean...this is a big game and—"

"Oh bullshit," said Torres, emphatically. "Sit down. I know how much you make, and you can afford to lose."

Ray started to take Voight's seat. He looked around at the other players, and then at Torres and said, "I was wondering if I could afford to *win.*"

Everyone burst into laughter. They knew exactly what he meant. Torres was laughing the most. "I'll tell you what," he said. "You play on my team and you can win all you want. Charlie, why don't you switch with Ray?"

Ray switched chairs with Charlie London, with everyone still laughing. He noticed Ed Morgan make eye contact with Torres and nod approvingly.

The game itself was uneventful. Ray won almost as many hands as he lost, and the rest of the team did well enough so that they barely won. He was surprised when Torres handed him $60, his share of the winnings. They must have been playing for two or three dollars a point. A big win, or loss, could have amounted to several hundred dollars.

"Sorry it couldn't be more," Torres apologized. "Hardly worth the effort."

Ray just smiled, breathed a sigh of relief, and went back to his room.

■ ■ ■

The plane ride back was generally cheerful because of the good reception all the Amsaco people received as a result of Ray's presentation—though they all knew that the Foreign Car Program sounded a lot better than it really was.

Dennison, Chessman, Wise, and Ray were sitting in the back, and Dennison kidded Ray, somewhat sarcastically. "That was a great presentation, Professor. Might not be a bad idea to actually sell a few of those foreign shocks."

"They'll sell...eventually," Ray answered.

"You guys really got your neck out on this one," Chessman pointed out. "You got Torres' attention, and don't think he won't check out how you're doing."

"How's he gonna know how much of our sales are foreign shocks?" Dennison asked. "We'll be OK as long as sales go up."

"He'll know," said Chessman. "You can't hide that stuff from the bean counters."

Dick Wise just smiled.

"Ralph knows what he's doing," Dennison countered. "With the Sears thing, and sales going up, no one's going to worry about why things are good. Dallas only worries about why things are bad."

"Yeah, that's true enough," Chessman answered. "But Ralph can't take credit for next year's results. They're based on what Emil did, not on Burch."

Everyone looked at Chessman with surprise. That was just what he wanted, and he continued. "I mean let's give credit where credit's due. Dave, you know damn well that Ralph's got nothing to do with the way things are going. He was against the Sears program, against the Foreign Car Program, against the Harrisonburg plant...just like Dick here. He's a bean counter."

Ray couldn't figure Chessman. He was tearing into his new boss in front of Dick Wise, who was certain to report it to Burch. On the trip down, he was praising Burch and ass kissing the new administration. Now he was "Truth" riding in on a white horse, saying what he saw as the facts, regardless of the consequence. It was not like Chessman.

Ray found out why a few days later when it was announced that Chessman was going to work for Dan McCormick at Commerce Yards, and Art Webb would be the new Vice President of Personnel. It made sense. At the meeting, McCormick must have offered this new job to Chessman. Undoubtedly that was the conversation that Ray had interrupted. On the flight back, Chessman could afford to alienate the "bean counters"—and he probably enjoyed doing it.

Chessman was packing his things into cardboard cartons and barely looked up when Ray entered. "You son of a gun," Ray said smiling. "You could have told me. At least I would have known what you were talking about on the plane."

As usual, Chessman ignored Ray's comment. "You guys are in for some rough times," he said with authority. "Putting Webb, a bean counter, in to fight the UAW is suicidal. They'll eat him up."

Ray had learned that it was useless to try to hold a logical discussion with Chessman. But he actually was beginning to like the guy, and could not resist getting in a few licks of his own. "He may not be that good at negotiations, but he certainly should understand the financial impact of the Personnel programs. And you said yourself that Burch wasn't married to the old ways. Maybe Art can do some good things...fiscally."

Chessman stopped packing and looked at Ray over his glasses. "You son of a bitch," he said slowly. "You're getting fuckin' dangerous."

Ray laughed.

Chessman resumed packing. "Don't any of you guys come looking for a job at the Yard, either. You don't know anything about boats, and Dan doesn't want to be a home for Burch's discards."

■ ■ ■

After two weeks of meetings and travel, Ray was in Mike Evans' office on a Saturday, trying to work out the yacht schedule. Dennison had not shown up yet.

"Do you think Burch should take Sanders on the boat?" Ray asked.

"I don't know," Evans replied. "Sanders isn't really a yacht type person. He's strictly business. If he wants Burch to see his operation, then maybe Kansas City is the place to go. And the yacht doesn't go to Kansas City. Maybe after they get to know one another it would be all right."

"I didn't know the Goodmans or the Belugas," said Ray.

"Yeah, but it's different. You're not the President. You're just a peddler entertaining the customers. When the Company President invites them on the yacht, it's an honor. When we do it, we're just hosts showing them a good time."

Ray thought about it for a moment and had to agree. He could not imagine the customers giving Emil, or Burch, as hard a time as they gave him.

"Well, who should Ralph take on the boat?" Ray asked.

"I'd like to see him take the ones Emil did. But maybe not. We really should sit down with Ralph...and Dave."

"I don't think Ralph likes to do that," said Ray. "I think we should make up a list of who he should take, and when. Then he could read it and say yes or no."

"Yeah, maybe you're right," Evans agreed. "It's not the way Emil worked, but things change. We should have Dave in on this...I don't know where he is. He was supposed to be here."

■ ■ ■

Ray found out where Dennison was the following Monday. He was called into Burch's office around 10:00 A.M. As he went in, Mike Evans was leaving. Mike said nothing, but just shook his head and rolled his eyes.

The look on Evans' face worried Ray.

Burch was sitting at his desk, going through a checklist. Ray could not help noticing how small Burch looked compared to Emil, who had sat in that same chair. It was like Burch was wearing a shirt with the neck two sizes too large.

"Sit down, Ray," Burch said as he put a check next to one of his notes. "I won't take too long…I've got a staff meeting set up this morning and I want you to sit in on it."

Ray was relieved to know that he was still part of the team, but he said nothing.

"Dave Dennison is leaving the company and I want you to take the Marketing job," Burch said. "There are a few things you need to know about it."

Ray sat there, not believing his ears.

"First of all, there's a lot more money. Your salary will be $75,000 a year, with a commensurate increase in your bonus. In addition, you'll come under the Untico Executive Compensation Plan. That includes another bonus, based on Untico's performance to goal, and a stock option plan, which could be worth a considerable amount over the years. The best part is that stock appreciation is considered a capital gain."

Burch looked at Ray, expecting some agreement. Ray just nodded. He was numb.

Burch continued. "The company wants their executives to do well financially, so they have hired Price-Waterhouse to handle taxes, and to be available for consultation on investments. I find that very useful." He looked at his checklist. "Let's see. Oh yes, we have an executive physical every year at Billings in Chicago, an excellent place. Part of the University of Chicago. And of course, there's the Management meeting. You know about that."

Ray was stunned. "I don't know what to say," he almost whispered. "I never expected anything like—"

"No, of course. But you have the business and marketing skills

I want. And Evans says you've gotten to know the customers pretty well." Burch noticed Ray's look of surprise. "In this case I've done something a little unusual. I've already spoken to Evans. You know, his connections become even more important now. You and I need his experience, at least for a while."

"Yes, we do. He's taught me a lot. And we get along well. You know, mutual respect."

Burch almost smiled. "Good, because now you're going to be his boss. He's agreed to stay on for a few years and go back to running Corporate Brand Sales. One of his assignments, and yours, will be to groom a successor."

Ray took a deep breath. "Let me digest this for a moment. Mike will be working for me? And Vince too?"

"And O'Brien for National Accounts and Crawford for OE Sales. Oh, one important change. Al Goldman and the International Operation will report directly in to me. I think it makes more sense, with his P&L responsibilities."

"Yeah, I agree. I never really understood why International was reporting in to Marketing. This makes more sense."

Burch was glad to see Ray agree. Not that it would change anything if he did not agree. But this was the right business decision and Ray recognized that. Ray was no "empire builder."

"OK, it's set then," Burch concluded. "I'll call O'Brien, Crawford, and Procino right after my staff meeting and tell them they have a new boss. And Goldman. I'd suggest you meet with your guys this afternoon. I'll have Stark put out an announcement. And, oh yes, I'll tell Beatrice, your new secretary. She knows something's up."

Ray was in a daze. He and Burch walked next door to the executive conference room. Jim Steele, Dick Wise, Art Webb, and Pete Stark were already waiting. Burch introduced Ray as the new Executive Vice President of Marketing. Ray was surprised when he heard his title—he had not even asked what it would be. The thought hit him that he had not even accepted the job. But he figured it best not to bring that up right then.

Dick Wise started the meeting with the financial report. Sales were holding at a level above forecast. It looked like the last two quarters of the year would more than make up for the slow second quarter, and the year would end up above forecast.

When he went through the sales details, he pointed out that foreign car sales were well below forecast. Jim Steele grinned when he heard that and was about to say something when he noticed no one else was smiling, so he said nothing. Ray saw this and also said nothing.

Profits were holding steady at budget levels because manufacturing costs were 2.31 percent over budget. All in all, Wise expected profits to end the year on budget.

Steele reported that costs were a little high because of preparations to supply Sears. However, once they started to manufacture the Sears shocks, the added volume would improve efficiency and reduce costs. It looked like next year would be very good.

The rest of the meeting was short and uneventful. Art Webb said that he was looking at alternative health plans to reduce costs. Pete Stark said he needed volunteers to speak at the Chamber of Commerce annual dinner next month. Burch told him to hold community commitments to a minimum because any executive who had time for that "shit" did not have enough to do in his job. No one volunteered.

Burch then told the group that Al Goldman would be reporting to him and would be around the following week to attend staff meeting. Ray figured that Burch must have spoken to Goldman earlier and had told him about Ray replacing Dennison...before even talking to Ray. This bothered him, but again he said nothing. He concentrated on what he had to do that day.

As soon as the meeting ended, he reserved the conference room and went back to his office. He asked Madge to call his new staff to a 1:30 meeting in the conference room. It was not necessary to tell her about his promotion.

"Congratulations," she said, without smiling. "It's hard to keep up with you. So you're going to be our new boss." With a slight smile, she added, "I hope you're not going to fire Mr. Evans."

"I'm not going to fire anyone. Didn't Mike tell you? He'll be going back to his old job."

"No. I haven't spoken to Mr. Evans this morning. He just went into his office."

"Then how did you—"

"Everyone knows."

Ray sighed. "They probably knew before I did."

Madge asked with a mischievous smile, "What time did you find out?"

Ray just shook his head and went into his office to gather his thoughts. He wondered why he did not feel elated. This was a great promotion. He was now one of the top five men in the company, maybe the top two or three...an *Executive* Vice President. His income would be beyond his wildest dreams. He was a legitimate member of the Untico Management Group. What was bothering him? The responsibility? No. He was responsible for sales, and sales were looking good. The challenge? No, not that either. Getting into OE Sales and National Accounts would be new, but interesting, and he was sure he could handle it. He could not see any problem in working with Vince, or Mike, or Ed.

Madge came in. "Could I talk to you for a second?" she asked.

"Sure. I'm just going to grab a sandwich before the meeting. Sit down."

"I think you should talk to Beatrice."

"Who?"

"Beatrice Donner. Your new secretary. Mr. Dennison's secretary."

"Oh, I hadn't even thought about that yet." He shook his head and took a deep breath. "I don't know where I am."

Madge nodded her head. "I can understand that. But I think you should talk to her as soon as possible. She's very upset."

Seeing Madge's serious expression, he said, "I'll see her right after the meeting..." She kept looking at him. "I'll go over there now." He was beginning to trust Madge's judgment. Beatrice was probably worried about her job.

He walked down the hall to Dennison's old office. Beatrice was sitting at her desk in the anteroom outside the office. She was a nice-looking woman in her early sixties, a little plump, with greying hair. She looked startled when she saw him approach. "Mr. Pendleton!"

"Hi, Beatrice," he greeted her, smiling. "Can we talk? In there." He pointed to Dennison's office.

"Certainly, Mr. Pendleton."

They walked into the office. It was twice as large as most

executive offices—only the President's was larger. Besides the over-sized desk and credenza, there was a large sofa and coffee table, a conference table with six comfortable chairs, and a large walk-in closet with room for several coats and six good-sized shelves. The two windows had floor-length drapes, the carpeting was plush, and one whole wall had customized floor-to-ceiling bookshelves.

This was now *his* office. He resisted the impulse to go over and sit behind the desk. He sat down at the conference table. So did Beatrice.

There was a brief silence before Ray said, hesitantly, "I...uh... I'm not sure just what to say, Beatrice. Ralph told me this morning that Dave was...retiring...and I would be taking his place."

"Yes, I know. Mr. Dennison called me last night," Beatrice said sadly. "He didn't want someone else to tell me. We've been working together for almost fifteen years, since Mr. Dennison was Regional Manager...I don't think he wanted to retire."

Ray could see she was ready to cry. He was sure Dennison did not want to retire, but he didn't want to upset her more. "Well... uh...I really don't know. Dave never talked about it with me. Maybe he wanted to spend time with the family or something." Ray did not even know if Dennison had any kids. Beatrice looked sadly down at the tissue in her hand.

"Anyway," Ray continued. "I just want you to know that your job is assured. I'll need someone with your experience and knowledge in the Marketing organization."

Beatrice looked up and smiled, just slightly. "Thank you, Mr. Pendleton. That was very nice to hear. Madge told me you were nice." Then she looked back down at her hands. "But I just don't know if I can go through a change like that."

Ray was surprised. Keeping her job was not her concern? "What do you mean?" he asked. "Nothing's changing. I mean, I might do things a little different, but the job's the same."

"No, no, you don't understand," she said looking down again. "It's not you...it's not the job. It's...oh I don't know. It's hard to explain." Tears started to appear and she dabbed her eyes with the tissue. She took a deep breath. "I came to work for Mr. Dennison almost fifteen years ago, a few months after my husband died. Mr. Gross had just been promoted to Vice President of Sales, and he brought Mr. Dennison in as Regional Manager in the Midwest. I was in terrible shape—a basket case. My husband and I had been married for twenty-seven years. Mr. Dennison was all nervous too, coming in to the home office and all. But he took the time to help me get through my first year back at work, even though he had his hands full in his new job." She smiled and shook her head. "Neither of us knew what we were doing. But we muddled through. And we've been muddling through ever since."

"Well," Ray said. "I intend to do some muddling myself."

She looked up and smiled weakly. "Oh no, Mr. Pendleton. You know much more, being a Professor and everything. You'll do just fine. It's me, you see. I don't know if I can...Over the years I've grown close to Mr. Dennison." She looked up at Ray. "It's not like I worked for Amsaco, as much as for Mr. Dennison. And now, just like that, he's gone. It's like I'm a widow again."

Ray did not know what to say. He could not understand how she could be making such a fuss about this. It was a job. He was not proposing marriage, and she was not a widow. He looked at his watch. It was almost 1:30. It would not be good to be late for his own staff meeting.

"Look, Beatrice," he said carefully. "I really don't know what to say. I'd like you to stay on the job. You can be very helpful to me and I respect your abilities." Actually, he had no idea about her abilities. "Let's think about it and talk again tomorrow. I hate to cut this short, but I have a staff meeting in two minutes, and a flight to catch at 2:30."

"Oh, certainly. I apologize. I didn't know your schedule. I shouldn't get all emotional like this and take your time. I—"

"That's OK, that's OK. I just had no idea what was going to happen today. We'll have more time tomorrow."

Ray was glad to get out of there. He was very uncomfortable talking personal issues—especially with a woman he scarcely knew who might burst into tears at any moment. He made a note to get back to her the next morning.

His staff meeting went well. After Ray made a short introduction, telling them he was more surprised than they were, the mood became less serious. Vince said he was confident Ray could be a good boss, because he was well trained when Vince was his boss.

Mike agreed, saying that Ray was doing very well in Mike's training program, and would probably graduate in a few years. Until then, Ray could not get in too much trouble as Executive Vice President, since not knowing anything was no handicap at that level.

Ed O'Brien laughed and offered his course in National Account Sales. Marv Crawford said it did not make any difference in his case, because at Amsaco, no one paid any attention to his OE Sales programs anyway.

Ray made appointments with O'Brien and Crawford, to have them bring him up to speed in their areas. After discussion of a few projects, Ray ended by saying he hoped they would just continue doing what they were doing.

After the meeting, he stopped by to ask Beatrice to help Madge start transferring his office. "You know, the phone and things. Then tomorrow we'll have time to talk."

When he and Evans got to the Falcon, it took very little time before they were leaning back in their seats, sipping scotch and sodas.

"Whew," said Ray, taking a deep breath. "This has been some day."

"Yeah," Evans agreed. "For a lot of people."

That seemed like an odd answer to Ray, but he did not question it. He asked, "Do you know what happened? With Dave?"

Evans looked at Ray, paused as if to make up his mind, and then answered, "All Ralph told me was that Dave didn't fit into his plans. I guess you do." They were quiet a moment. Then Evans added, "He bought me."

"What?"

"He bought me. Without Dave and Emil, he needed me to maintain ties with our traditional customers."

"He's right," said Ray thoughtfully.

"Damn right he's right. At least for a while. Until you and him get established. So he bought me for a couple or three years. I feel like a whore...but I guess we're all whores."

Ray felt uneasy. "Why didn't you retire?" he asked apprehensively. "You were planning on retiring."

Evans looked at Ray and smiled. "Well, you're such a nice guy that I didn't want to leave you hanging in the breeze. But besides that, let me show you some arithmetic. You're my boss now, so you'll see all my salary figures anyway. Yesterday I was making $60,000 a year. If I retired, I'd be bringing home about $25,000. He offered me $90,000. That's a big difference."

"Yeah, it sure is. Even if it's only for a couple of years."

"But it's more than a couple of years. My retirement salary is based on two things, the number of years with the company, and my salary for the last five years. With a few more years and the big jump for the last five, I'll be taking home $40,000. And that will be for the rest of my life…if I live that long."

Ray shook his head. "I didn't think Burch was that generous."

"He ain't. Just take what I'm making now, plus what you're making—"

"Not as much as you."

"I wouldn't think so. But add that up and compare it to what we were making, plus Dennison's salary, which had to be pretty big, probably six figures." Evans paused to let Ray do the arithmetic. "The company's still saving a bundle."

"Yeah," said Ray. "You've got to give Burch credit. He knows what he's doing."

"Yeah, you've got to respect that. He sure does know what he's doing…the prick."

They both laughed and then sat back to relax. It would be another hour before they got to Des Moines. Ray thought about his new position. Executive Vice President—holy shit! He never imagined anything like that when he came to Amsaco. When he and Dorothy had visited the…"Dorothy," he thought. "Oh my God!" He had not even called Dorothy, much less discussed whether to take the new job. How could he have forgotten? He had to call as soon as they landed.

"Hi, honey," he said when he got through to her at her office.

"Hi. I thought you were going to Iowa or someplace."

"I did. I'm in Des Moines now. Look, I won't get back until late tonight, but tomorrow night we have to go to Schuler's. We've got something to celebrate."

There was silence for a moment, and then she said, "It must be something good. Let me guess. You got fired and you're coming back to your family."

He did not really need the sarcasm, but went along. "No. Not that good. But how does Executive Vice President sound? Of Marketing."

"Isn't that Dave Dennison's title?"

"Dave's retiring. At least that's what Burch told me...I don't know really. But Burch called me in this morning. I was never so surprised in my—"

"This morning?"

"Yeah. I'm sorry I didn't call you sooner, honey. But I've been running around like crazy. Had to go right to Burch's staff meeting, and then call one of my own. And Beatrice was upset—"

"Beatrice?"

"Dave's secretary. She's been with Dave for a hundred years, and now she says she feels like a widow and—"

"I know the feeling."

Ray took a deep breath, feeling frustrated. "Anyway, I barely got out of there, and I was late for the plane. This was really the first time I could call."

"Well, I was in meetings most of the day, myself. You wouldn't have got me anyway. And we can talk about it tomorrow. I'll make reservations at Schuler's. At least we get to go out to dinner, alone."

Ray hung up the phone. He sighed and shook his head. This was a great promotion, with a big increase in salary, and he felt he had to apologize to his wife. Something did not make sense.

It was after midnight when he got home. Dorothy was asleep. He was up early the next morning. Before he left for work, he said little to Dorothy except "See you tonight."

■ ■ ■

There was a message to come to Burch's office.

"I understand Beatrice might be leaving," said Burch, coming right to the point. Without waiting for an answer, he continued, "This could actually work out well. Betty Johnson is not really a financial-type secretary, and Dick would like to promote Lorraine Cutter, his old girl. So you could have Betty, who knows all the customers and the field force. She's very strong in Marketing and could be a big help to you. I think that it—"

"Beatrice hasn't said she'll be leaving," Ray interrupted. "She just has some concerns. I'm going to talk to her this morning."

"Hmm," said Burch looking away from Ray. "Well, I think it

might be best if she did leave. You're free to offer her a generous retirement package. Check with Art and tell him I authorized it. Let me know how it works out."

With nothing else to say, Ray started to leave. Burch added one more comment as he left. "The best business decision would be to make these changes."

Ray had no doubt what his boss wanted. He went over to Art Webb's office before he spoke with Beatrice. Art was very cooperative when Ray told him what Burch had said.

"Sure," he said, looking at Beatrice's file. "We can do quite a bit for her. Let's see, she's 62, so she could take early retirement. But we could waive that and give her full retirement, what she would get if she retired at 65. We could even stretch that to 66 so she would have enough time to qualify for full medical benefits for the rest of her life. That would be the most important benefit."

Ray knew very little about the retirement policy. He was impressed by how easily the policy could change at the request of the President. He wondered briefly what would happen if some other 62-year-old wanted to retire with the same package. But it was not worth troubling himself about now. He would worry about that when he was 62.

When he got over to his new office, he asked Beatrice to come in. This time he sat down at his new desk, and Beatrice sat across from him. It was a big curved desk and she was five or six feet away from him. In the new chair he was much higher than Beatrice. He had forgotten that Dennison had made his own chair higher than the ones on the other side of the desk. Ray felt strange sitting at that level, looking down at Beatrice. Like a king on a throne. Beatrice did not seem to mind. She seemed much calmer and smiled when Ray started to speak.

"Beatrice, I've been thinking about our conversation yesterday."

"Yes. So have I," she said shaking her head. "I shouldn't have burdened you with my problems."

"Oh, that's OK. No problem. I understand completely. This is a major change and you may choose not to go along with it. I understand."

"I think maybe I shouldn't have said anything," she said, still smiling.

"No, you were right in telling me. You have a big decision to make, and I've checked it out to see what the company would do if you chose to retire."

Her smile disappeared and she looked surprised.

"I talked with Art Webb this morning and—"

"You did?"

"Yes, and I think he was very reasonable. Because of your important position, he said we could give you a retirement package as if you were retiring at age 66. That means you would get 100 percent of your retirement benefits, including medical for the rest of your life."

"That's very generous."

"Yes," he continued. "I was kind of surprised myself." He looked at the blank expression on her face. "But that doesn't mean you have to retire. I just wanted you to know what your options are. I would be pleased if you stayed."

She stood up. "I'll have to think about it," she said sadly, as she walked slowly out of the office.

"What's the matter with her?" Ray thought as he watched her leave. "All I did was give her her options. And either way she does all right. What else could I do?" But deep inside he knew what would please his boss. And he liked the idea of getting Betty Johnson as his secretary. Somehow he felt guilty.

Later that morning, Beatrice thanked him for everything and told him she would be retiring.

In the afternoon he interviewed Betty Johnson. He was very uneasy. He did not know how he could keep her busy with secretarial work. He did not write that many letters or memos. Travel arrangements were relatively simple since he used the company plane most of the time. And he was uncomfortable asking her to serve coffee. Back at Harvard, everyone took turns making coffee in a most informal atmosphere. This hierarchy was difficult for him.

He mentioned all this in the interview. She just smiled and told him not to worry. She had no problem serving coffee and she knew many useful things to do that would help him do his job. As long as she received her paycheck every week, and regular pay increases, there would be no trouble. She also added that she already knew his personality from Madge and there would be no trouble there, either. Also, it was too bad about Beatrice, but Ray would be much better off with Betty. Beatrice was very nice, but she was also very slow and was not really very smart. Betty then advised Ray to ask her about any Amsaco-related subject and she could probably help. After Ray's experience with Madge, he readily believed her. She then ended the interview by saying she would address him as Ray, except when others were present. Then he would be "Mr. Pendelton" if that was OK with him. He agreed, and the interview was over. Ray felt like Betty had been the one conducting the interview and had made the decision to allow him to be her boss...which was not far from the truth.

■ ■ ■

Ray was not expecting any wild celebration that night at Win Schuler's. Everyone at the office was congratulating him, recognizing what a great promotion he had gotten. He was now top management, a goal that 99 percent of them would never attain. He was an Amsaco celebrity. But Ray knew Dorothy would have other concerns. Would this require more travel and more time away from her and the kids? Would it require more of her time for entertaining? What effect would it have on her job? And Ray didn't know how he would answer those questions. He was apprehensive when they sat down to eat. Dorothy, however, seemed calm and not argumentative.

"We'll have the Côtes du Rhone, 1976," he said ordering the wine. Then turning to Dorothy he explained, "That's the wine we had at the Untico Management Meeting. I made a point to remember."

"We've come a long way," she laughed.

As they sipped the wine, he went over the salary increase, the bonus plans, the stock options, the annual physical, and the Price-Waterhouse tax and consulting service.

Dorothy just shook her head. "Unbelievable." She repeated, "Just unbelievable. Is anyone actually worth that much money?"

"You mean, aside from me," he joked.

"Especially you. You're still the same person who sat here celebrating with me when you made half that amount. Is what you're doing now so much more difficult...or important?"

He looked at her serious face. "I don't know, hon. I really don't know. Actually, I've wondered about that. When we were at the Untico Management Meeting, with all those top executives and all, it dawned on me that while we were all there, the companies were all operating very well without us. If a bomb exploded in that room, everything would still go on. We wouldn't even be missed. It seems that all the productive work is done at lower levels." He laughed. "I didn't mention this to anyone down there."

"But you're working six and seven days a week."

"I know, I know. And we're doing things, important things. Like we entertain Joe Beluga. We spend three days with him and we spend all kinds of money. But if we didn't, he still needs to buy shocks. And our Territory Managers will go in and tell him about all of our programs. And they'll check his stock and write up the order. And the programs they talk about were developed by Vince's group. I'm not really needed. And neither is Dick Wise or Jim Steele. Their operations will go on without them."

He was thinking this out logically and Dorothy just watched him and listened. "We're supposed to give direction. We make sure our Managers don't make bad decisions. But we'll make a lot of bad decisions, especially if we don't listen to our Managers. And yet," he said, "all the cases I taught at school were about Top Management decisions and how they determined the destiny of the company."

"Top Management or Presidents?" she asked. "I remember those cases were always about Chief Executive Officers."

"Right," he agreed, smiling as he thought how well she went right to the heart of the matter. "It's always a strong personality, CEO, or someone else. Someone who actually changes the character of the company."

"Then Ralph Burch is determining the character of Amsaco?" she reasoned. "That's scary."

He thought of his second conversation with Beatrice. He and Art Webb were really only carrying out Burch's directions. Art was in charge of all the Personnel functions in the company, and Ray was in charge of all the Marketing and Sales. And yet, they only did what Burch said they could.

"It *is* kind of scary," he agreed. "You don't really make the decisions unless you're the President."

"Then why do they pay you so much?"

"I don't know," he said. "Maybe the more they pay me, the more they can pay themselves. That makes sense. Because it goes on that way to the top. Everyone makes more than the guy reporting to him. And it carries over when you switch jobs. The other companies have the same salary levels. And no one wants to change it, because then they couldn't justify their own salary."

"Sounds like a conspiracy. Like some secret fraternity."

He laughed. "Yeah, the 'establishment.' You know, until now I never knew what 'establishment' really means."

"And now, you're in it."

"We're in it."

"Bullshit. I don't want anything to do with it."

He did not answer, but just smiled. "It seems like an evil group, doesn't it? Why is that?"

"Because it's not fair. You have all the employees working hard all day and then trying to make ends meet at home. And then you have the executives making enormous amounts of money, only because they have the power to decide how much they make."

Ray did not disagree with the idea of unfairness in compensation, but he took issue with the idea that anyone was working harder than he was. He was about to argue when the waiter came to take their order. This was a celebration, so he ordered the most expensive dinner, the surf and turf. Dorothy ordered the red snapper.

As the waiter left, Ray said, "Look, I don't know what's fair and what isn't, but I work pretty hard. I work long hours, and travel, and work under a lot of stress. I deserve more money."

"That much more?"

"Who knows?" But if the compensation system in the country is unfair, I'm not about to change it. I'm not *able* to change it. And if this is the way it works, I'd rather be on the Management side, the overcompensated side."

She paused and bit off the end of a breadstick. "I don't know," she said pensively. "Feels like prostitution."

Ray laughed. "That's what Mike said." He explained Burch's financial incentives to keep Evans from retiring. "Mike said he was bought. That he felt like a whore. But that he guessed we were all whores."

Dorothy looked at him sternly. *"I'm* not a whore."

Ray could think of nothing to answer. He was not calling her a whore. He was calling himself a whore. If she did not want to see the humor, he was not about to explain it. They were quiet for awhile. The waiter brought them their salads. Dorothy poked at hers and said, "So, Mike Evans is making more than you, and you're his boss."

"Well, he's making more salary. But when you add the bonuses and the other perks, I'm making more. I'm happy with what I'm getting, so why should I care if Mike's getting a good deal? He's been with the company for many years."

"But why just Mike? Dave Dennison had even more years."

Ray had no good answer. "I don't know. I have no idea what happened with Dave. I guess the difference is Burch wants Mike."

She continued her questioning. "But why was it so important to keep Mike? Burch doesn't spend money for no reason."

Ray knew his answer could lead to trouble, but he answered truthfully. "With Emil and Dave gone, and Burch not knowing the customers personally, that left just me...if Mike left. And I don't know the customers that well."

Ray watched her think as she finished her salad. "Let me see if I understand this," she said carefully. "You used to have Emil, Dave, Mike, and you to entertain the key customers...and Emil was very active."

Ray nodded. He could see where she was headed.

"And now there's just you and Mike and Burch, and Burch is not real active." She looked right at him. "My God, Ray, you're going to be busier than you are now."

Ray nodded. That was one of the things he loved about her. She was smart. He was glad he had not tried to lie.

"There's more." he said, almost apologetically. "I also have responsibility for National Account Sales and OE, the car companies. I'm not sure how much entertaining that will require, but there will be some. And I know there'll be a lot of meetings. Yeah, I'll be busy. But that's why they're paying me so much."

"Can't you do something about that?" she asked. "Delegate or something?"

"Oh sure, definitely," he said, looking for something good to talk about. "I don't have to run the National Sales Meeting anymore. Mike will. I just have to make a speech. And I don't have to do a lot of the Sales administration. In some ways I'll have less to do because I'll have experienced executives handling a lot of the work." He paused, thinking maybe he should stop there. But he had to be honest with Dorothy, and leaving something out was like lying. "With customers, I can't delegate. And neither can Ralph. Important customers want to talk to the top people. And Ralph's the top executive, and I'm the top Marketing guy now."

"We'll see even less of you. The kids will forget what you look like."

Ray was getting irritated. Why did he have to defend himself for getting a promotion? Why couldn't she just congratulate him and tell him how proud she was of him? They were silent as the main course was served. Ray poured Dorothy some more wine.

"You know, honey," he said carefully. "Of course, I don't know this for sure until I'm on the job for awhile, but I will have a lot of autonomy. In many ways I can make my own schedule, except for the industry events...and the company events. Maybe I can arrange to be home more."

She dismissed the idea with, "I'll believe it when I see it."

They ate in silence. Ray could see that Dorothy was thinking. Finally she asked, bluntly, "What's my role in this new job?"

He stopped eating and looked at her seriously. This was the most sensitive part of the evening. He did not want to screw it up, but the only way he knew to proceed was to tell the truth. "It's important...very important. It's everything that it's been, plus more contact with the other customers—the Sears-type accounts and the car companies. Marv Crawford says there's not that much entertaining with the car companies, at least for wives. But there's quite a bit with the national accounts. We'll be entertaining the top people at Sears, Penney's, Ward's, Kmart, you name it."

Dorothy ate slowly. "What happens if I don't go?" she asked, looking straight at Ray.

"Damn it," he thought. "Why does she do this?" This was the reaction that he feared, and it made him angry. But he took a deep breath and controlled his answer. "I don't know. It would be very awkward. It doesn't happen. Most wives love to get wined and dined...to go to the fancy resorts...the yacht. They want to be included."

"Aren't there any single men or divorced men?...Or men who have wives that are working and can't take time off?"

He was getting angrier, but he kept control and answered as best he could. "Not many. I don't really know. Art Donnelly of Federal Mogul was divorced recently and attends some stuff by himself. But he stands out like a sore thumb. I don't know. There may be others. But Christ, Dot, what are you saying? That you want me to do this alone? Burch probably wouldn't have offered me the job if he thought I'd be entertaining customers by myself. We're in this together. It's a package deal."

"But no one asked me," she blurted. "I'm being pushed into this crazy lifestyle because it's what you want. And nobody's asked me what I want."

"Well, what the hell *do* you want? There! I've asked you."

"You don't have to be nasty."

"Well, what the hell do you expect?" He was talking louder now. "I'm promoted to maybe the second-highest position in the company, with a hell of a lot of money, and recognition throughout Amsaco and Untico…and even the whole industry. And the only one who's not impressed is my wife."

"Oh, I'm impressed all right. I'm impressed with how you've become totally immersed in Amsaco. Nothing else matters. The kids could be at boarding school as far as you're concerned. And me, I'm nothing. I don't have any skills. I don't make any money. You laugh at the money I bring home. And the last thing you worry about is how I feel. My feelings are insignificant compared to Amsaco. They own you. Amsaco and Untico and any other 'Co' own you. Sure I'm impressed."

"Damn it," he said in total frustration. "What the hell do you want me to do?"

"Nothing. I don't want you to do anything," she said, looking away with tears in her eyes. "Just take me home."

They left without finishing their dinners. Neither of them said a word on the way home.

The kids were already in their rooms. Ray didn't go up to see them, but just sat down in front of the TV, without knowing what was on. Dorothy cleaned up in the kitchen and went directly upstairs. Ray heard her talking with Paul before she went to the bedroom. He sat in front of the TV for awhile, then turned it off and went upstairs. Everyone was already sleeping. He looked in on

Barbara and then Paul, but did not wake them. He went into the bedroom, undressed, and got into bed. Dorothy was lying with her back to him, apparently asleep. Actually, they both lay awake thinking for a long time.

■ ■ ■

Dorothy had to talk to someone, and she knew Helen Bloom would be understanding, more so than her mother or any of her other friends. In the past year they had met a few times for lunch, as well as the business dinners. Dorothy respected Helen's intelligence and independent thinking.

Over lunch, she told Helen about Ray's latest promotion and her fears that the company's demands on Ray's time could ruin their marriage. "What's left of our marriage. I'm almost ready to give up," she explained. "It seems like with each promotion he moves further away from me and the kids. And he keeps getting promoted."

Helen smiled. "He's not trying to move away," she said, touching Dorothy's arm. "He's just part of the system and the system makes the rules. Paul and I were lucky. He was all gung ho in the beginning; always meeting with this one or that one, joining industry associations, going to industry meetings. But we owned our own business, and when we saw what was happening, we could stop it. Not so in a big corporation."

"Then I just have to accept it?"

"Lots of others did. Marilyn Gross watched Emil grow with Amsaco." Then realizing what she had said, Helen laughed and added, "Literally grow."

This did not console Dorothy. "Marilyn just lived a separate life," she said. "like Ann Dennison and Irene Evans. I don't think I want that...only seeing my husband at company functions... raising the kids by myself. I mean, they're teenagers." She thought for a moment. "Ray and I talked a lot about how we had to stick together when the kids became teenagers. Now I have to handle things myself."

"Maybe you do," Helen stated simply. "But maybe you don't. What are your alternatives? Compare the alternatives with what you have now. What would your life be like if you ended your marriage?"

"Got a divorce?"

"Yes, you can't compare your present life with nothing. Maybe the alternative is worse. What would it be like? What about financially?"

Dorothy thought for a moment. "I don't think there would be any trouble financially. If Ray gave me half of what he makes now, it would be a lot more than we made at Harvard. We're not big spenders. No, I wouldn't see any problems financially."

"What about the kids?" Helen asked. "Could you handle that alone?"

"I'm doing that now," Dorothy answered. "That's the problem. I'm doing everything alone. In some ways it's like we're already divorced."

"Not quite," Helen countered. "You still sleep together. You have a man to make love to you."

"Not very often. It's like we're a threesome in bed—me, him, and Amsaco. Most nights we fall asleep angry, with our backs to each other."

"That's because you're in the middle of this thing." Helen explained. "Nothing's resolved. Once you make a decision, either way, things will be better. It may not be perfect, or the way it used to be, but it'll be better...either with Ray or someone else."

Dorothy laughed. "Someone else?"

"Is there someone else?"

"No."

"Could there be?"

"I suppose Emmett...Dean Clarke is a...possibility," Dorothy said, smiling. "He's been very warm to me." She paused. "In fact, he's been coming on to me, but I've been holding back. Nothing's happened."

"Could something happen? I'm not trying to be nosy, but if that is a possibility, then you have to bring it out in the open."

Dorothy smiled again. "I suppose. He's very nice. Something like Ray, actually. He's quiet and pleasant."

"Married?"

"Divorced. He has a daughter Barbara's age. He said his wife left him three years ago...wanted more excitement. Maybe we should just switch spouses. She can have Ray and all the excitement."

"Don't knock it. A lot of women would love to be in your position."

"I know, I know," Dorothy said with frustration. "Is it me? Am I being unreasonable?"

"No, you're not being unreasonable. You're in a situation you don't like, and you're the only one to decide if you are going to accept it. But you have a choice. You can stay or you can get out. And here's some advice…the only advice I'll give you. Don't stay and be miserable and make everyone else miserable. Either go along or get out. I'm not suggesting you go one way or the other. That's entirely up to you." She reached into her purse for her address book. "Here's a name of a friend of ours, Edgar Weintraub. He's an attorney, and a good one. If you want to get out, call him. If not, throw it away. It's your choice."

■ ■ ■

Back in her room, Dorothy stared at the piece of paper in her hand. "Edgar Weintraub, Divorce Attorney," it said ominously. She stared and wondered. What would it be like if she went to this attorney and got a divorce? She could become independent of Amsaco and free to make her own life. She could find another companion. If it wasn't Emmett, she was attractive enough to find someone else. As she told Helen, she could swing it financially with no trouble. Ray was making enough now to pay generous child support and the rent. She could make a decent salary at the university if she could work full time. Several women at school were divorced and getting along fine. One of them had told her how great it was to be free from her asshole husband.

But Ray was not an asshole. She still cared about him very much. She just couldn't go along with him on his corporate journey. Maybe he could find someone else who loved the wining and dining, and she could find someone to be with her. But Ray was still a good person. She did not want to hurt him.

Even Helen had said she liked Ray. "And Paul does too." she added. "Paul thinks he's honest, and with Paul that's everything."

It was not that she was starting to hate Ray. She was losing the Ray she had married. He was changing into a clone of a corporate executive. His life was not his wife and family anymore. It was the corporation: the sales, the profits, the market share...this corporation which did not value wives, except as ornaments or maids... where her life was insignificant...a closed men's "establishment." She was losing Ray to the corporation. She was not really leaving him; he was leaving her.

OK then, she would go see this Weintraub and find out what was involved in getting her freedom from the corporation. If Ray was happy with Amsaco, he could stay. But she wanted out. As Helen had said, "You have a choice."

She reached for the phone and then stopped. Did she really want to go through a divorce? Could she really do that to Ray? He would be shocked...stunned. He knew she was unhappy, but she knew divorce never entered his mind.

And the kids! They would be devastated. She knew some families that had gone through divorce. Their children's lives changed overnight. Their schoolwork and athletics had suffered. They became sullen and lost friends. All sorts of psychological problems arose. Her old friend, Jenny Gutkin, had told her that she had handled her divorce very well, but the kids were never the same. Could she do that to Paul and Barbara?

But what about her? What about her feelings? What about her life? She wanted someone to help her. Her mother wouldn't. Helen couldn't. She was all alone. She needed Ray....But he was the problem!

She lay down on the bed and started to cry. She thought about what it would be like for the kids and cried harder. She thought about being without Ray and she cried some more. The more she tried to stop, the harder she sobbed.

About an hour later she got up and went over to the phone.

■ ■ ■

When Ray came home that night, she told him they had to talk. He agreed and they went into the living room. He sat down on the couch and she sat in the chair, facing him.

"Ray, I can't stand the way things are going. We've got to talk about it."

"Good. I feel the same way."

"OK then, I have to tell you how I feel about your job and its effect on our marriage." He just nodded. She took a deep breath and continued. "It's ruining our marriage. The higher you go, the less marriage we have. We've turned into strangers in our own home."

"Oh, now Dot, I know it's a problem," he replied. "But it's not that bad. It's something we can work out. I can—"

"It is that bad," she interrupted. "Listen to me. Hear what I'm saying. I don't like what's happening to our life. And I don't see anything coming up that might change it. We're turning into Emil and Marilyn—we lead separate lives."

"Oh c'mon Dot. Our lives have changed. It's not the same as it was. But a lot of the changes are good. We do go to some pretty nice places, and we're living pretty—"

"I like the benefits. I like not having to worry about money. I like the prestige of being the wife of a successful executive. But the price is too high. We're not a family anymore. We're not—"

"We are too a family," he interrupted this time. "We're a family where the husband is working long hours, temporarily, until I get things under control."

"Temporarily?"

"Yes, temporarily. I'm still new at this sales game. Give me a chance to get to know the job. Then I can get some control of my schedule. Right now I'm just doing what everyone tells me to do. But eventually I'll understand the whole picture and then I'll decide what I'm going to do. Give me some time."

Dorothy looked sternly at Ray. She took another deep breath and said carefully, "OK Ray. I'll give you some time." He started to smile, but she added, "But this is serious, very serious. Now listen, listen carefully. I have been seriously considering divorce."

"You what?"

"I got the name of a divorce lawyer from Helen and—"

"You called a lawyer?"

"No, I didn't. But I've been considering it."

His arms flew up in the air in frustration. "Where the hell does Helen Bloom come off, telling you to see a lawyer?"

"She didn't. She just gave me the name and told me I have a choice."

"A choice?"

"Yes. I can accept my life or change it. I don't have to go blindly along with whatever you do. And if you won't listen, I can get out."

"But divorce, for chrissake."

"It's a choice," she said with tears forming in her eyes. "I thought about it, but I don't think I can do it. I thought about what it would do to the kids. The kids see us argue sometimes, and they want to see you more...but they really have no idea what's going on. They would be shattered." She looked straight at Ray and added. "I thought about how it would hurt you, and I decided I couldn't."

He did not know what to say.

"So," she continued, a little more calmly. "I've decided to try to make the best of the situation. To try and enjoy being a corporate wife, at least for now. I called Emmett and told him about the situation. He was very nice and we agreed I could work part-time. But I can't handle regular work, with dead-lines...the important stuff."

Ray heaved a sigh of relief and looked lovingly at his wife. "You scared the hell out of me."

"Good. Maybe then you'll do what you said you'd do...get your work under control so you can be a father and a husband again."

"I will, honey," he promised. "I swear I will."

He got up and walked over to her chair. He knelt down on one knee and took her hands. "It'll be all right. You'll see. But no more divorce talk. We're together for life. I'll do my part, I swear. But meanwhile, let's be happy. Let's enjoy the good parts of the job...the yacht, the resorts, the nice people..."

"Sure," she said, smiling a little and holding his hands. "And the money."

He laughed. "Right. We'll put a lot of money in the bank and maybe we'll join the country club, and get a new car, and—"

"And buy a new washer and dryer," she interrupted. "And new drapes, and stay at a nice hotel when we visit Boston."

"Yeah, if it will impress Henry, it's a good way to spend our money. And I think I should get a new suit...custom tailored...two suits."

"And I'll look for a new house...near the country club."

They both laughed. "You feel a little better now?" he asked.

"A little," she said, looking more serious. "I guess maybe I am a whore."

20. While You Can

Everything had been good since Ray's promotion. He was a celebrity at the National Sales Meeting. Congratulations came from all directions.

"Well deserved," said Al Donaldson.

"Now we've got some brains running the outfit," was Walt Morris' comment.

"Just watch us go now," Sam Kemper said enthusiastically.

"I hope y'awl will still play poker with us," drawled Elgin Cramer.

Ray did, and he really enjoyed himself. This was Ray's third year at the meeting and he knew almost everybody. Plus, this year he was everyone's boss, and a hero to boot. The salesmen were all happy because 1978 had been a good year and bonuses were substantial. They each had something good to say, and Ray's ego was inflated a little more by everyone he met.

Mike Evans was enjoying the meeting as much as Ray, but he had enough experience to know why. "Sure is fun when sales are up," he said to Ray at breakfast.

"Sure is."

"Enjoy it while you can."

■ ■ ■

Ray was scheduled for three trips on the yacht over the winter. He had the extra "yacht duty" because Mike thought it best that Burch go on the "American Trip" and meet several customers. "It's best if he's not thrown in too close with a customer until he knows him better. And I can watch him. You handle the yacht."

"OK, I'll make the sacrifice," Ray joked.

On the first trip, they entertained Doug Wilmot and his wife

Louise from Montgomery, and Irwin and Melanie Rodbell from Marietta, Georgia. Doug and Louise Wilmot had a warehouse and several jobbing stores in Alabama. Doug was in his late sixties and had carried Amsaco shocks for over thirty years. Dave Dennison had never considered him very important, so he had never been invited on the yacht. Mike Evans did not agree. "He's a good loyal customer," he told Ray. "And he gives us steady business year after year with very little trouble. I'd like to have more like him."

The Rodbells were thrilled to be on the yacht. They were Ray and Dorothy's age and had a small warehouse in Marietta, Georgia, which did a small amount of business in the Atlanta area. When Richards dropped the Amsaco line, however, Mike Evans took Irwin into every Richards Jobber and saved quite a bit of business. Many Jobbers had customers who liked the Amsaco shocks and were not about to change just because Richards did. With the Amsaco shock line as his lead, Irwin took advantage of the situation and was supplying products to these new accounts. His business had grown considerably and the yacht was icing on the cake.

There was no tension with this group. The Rodbells enjoyed the expensive liquor, trying a little of each. They praised Donald, the cook, when he served them his gourmet conch chowder, followed by the best-tasting grouper they had ever eaten. They even won a little money at the casino on Paradise Island.

Doug Wilmot just went along saying, "Lord a'mighty" as he watched all the money being spent. He carefully inspected the expensive liquor, but then chose to sip the Jack Daniels with a little water…very little. At dinner, he asked Donald what the expensive-looking bottle of wine cost. When he heard, "about $80 a bottle," he said, "Lord a'mighty" and would drink none of it. "That's one habit ah don't want to git into." The casino also impressed him. "Ah never saw so many people tryin' so hard to throw away their money," he said.

"I understand your customers are like that when they come into your stores," Irwin kidded.

"Well, sure," Doug went along. "But at least their buggies run better when they're done."

When they were getting ready to leave, Doug hugged Dorothy and said to Ray, "Sonny, you treat this lady raht, you hear?"

Louise took Dorothy's hand in hers and said warmly, "Ah really would like to have y'awl visit us. You come with your husband next time he comes down on business. We would be proud to have y'awl stay in our home."

"We'll show y'awl what southern hospitality is all about," Doug agreed. Then, putting his arm around Ray's shoulders he added, "Yer not 'fraid of snakes, are ye?"

Ray did not even want to think about what Doug had in mind.

■ ■ ■

Ralph Burch held the Christmas party at the Jackson Country Club for company officers and wives. The men wore their best suits, while the women could dress up as much as they wanted, short of wearing evening gowns. The hors d'oeuvres were excellent, ranging from gigantic shrimp to oysters Rockefeller to many that Ray had never seen before. When Ray commented that the filet mignon was slightly overdone, Dorothy laughed. "I remember when you couldn't spell filet mignon." The meal was complemented by good wine and champagne, and topped off with a chocolate soufflé.

Socially, however, it was less successful. This was the first meeting of the new executive group and most of the wives did not know each other. Dorothy knew only Irene Evans. Ralph Burch spent time talking to each couple, as a host was supposed to do, and he made a brief speech about how well the company was doing. He went through the motions, saying all the right words.

"He was like a robot," Dorothy said later.

■ ■ ■

When it came time for the year-end bonuses, Ray expected mostly some kind words, such as "You're doing a fine job," or "Keep up the good work," or even, "Untico is pleased with your work." He was not expecting much money.

When Burch called him into his office, he explained that Ray's Amsaco bonus was prorated on the number of months he was in each position, and therefore only came to $15,000. With a full year as Executive Vice President he could expect more…as long as they surpassed budgeted profits. He handed Ray the check. He then explained that the other bonus, the Untico bonus, was based on only three months in the plan, so was really only a token payment. The "token" was $10,000.

When he showed the checks to Dorothy, she stared at them and then at Ray. "That's just about what you were making as a Professor," she said in disbelief.

"And next year it should be more…a lot more," Ray added, still in shock. "This should be a very good year."

■ ■ ■

The second yacht trip, in February, was not as friendly as the previous one. Dorothy was happy to take Helen and Paul Bloom because of her friendship with Helen. Ray was a little uneasy because the Blooms knew about their marital problems. The other couple, Jack and Rene Maluk from Cleveland, were nice enough, but the overall atmosphere was cold.

Both customers were big—in Amsaco's top five every year. They had been on the yacht before with Emil, so Ray was like a substitute. Their importance justified the presence of Amasco's top executive, but Burch was off somewhere in the Greek Islands with other customers. To them, Ray was just a "peddler" playing the host.

There was little Ray could do for them other than host. Both Bloom and Maluk knew their business better than Ray, and there were no real issues to discuss. There was also nothing that Ray could tell them about the yacht or the Bahamas. They knew Reuben the captain, Donald the cook, and Patrick the first mate. There were warm greetings when they came on board. And they knew what they wanted to do. In fact, they introduced Dorothy and Ray to Chub Cay.

It was Helen's idea to cruise over to Chub Cay where there was a beautiful beach and solitude. They docked in the harbor on the southwest end of the little island. Nearby there was nothing but an office/general store and a weathered tennis court. Ray was not impressed until they walked over to the east side and saw the beautiful white-sand beach stretching as far as he could see, with no other person in sight.

"It's beautiful," said Dorothy. "Perfect."

Helen smiled. "And the water is absolutely clear. This is my favorite place in the Bahamas…maybe anywhere."

Donald had packed them a picnic basket with delicious hors d'oeuvres, sandwiches, fruit, cheese, and wine. They laid the food out on the blankets, opened the wine, and enjoyed the peaceful lunch. Then they swam, snorkeled, sunbathed, and sipped more wine. "This is heaven," Dorothy said as she stared at the clear blue sky and absorbed the warm sun.

They were relaxing for about an hour, when Jack noticed someone else further north up the beach. Two people were walking along the water's edge toward them.

"Are they wearing what I think they're wearing?" asked Jack.

They all looked up. Dorothy gasped. "I don't think they're wearing anything."

"Yeah," said Jack. "That's what I thought they were wearing."

Paul reached into the carrying bag and pulled out the binoculars. "Yep," he said, looking up the beach. "They're getting an even tan. Nice-looking young couple."

"Put those away," said Helen, grabbing the binoculars. "Let them have some privacy. We're the intruders here."

"We're not intruding," Paul argued. "We're just using the beach. They're the ones coming toward us. Maybe they'd like a glass of wine."

They did not find out, however, as the couple disappeared into a small cabin hidden back in the trees.

"Isn't that beautiful?" Dorothy said softly. "Vacationing on this isolated island where you don't even have to wear clothes. Just the two of them."

"I hope we didn't spoil their vacation," said Rene.

A short time later the couple came back out, still naked, and ran into the water. Then they ran out and rolled around in the sand, then ran back into the water. They were far enough away to ignore the "intruders," but close enough that their laughter could be heard.

"They must be right outside their cabin," Dorothy figured. "Maybe we should move. This might even be their honeymoon."

"Good idea," said Helen.

They picked up their blankets and food and moved another 200 feet or so away.

Paul kept kidding Helen by reaching for the binoculars, but she would just hit his hand and say, "Leave them alone."

Walking back to the boat, Dorothy grabbed onto Ray's arm, put her head on his shoulder and said, "Isn't that romantic?"

Ray looked at his wife lovingly. This was the first time in quite a while that she had talked to him like that. He smiled at her and was about to answer when Jack walked by. He had heard Dorothy, and commented, "Yeah, except for getting sand up your ass."

Ray made the mistake of laughing. The moment was spoiled.

Dorothy let go of Ray's arm and walked back in silence.

■ ■ ■

Aside from the money, the best part of the job for Ray was enjoying the results of good sales. The whole industry had been picking up since summer. Some people said it was because of the early winter. Others said that high new car sales five years before meant that a lot of cars were getting into the four-to-ten-year-old range, when replacement sales peaked. Still others tied it into the national economy, or the high interest rates that prompted people to repair their cars rather than buy new ones. Ray had no idea why sales were increasing. He knew it was not because of his Foreign Car Program.

But it did not matter why sales were up. They were up and that meant the factory was busy, which meant they were running more efficiently, which meant profits were up. With profits up the Amsaco management looked good in the eyes of Untico's executives. Everyone was happy.

The customers were happy. Ray's reception was warmer and more congenial when he visited them, or met them at meetings, or took them on the yacht. As long as Amsaco could deliver product for them to sell, they were content. The new plant in Harrisonburg and the new equipment gave Amsaco more than enough capacity to meet these demands. The foreign shock sales were insignificant, but the added capacity to build them proved crucial.

Amsaco customers were especially happy because they were doing better than their competitors, who were having a big problem with delivery. Closing down their Columbus plant was giving Blackwell more problems than they bargained for. They could not supply enough internal parts for their shocks. While the Kinston, North Carolina, plant had enough assembly capacity to meet the demand, they had never tried to build the parts. Columbus had always supplied parts to all the smaller plants.

Anticipating this, Blackwell had Columbus build a stock of key parts to last until the machinery and tools could be shipped from

Columbus and installed in Kinston. What they did not consider were the bitter feelings involved in closing the plant. Actually, Tom Sunday, the Production Control Manager in Columbus, did know of the bitter feelings, and shared them, thinking his own job might be in danger. When his top aide told him there might be more problems than company Management expected, he said. "They told me to build three months of parts. And said they had a good termination agreement with the union...a hell of a lot better one than we'll get when we get canned. Fuck 'em. Three months is what they asked for and three months is what they'll get."

The machinery arrived in Kinston with all sorts of problems. Sensitive dies had deep scratches, making them useless. Electrical connections were switched on old machinery for which they had no electrical drawings. Key machine parts were missing. Much of the equipment was old, with replacement parts very difficult to find, and the more important the part, the more likely it would be missing. The UAW officially denied any sabotage, but there was no doubt some people, who knew what they were doing, were making sure there would be no production without the Columbus plant.

By the time the Manufacturing Group realized what was happening, they were in deep trouble. They immediately went outside the company to try to buy parts. Some they could get quickly, but for others it required months to get tools and dies built. They frantically tried to get their equipment to turn out whatever they could, working three shifts, seven days a week. They also looked to buy complete shocks outside.

Jim Steele was approached to supply certain Amsaco shocks that were interchangeable with Blackwell's. He informed everyone at Burch's Saturday morning staff meeting. "They're in bad shape," he explained. "They'll take almost anything and pay top price. We can almost choose what we want to supply, make good production runs, and ship them bulk. Blackwell will package them. We can make some good money for six months to a year." He chuckled. "It's a manufacturing man's dream."

Ray was against it. "I'd rather have them face the marketing man's nightmare," he declared emphatically. "Failure to deliver! This gives us a chance to pick up some market share. Every shock we don't ship them increases our market share."

"Not necessarily," Steele argued. "They can still buy from Crane."

What Steele did not know was that Crane was having their own problems. When Crane lost the Sears account, Lorenzo had closed down a shock assembly line and replaced it with new water pump and rocker arm lines. This reduced their shock capacity more than just the Sears volume. They still had more capacity than they needed when sales were down, but with the pickup in sales, they were scrambling to deliver—not as badly as Blackwell, but certainly they were not in any position to supply a competitor.

Ray argued against helping Blackwell. "It's a major opportunity," he said. "With the addition of Sears, we should push to 23 or 24 percent of the market, maybe 25. But Blackwell's still over 40." He paused to let the numbers sink in. "But if we can take some business directly from Blackwell, they go down while we go up. We'll be approaching 30 percent and they'll drop into the thirties. And some of that will be permanent, depending on who we can change over. We shouldn't look at immediate profits. Market share is what we should aim at...long term."

Burch was quiet, letting them argue. He liked the idea of the immediate profits. You could put those in the bank. But he also understood the idea of market share. They would make plenty of money this year anyway. Market share would improve profits every year. That would be good to report to Dallas. The Professor knew what he was talking about. But there was another factor to consider. Blackwell was battling the UAW, and Burch did not want the UAW to win. It would be a bad precedent, especially if Amsaco ever wanted to close their own expensive UAW plant in Jackson. And if they ever did, they might need Blackwell's help. Helping Blackwell now would be good business, and understood as such by Blackwell's Management.

"Sell them what you can," Burch interrupted, ending the argument. "Just be sure you don't get us overextended."

Since Burch didn't bother to explain his reasoning, Ray was frustrated. He could not understand why market share was not the prime factor. In his mind, Burch was greedy for immediate profits at the expense of long-term growth.

Even with help from Amsaco, however, Blackwell could not deliver to meet the increasing demand. As they had difficulty filling complete orders, the customers would increase the size of their orders, and Blackwell slipped behind even further. Many Blackwell customers were unhappy. Reuben Bennett in Miami was talking about switching to Amsaco, and Mike Evans was going down to Kansas City to speak with Harry Liscio.

"Harry is really pissed at Blackwell," he told Ray. "Feels they should give special service to a long-time customer like him. It really grinds him when one of his Jobbers calls a competitor because Harry can't deliver. We've been after Harry for a long time. This might be our chance."

■ ■ ■

On his third yacht trip, in early March, Ray sat up on the top deck with his back to the wind and the drizzle, looking out at the rough seas. He had been feeling a little queasy below and came up to breathe fresh air. He was feeling better and enjoying his solitude.

The others were down below socializing as they made the three-hour trip from Lyford to Chub Cay. He felt somewhat guilty, leaving Dorothy alone with the Bermans. But she could have come up with him if she chose. Actually, she had gotten to like Gina, once they could talk without Ron dominating the conversation. She liked Elaine too.

It had worked out well so far, having Sid and Elaine along as well as Ron and Gina. Ron was not so obnoxious when his father was there. Mike Evans had suggested this arrangement when Ray had protested taking Ron on the yacht.

"You've got to take him," Mike had told him. "He'll be the boss when his father retires, and he knows about the boat from Sid. It would be an insult not to invite him."

"But cooped up with that guy for three days? Dorothy will divorce me."

"Take Sid and Elaine too. Anyway Sid needs some stroking, with Emil gone."

Ray thought for a moment and asked, "Can we take two guys from the same company?"

Mike looked at Ray quizzically. "I don't know. I'll check with my boss."

Ray laughed. Mike said, "We can do whatever we want. We run Sales."

Dorothy and Ray had no trouble with Ron as they made a point of not being with him except when his father was around. Ron caught Ray a couple of times, but Ray just listened politely until he could get away. Dorothy escaped entirely.

When they told the Bermans the Chub Cay story, Sid and Elaine decided to go over there. They did not expect to see any naked couples, but the quiet white-sand beach sounded appealing.

Ron was looking forward to some kind of sexual adventure, even if it only involved looking. "After awhile," he explained when he caught Ray alone, "you get tired of looking at the same pussy every night."

Ray did not think Ron would follow him up to the top deck in this bad weather and he felt secure. Better than secure. He was quite comfortable in his rain gear. The salt air smell was clean and natural. The whitecaps were breaking in a mesmerizing rhythm for as far as he could see. The boat surged up and down with the waves, and Ray felt safe with Captain Reuben at the helm. He leaned back with his hands behind his head, looking out at the horizon. Life was good. When sales were good, life was good. He had never thought about that when he was teaching.

At school, he would just look at the situation analytically. What was happening in the market? What were the present capabilities of the company? What were the choices available? Therefore, what action should be taken? Personalities were not considered. Neither were the personal ambitions of the people involved, or the politics, or fears, or moods. Emotions played no part in the analysis. The important thing was to understand the situation so that intelligent decisions could be made.

His customers, however, were not particularly interested in the reasons why things were good or bad. Their businesses were their livelihoods. It put food on the table, put the kids through college, and paid for membership in the country club. They wanted results...good results. And they did not care why or how.

The same was true with Amsaco's executives. They wanted profits and returns on investments and company growth. These results enabled them to keep their jobs and advance to better ones. When things were right, everyone was happy, everyone was a hero. Besides his happy customers, his own field force loved Ray right now because bonuses were good and prospects were even better. Untico was happy because sales and profits were growing. They did not care if the Foreign Car Program was doing well, or how they had gotten the Sears account. They wanted results and Ray was giving them outstanding numbers—it didn't matter how.

He wondered how things were going at Blackwell and Crane. The Blackwell field force must be going crazy trying to explain why they could not keep up with the orders. He would not want Dave Brown's job right now. Even Andy Wilson must be in trouble with the board, trying to explain the disaster at Kinston. And George Lorenzo at Crane—he had to be in trouble for losing an account like Sears. Ray remembered how depressed he had been a year ago when things were going badly for him, and now he felt a little sorry for "Brownie," and Wilson, and Lorenzo. He needn't have.

21. Balls

At Crane, Lorenzo had been surprised when Markham told him they were losing Sears. He thought Sears had reluctantly accepted the increase and it was a closed issue. He never thought they would change lines. Either he had miscalculated or Markham was sabotaging him. He was not sure. At any rate, he had to figure out what to do.

He had already prepared a presentation for Grady Leach, President of Crane, bragging about the increased profits from the price increase. Now he would have to explain why it was better to lose the Sears business. He did not look at this task as "damage control." It was more in the line of turning this "sow's ear" into a "silk purse." Not a big problem!

What he had to do was show the company was making more money by not wasting capacity on the low-profit Sears business. The first thing was to fill in the production void. Luckily, business was up on almost all lines. He needed more capacity for many products, so he shut down a shock assembly line and replaced it with rocker arm and water pump lines.

Now he was running almost all lines at capacity, and they all had higher margins than the Sears shock business. Since all automotive parts were selling well, sales were higher than the year before, when they had the Sears business. With the higher margins, profits were higher than the year before also. Of course, if they had the Sears business in addition, profits would have been even higher. But Lorenzo covered this by stating they would not have had the capacity for that much business, which was very difficult to prove.

He presented this scenario to Grady Leach, who was so impressed with Lorenzo's "efficient use of assets," that he asked him to present it to the Board.

"Sometimes smaller is better," Lorenzo told the Board. "Most Managers think sales volume is all that is needed to generate profit. But we're a little more discriminating. We want more business as much as anyone, but it has to be worthwhile. It has to be profitable. When I looked closely at the Sears business, it did not measure up to our profitability goals. And Sears was very arrogant. 'This is the way we do business and you have to do it our way,' was their attitude. Well we didn't. We made a calculated decision to make that business worthwhile or put our efforts elsewhere. Sears is a big company, but they don't run our business."

Lorenzo looked at the smiles of approval and continued. "Since we parted company with Sears, we've not only eliminated the costs of serving this large account, but we've made up most of that shock business with more profitable shock business. In addition, we've used the additional capacity for other more profitable products."

He then showed slides of the numbers, ending with an estimated net profit increase from the year before of almost one million dollars. He attributed this mainly to dropping Sears. The Board was impressed, and congratulated Lorenzo and Leach for having the "balls" to stand up to Sears.

Markham, who had been invited to the presentation, just sat listening to the praise. Here Lorenzo had lost the biggest shock account in the country through his own stupid miscalculation, and he was being congratulated by the Board. Markham had enough experience, however, to go with the flow. He stood up smiling and shook hands with several Board members. "That's our leader," he said, putting on a proud expression.

■ ■ ■

At Blackwell, Andrew Wilson was in a similar position. He had a Board meeting coming up and he did not want them to know what a disaster they were facing as a result of closing the Columbus plant. Not only had he closed a plant just when they needed the capacity, but he had chosen the key plant that supplied parts to all the other plants.

"How bad is it?" he asked Jeff Baldino, his Vice President of Manufacturing, at an emergency staff meeting.

"We're in trouble," Baldino answered nervously. "Up to now we've had some back-order problems because of no production from Columbus. But we can handle that. The trouble is that Kinston's trying to ship at 118 percent of capacity at the same time they're trying to install the Columbus equipment. If we can't get that equipment up, the worst is yet to come."

"How long before that equipment's working?"

"Some of it pretty soon, but some of it never." Wilson and the others looked shocked.

"This is what we're doing," Baldino explained. "We're fixing up the equipment we know we can fix. We'll have more equipment up and running each month...each week, actually. And 40 to 50 percent of our parts will be produced within three months. At the same time we've got eight different vendors working overtime, tooling up for the other parts—to replace the worst machines. We'll have some parts dribbling in the next few months, but on some critical ones we're looking at six to nine months, maybe a year."

Brownie moaned.

"But we're also looking outside to buy complete shocks," Baldino continued. "Europe, South America, even Japan. And it looks like Amsaco will sell us a bunch."

"Amsaco will sell us?" asked Wilson and Brownie almost simultaneously.

"They said they will. Crane won't because they don't have the capacity. They shut down a line when they lost Sears. But Amsaco opened their new plant in Virginia, so I guess they're glad to get the volume."

"Those lucky bastards," Wilson muttered. "They open a plant while we close one...just before the market opens up. They're not that smart...just lucky."

"Evans is smart enough," Brownie said thoughtfully. "Smart enough to use this to take business." He looked at Wilson. "If it takes us a year to get out of this, those bastards will be bigger than we are."

Wilson nodded. He looked at Morgan Farnsworth. "What will this do to us financially?"

"Not as bad as you might think." Farnsworth answered. "Don't forget, we're coming off a few bad years. This would have been a fantastic year if we could have shipped. But as it is, we'll sell everything we can make and everything we can buy. If we can partially recover by the middle of the year, we should still be profitable…if our customers don't panic."

"They won't panic," Brownie stated emphatically. "We'll lose some, but most will stay with us."

Wilson sat back and thought. "OK," he said. "As long as we can stay profitable, I think I can handle the Board."

■ ■ ■

"We're in a war," he told the Board after carefully explaining the situation. "And this is just the first battle. The UAW is pulling everything they can to beat us, because the stakes are high… survival. But we're gonna win. We're gonna have casualties, but we can handle them. This year will be the toughest. Our costs will be high. We're gonna lose some customers. But, even with all that, we're still gonna show a profit, and we'll still be the top shock absorber company in the industry."

He stopped to let that sink in. Several Board members nodded in approval.

"But next year," he continued, "and every year after that, we will be even stronger. We'll have a low-cost operation and our competitors will not be able to keep up with us. We'll regain any market we lost, and we'll be more profitable than we've ever been. We'll run our business the way we want to, the way it should be run, without the UAW to hold us back."

Stan McCloud stood up to get the attention of the Board. "I'd like to say something," he said, looking around. "Something I think we are all thinking. We're lucky to have a CEO like Andy, with the balls to stand up to the UAW."

"You bet," said Charlie Anderson.

The others joined in, voicing their approval. The meeting halted as they walked over to shake Wilson's hand.

"You can count on our support," McCloud promised.

No one asked why they did not choose a less-busy time to take this dangerous action, or why they did not find outside sources *before* the move. They were in a war, and they were backing their general.

■ ■ ■

Ralph Burch sat at his desk, punching numbers into his calculator. He was double-checking Dick Wise's estimates for the year, before next week's meeting in Dallas. The numbers looked very good. Even his worst scenario showed a 30 percent increase in profit over last year. More likely it would approach 50 percent.

Everything was going well. The Sears account and the booming automotive business boosted sales way above last year's. Blackwell's production problems added even more to sales. Partly this was what Amsaco was shipping directly to Blackwell. More important were the shocks Amsaco's distributors were selling to Blackwell's Jobbers. It was extremely frustrating for Blackwell's distributors, not being able to deliver to their own customers. Some were unhappy enough to consider a change. Harry Liscio had given Mike Evans the go-ahead to change him over, right after the Academy dinner.

"I don't want this to be the topic of conversation at the Academy," he told Mike. "But I've had all I can take. Schedule the changeover a week or so after the dinner." Evans scheduled it seven days after the dinner.

Burch was pleased. Emil had been after Harry Liscio for years. "He's the perfect customer," Emil had said. "He owns the Kansas City territory. No one comes close to him. And he doesn't change lines very often; he's loyal. All you have to do is do your job. Give him a fair price, give him manpower help to run his programs, give him a good product, and deliver it on time. He'll stick with you. Some day I'm going to get him."

Emil never did, but Burch did, and he intended to take credit for it in Dallas. He would also take credit for the reduction in costs resulting from Jim Steele's new equipment and Bob Simpranian's product standardization and consolidation. Burch knew that he was not responsible for these successful programs, and he understood very well that he would have vetoed the appropriation when it went through, if he had been at Amsaco at that time. It was this very expansion when sales were down that cost Emil his job. Emil knew that sales would eventually turn up, but they did not until Emil was out and Burch was in. And of course, no one knew that Crane would shut down a shock assembly line and Blackwell would close their key plant.

Everything was going Burch's way. Even the Jackson plant was running better. The UAW in Jackson was nervous because of Blackwell's closing of their Indiana plant; they did not want that to happen at Amsaco. All of a sudden Jackson became more efficient. Production increased just when it was needed. Overtime was worked without complaint. The number of grievances went down. The foremen could not believe the cooperative attitude.

Although Emil would have called Burch a "lucky bastard" for taking over just when things turned up, Burch did not consider it entirely a matter of luck. These events were happening while he was in charge, and he was taking steps appropriate to deal with them.

He was not excited or overjoyed. He knew that if this year was very good, next year could be less good and would be measured against it. His job now was to maximize profits for next year. It was not something to be emotional about; it was his job.

■ ■ ■

At the Academy dinner, Andy Wilson had collared Burch at cocktails. He described his presentation to his Board. "They congratulated us on having the balls to take on the UAW," he told Burch. Even though Wilson had been drinking, he knew exactly what he was saying. He wanted Burch to believe that Blackwell's problems were a result of a planned fight with the UAW, not mismanagement. In that respect, they were allies, and Burch might need Wilson's help some day. Burch understood the message. He also understood that Wilson had gotten himself into a position where he had to wave the flag and fight the union in order to justify what was happening to Blackwell. Burch was somewhat jealous of the image that Wilson had developed as a result of these events.

"They're equating 'having balls' with making poor business decisions," he told Ray after the dinner.

The same evening, Joe Markham had told Mike Evans about Lorenzo's presentation to Crane's Board. "You got to understand, Mike, Lorenzo fucked up royally. He was acting as if he knew every-thing and Peterson and I were idiots. I just followed his orders and figured we'd lose Sears…and Lorenzo would go out with 'em." Evans nodded his understanding.

"Then the bastard turns it around so the Board thinks he knew what he was doing. They congratulate him on having the balls to stand up to Sears. He's got balls all right. He'll probably drive us right into Chapter 11...and then they'll make him President."

When Mike told Ray and Burch about his conversation, Ray laughed. "And I thought it was my ingenious Sears plan that got us the account."

Burch was not laughing. He just shook his head and muttered, "Balls."

Back in his office though, he thought more objectively about the situation, especially about Sears. No matter how they had gotten Sears, there was no doubt that Sears was a good account. Their sales volume made a significant contribution to profits, even if the profit margin was low. By the same token, however, even a small increase in price would significantly improve the profit picture. And that would be needed in 1980, if they were to improve on 1979. Some way, they had to get more out of Sears. In fact, price increases would be needed with all customers. Sales could not grow in 1980 as much as they had in 1979. Therefore, additional profits had to come from price increases and cost reductions.

Yes, 1980 looked like the time to get started on cost reductions. The organization would be in position to handle some cuts. In fact, they would need some to keep from getting too fat. The original plan had been delayed because of increased sales, but now it was time.

Burch was uncomfortable with customers and did not like to work on increasing sales. Let the salesmen do that. Cutting costs, however, was not only enjoyable, but he was good at it. Some Managers had a hard time with cost-cutting, especially reducing staff. From Burch's view, they did not have the strength to make the tough decisions...they did not have the "balls." But he did. If necessary, he could be ruthless. Carl Buzzard had once complimented him by saying, "You're the most ruthless Manager I know." And he was right. Burch could fire his Managers, make drastic cuts in headcount, significantly reduce expenses, and even close down a plant, if it would improve profits.

As he sat contemplating what was to happen, he was overcome with a warm, comfortable feeling, and he almost smiled. "I'll show them who's got balls," he thought, as he picked up the phone to call Carl Buzzard.

22. Buzzard

One Saturday morning, Burch walked into the staff meeting with the meanest-looking man Ray had ever seen. His high cheekbones, craggy complexion, and squinty eyes, together with large teeth in a large mouth, gave him a prehistoric look, like the pictures Ray had seen of Neanderthals. But this one was wearing a suit and tie.

"This is Carl Buzzard," said Burch with no emotion. "He will be taking over for Jim Steele, who is retiring." Burch said no more and no one asked any questions.

But Ray had plenty of questions. Why was Jim leaving? Had he done something wrong? As far as Ray knew, Jim was the most capable executive in the company. All his plants were running well, including the new operation in Harrisonburg. Ted Lyons had done so well starting the new plant that Steele had made him permanent Plant Manager. And Lyons had the new equipment running well, producing Bob Simpranian's new line of standardized, consolidated shocks. While their competitors were in trouble, Steele was delivering good product, on time, and Amsaco customers were happy. Ray knew that this production complex was all the result of Steele's vision and his professional ability to put his vision into practice. Why was he retiring? Was there something wrong with his health? Did he have a disagreement with Burch?

Ray thought Dick Wise might know and asked him after the meeting.

"Steele's costs are too high," he answered curtly. "There's too much fat in Manufacturing...and Engineering too."

"That's it?" Ray asked incredulously. "His costs are high? I always thought he ran a solid organization. Couldn't Burch just ask him to reduce costs?"

"He can't reduce costs like Buzzard. You watch. That's Buzzard's strength. He and Ralph got their MBAs together. He's real strong financially, and he's the guy Ralph wants on his team."

"Strong financially? You mean he's an accountant?"

Wise smiled. "Sure. Accountants know how to run the business."

"They'd better," Ray answered, shaking his head slowly. He thought for a moment and added, "I'm the only one in that meeting now that's not an accountant."

Wise smiled even wider. "I told you we were taking over."

■ ■ ■

Ray got to see Buzzard in action on a trip to Harrisonburg. Buzzard was taking Bob Simpranian and Ken Swanson to meet with Lyons and his staff in an effort to reduce inventory costs. Mike Evans and Ray were heading for Atlanta to see the Rodbell's operation. They also had been contacted by Les Richards, who asked if they could drop by to see him right away. This was a chance to get both visits in on the same day.

"I think Rodbell's killing him," Mike surmised. "He may want some sort of truce...might even want to come back. He made a bad move, leaving Amsaco.

"I don't know if we should take him back," Ray argued. "I like Rodbell. He's done a great job for us. That's the type of guy you like to work with."

"Can't let that get in the way of business," said Evans. "If we can get Richards back, we move. We don't ask questions. Richards is several times bigger than Rodbell. And besides, look at the message that sends to anyone else who thinks of leaving us."

"But after everything Rodbell's done for us...when we really needed him? We just throw him to the wolves?"

"No, no. We stay with him. He'll be all right. Some of his additional business will stick with him, and he'll be a lot bigger than when we started. But Richards is the top account. Rodbell will be the first to understand when you tell him."

"When *I* tell him?"

"Sure. You're his boat buddy. What do you think that yacht's for, just to have a good time?" Evans laughed. "But seriously, we don't know what Richards wants. He may only want to chew us out...or give a message to Rodbell. We don't know. But if he does come back, there might be some sort of agreement they can come to…to stay out of each other's hair. But we don't want to get involved in that. It's illegal."

"And immoral," Ray added.

"And fattening." Evans saw Ray's questioning look, so he explained. "Everything we want to do is either illegal, immoral, or fattening."

■ ■ ■

Ray had agreed with Buzzard that they would take the Falcon into Harrisonburg and tour the plant. Then he and Evans would fly down to Atlanta for their meetings and pick Buzzard up on the way back. They were leaving at 6:00 in the morning so they could make the trip in one day. This would be an efficient way to use the Falcon, and saving money for Amsaco was getting to be more and more popular.

Besides, Ray wanted to see the Harrisonburg plant in operation and give Ted Lyons a chance to show off his new equipment and his new people. This did not happen. Buzzard did all the talking on the tour. As far as Ray could see, the operation was neat and clean, the equipment was impressive, and the people were working pretty hard. Buzzard did not notice any of that.

Instead, he found all sorts of things wrong. He started at the airport. Ted Lyons picked them up at the airport in Staunton in the company station wagon. They were a little crowded with six people, and this seemed to irritate Buzzard. Rather than crowd three people in the front, he made Swanson sit in the folding seat in the back, facing the rear. Simpranian volunteered to sit back there with him, so Lyons drove, Buzzard sat in front with him, and Ray and Evans sat in the backseat. Buzzard then heckled Lyons for driving too slowly. "Can't this fuckin' truck go any faster?"

When they got to the plant, they had to wait for the guard to open the gate. He had been doing something at the tractor shed about fifty yards away, and was not too fast getting back. As they were getting out of the car, Buzzard reprimanded Lyons in front of the guard. "Look, I'm runnin' this fuckin' outfit now and I don't have a lot of time to waste waiting for an old man to come and let me in. I don't know why the fuckin' gate has to be closed in the daytime, anyway. Or why you need a fuckin' guard."

"Our security system follows an Untico standard," Lyons said. "Ever since the sixties, anyplace there's an American flag flying, you have to have security. That's the rule."

That made Buzzard even angrier. "Well take down the fuckin' flag and open the gate,…and get rid of the old man."

Ray did not know if that was a direct order, or just a remark made from frustration…and neither did Lyons…or the guard.

When they toured the plant, Buzzard was annoyed with everything. Walking through the warehouse, he concentrated on Swanson. "Look at all this shit," he said, gesturing emphatically. You ought to get by on half of it."

"Half our finished goods? Half our inventory?" Swanson was stunned. "That would be asking for disaster. We'd lose our reputation for delivery. Our service level is 96 percent," he said proudly.

"Who the fuck needs a 96 percent service level?"

Swanson looked toward Ray for help. Ray responded with, "It's one of our big selling points, Carl. Right now these guys are doing a great job of supplying our customers while Crane and Blackwell are having all sorts of trouble…and we're picking up business."

"Yeah, but I'll bet Crane and Blackwell are making more money," Buzzard countered. "Or at least a better return on investment, 'cause they don't have all this fuckin' inventory." Then turning back to Swanson, he continued, "I'll bet I could find lots of stuff that's been sitting here for months, that you didn't need to stock…lots of stuff."

"You'd find some," Swanson agreed. "But that's because we don't know exactly what's going to sell all the time. We know a lot, but there's always surprises. And if we don't have it, we go on back order. Sure, you can look back to see what we didn't need. But tell us what we're not going to need next year…or next month… or this month for that matter." He stopped and looked right at Buzzard. "Tell us that."

Swanson made sense, but that did not seem to faze Buzzard. "That's your fuckin' job," he said, ending the conversation. They walked into the manufacturing area and he turned his attention to Lyons.

"You've got too many fuckin' operators over there in valve sub-assembly," he pointed out. "With a good methods improvement you could get rid of three of them."

"But this was set up by our Industrial Engineering Department," Lyons protested. "They *did* a methods improvement analysis." In fact, Lyons knew that this was quite an improvement over the way they were doing it in Jackson.

"Make 'em do it again," was all Buzzard said.

At the welding area he looked at some brackets being MIG welded. "Look how long it takes them. Why the hell don't you spot weld the fuckin' things?"

Lyons did not know what to say. He looked to Simpranian for help. "We specify that, Carl," Simpranian explained. "Manufacturing doesn't make that decision...and the MIG weld is needed for strength."

"That's bullshit," Buzzard countered. "You engineers overdesign everything just to cover your ass." Then turning to Lyons, he instructed him, "When you see a way to save some money by changing a design, you do it. Tell these fuckin' engineers what you want to do and let them change the specs. And if they don't, you go ahead and do it anyway. You can't use the engineers as a fuckin' crutch."

Lyons and Simpranian just looked at each other, but said nothing.

In each area there were bins of parts and partially assembled shocks waiting for the next operation. "What the hell are these for?" Buzzard asked, picking out one bin.

"They get assembled to the forks over there, on the Minster," Lyons answered.

"But the Minster is working on that other stuff."

"Well these must be up next...or soon."

"Meanwhile they're taking up space...and money, just sitting here."

He repeated this several times with other parts and then stopped, right about in the middle of the plant. "Listen to me," he said to Lyons. "And listen good. You've got too much fuckin' in-process inventory and you're gonna reduce it in half."

"In half?"

"Right, half! Up to now you've been building too far in advance, or ordering parts from Jackson or outside, way too early. That's just to give yourself a fuckin' cushion, for when you make mistakes. Now you're gonna get rid of that cushion and fine-tune this operation."

Lyons just stood there with his mouth half open. Buzzard put a hand on his shoulder and pointed toward one end of the building. "Now when you get rid of all this excess inventory, you're gonna have all sorts of room. And to prove it, I want to see an aisle from that wall over there all the way through the middle of the plant to that wall over there."

"But—"

"I want to stand over there the next time I come here and be able to see direct from one end to the other."

"But—"

"And the only way you'll be able to do that is to cut back on all this fuckin' in-process inventory. And if you can't do that, I'll find someone who can."

When they got back into the plant office, Lyons got a driver to take Ray and Evans back to the airport and went into his private office, where Buzzard was waiting. As Ray left, he heard Buzzard yell something at Lyons that ended with "too many fuckin' heads." Everyone in the office heard.

Mike and Ray flew into Atlanta, where Travis Puckett, the District Manager, met them and drove to Marietta to have lunch with Irwin Rodbell. After lunch they toured the warehouse, which he was expanding. Ray was favorably impressed with the neatness and the hard-working employees. Rodbell was turning into a good customer.

"You've got a nice operation here," Ray said to Rodbell. "Mike says you're doing quite a job for us."

"I have to," Rodbell said smiling. "Otherwise you won't take us on the boat anymore and Melanie would kill me."

About 3:00 P.M. they met with Les Richards in his office in Atlanta. Richards had a large warehouse on West Peachtree, with one of the classiest offices Ray had seen in a warehouse operation. He had dark mahogany paneling and a plush white carpet. Ray wondered how he kept it clean. There certainly could not have been much traffic in there from the warehouse. Richards was on the phone in a big comfortable chair behind a large mahogany desk. He waived them in, pointing to a leather couch and two chairs. Travis moved some golf clubs, and the three of them sat down.

Richards hung up the phone and spoke to them from across the room. "Well Travis, you've been doin' a lot of running around for Mr. Rodbell lately."

"Just doin' my job, Les," Travis answered. "I'd just as soon be doin' that for you. Ah always liked workin' with your boys."

Richards did not smile. "Yeah, well we might want to talk more about that some time. Ah haven't been real happy with Crane. A lot of back orders...lot of 'em. But that's not what I wanted to see you boys about today. Ah've got something that might be very interesting for you. Let me get raht to the point. Ah have to leave pretty quick."

He got up and walked over to the bookcase on the opposite wall and opened a cabinet door. Inside was a small bar. "Can ah offer you boys something to drink?" he asked. They all declined, so he poured himself a little scotch, took a sip, and continued. "Ah golf pretty regular at the Atlanta Country Club. Fact is ah'm goin' there as soon as y'awl leave."

Ray was getting a little fidgety. He wished Richards would get to the point.

"Well, last Saturday ah played in a foursome with Jesse Tucker...you know, from NAPA."

"He's the number-two man at Genuine Parts," Evans explained to Ray.

"Yeah," Richards agreed. "And some day he'll be running the whole company...some day soon. Well, we got to talkin' about business, and you know, he's got problems just like me, only bigger. You see, Blackwell's got more shocks on back order than Crane, and that really kills NAPA. They want to supply 100 percent of what their Jobbers need...100 percent. But if they're out of something, the Jobbers got to get it from someone else. Ah know. Ah do a lot of business on the few things they can't deliver."

He paused. "We talked about the industry and the back-order problem. Ah told him that the best company ah know of, as far as fillin' orders is concerned, is Amsaco."

"That's real nice of you," Evans said, somewhat surprised.

"Well, that's the facts. Travis here always gave me service, and the factory shipped me what ah wanted, when ah wanted. These Crane boys gave me a lot of promises, but they ain't hardly delivered on any of them."

Evans had to step in. "Well Les, we can do something about that. You know we still love you."

Richards just smiled slightly. "Well, ah appreciate that, but that's not what ah wanted to talk about today. Travis, maybe we could have lunch next week some time and talk about it."

"How 'bout Monday," said Travis, pulling out his appointment book.

"Fahn. That would be just fahn. But look here, let me tell you about my talk with Jesse. Jesse knew full well what ah was talkin' about. He said he knew Emil pretty good, and Emil was a Marketing man. He took good care of his customers. Jesse thinks Amsaco might be a good supplier to NAPA."

Ray said quietly, "Wow."

This time Richards did smile. "You bet. NAPA's the best customer you could have. It would be like putting on twenty warehouses as big as mine, and I'm pretty big. Anyway, ah told Jesse ah knew you boys and would be glad to pass on any messages. He said he'd be obliged if ah would do that. That he'd like to talk with you, but not at his office. Find some place out of the way, just to talk a little. Just let me know and ah'll contact him. And he'd like to meet your new President."

"I'll talk to Burch tomorrow," said Ray. "And we'll propose a place.'

"Fahn. Just call me in the morning."

"But Les, I'm wondering. Why are you doing this? Aren't they a competitor?" Ray was just being honest. It was a question on Evans' mind also.

"Just doin' something to help a business associate," Richards explained. "They're not really a competitor of mine. They have their Jobbers and ah have mine. Ah can't be concerned with a few dollars. But Jesse is a fahn fella, and NAPA is a fahn organization. Besides, Lori has a lot of stock in Genuine Parts. They run the NAPA program, pretty much. Her daddy bought in right in the beginnin'. We've known those boys a long time."

Travis laughed and said to Ray, "Anyone in Atlanta who has any money has stock in Genuine Parts or Coca-Cola."

Richards nodded in agreement. "Two fahn companies."

■ ■ ■

On the flight back to Harrisonburg Ray commented to Evans, "This NAPA thing sounds fantastic. Are they really twenty times bigger than Richards?"

"More than that," Mike responded. "If we had NAPA, we'd be the biggest in shocks. We'd be bigger than Blackwell."

"Wow," Ray said again.

They just thought about it for a few moments. Then Ray changed the subject. "Sounds like Richards has quite a bit of money."

"No, I don't think he does," Evans answered. "But Lori does. Or at least her 'daddy' does. But Les fits right in. He's comfortable with her daddy's money. Belongs to the Atlanta Country Club and all that...southern society. Old man Mooney, Lori's dad, could care less. He built the business from nothing, just using his head and putting in a lot of work. Travis says that old man Mooney was the best salesman he ever knew—anywhere. He built up the business, and I guess he made some good investments. That Coca-Cola stock is no joke. Made a lot of people rich in Atlanta."

"So he moved into Atlanta society."

"Not the old man. His wife did, and Lori...and Les."

Ray laughed. "I learn something new everyday. You know, I never thought of WDs as being wealthy. I mean, not big-time wealth. I figured guys like you and me, we're officers of a big corporation, with our jets and yachts and big salaries and bonuses. I thought we were doing pretty good. But some of our customers do better."

"Much better," Evans emphasized. "The WDs makes us look poor." He paused, thinking. "Well, not all of them. They fall into two classes. Either they make a hell of a lot more than we do, or they owe a hell of a lot more than we do."

Ray was thinking about that as they landed in Staunton. He was proud of being an Executive Vice President of a big company with a couple of hundred people working for him and millions of dollars in his budget. Yet, his WD customers looked on him as just an employee of Amsaco, with use of the jet and the yacht, but no chance of making any real money. It was somewhat ironic. Maybe his brother-in-law was right. Maybe he was just a "flunky."

They had to wait about fifteen minutes at the airport until

Buzzard, Simpranian, Swanson, and Lyons arrived. Lyons looked pale. When Buzzard went into the men's room, Ray asked Lyons how the afternoon went.

"It was even worse than the morning," Lyons replied, almost in tears. "Nothing was right as far as he was concerned. No one had any brains. Everything would have to change. It was a nightmare." He paused, thinking for a moment, then added, "It's like having Chessman for a boss."

Ray laughed just a little. "Nothing could be that bad."

"To tell you the truth, I'd rather have Chessman. I mean every little thing. My staff is totally demoralized. You know, we have the best efficiency numbers in the company, and our service level is great. And all this while we tooled up for a new line and supplied Sears with their pipeline. I mean everyone should be praised for doing such a great job. They should get a medal. Instead, everyone's scared shitless."

Ray did not know what to say. "So what are you going to do?"

Lyons calmed down and thought for a moment. "I think I'm going to put a fuckin' aisle down the middle of the fuckin' plant, from one fuckin' wall to the other. It'll take a lot of fuckin' time, and it won't do any fuckin' good...but that's what he fuckin' wants and that's what we'll fuckin' do...if everyone doesn't fuckin' quit."

"Sounds like you understand the situation," Ray said laughing.

"The fuckin' situation," Lyons corrected him.

Ray was very concerned. Besides the moral side of Buzzard's apparent disregard for anyone's feelings, Ray did not want to see any disruptions in the plant's service level. The afternoon's meeting with Richards had confirmed the effectiveness of service level and delivery. Ray spoke to Buzzard about this on the plane. "Do you think maybe you scared everyone too much?" he asked. "If their morale is low, it could affect performance."

"Nah," Buzzard dismissed the thought. "They work harder when they're scared."

Buzzard was a different person on the plane. He did not yell or curse. He was courteous to the pilots, as well as to Ray and the others. Ray could not figure out which was the real Carl Buzzard and which was just an act. Did Buzzard really know what he was doing? Ray got a clue during the bridge game.

Buzzard wanted to play bridge, so Simpranian and Swanson agreed. Swanson was not much of a bridge player, but Simpranian had played quite a bit in college. He had even earned some fractional master points in local tournaments. Ray had also played a lot of bridge at school. He did not have any master points, but he had played with people who did, and he knew what he was doing. Evans had no desire whatsoever to play and took his scotch and soda to the back of the plane to relax.

Ray agreed to play and Buzzard gave him Swanson as a partner. Simpranian asked Buzzard what conventions he used. "I don't use any of them," Buzzard answered. "But I've made a lot of money beating guys that did."

Swanson laughed. "I don't know any of them."

The first two hands were played by Ray and Swanson. On the first one, Swanson played terribly and they went down three at three hearts. Buzzard took his tricks emphatically with comments like, "You're not going to sneak that queen through me," and "You're down one and we're not through yet," and "Down three. You're not playing against little boys."

Ray played the second hand and made five spades when they only bid three, Swanson doing the mis-bidding. Ray said nothing to Swanson, because it was obvious Swanson did not know bridge very well. Buzzard had comments, however.

"You blew an easy chance for game," he criticized. That had been obvious to Ray and Simpranian as soon as Swanson laid down his hand. Swanson should never have passed at three, but should have bid four spades. They had not said anything because Swanson was not a bridge player. Buzzard however, turned to Ray and said, "You should have jumped right to four."

To Ray, that would have been overly aggressive and could have led to an overbid. It was also obvious to Simpranian. But they just looked at each other and said nothing.

Any doubt about Buzzard's knowledge of bridge was settled on the next hand. Buzzard opened with one no trump, and the bidding ended at four hearts, with Simpranian playing. Buzzard laid down his hand and Simpranian was surprised to see it contained only twelve points. Ray was equally surprised and asked Buzzard, "How can you open one no, with only twelve points?"

Buzzard looked disdainfully at Ray and answered, "I can if I have even distribution."

Ray had no answer. He looked at Simpranian, who just grinned and started to play the hand. They both saw how little Buzzard knew about bridge. He just talked like he did. Was this also true about Buzzard's knowledge of manufacturing? And distribution? That was not amusing—it was frightening.

■ ■ ■

It was after 11:00 P.M. when Ray got home. The kids were in bed, but Dorothy was waiting up for him.

"You must be exhausted," she said, giving him a hug. "What time did you get up, 4:30?"

"Closer to five."

"Oh, I stand corrected. You're probably not tired at all then. And I was going to give you a massage." She started to rub his neck and shoulders.

"I just need a drink," he said, walking away from her to the bar. He poured himself some scotch. "It *has* been a long day. All sorts of things happened. I don't know whether to feel elated or depressed. It's like the good news/bad news stories."

She sighed and sat down on the couch. "Tell me the good news."

He told her about the meeting with Les Richards and the NAPA inquiry. Her reaction was personal. "I was kind of glad when the Richards left," she said. "It meant we didn't have to take them to dinner. But Melanie Rodbell was sweet. I hope the Rodbells don't leave."

"No, they won't leave. Mike says they'll be a lot better off than they used to be, even if Richards takes back some business. But Richards isn't even what makes it so exciting. NAPA is! They're really big. Bigger than Universal."

She smiled. "I don't think that's so exciting. Now if you said you were taking tomorrow off, and we would be home alone all day… and we could run around naked, that would be exciting."

"Have you been drinking or something?"

"Just a little wine." She giggled. "Let's go upstairs."

"I haven't told you the bad news yet."

She groaned. "OK, go ahead. I guess I have to hear it all."

He told her about Buzzard; how he abused the guard, and

Lyons, and Swanson, and just about anyone he came in contact with. He thought she would be angry about the abuse, but she laughed, especially when he told her what Lyons had said about "building the fuckin' aisle."

He had to laugh too, but he said, "It sounds funny, but it's serious. We have this 'loose cannon' running around, just when everything is going so well and we have a chance at NAPA." Then he told her about the bridge game.

"So he can't play bridge," she said with disinterest.

"That's not the point," he explained. "If he talks as if he's an expert in bridge, and he doesn't know anything, maybe he doesn't know anything about manufacturing either. Maybe he's just a fraud. But he's got the whole plant running around doing everything except getting shocks out the door. It's frightening."

"Well, there's nothing you can do about it tonight," she said, trying to calm him down. "Except cultivate an executive ulcer. Why don't you finish your drink and we can go upstairs…and relax."

That was no answer as far as Ray was concerned. But he did not know what else to do, so he gulped down the rest of his drink and went upstairs.

As he was already getting in bed, Ray said. "I've got to talk to Burch in the morning. I don't know if he realizes what Buzzard's doing."

"Ray, put it away," she replied. "You've been going since 5:00 this morning. Let it go." She sat down next to him and gently clasped his hand. "Relax a little. You're going to make yourself sick."

He looked at her, took a deep breath, and nodded his understanding.

She spoke quietly. "Now look. You've got to unwind." She put her hands around the back of his neck and rubbed slowly. "I still owe you that massage…and who knows where that might lead." She smiled, kissed him softly and got up to go change into her nightgown. "Don't go away."

She pulled out one of her sexiest nightgowns and went into the bathroom. She brushed her teeth, straightened her hair, and came back in, smiling. Ray needed some loving…and so did she. She crept into bed as her eyes were adjusting to the dark. As she reached over to touch him, she heard him snore, softly at first and then a little louder. She froze, not knowing whether to wake him or let him sleep. Then she turned away and put her head on the pillow, facing away from Ray. Tears formed in her eyes.

23. They Don't Teach This at Harvard

Ray was up early the next morning. He wanted to get some facts straight before seeing Burch, so he called Vince Procino to come into his office. Other executives would have had their secretary call, but Ray could not see the efficiency in this. He was perfectly capable of picking up his phone and dialing Vince. It seemed to him that having Betty call would be just a method of letting Vince know that Ray was a big executive. Some executives, like Buzzard, did that all the time, for exactly that reason.

"I want to talk about NAPA," Ray told him. "What are they all about? How big are they? Where are they?"

"I've got some stuff on that," Vince answered. "Can I ask why? We have something going with NAPA?"

Ray filled him in on the meeting with Richards.

"Holy shit, Ray. That's big time."

"I know, but how big? I'd like to know what it would do to sales volume and market share before I talk to Burch."

"Give me a half hour."

When Vince came into his office, Ray asked Betty to come in also. "I just want you to know what's going on," he told her. "And fill us in on what you know, including anything that Emil might have had going."

Since starting to work for Ray, Betty had delivered on all her promises. She would type his letters and memos off the Dictaphone with no mistakes, and very often with improvements on his wording. Occasionally she would even question what he was saying or how he was saying it. She made all his travel arrangements, sometimes talking directly with customers, whom she knew. Every morning, the latest sales figures were on his desk, and his mail was sorted as to importance. Many times she would read the important letters to him over the phone when he was travelling. He did not have to ask for flash reports from his staff. They were on his desk by Friday afternoon so he could be prepared for Burch's Saturday meetings. Often there was an addendum that she had asked for after reading the reports. She screened his telephone calls, called his wife when his plans changed, helped him by discussing marketing problems, and performed many other important tasks...and she served coffee. She was a capable business associate. Ray was grateful to Burch for forcing Betty on him.

"We have a chance of getting NAPA, " he explained to her when Vince came in. "They want to talk to us because Blackwell is really screwing up deliveries. I'm supposed to set up a meeting for them with Burch. But before I talk to him I want to know more. What should I know?"

"NAPA is big time," Vince repeated. "This isn't like putting on another WD. It's like putting on twenty or twenty-five big WDs. They supply over 5,000 Jobbers. It's big."

"Mr. Gross had great respect for NAPA," said Betty. "He said only the best companies could be major suppliers to NAPA. If he was a Jobber, he'd be an NAPA Jobber because he'd be sure he had good products. The companies would stand behind them."

"That's right," Vince agreed. "You have to have a quality product, good delivery, and a field force capable of working with their whole organization...besides good prices."

"How big a field force?" Ray asked.

"Twice as big as for Universal. Maybe more. Universal is just one company. They do everything one way from one office. NAPA is a bunch of companies...big WDs. Genuine Parts is the biggest. And GAPCO is big." Then, looking at his notes, he added, "Then there's Quaker City, NAPA Pittsburg, NAPA Hawaii, Britain Brothers, NAPA Des Moines, and Standard Unit Parts around Chicago. And these are multilocation WDs. Even the smallest is real big. Our field force would have to work with all these different WDs, as well as 5,000 Jobbers. This is big time."

"And supply all these guys," said Ray, beginning to understand. "What about our capacity to supply them?"

"With the addition of Harrisonburg we might have a chance." Vince paused. "I'm no manufacturing man, but with some new equipment and our three plants, I think we might have a chance."

"A chance?"

"Well, I can't be that accurate. The new guy, Buzzard, will have to answer that."

Ray groaned and Betty laughed. "I heard about yesterday's visit," she said.

"It doesn't take the 'underground' very long, does it?"

"About an hour."

Ray described Buzzard's visit to Vince, holding back on some of the language out of courtesy to Betty. "He really shook them up," Ray explained. "I mean he found fault with everything...everything. Said they could get by on half the inventory, and they didn't need so many people assembling this or that, and there were too many heads in the office. And swearing at the top of his lungs. Everyone heard him."

"Nice," Vince said sarcastically. "But maybe he knows what he's doing. Maybe he'll improve the operation."

Ray nodded. "Yeah, I thought about that, but I got a different signal on the plane ride back." He told them about the bridge game. "He sounded just as expert, just as arrogant about bridge as he did about manufacturing and distribution. But he knew nothing about bridge. I don't know what to say to Burch."

"I wouldn't say anything bad about Mr. Buzzard," Betty said. "Mr. Burch brought him in."

"Betty's right," Vince agreed. "He's Burch's man. You won't convince him to change his mind just because Buzzard's shaking things up a little. That's probably just what Burch wanted him to do. But Burch can understand what adding NAPA can do for profits. He understands the power of market share. Just talk positive...about profits. If Burch buys in, he'll control Buzzard."

"Yeah," Ray agreed as Betty also showed her approval. "And exactly what *will* this do to market share?"

"It would make us number one," Vince answered. "Just what Emil always wanted. I never thought it was possible. And I sure never dreamed NAPA." He turned to Ray. "Right now with the addition of Sears and with a temporary chunk resulting from

Blackwell's troubles, we're in the high twenties, maybe 30 percent. And Blackwell's dipping into the high thirties. The numbers won't come out for another month. But figure that Blackwell will recover at least a portion of what they lost. Even so, if we add NAPA volume and they lose it, we'll pass them. I think we'll be in the high thirties and they'll be in the low thirties. That's how big NAPA is."

"Mr. Burch has to be impressed with that," Betty concluded.

"He can turn those numbers into projected profits," Ray agreed. "I guess that's all I can do. Present the possibility of getting NAPA and the opinion that we can handle it. The rest is up to him. Betty, why don't you see when I can get in to see him."

She started to leave, then stopped. "I don't know how you value the information from the 'underground,' but there already is an opinion on Mr. Buzzard."

Ray smiled. "I'm valuing the 'underground' more and more. What's their opinion?"

"Your bridge evaluation looks accurate."

"You mean he's a fraud?"

"A fuckin' fraud." She smiled sweetly and left the room.

■ ■ ■

Burch's reaction to the news of the NAPA contact disappointed Ray. While Ray did not expect any great praise, Burch acted irritated, even angry. "NAPA is a difficult customer," was his initial response.

"Yeah, but look at their size," said Ray, figuring that maybe Burch did not understand the situation. "It's like taking on over twenty big customers. It's the biggest—"

"I know what NAPA is," Burch interrupted, "and I know what you have to go through to service them. I've spoken with some of the financial men from Walker and Echlin. There's a lot of costs involved."

Ray was astonished. "You mean you're not interested?"

"Of course I'm interested. How could you not be interested in an account like NAPA? But you can't measure an account just by the sales they generate. There's costs involved too. And how does it fit within our organization? There's a lot of things to consider."

"I know. I agree. I know we'd have to develop a Sales organization just for them. And we probably need to expand our facilities. But I think Harry Fitzimmons has a good feel for servicing a large organization. At least we'd have a good start. And Vince could handle the promotion and advertising with just a little more help. The big question is in Operations and Buzzard would have to handle that."

"Right! And that could cost a lot of money," Burch said, as if his point was being proven. "Both an initial capital investment plus the operating costs to service their organization."

"Yeah," Ray said with a smile. "But in the end, we'll have the biggest market share. Amsaco will be number one in shocks."

"Number one doesn't show up on the balance sheet," Burch said, refusing to go along. "We're not playing football. If an appropriation shows a good return on investment, then we'll do it. Otherwise we're better off being smaller and more profitable."

The wind was out of Ray's sails. "Yeah, sure. Of course. But it just *has* to show a good return."

"Don't be too sure."

"Should I get an appropriation started?"

"No. I'll put Wise on it."

This made Ray a little nervous, but there was nothing much that he could do. "OK," he said. "What about the meeting? Jesse Tucker wants to meet with us...wants to meet with you especially."

Burch looked annoyed again. "Set it up in Vegas, at AWDA."

"But that's not for three weeks."

"That's OK. It'll give us a chance to look at the numbers."

"But—"

"Set it up at AWDA," Burch repeated. He turned away and looked at some papers, essentially dismissing Ray.

As Ray left, he could not help thinking they were sending the wrong message to NAPA. They were saying that NAPA was not worth a special trip...that Amsaco could meet them at AWDA, when they met all their other customers. They should be setting up a meeting within a few days to show their enthusiasm and their ability to move quickly. They should strike while the iron was hot.

When he told Mike Evans about the problem, Mike said, "Make up a story. Tell them Burch will be out of the country or something. Then make a big deal about the meeting in Vegas. Get a private dining room away from the strip, with fancy food. No showgirls. Not with NAPA. Call Walt Morris. He can find the right place."

"I guess so," said Ray, reluctantly. "But it's like I have to outsmart my own boss."

"I do it all the time."

Ray smiled. "I guess it's the best we can do. But I don't like it. I'm not happy."

■ ■ ■

Burch was not happy either. His plan was to reduce costs. He could not do that when the new plant was opening, they were putting on Sears, and the industry sales were going up. He had to go along with increased sales and increased costs. But now, with things getting back to normal, it was time to get these costs under control. But he could not do that if they were expanding to handle NAPA. A project like this would emphasize production at all costs— putting in new equipment and new people and struggling to get product out the door. It would be a year or two before things came back to normal. He wanted to establish his reputation as a tough man on costs...a man with "balls." He was good at that and he enjoyed that. He did not want to wait that year or two.

He had to discourage this venture. It probably would not happen anyway. NAPA hardly ever changed major suppliers. It wouldn't take much to kill the idea. He could do it just by dragging his feet.

Burch's plan probably would have worked except for Dudley Graham. Graham was the President of GAPCO, the second-largest distributor in NAPA, with the home office in Dallas. He belonged to the Dallas Country Club, as did several Untico executives, including Max Simpson. They were not close friends, but they knew each other and had talked about the automotive after-market, along with other business subjects. They were having a few drinks on Saturday after golf when Graham asked Simpson, "Amsaco's part of your responsibility, isn't it?"

"Yes."

"Well, we've made a contact with them, and their response was... surprising. I was wondering if you could shed some light on it."

"Go ahead. I'll try." Simpson was apprehensive. He knew nothing about any contact with NAPA. Anything that important should have been reported to him.

"Well, Max," Graham started to explain. "I don't know how much you know about our organization, but we're pretty big in the automotive aftermarket."

Max smiled. "I'm well aware of NAPA." Actually, Untico had

looked into buying Genuine Parts. They were discouraged by the split ownership of NAPA by the various distributors. They considered buying all the NAPA distributors, but that got too complicated. He did not mention this to Graham.

"OK," Graham continued. "So you know we're the best customer any manufacturer can have in the automotive aftermarket." Simpson nodded. "So our suppliers are very loyal to us, and we're loyal to them. We don't change a major supplier unless there's an absolute need. Well, we think there's a need…with Blackwell, our shock supplier. They've been really screwing up."

"In what way?"

"With delivery. That's our number one requirement. Our business is to supply parts to our Jobbers. We don't want to miss a single sale. We don't want our customers to buy anything outside our organization." He paused and shook his head. "Well, Blackwell's made some internal changes that have really screwed up their delivery. And it looks like it won't change for a while. Now, ordinarily, when a manufacturer gets into trouble, we'll stick with him. We understand things can go wrong. But we've been dissatisfied with Blackwell for some time now. It seems they're getting 'financially oriented.' They're more interested in squeezing out a few more bucks in profit than in taking care of us. It's been building for a while."

Simpson just nodded. "And Amsaco?"

"Things seem to be just the opposite with Amsaco. They've just opened a new plant, took on Sears, and everyone in the industry says they're delivering shocks as fast as you order them."

Simpson said, "That's true."

"Now we don't make a major change like this just based on current events." Graham continued. "We're well acquainted with Amsaco. Emil Gross has built them into a good customer-oriented company, the kind we like to work with."

"Well you know Emil's not—"

"Oh yes. We know there's a new President. That's why we want to talk with Amsaco…to see what this new guy is like. But it's got to be secret. We can't risk making a big thing out of this until we're ready. So we sent out feelers through a discreet industry contact that we want to meet with Amsaco, with this guy Burch."

Simpson was getting angry. He should have known about this. But he said nothing except, "I understand."

"Well, the feelers went out through Jesse Tucker…at Genuine Parts. We thought Amsaco would be in Atlanta the next morning. But the message we get is that they'd like to talk to us in Las Vegas, during AWDA…as if we were like any other distributor. I don't understand. Am I missing something?"

Simpson thought for a moment, then answered, "Dudley, I'm a little embarrassed. I don't really know what happened…but I will."

■ ■ ■

Ray got a call at home from Burch that afternoon. Burch was angry as he asked, "Pendleton, have you talked to anyone at Untico about NAPA?"

Ray thought for a moment, trying to figure what this was about. "No, I haven't spoken to anyone."

"Well, I just got off the phone with Simpson and he knew about it. He wants the two of us in his office at 8:00 A.M. on Monday to explain what's going on with NAPA. You sure you haven't spoken to anyone?"

"No, no one except Les Richards like we planned. And Walt Morris…to set up the meeting in Las Vegas. But Walt knew it was a secret. That was the whole idea of him finding us a place."

Dorothy yelled in from the kitchen, "My God Ray, you just got out of your Saturday meeting. Can't he leave you alone?"

Ray covered up the speaker as Burch told him, "Well, somehow he knows about NAPA and he's pissed. He wants the two of us in his office. We'll have to leave tomorrow around 5:00. Peggy will make hotel reservations. I'll see you at the plane."

When he told Dorothy about the call, she reacted with anger. "But Barbara's piano recital is tomorrow…at 3:00."

"Maybe I can leave right after she plays. It'll only take me a half hour to get to the airport. How long is the recital?"

"Last year it went over three hours. It won't be over until after six. And Barbara will be one of the last ones to play."

"Couldn't she ask if she could play in the beginning? Then I could leave."

"In the beginning?" Dorothy was getting angrier. "No, she can't. They start with the younger kids, the beginners. It would be humiliating for her. She's one of Mrs. Cutler's best students now. She can't play with the little kids. Why can't you just leave a little later?"

Ray thought about that. As far as he was concerned they could leave later. Leaving at 5:00, he figured three hours flight time and a half hour to the hotel. They could leave at 6:30 and get in at 9:00. That would be fine. But Burch was in charge, and he said 5:00. And sensing Burch's bad mood, Ray did not want to speak to him at all, much less ask him to change the time. Burch was the boss and he set the time.

"I can't change the time, honey," Ray said sadly.

"Then you'll have to miss it…and don't call me honey."

The next day Ray stayed at home while Dorothy took Paul and Barbara to the recital. He stood at the window watching the car pull out of the driveway, feeling guilty that he was letting down his little girl. He sighed, pulled out some papers from his briefcase, and started to figure out what the NAPA account would require in additional manpower. He worked for about fifteen minutes when he realized he needed information that was in his office. He sighed again, grabbed his briefcase and his overnight bag and drove to the office, figuring he might as well work there. It was a hell of a way to spend Sunday though.

■ ■ ■

It was a long plane ride. After Burch interrogated him once more on how Max Simpson found out about NAPA, they hardly said a word. Burch pulled out his calculator and some papers and went to work. Ray did the same, but without the calculator. They arrived at the hotel before 8:00 and, as Ray had expected, there was nothing planned. He just walked around the hotel lobby, stopped at the bar for a beer, then went up to his room.

They were at Simpson's office at 7:45 and waited with his secretary in the anteroom. Simpson came in right at 8:00, talking with Alan Tracy. Tracy greeted them, then kept going to his own office. He told Burch, "Stop in to see me before you leave."

Since his secretary had already given them coffee, Simpson wasted no more time. He told them of his conversation with Dudley Graham. Ray made eye contact with Burch to confirm that Graham was Simpson's source of information, not Ray.

"How could you get an inquiry like this and not tell me about it?" Simpson asked, angrily. "When Dudley saw that I didn't know anything about it, he must have thought I was an idiot...or at least an incompetent executive."

"I was going to tell you, Max," Burch started to explain. "But I wanted to get all the facts together."

"What facts?"

"Well, first of all, if there was anything to this. I wanted to meet with them, see what they had to say, see if they were serious—"

"*Serious?*" Simpson was getting angrier. "Why the hell would they contact you if they weren't serious? And if you were wondering, why the hell didn't you get your ass right down there and find out?"

Before Burch could answer, Simpson turned to Ray. "And you should know that you have to strike right away...when the opportunity's there. That's Basic Selling 101."

Ray did not know what to say. Simpson was right. That was what Ray wanted to do, but Burch had overruled him. He could not say that though. He could not undermine Burch in front of his boss. He looked at Burch for help, but Burch just sat there expressionless.

"We, er...we considered that," Ray stammered.

"Well you better goddamn reconsider it," Simpson roared, thereby saving Ray from having to explain. "You better get your asses down there this week—tomorrow. You tell them you misread the message or something, but you let them know you want their business." He turned to Burch. "Then you'll find out if they're serious."

"Sure Max," Burch said quietly. "Ray will contact them as soon as we leave here. I'm sorry I didn't bring you up-to-date, but I wanted to have the complete picture before I called you. Estimated costs as well as estimated sales...and what kind of investment would be required."

"You mean for additional capacity?"

"Yes. We have some extra capacity, but I don't know if we have enough to serve NAPA."

Happy to be changing the subject, Ray added, "I'm sure we'd have to add capacity." They both looked at him. Apparently he had not brought Burch up-to-date on this.

"How much capacity?" Simpson asked.

Ray realized he had spoken too soon and tried to backtrack. "I don't really know for sure. It's just a salesman's estimate," he joked. "Carl Buzzard would have to figure it."

"What's your 'salesman's estimate'?" Simpson asked, somewhat sarcastically.

Ray looked at Burch, who said nothing, so he continued. "Just roughly, we figure we need a 25 percent increase in our present capacity. Now I don't know that for sure. It depends on the actual NAPA volume, and our actual capacity. We'd have to tie that down. But I can't see us having anywhere near that capability. We'd have to expand. And the way I see it, Seward is the place to expand."

Burch and Simpson both looked surprised. "Seward?" Simpson asked. "Your Nebraska plant? I thought that was just a mini-plant, for specialties. I thought they had failed as a major facility."

"It is a specialty plant now," said Ray, with a little more enthusiasm. "But it can be expanded. We have a good Management team now, and plenty of room. And there's plenty of labor...nonunion. It's a good location for shipping nationally. And we can't get much more out of Jackson or Harrisonburg."

Burch thought for a moment and then joined in as if he had known about this all along. "Seward has been an efficient operation for several years. They have a good staff."

"Sure," said Ray, smiling. "We'd need bricks and mortar and more equipment, but they could handle it."

Simpson sat back in his chair. "Fine. You won't have any trouble getting the funds from here."

Ray felt better. The idea had come from Vince Procino, but Ray had not gotten a chance to discuss it with Burch. In his office and on the plane, Burch had not wanted to talk about these details. Ray was a little worried that Burch might be angry that he was bringing it up now, in front of Simpson. But Burch almost seemed enthusiastic about the Seward idea himself. And now they would be going after NAPA, as Ray had wanted all along.

They discussed other ideas and details for about an hour, when Simpson ended the meeting. "We have a staff meeting with Torres at 10:30," he said to Burch. "And Tracy wants to see you. When you're done, use my phone here to call your contact with NAPA."

As Burch left, Simpson called in his secretary to get more coffee. Then he leaned back in his chair again, looking at Ray, with a peculiar smile. "I get the impression, Ray, that you're hot on going after NAPA."

"Yeah, sure. It would make us number one in shocks, with a big improvement in the bottom line. Yeah, I'm hot."

"And Ralph isn't?"

"Well, I don't know," Ray said, somewhat taken back. He was not about to speak for his boss. "He's cautious."

"Cautious, hell. He's a fuckin' accountant."

Ray was stunned and said nothing, so Simpson continued. "All he thinks about are costs. He can't see going after NAPA because he'll have to spend money." He stopped and smiled at Ray. "I know. You're not about to say anything. But you know what I'm talking about. I'm basically a salesman and I've been fighting accountants all my life. I know what you're going through."

Ray did not know what to say. He wanted to be friendly with this important man. He understood what Simpson was saying and he basically agreed with him. Ray was having difficulty working with all the accountants who were running Amsaco, and it was getting more difficult every day. But Burch was his boss and Ray had to be loyal to his boss. He tried to joke his way out of the subject. "You have to remember," he said with a smile, "at Harvard I learned to tolerate all the financial wizards. I'm immune."

Simpson smiled back, then leaned forward without the smile and said, "Forget that Harvard shit. They don't teach this at Harvard. Forget being nice and being loyal. You're in a war zone now and you have to decide which side you're on. Simple as that. If you're on my side, you have to do what I need. And there are rewards—big rewards. If you're against me, you better find someone to protect you, 'cause you're not strong enough."

"But I don't understand," Ray said, his head spinning. "What can I do for you? What war are we in?"

"I'll tell you," Simpson said, sitting back again. "Now listen to what I'm saying. Listen good. In my career, I've always been successful. Whenever there was a job open that I wanted, I got it. At Berringer, at several companies before Berringer, and here at Untico. And what got me here was performance. I always did a good job, sometimes outstanding. There's always been others who wanted what I wanted, and there was all sorts of in-fighting and politics...and I can hold my own with that politics shit. But my major weapon was always performance, 'cause that's real...no bullshit. I became President at Berringer because I was the best damn salesman they ever had. I remember Kessinger, the financial guy, and Marchese in manufacturing, both wanted the job. But they had to give it to me because I had brought in more customers and sold more paper than ever before. I performed. And they knew I'd perform as President. And I did."

He paused and looked at Ray. "And I'm aware that you're doing that too. You've got a good track record."

Ray smiled and said nothing.

"Now, here at Untico, I'm following the same course. But my performance is based on what my companies do—on the profits they produce. And I'm not going to be President of this outfit with the horseshit profits they've been producing. I figured that out right away. But I'm working on it. Berringer is a problem with that damn EPA on our back. It's going to cost us some money. But that's only temporary. All the paper companies are having the same problem, and it's going to cost them all. Some won't make it. But we have the money to get through this, and then we're gonna make a lot of money. There'll be fewer competitors, and all of us have to make back our investment. The prices will rise and we'll all make money."

He paused again to let the logic sink in. Ray just nodded. "And the shipyard," Simpson continued. "The Yard has been a loser for a long time. But McCormick's going to turn that around. He's started already, bringing Chessman in to fight the union." He laughed. "You know the first thing Dan did? There was this big bronze plaque in the lobby, under a big portrait of Everett Beaumont, the founder. It said, 'Quality ships—no matter the cost.' Dan took down the plaque and the portrait and sent them over to the local museum. Then he called in the Management team and gave them the new message, 'Quality ships—at costs below selling price.' Dan never should have been an accountant. He communicates too well."

Ray laughed along with Simpson. "Yes, and he's honest too. He was a good boss."

"Well, he'll get the job done at the Yard. He'll have some rough spots, but there's so much room for improvement. And we'll help him in Washington…get him some good contracts."

Simpson paused, collecting his thoughts. Ray said nothing, and Simpson continued. "So that's Berringer and Commerce Yards. Leaves the tire company and Amsaco. The tire company goes along with the automotive industry, which is on the way up. So they'll be all right. Nothing spectacular, unless they get some special customers, like Sears or NAPA." He stopped and held up his hand. "I know—I know. NAPA is not that big on tires. But they could be. They've got more power than they know what to do with. And if we're a major supplier to them they'll listen to any ideas we have... There's all sorts of opportunities. Anything from a tire program for NAPA...or Sears, to buying other automotive companies, or getting into a retail operation. It's wide open. And I think you could find the opportunities—stuff I haven't even thought of."

Ray was impressed. This guy was smart. And he knew the automotive market much better than Ray had realized.

Simpson continued. "So if Amsaco could actually get NAPA, it not only means you become 'number one,' but it could mean some synergy with the tire company, or other opportunities...and major profits all around." He paused again, then said very carefully, "And this all will begin to gel in two years or so, just when Untico is going to look for a new President. The paper company will be turning profitable, the shipyard will be a modern, aggressive organization, generating profits. There'll be new life in the tire company, the shock absorber company will be the leader in the industry, after years of just hanging around,...and who knows what other automotive ventures we'll have. Torres and the Board can't ignore performance like that."

Simpson stopped, leaned back in his chair, smiled and asked Ray, "You want to be on my team?"

"Well, yeah, sure," Ray stammered. "I, er, I thought I already was. I mean Ralph and I both are—"

"Don't give me that bullshit," Simpson said angrily. "Burch doesn't see things the way I do...the way we do. He's not going to spend money to grow...not willingly anyway. He thinks in terms of costs, only costs. He thinks small. I don't know why I let Tracy talk me into him anyway. I can't let him determine my future." He stood up and walked around the desk to Ray. "I think you can do what I want done...maybe better than I can."

"But Ralph's my boss."

"Forget that shit. I want you to do what I want, not what he wants. Forget the organization chart. If you want to be loyal, be loyal to me. You'll be much further ahead."

Ray was flattered, and he understood what Simpson was saying, but he was still confused. "But what do you want me to do?" he asked.

"I want you to get NAPA," Simpson responded quickly. "This is an opportunity that does not come along often. We can't blow it."

"Well, sure," Ray agreed. Getting NAPA would not be disloyal to Burch. "But I'm just one man in the organization and—"

"And I'm another, a very important one. Burch will do what I tell him, if I know what to tell him. And to do that, I need to know what's going on. This whole thing would have slipped right by if I hadn't golfed with Graham. That can't happen again. I want you to keep me informed from now on—without Burch knowing."

Ray took a deep breath. "What type of information?"

"Everything! Everything that could affect getting NAPA. Prices too high, slow to react, Burch's glowing personality...or lack thereof. Anything that's important. I trust your judgment."

Ray nodded.

Simpson sat on the edge of his desk. "Now first of all, there's this expansion. At Seward was it? If we need an appropriation, I want it on my desk in two weeks—not two months. We have to show NAPA we're ready to go. You let me know if it's being held up."

Ray nodded again.

Simpson stood up and picked up some folders on his desk. "I have to get to a staff meeting. You can wait here until Burch gets back. Use my phone to set up the meeting. You let me know when that meeting is set. I want to call Graham...this afternoon."

He started to walk out, then stopped and smiled at Ray. "And don't look so glum. Us Marketing guys have to stick together. And we're gonna make corporate history."

Ray watched him leave without saying anything. He was still in shock. Simpson was definitely right about one thing. They did not teach this at Harvard.

24. Still the King

Ray was worried about following a course that apparently was not the way his boss wanted to go. And Burch must have been embarrassed to be reprimanded in front of Ray—especially since Burch knew that Ray was in agreement with Simpson's thinking. That would cause friction between Ray and Burch.

And now Ray was essentially Simpson's *spy* at Amsaco. This not only scared Ray, it bothered his conscience. He should be loyal to his boss, even if Burch was a "creep."

On the other hand, he was glad they were now going after NAPA full steam. That made sense. It was what Ray would recommend if he were teaching the case at Harvard. More important, Simpson agreed, and Simpson was a higher authority than Burch. And Simpson was promising "rewards" for Ray.

What about these "rewards?" The basic concept made Ray feel guilty. Was he doing this for the "rewards?" And what were they? A bigger bonus? A promotion? The only promotion he could get at Amsaco was Burch's job. Ray did not even want to think about that. Maybe Simpson meant a bigger job at another Untico company. No, Ray knew better. Simpson was a Marketing man and looked down on Financial men, and Burch was Financial…and Ray was Marketing. It was logical that Simpson would like to work with Ray as President. But going around Burch's back to take his job made Ray feel guilty…and tainted.

To rationalize his actions, he logically concluded that what he was doing was best for Amsaco. Ignoring any personal rewards, this was still the proper business decision. Therefore, he was not doing this for personal gain. He was being loyal to Amsaco.

When he tried to express his dilemma to Dorothy, nothing came out right. "Are you trying to get Burch's job?" she asked.

"No, no," he replied, shaking his head. "I don't want Burch's job. I never even wanted my present job...or the one before that. It's like I'm being carried along by the current, through the rapids. I have no control."

"We're being carried along by the current," she corrected him. "I have less control than you do. Maybe you can understand how I feel." She thought for a moment and added, "And Paul and Barbara don't even know we're in the river."

"Yeah," he said, pausing. "But at some point, I'm going to get it back under control."

"If we don't all drown first."

■ ■ ■

Worried as he was, Ray was pleasantly surprised when Burch turned out to be very cooperative. At their meeting with NAPA, Burch was pleasant and positive about Amsaco's ability to supply. While he did not have the personality of Emil Gross, he knew what to say and showed confidence that he was running Amsaco, and he was running it to serve the customers. Ray smiled as Burch explained the logic behind opening the Harrisonburg plant. He wanted to assure good customer service.

He went further, stating that to be certain that Amsaco could serve NAPA, they were prepared to add more capacity by expanding the Seward operation. In fact, the plan was to have the appropriation down to Dallas in two weeks, and Untico had already indicated approval. Ray smiled again. Simpson had obviously talked in detail with Burch.

Jesse Tucker was impressed. While he would not commit, he was encouraging, suggesting that Amsaco go ahead with their plans. Burch surprised Ray even more by stating that Amsaco was confident enough in the future that the expansion would take place without any NAPA commitment. When Ray next called Simpson, he could report that things were going very well.

Besides keeping Simpson up-to-date, Ray had quite a lot to do. His first priority was to work with Carl Buzzard, Vince Procino, and Dick Wise on the appropriation. Wise was very cooperative as Procino estimated the sales volume and the distribution requirements. Buzzard seemed annoyed at the whole project. "Who needs all this expansion garbage," he said. "We're trying to control our costs."

Ray tried to explain the profits that would be generated by the additional sales, but Buzzard would not buy it. "Sales, sales," he ranted. "All you think of is the fuckin' sales. We're gonna spend all our time and effort on adding capacity instead of reducing our costs. And you're gonna give it all away anyway. At the end of the day, we're gonna be bigger, but not more profitable."

Dick Wise just smiled and went ahead with the appropriation. Buzzard reluctantly went along. Apparently they had their orders from Burch.

Ray's second priority was to put together a proposed NAPA Sales and Marketing team. Talking with Evans and Procino, they agreed that Harry Fitzimmons should head it up. "Harry's the best man we have," Evans stated. "He knows that type of operation and, in fact, he knows a lot of the NAPA people. He's perfect." Evans thought for a moment and added, "And Roger Tufano is ready to take Harry's place."

Procino nodded in agreement. "Roger's been ready for a while now. Universal will have no trouble accepting Roger."

"OK," said Ray, thumping the desk. "We're moving. Let's talk to Harry and let him start thinking about his organization. But he's to keep it to himself. We can't say anything to Roger or anyone else at this time." They both nodded. Turning to Vince, he asked, "What about the marketing support? What will you need?"

"Not that much," Vince answered. "I think two full-time people for advertising and promotion. Then our regular group can support them. It's hard to say because I'm not sure just what the programs will be. But two heads should be figured in the appropriation."

"I'll tell Wise," said Ray. "And we'll need Harry's estimate on the field force."

"I'll get with Harry," said Evans. "We'll have some numbers for you tomorrow."

"Good. And Vince, give some thought to what our promotion programs might actually be. We'll look smarter if we actually propose something. Maybe you can check with some other NAPA suppliers and see what they do. But keep it quiet."

"I have some connections," said Vince, smiling. He turned to Evans. "Looks like we've trained the Professor pretty well."

"He'll make it."

Ray was enjoying this. Taking action was the most fun. He felt like a quarterback, leading his team down the field to a touchdown. This was what he imagined big business should be. He mentioned this when he called Max Simpson.

Simpson laughed and agreed. "I know exactly what you mean. And there's a whole lot more fun to be had. This is just the first game. You'll be all-pro by the time I'm finished with you."

Ray's third priority was more time-consuming and much more work. Jesse Tucker wanted him to meet all the NAPA distributors, since they all would take part in the shock supplier decision. Genuine Parts could have made the decision by working through the proper NAPA committees, which they controlled. But they did not like to work that way. They would rather have consensus on a major decision. So Ray took Fitzimmons to visit each NAPA distributor.

This tour itself was a major undertaking. In addition, Ray had other important business meetings. Ed O'Brien had a meeting set up in Chicago with Ed Purcell at Sears. Purcell wanted to review the status of the changeover. It was supposedly complete, but delivery problems were popping up at some stores in the Northeast. O'Brien said that Purcell was not worried, that it was probably just some "startup wrinkles." But Ray wondered if it could be because of Buzzard's affect on morale at Harrisonburg. This was a real possibility. Regardless of Management actions, it took the cooperation of everybody at Harrisonburg to make the new delivery system work. He decided that if he ever did become President, the first thing he would do was get rid of Buzzard and see if he could get Jim Steele back.

There were other meetings. Marv Crawford set a date for Ray with Ford, in Detroit, followed by one with Chrysler. Then Mike Evans suggested that a visit to Harry Liscio in Kansas City might be worthwhile to thank him for the changeover. Plus Ray was still meeting customers he had not yet gotten around to meeting, and he had to stay in contact with the ones who had become his friends. Doug Wilmot wanted Ray and his "pretty woman" to attend his open house in Montgomery; Paul Bloom wanted them to visit in Detroit.

In addition to all this there was AWDA week in Las Vegas, where he met with almost all the Amsaco customers. For a three-week period, he was home only once, for one Sunday, and even then he had to go into the office to sign the Seward appropriation. Ray's work was piling up in his office, Burch was irritated that he had missed Saturday staff meetings, and Dorothy had just about given up.

"This can't go on like this," she told him in frustration. "You said you would get things under control. That as Executive Vice President you could make your own schedule. But it's getting worse. You're not even here on weekends. Do you understand how ridiculous this is?"

"I know," he agreed. "I know, I know. It is ridiculous. But it's only temporary. It's the NAPA stuff. Let me get through this and then I'll cut down on my travel. I'll get control of my schedule."

"You say that every time. For two years you've been saying that."

"I know, but something unexpected always came up." He sighed. "But I'm beginning to understand the job now, and this time I'll do it. I swear it."

Ray was honest when he said that. He really meant to make that his top priority when this big surge was over. But deep down inside, he was beginning to have doubts. Some other emergency always seemed to pop up after one was brought under control…or some other opportunity. Like what did Simpson have in mind with the tire company and other acquisitions? Would that add more barriers to getting his time under control? As he was "climbing the corporate ladder" his workload was climbing right along with him…only faster. Would another promotion add even more? Ray saw what was happening, but he just did not have the time to address that problem. He would get to that later. Dorothy would just have to understand.

There was another side to the situation, an important one… one that he tried to ignore. He had to acknowledge that he was enjoying himself. While he missed the warmth of family, when he was out on the job he was pleased with his life. As a senior officer he traveled first class. He used the company jet most of the time, but even when he had to fly commercial, he went first class. He stayed at the best hotels and ate at the best restaurants. In Las Vegas he got the best seats at the best shows. He gave out generous tips and received the best service wherever he went. The field force, the plant personnel, and the home office all treated him like a king. He was "Mr. Pendleton" at the office and at the plants. At the Management level they would call him "Ray," but with the respect for someone who had attained the goals they were all aiming for…and never expected to achieve.

Things were great with the customers also. Business was good. The customers were able to pay their country club dues and college tuition for their kids. At AWDA almost every customer was telling Ray what a great job he was doing and that Amsaco was a great company. Of course, they also added that their distributor discount should be higher.

"That's healthy," Evans told Ray. "If business is bad, they want you to reduce the customer price, to increase sales. What they're saying now is that business is fine and they're making some money, but they want some of our cut. They're greedy as hell…but then again, so are we. But we're in charge of maintaining the discount structure."

Ray laughed. "I keep learning things."

"Well, if you can't teach your boss, who can you teach?"

Ray kept on learning things. As he toured the NAPA distributors he learned how different they were from each other. Their approach to selling was vastly different because their customers were different. In the Southeast, Genuine Parts would stick to the programs and the pricing, playing by the book, as they served some big Jobbers. In New England, the Genuine Parts Distribution Centers would wheel and deal to compete with the independent distributors in cut-throat competition. In Chicago, Standard Unit Parts was looking to serve chain operations, while in Texas, GAPCO sold the program, following the rules in rural communities. The business was highly social in Hawaii. As long as the products had quality, the Jobber customers were friends with Don Wang, and would do business with no one else.

■ ■ ■

Walt Tabor, the Regional Manager for the Southeast Division, looked very smug when he welcomed Ray and Harry to tour the Genuine Parts Distribution Center in Jacksonville. "I'd like to run over to Tampa and introduce you to our biggest Jobber, a six-store operation. You don't understand NAPA until you understand our Jobbers." Ray agreed. He wanted to know some NAPA Jobbers who were the core of the NAPA concept. What were they like? What did they think? What did they need?

They drove over to a nice-looking store with a big NAPA sign. The building looked newly painted. There was plenty of parking space, and it looked like it had a very large area in the back for inventory. A new Cadillac was parked by the side door.

"That's the new owner's," Tabor said.

Tabor greeted the counterman as they went in. They were apparently expected and were waved into a big office in the back. As they entered the office, the owner swiveled his chair to face them. There was Emil Gross with a big smile on his face.

"You bastards gonna buy me lunch?"

Ray's jaw dropped. Harry, smiling broadly, went over to shake Emil's hand with both of his. "You son of a bitch. We were wondering where you disappeared to." Tabor just watched and laughed.

Ray finally gained his composure and shook Emil's hand. "Son of a gun. You said you'd do something like this. Six stores. That's great. Are your boys in it with you?"

"You bet! And my son-in-law," Emil explained. "We bought a three-store operation and added three more. My two sons each manage a store, and my son-in-law…plus the three managers stay on… to run the other three stores and train my boys. I run the warehouse, and Walter here, makes sure we're doin' it right. Can't lose."

Ray was now smiling broadly. "Wait'll I tell Dorothy. How's Marilyn like it?"

"She wasn't crazy about moving away from her friends. But this way our kids all have good jobs. And that's a first. And she's tickled to death to have her grandkids so close. Besides, she's got to do what I tell her."

"Sure."

"Anyway, I think a lot of her friends will end up down here, or near here. They'll visit for sure. That's why I needed this office…to have some place to escape. Let me show you around."

Emil grunted as he raised his large frame from the chair. "I've been getting in shape," he boasted. "Playing golf a few times a week. When you have some time I'll take you over to the club."

"I haven't even had time to read my mail," Ray said sadly.

"That's what happens when you have a prick for a boss," Emil said laughing. "C'mon, this is the store." He first showed them the front of the store with the retail displays and the parts counter. It was neat and attractive, but not very busy. "Things'll pick up here around noon. Right now our truck's out delivering to the service stations and garages, but it doesn't get crowded in the store until later. But let me show you where the money is."

He took them back to his office and went out through another door. Ray thought it was a bathroom door, but it entered into the warehouse, a surprisingly large warehouse.

"This is the American Barrel Warehouse," Emil announced proudly. "ABW."

"I don't want to hear this," Tabor said, with a smile. He grabbed Fitzimmons' arm and walked away from Emil and Ray.

Emil smiled at Ray. "Having the front separated from the back makes this a legitimate warehouse. So I can buy direct from the manufacturers at WD prices. That's what separates this operation from anyone else's."

Ray was not surprised. He knew that Emil would be working some angle that was different.

"I sell to other Jobbers around town," Emil continued. "So it's a legitimate operation. I also stock the NAPA products for my own stores. But there's nothing to stop me from supplying the non-NAPA stuff to my own stores. At WD prices I make a much bigger profit. That's what Tabor didn't want to hear."

"Is that legal?" Ray asked. "What about your NAPA contract?"

"It's perfectly legal," Emil answered. "And my NAPA contract is a handshake, agreeing to use most of the NAPA program...or all of it if I want."

"A handshake?"

"That's right. Just a handshake. That's the NAPA deal. A gentleman's agreement." He noticed Ray looking at him a little strangely. "But I keep my end of the bargain. I buy an awful lot of the NAPA products from their distribution center...a hell of a lot more than the old owners did. I use ABW mainly for special deals or emergencies...and for insurance. If I ever leave NAPA, I have my supply all set for my stores. And it sure has come in handy with their shock supply problems. I've been buying quite a bit of your stuff the last few months. I bet I've become a pretty big customer for Amsaco. You may have to take me on the yacht."

Ray ignored this remark. "The arrangement is all right with Genuine Parts?"

"Sure. I told Jesse Tucker what I planned to do before I bought the stores. It's OK with him as long as I don't go overboard with the warehouse stuff. I just don't make a lot of noise about it." He thought for a moment. "You know it actually was my talking with Jesse that got him interested in Amsaco."

"You got him interested?"

"Yeah. When Blackwell started screwing up, and Crane was showing the same signs, I told him Amsaco was shipping just fine. He asked me if I would contact you, but I turned him down. Told him there was no way I was going to call that prick Burch. How *did* he get in touch with you guys? Did he just call you?"

"No. It was through Les Richards, of all people," Ray said, smiling. "Les might be coming back to us. Anyway, Les knows Jesse from their club, and he relayed Jesse's message. Seems that Jesse was concerned about Burch. He wanted to meet him...to see if Ralph was customer oriented, like you."

"Yeah, sure. Ralph's left toe is customer oriented."

"Actually, he did pretty good," Ray pointed out. "He said the right things to Tucker. I think he said the same things you would have said." Ray stopped and grinned at Emil. "Of course, it might have been because of the instructions he got from Max Simpson."

"From Max?"

Ray explained the meeting between Dudley Graham and Simpson and the subsequent meeting in Simpson's office. He only mentioned Simpson's angry conversation with Burch, not his private conversation with Ray.

Emil smiled as Ray told his story. "Good," he said. "Serves the bastard right." Then he thought a moment. "But it surprises me about Max. He never was that involved in our business before."

"He had his reasons," said Ray, debating whether to tell the rest of the story. There was risk in telling anyone. But Emil was now a friend, a friend with a good deal of knowledge about the politics involved, as well as the business aspects. And there was not much risk in Emil telling Burch. He filled Emil in on the rest of the meeting with Simpson. When he told him about his role as a "spy," Emil just nodded.

"He doesn't trust Burch. That's smart." Then Emil smiled at Ray. "But it looks like he has plans for you. That's good. You're my protégé."

"I'm just his spy," Ray said modestly.

"Oh no. He's got plans for you. Sounds like he wants to expand in the automotive aftermarket, and he'll do it through you. This could be a real good move for you."

"You think I did the right thing then?"

"Of course," Emil said, as if it were a silly question. "You have a choice of hooking up with Simpson or Burch. That's a 'no brainer.' Especially since you're not an accountant." Emil laughed at his own joke, then put his arm over Ray's shoulders. "When Jesse told me he was concerned about Amsaco because I was no longer involved, I told him not to worry, that the 'Professor' would take care of him."

Ray laughed. "I suppose that was all he needed."

"Really. It was important. He said he had heard a lot of good things about you."

"About me?"

"Yeah. These things get around the industry pretty quick. You're a hot item." As Ray thought about that, Emil could not resist adding, "Must be your Foreign Car Program."

That evening, Ray thought about his conversation with Emil. It was exciting to think of himself as a "hot item" in the industry. But if Jesse Tucker had heard about him, it must be all around. People knew about him and thought he had a lot to do with Amsaco's success. If he had respect like that, maybe he could do a lot for Max Simpson. Who knew where it was all leading. This was exciting.

■ ■ ■

Ray would not have been so excited if he could have heard a conversation between Burch and Buzzard. It had been a frustrating few weeks for Carl Buzzard. He had to put through a rush appropriation on something he did not want to do in the first place. His plan was to shrink the operation, not expand it. He could personally take credit if he could reduce the headcount by

30 percent, or 20 percent, or even 10 percent. The same with inventory. These reductions would be attributed to how he ran the operation as compared to Jim Steele. Even the people who did not like his style could not argue with his results. He imagined himself speaking at the Untico Management Meeting, explaining how efficiently his fine-tuned organization was operating.

Expanding the operation, with more heads and more inventory would not result in personal gain for Buzzard. It was a no-win situation. If it did not go right, he would be to blame for the cost over-runs that would eat into the profits. If he did everything perfectly, it would go unnoticed, as Pendleton got the credit for the big increase in sales and the resulting increase in profit. Even if he improved the efficiency in the plants, it would still be attributed to the increased volume obtained by the Professor. Buzzard was not happy.

He felt that Burch was letting him down and siding with Pendleton. He had no animosity toward Pendleton, whose job it was to increase sales. But Burch had brought him in to cut costs, and now was ordering him to do just the opposite. And he did not know why. Burch had just walked into his office one day and told him to get with Wise and Pendleton and put together an appropriation to expand the Seward plant. When Buzzard protested, Burch just said, "Do it."

People thought that Burch and Buzzard were very close because they knew each other from before and Burch brought him in at a very high level. This was not true, however. Burch was not close to anyone. Since Buzzard had come in, he had heard very little from his boss. This was OK with Buzzard most of the time, since it left him free to do what he wanted. But this Seward expansion was irritating him more and more. Finally, he just had to bring it up.

He walked angrily into Burch's office and said bluntly, "What the hell is the deal on this Seward expansion? I thought we were going to cut costs. Why are we increasing costs?"

Burch was sitting at his desk, calculating some flash report numbers. He looked up surprised, then said without emotion, "We are going to cut costs. Nothing's changed."

"But look at all the money we're gonna spend on Seward...not to mention the time and effort. How can I cut costs when all my engineers are figuring out how to ship NAPA. They're all running around all excited about spending money. There's no way I can get them thinking about saving money. And worst of all, I was planning on cutting back at Jackson, but how can I do that when we need more production? And Jackson's our high-cost plant."

Burch put down his pencil and sat back in his chair. "I know what I'm doing," he said, looking sternly at Buzzard.

"Well maybe you can tell me so I'll know what's going on."

Burch thought for a moment and then asked, "What are your plans to cut costs?"

"I've got lots of plans. Cut a bunch of heads in Harrisonburg, and reduce the inventory, and—"

"What's your one biggest move? The one that's going to save the most. The one that's the most difficult, but will give the best returns."

Buzzard stopped to think. Burch was thinking something specific. "The one biggest move would be to close Jackson," he said carefully. "We talked about that before I came on. With the union, it's our most expensive plant. We can save the most by closing Jackson. But how the hell can I do that if we're adding NAPA's volume?"

"Don't jump ahead," said Burch. "Let's take it one step at a time. You want to close Jackson. OK, if we do, what happens to our capacity? Do we have enough capacity to handle our customers? Forget NAPA. Our present customers, can we handle them?"

Buzzard had to think about his capacity figures. "No. Not quite. We do too much at Jackson."

"So, what would you have to do to close Jackson?"

"I'd have to move most of the Jackson equipment to our other plants."

"You have room for all that equipment?"

"No. We'd have to expand one of the plants."

"And that would be Seward, right?"

Buzzard was beginning to catch on. "Right. Harrisonburg is too big already."

"OK," Burch continued, almost smiling. "So, in order to close Jackson, we have to expand Seward." He paused to let that thought sink in. "And what are we doing now at Seward?"

"Expanding," said Buzzard, still standing and still trying to figure it out. "But we're expanding to handle the NAPA volume. We're gonna need every bit of Seward."

"Just wait there," said Burch, holding up his hand. "What we're doing now is expanding Seward. We've got approval from Untico to expand Seward." Burch stopped and smiled just a little. "And that approval was pretty easy, wasn't it?"

"Yeah."

"Now what happens if we don't get NAPA?"

"We'd have too much capacity," Buzzard said slowly. "More than we'd need."

"And what's the logical thing to do if we have too much capacity?"

"We close a plant," Buzzard said, starting to smile.

"And if we have one old expensive plant," Burch continued, this time actually smiling, "and two new modern and efficient plants, which one do we close?"

"Jackson," Buzzard said, sitting down. "But how do we keep from selling NAPA? Wise said the push to sell them came right from Dallas. And Pendleton is red hot on selling these guys."

"There are ways," Burch said, not smiling anymore. "We haven't agreed to anything definite yet. Terms, prices, support services, packaging...they all have to be negotiated. We want NAPA, but only if they generate good profits. And we determine what good profits are...me and Wise. The Professor is liable to have a very difficult negotiation."

Buzzard smiled broadly, showing his large teeth. "I apologize for doubting you. You are still the king."

Burch ignored the compliment. "The best part is that everyone thinks we're expanding for NAPA...Dallas, the Professor, the UAW, everyone. You can even sneak some stuff through. You can transfer some critical equipment from Jackson to Seward before the UAW knows what's going on. Then when negotiations fall through, it's not our fault. It's the Professor's. And then we step in and make the most out of a bad situation. We turn disaster into a profitable course of action...we make a good business decision. We 'reluctantly' close our oldest plant. We show we have the 'balls' to do what has to be done."

Buzzard just nodded in admiration and agreement. Then a

thought hit him. "But won't Pendleton sense something's wrong? Won't he see our change in attitude towards NAPA?"

"Not for awhile," said Burch, who obviously had already considered that. "And when he does, what's he going to do about it? I'm his boss. I can handle the Professor."

25. Showdown

On a Saturday morning before the staff meeting, Ray was going over the 1980 sales forecast with Dick Wise.

Wise suddenly flashed a surprised expression. "You've got a lower sales figure for the rest of this year," he said looking at the forecast. "The 1980 figure is wrong, because you're starting out lower at the end of '79. Why aren't you sticking to our '79 forecast?"

"I've got lower than forecast prices," Ray answered, respecting Wise's ability to quickly analyze numbers. "I thought we should skip the August price increase."

"Why the hell would we want to do that?"

"Well, we're having a hell of a year, and we'll be way over forecast, and profits will be high, even without the price increase." Wise was looking at Ray with a quizzical expression, as if Ray had not yet answered the question, so Ray continued. "President Carter is asking business to hold back on price increases to try to stem inflation. And some of our customers are complaining about the cost of inventorying our shocks with the high interest rate and all. And the interest rate won't come down until inflation comes under control." Wise still just stared at Ray. "So I thought we could get some good customer relations from some publicity about Amsaco trying to help the President stop inflation...you know, we'd look patriotic."

"Our customers don't want a price freeze," Wise answered, shaking his head in disbelief. "They just want longer terms."

"We'd have to explain it to them...that we're taking this step to try and get interest rates to go down."

"Boy, you sure get some weird ideas. But take it up at the staff meeting if you want."

Wise knew exactly how Burch would receive Ray's idea. "Jimmy Carter's not running this company," Burch said angrily. "We are. And our job is to maximize profits. Our costs aren't slowing down. Tell the President to ask the UAW to stop asking for more money. Then we'll stop raising prices." He pointed his finger at Ray. "Now listen, and listen good. You put through that price increase, and do it sooner than planned...tomorrow if you can...today even. And then you put another one in as soon as we can after that. In an inflationary period, our job is to raise our prices faster than anyone else. That's the way to maintain and improve our margins. Do you understand? We want more and bigger price increases."

Wise was smiling at Ray, who just nodded his head and said nothing. The meeting went on to the next subject. After the meeting, Wise invited Ray into his office. "You know the only thing that will stop inflation?" he asked.

Ray was not in too good a mood, but he asked, "What?"

"Unemployment," said Wise, rather smugly. "Asking corporations to hold the line on prices is futile, as long as labor costs are continually rising. The Fed will have to raise interest rates until there's a recession...and unemployment." Wise smiled. "Meanwhile we build parts overseas with cheaper labor. That helps both ways. It puts pressure on American labor to hold wages down, and it adds to unemployment. That's a short course in inflation."

Ray did not like the idea of purposely using unemployment to reduce inflation. It seemed unfair, cynical, almost unpatriotic. At the same time, Amsaco's very success—increasing production and employment—would lead to higher wages, then higher prices...and inflation.

He bounced the problem off Max Simpson when he told him of Burch's orders to raise prices and Wise's ideas about unemployment. "Yeah, you need unemployment to reduce inflation," Max agreed. "And Burch is right. Your job is to raise prices as high as you can get away with."

"But what about inflation?"

"Inflation's got nothing to do with your pricing strategy," Simpson answered, sounding a little impatient. "You're the Professor. You should know that. Pricing depends on what your competitors are selling at and what the customers will actually spend. Right?"

He answered without waiting for Ray. "Of course! And even us peddlers can understand that that additional price goes right to the bottom line. Your costs are already determined. Now every penny you can add to the price is profit. Burch is right."

Ray received no more satisfaction from Vince Procino. When he told Vince to go ahead with the price increase, Vince just smiled and said, "We're all ready."

"You don't seem surprised," Ray commented.

"No, I can't say I am." Then he smiled a little wider and added, "You can advocate the overthrow of the government, or say bad things about Burch's mother, but don't mess with a price increase."

Betty Johnson laughed when he told her his dilemma. "Yes, there certainly is something sacred about a price increase," she confirmed. "I don't know about the economics of inflation, but Mr. Gross always paid a lot of attention to prices. He would have Mr. Sudarsky and Mr. Burch come in to talk price increase. Mr. Burch would have his calculator, Mr. Sudarsky a lot of reports, and they would meet for a long time. I would usually get them lunch. Sometimes Mr. Chessman would come in to play cards, then just hang around and listen. One time he told Mr. Gross that the financial job wasn't so hard, that he could handle most everything, except he would have a little trouble with pricing. Mr. Gross laughed at that for a week."

"That Chessman was something. But I bet Burch wasn't laughing."

"No, but that made it even funnier to Mr. Gross." Betty laughed. "One time I asked Mr. Procino what made pricing so complicated. He said it was mostly because of consolidation."

"Consolidation?"

"Yeah. We base our price on what the car companies set for their replacement shocks. But we might have one shock that fits five OE applications with five prices. What do we charge? The highest? The lowest? The most popular? And then there are all sorts of price discounts for Jobbers and WDs and garages, And our competitors don't do it the way we do. So we all end up with different prices to the consumer, and some of them could look pretty ridiculous."

"Sounds like you know the subject pretty well."

"No, I don't really," she answered. "I don't understand how they decide everything. But when they're all done, they can add up what we sell each item for, and how many we'll sell of each, so our total sales can be figured. Sometimes Mr. Gross would tell Mr. Sudarsky to get another 2 percent…and he would."

"I'll bet he did."

Ray noticed one thing in the process that Betty described. Inflation was not even considered. That did not seem to bother her, or anyone else but him, apparently. Maybe the basic task of Managers was to maximize profits, period, just like Burch said. Considerations like inflation or environment or loyalty to employees or consumers seemed to be matters of lip service. He wondered how he would have handled this subject in class. Would he assign advocates of one side to present the arguments of the other? He could certainly present the argument of Burch and the others. But no one seemed to care about his view. Maybe he should just enjoy his executive position, and forget this inflation thing.

He thought of talking it over with Dorothy. She would understand. Or would she? Lately she had not said anything supportive. She would criticize Burch and Simpson and their demands on Ray. She did not like Ray's role as "spy," and was critical of these executive "games." Since Ray was in the middle of this "game," she was also critical of him.

"Why don't you just tell them to leave you out of their games," she said. "Tell them you'll just do your own job."

While Ray agreed with her, there was no way he was going to tell that to Simpson or Burch. He did not make the rules. He knew if he did not like the game, he could leave. Dorothy did not seem to understand that…or would not. If he brought up the inflation dilemma with Dorothy, she would probably criticize him for even considering that Burch might be right. She would probably accuse him of giving up his ideals, of becoming a "Republican." No, he'd better not bring it up.

■ ■ ■

Ray's next run-in with Burch was over the size of the proposed NAPA field force. Harry Fitzimmons had proposed an organization of forty people to cover all the NAPA Distribution Centers. "These guys need personalized service," he told Ray as they were flying to meet the NAPA Pittsburgh group. "Each NAPA group has its own method of doing business. And we've got to learn what they do and how to work with each one of them."

"I agree with your logic," Ray answered. "But we just can't do that. We've got to have fewer salesmen per customer for NAPA. That's the whole concept of NAPA. We don't have to sell the Jobbers or look for more Distribution Centers. That's what NAPA does for us. We give them a better price, but that's justified by our lower costs...or it's supposed to be."

"Yeah, I understand that. But how many men can I have?"

"I don't think you can have more than thirty. I can try to get a few more, but I don't think I can sell it to Burch. He's told me to watch our costs. Can you do the job with thirty men?"

"Sure," Harry said, almost glibly. "I can do the job with ten. It's just a matter of how many times they visit each customer. We have to service about 5,000 Jobbers. If our Regional Managers service the Distribution Centers, we can have, say, 25 salesmen for the Jobber. That's about 200 Jobbers each. Comes to about one day a year for each Jobber, if you consider vacation and travel and meetings and stuff. One day a year's not a lot, but if they plan right, they can handle it. They can see four or five Jobbers in a day and then return every three months or so. We can do it."

"Good," Ray said nodding. "I'll go in for thirty-three."

"Remember," Harry added. "These are mainly service type guys, not super-salesmen. Their salaries should be lower. This might even be considered a training ground for Amsaco salesmen."

Ray used that logic when he presented his plan to Burch. He had already gone through the numbers with Dick Wise, who agreed the costs were reasonable. Ray had explained Harry's original request and how they had reduced that number. Wise could see that Ray was taking a reasonable approach and was trying to hold costs down.

"Thirty-three heads will be OK," Wise agreed. "But you have to keep their salary levels down. Harry's right that this should be a training ground...so pay them apprentice wages."

Burch was not so agreeable. "Too many heads," he said curtly. "Just too many. We don't need more than twenty to service NAPA. These guys aren't selling. All they're doing is servicing the accounts. They don't have to wine and dine the Jobbers, or call on all the service stations to solicit business for the Jobbers. We give NAPA a better price because they do all that. Our guys just visit the Jobber once in a while and go over our programs."

"I agree," said Ray. "But, twenty is just not enough. Harry started with forty, but I cut him back to thirty-three, and Wise agreed with that." Ray was ready to settle for thirty.

"No way," was Burch's answer, with no further explanation.

Ray thought he would try some numbers. Burch liked to decide things based on numbers. "With only twenty," he said, figuring out loud, "and 5,000 Jobbers, we'd be averaging 250 Jobbers to each man."

"Fine," Burch joined in the calculation. "That's five Jobbers per week, or one a day. That's enough."

"But they have to put in time with the Distribution Centers, and travel, and meetings—"

'Twenty's enough." Burch looked down at some papers. The meeting was over.

Ray had no other arguments anyway. But he was afraid Jesse Tucker would not like that number at all, and it could end the negotiations. He expressed this fear to Max Simpson over the phone.

"That dumb son of a bitch," Simpson muttered. "This is a big deal and he's looking to save pennies."

Ray was embarrassed. While he agreed with Simpson, Burch was still his boss and he did not think it right to be having this conversation about his boss. Still, the fact was that he was calling Simpson to report on Burch's actions. What the hell did he expect.

"I've got to talk to him," Simpson continued. "There's no chance of you convincing him?"

"I don't think so, Max. He's got all the numbers in his calculator."

"Well, he's gonna have to recalculate. I'll call him." There was a pause. "No, he'd know you told me. I'll tell you what. I'm going to be in Chicago tomorrow. I can be in Jackson tomorrow night. I'll set up a dinner meeting for you two guys to bring me up-to-date on NAPA. You just make sure you slip up and let me know you don't agree with the manpower level. Just stutter a little or something. I'll jump all over you and we'll get a good argument going…and I'll win."

Simpson did win, and Burch was not happy about it. Contrary to Burch's wishes, Ray left the dinner with instructions to use thirty-three salesmen dedicated to NAPA in his proposal. There had been two meetings of the three of them, and both times Burch's decisions had been reversed. As far as Burch was concerned, it was him against Simpson and the Professor, and he was losing…so far.

■ ■ ■

While Ray was preparing the final proposal for NAPA, everything else was going well. The Seward addition was going up surprisingly fast. Ray had thought Buzzard might drag his feet on this expansion. Buzzard had not kept secret his opposition to the whole NAPA idea. But the addition to the building had been put up in less than three months, and some equipment had already been transferred from Jackson. New equipment was scheduled to come in through July and August. It looked like everything would be installed, debugged, and running smoothly in the fall.

Harry Fitzimmons was preparing for his new staff of thirty-three salesmen. He was looking through his own Universal people in addition to others on the corporate field force. He was also looking for new hires at "apprentice" salaries.

Vince Procino was also looking, and Ray got a pleasant surprise when Vince called him about a candidate he was interviewing. "I was asking him if he knew much about us," Vince explained. "And if he knew anyone here. He said when he graduated, he heard that one of his professors had gone to work for Amsaco. Asked if Professor Pendleton worked here."

"No kidding? What's his name?"

"Rasche, Phil Rasche. You know him?"

"Yeah, sure. I remember Phil. He's a smart kid. Is he here now?"

"Yeah. You want to see him?"

"Sure. C'mon over."

Ray sat back in his chair smiling. Phil Rasche, one of his students from what seemed like a hundred years ago. It would be good seeing him, if only to show off a little. Rasche should certainly be impressed with Ray's position, if not with the fancy office and secretary.

"Welcome to the real world of marketing," Ray said when Rasche came in. He stood up and walked around his big desk to shake hands.

"Wow," said Rasche as he looked around.

Ray laughed. "A little different than my office at school. But I earn every bit of it. I work three times as hard as I did at school."

"Ray's just an average worker," Vince joked. "But I trained him well, so he's moved ahead."

"That's right," said Ray. "I suppose Vince told you that I worked for him when I came here. Just do everything Vince tells you to do and you can do this too."

Phil looked around at the big desk and credenza, the couch and drapes and carpet. "OK, who do I have to shoot?"

They all laughed. "I told you he was pretty sharp," Ray said to Vince. "But fill me in, Phil. What have you been doing since graduation? Seen any of the others?"

"The only one I've had contact with is Gene Perlow," Phil answered. "We both went with G.E. So, I've seen him a couple of times. But he's been out selling and I've been in Advertising and Promotion, so we don't see each other much."

"How do you like G.E.?"

"It's been fine. I've learned a lot. But I get lost in such a big company. I would love to work here, where people know who you are."

Vince broke in, saying, "It looks pretty good. Phil's got the basics that we need, and he seems willing to learn how we work."

"Good," said Ray, smiling. "I know he has a good education." Then turning back to Rasche he asked, "You don't hear much from the others?"

"No, we're all scattered. Orlowski went to New York with Arthur Andersen's consulting division. Berman's in Chicago with Sears. A lot of guys went with smaller companies." Suddenly his face lit up and he chuckled. "The most interesting was Sylvia Gregory. You remember Sylvia?"

"Sure. Smart gal."

"Well she was smart enough to go with Bulova."

"No kidding."

"Yeah. When they came to school to interview, she figured she knew so much about them that she could really have a good interview, and she did. She got some kind of Assistant to the President job. Strategic Planning or something."

Ray laughed as Phil turned to Vince and explained how Ray

had handled the Timex-Bulova case. Ray was surprised how clearly Phil remembered everything.

"I'll never forget that case," Phil concluded. "Learning to understand the opposing side has stayed with me. I do it all the time, and not just in business situations. It's helped end a few fights with my wife. But it helps most with my boss. I do what he wants because I understand where he's coming from. I fight with him sometimes, but I do what he wants…and I know why."

"That's an excellent quality, doing what your boss wants," said Vince. "You're hired."

Ray felt a little guilty, considering his relationship with Burch, but he went along with Vince's joke. "We should do a little more of that around here."

They talked for a little while longer, when Betty interrupted, saying Ray had a call from Max Simpson. Rasche and Procino left while Ray took the call. He assured Simpson that they were sticking to the thirty-three-man field force. "Good," Simpson said. "I've been talking with Dudley, and he says that a company like ours should have at least thirty salesmen for NAPA."

When Ray hung up, Vince was waiting to come in. "What's up?" Ray asked. "Will Rasche be coming with us?"

"Yeah, we have an agreement. He was pretty excited…and quite impressed with your position. Especially your office."

Ray laughed. "We can thank Dennison for that. He had pretty good taste."

Vince changed the subject. "Ray, could I ask you something? If you don't want to discuss it, just say so."

"Sure," said Ray, taking note of Vince's serious look. "What's on your mind?"

"It's the call from Simpson," Vince said, coming right to the point. "It's unusual that you should be having so much contact with him."

"So much contact?"

"There's rumors running around. A lot of calls between you and Simpson. More than between Simpson and Burch. People are talking."

Ray was surprised, but tried to downplay the significance of the rumors. "You can't stop rumors. I can't worry about what people say. Geez, this company spends a lot of—"

"Ray," Vince interrupted. "I know all about rumors. That's not the point. The problem is if I've heard them, then many others have also. And they're bound to get upstairs…if they're not there already."

Ray looked seriously at Vince. He knew Vince was only telling him this for his own good…as a friend. Maybe this would be a good time to talk over the situation. Vince might have some helpful ideas. He trusted Vince. "Sit down, Vince," he said as he walked over to close the door. "Let me tell you what's going on."

He walked back to his chair and sat down. There was silence as he thought what to say. "You've probably been my best friend here…so I'll tell you what's going on, because I really don't know what to do. Or more accurately, I don't know what to do other than what I'm doing."

Vince just listened as Ray rambled on about the meeting in Max Simpson's office, the dinner meeting with Burch and Simpson, and all the telephone calls. "I don't know, Vince. I'm in the middle of this company intrigue. I'm Simpson's spy. And I don't want to do this. But what else can I do?"

Vince shook his head. "You sure are in the middle. I don't know what to tell you."

"I told Emil about it when I was in Tampa. He said that I had to join either Burch or Simpson, and as far as he was concerned, it was a 'no brainer.' You know, like in gin rummy."

"I know what a 'no brainer' is," said Vince. "And Emil is probably right. Simpson's a lot more powerful than Burch. I don't know what else you could do. Morally it's a dilemma, but from a practical view, you sure as hell can't tell Burch what's going on."

"Yeah," Ray agreed. "And Burch is my boss. I hate that. I hate being in this position. But it just happened. Everything just happened. I keep getting new jobs and new bosses, and—"

"And new salaries," Vince interrupted. "And new bonuses and new offices—"

Ray laughed. "Yeah. I guess you don't feel sorry for me. But that's not the point. I'm not looking for sympathy. It's just…I don't want to be anybody's spy. I want to talk honestly with my boss, but I'm working behind his back. I want to spend more time with the family, and instead I'm flying from one crisis to another. And when's the last time we talked over new marketing ideas?"

He stopped and looked at Vince who was smiling. "Things'll be better once this NAPA thing is behind us," Vince said encouragingly. "Until then you'll just have to travel first class, endure the Untico yacht, and put all that money in the bank. Then things'll get better."

Ray smiled and calmed down a little. "I'm sorry, Vince. I guess I don't have so much to complain about."

"Ray, your problem is simple. You're too honest. You're doing things that you're not proud of. And maybe you don't like yourself for doing them. But if it's any consolation, I'd be doing the same thing. What else can you do?"

"I don't know. I don't know." Ray looked seriously at Vince. "But that is a consolation. I don't feel so evil. Actually, what you're saying is just about what I said to my class back at Harvard. But I never realized how difficult it could really be." He paused, thinking back. Then he looked at Vince. "Anyway, thanks. You really are a friend. You don't give me a lot of advice, but I appreciate your listening to me."

"Well, don't get all mushy," Vince said. "Maybe I'm just sucking up to the next President of Amsaco."

"Don't even say that."

"OK," Vince said laughing. "But there is one piece of advice I can give you."

"Yeah?"

"Don't call Simpson on the company phones."

■ ■ ■

Things were going well enough that Ray agreed to take the family on a vacation over the Fourth of July. The plan was to take a full week, drive down to Washington, D.C., and tour the Capitol. With the fourth falling on Wednesday, they could take a full nine days and Ray would only miss four work days. When he talked it over with Burch, he was reminded that he would also miss two Saturday staff meetings.

"Look, how does this sound?" Ray bargained. "I'll finish up a draft of the NAPA presentation before I leave. Then you can go over it while I'm gone and we can finalize it when I get back. We can wrap up the whole agreement by the end of the month. Then I'll really be busy. This might be my only chance this year to take the family on a vacation."

"OK," Burch agreed reluctantly. "But make sure we can get a hold of you."

"Just check with Betty."

Dorothy was happy to get Ray away from the company to spend a week with the family. "But why not two weeks?" she asked. "Then we could go up the coast and visit my mother. And your parents. You said we would, remember?"

"I know," he answered, a little annoyed at being on the defensive again. "But I just can't take that much time right now. I had to fight to get this week. We can either visit family or go to Washington. And I think the kids would prefer D.C. Maybe we can visit the family during the holidays. Things should calm down by then."

"Yeah, sure. I'll believe that when I see it. But OK, we have one week, with just the four of us. Let's not fight. Let's enjoy it."

Ray was happy to go along with that idea. "Yeah. Tell you what. Let's get two rooms at the motel. Let the kids have their own room. What the hell, we're rich."

She looked at Ray, surprised. "That would be wonderful."

They left early Saturday morning, travelled all day with only three stops, and got to their motel in late afternoon. The kids wanted to get into the pool as fast as they could, which was fine with Ray. He and Dorothy just relaxed and unpacked.

"I'm all hot and sticky," she said. "I think I'll take a shower before dinner."

"Sure. The kids are in no hurry to eat."

Ray sat on the bed going over the tourist brochures as Dorothy went into the bathroom. He wanted to plan out their agenda for the next day. When he heard the shower running, a crazy idea went through his mind. He took off all his clothes, walked into the bathroom and pulled open the shower curtain. "I'm hot and sticky too," he said with a mischievous grin.

They showered together for the first time in years, and then made love for the first time in weeks. Afterward, she snuggled in his arms and laughed when he started to snore.

They started out early on Sunday, following Ray's plan to see everything. They walked in the hot sun from the Lincoln Memorial to the Washington Monument, and then to the Smithsonian. By midafternoon they were pretty tired.

"OK," said Ray, looking at his schedule. "We're in no hurry. We can come back here tomorrow and then go to the Capitol...or maybe the Mint, and hold the Capitol for Tuesday."

"Let's go swimming," said Barbara.

They drove back to their motel, and it did not take long before the kids were in the pool. Dorothy and Ray were relaxing in deck chairs, sipping gin and tonics, and watching the kids socialize with new friends.

"This is great," said Ray, leaning back and closing his eyes. "It's like being on the yacht."

"Except we don't have the pressure of entertaining customers," Dorothy said, also leaning back and closing her eyes.

"That's true."

Ray looked over at his wife in her bathing suit, lying back in her deck chair with her eyes closed. He looked at her legs, then up to her bathing suit to her breasts, then to her pretty face, then back to her breasts. "It sure is hot and sticky," he said.

She opened her eyes to see him looking at her. She smiled and said, "Maybe we could take a shower before dinner."

"Yeah."

They enjoyed dinner at Denny's that evening, then took the kids to a movie. Both Barbara and Paul brought a friend they had just met that day. The next morning they were up early to continue Ray's schedule. The kids were giving him a little more trouble, however. They could take just so much of the educational opportunities in the nation's capital. The social life back at the pool at the motel was more attractive.

Dorothy did not put up too much resistance. "Why push it?" she asked. "We have the rest of the week to see everything. Let's spend the rest of the afternoon by the pool."

Ray reluctantly agreed.

"And later on," she added as an incentive, "we can take a shower before dinner."

When they got back to their room, there was a message to call the office.

"Don't call," said Dorothy.

"I have to."

"What if we didn't get back until 6:00? Call back at 6:00 and if no one is there, call tomorrow."

"I can't, Dot. Someone wants to talk to me. And it must be important or Betty wouldn't call me here."

"Damn," Dorothy muttered under her breath. "I knew something would come up and ruin everything."

"Nothing's ruined. Just let me call and find out what it is."

He called Betty, who apologized for bothering his vacation, but said that Burch wanted to talk to him right away.

"What's up?" he asked when he got through to Burch.

"It's this damn price structure," Burch said, getting right to the point and expressing no interest in how Ray's vacation was going. "You're giving them a 22 percent discount off of Jobber price, plus another 7 for ordering at truckload quantities. And that's in addition to the thirty-three-man field force and the 3 percent advertising allowance...and special packaging. My god, Pendleton, what else can you give them?"

"But it's in line with what NAPA always gets. We checked it out pretty good with their other suppliers and with their Distribution Centers. This is pretty close to Blackwell's prices. We're not buying the account. We're just being competitive."

"I don't give a shit about the other suppliers, or Blackwell. I've gone through the figures, and I don't see any reason they should get any more than the 15 percent redistribution discount we give all our other WDs."

Ray gasped. "They would never go for that. They'd throw us out of the office. The extra discount's there because they do all the selling to the Jobbers and they add Distribution Centers without any help from us. It costs us much less to sell them, so they get a better discount."

"It doesn't cost us less with a thirty-three-man field force," Burch countered. "And all that other shit. If you and Simpson want thirty-three men, then we have to save someplace else. And that has to be in the discount. I don't see us going much above 15 percent...17 percent maximum. Now you figure out how to sell them at these numbers. Dazzle them with how they're better off with our quality product, delivered on time, and all that shit. It's time you did some selling. Anyone can give our stuff away."

Ray was starting to panic. He could not imagine going in to see Jesse Tucker and trying to sell a program with a 15 percent discount, when they were already getting over 20 percent. Jesse would think he was crazy, or incompetent, or both. "Maybe we could back off a little on the field force," he offered. "Or some of the other expenses."

"Well, you think about that. And put a package together that we can make some money on. But I'm not going along with this. I'd rather not get these guys than give the stuff away."

Ray was confused. He could see an argument over one or two percent of the discount. But this was way out of line. Everyone knew going in that NAPA would get a significant discount. That was the whole concept of NAPA. They guaranteed a big volume of business, where the manufacturer had to do little or no selling, and that reduction in cost got passed on to the Distribution Centers, who used it to sell the whole NAPA program. Burch knew this better than Ray, so what else could he say? "Let me think about it," was all he could come up with.

"You do that."

When he hung up the phone, Ray just sat on the bed, thinking. Dorothy was coming out of the bathroom in her bathing suit. She looked at his sad expression and asked, "What's the matter?"

"Burch doesn't agree with the discount I proposed for NAPA," he said without looking up at her.

"And that couldn't wait until you got back?"

"It's important. The numbers he wants would kill the whole deal. And he knows that. I don't understand him."

"It won't be any different next Monday. Why doesn't he just leave you alone?"

Ray put his hand to his forehead and closed his eyes, thinking. He did not answer Dorothy, but said with a sigh, "I've got to call Max."

"Oh, for chrissakes," Dorothy said in frustration. "I'm going swimming." She slammed the door as she left.

As Ray expected, Max was not happy to hear the news. "What do you mean he's raising the price?

"He's backing off on the discount we give NAPA...big time. This isn't just a negotiation trick. He's talking numbers where we'll just get thrown out of Jesse's office. There's no chance of them even talking about it. We might just as well call them and tell them we don't want to sell them."

"That son of a bitch," Max said angrily. "He doesn't learn. Well, I've had just about enough."

There was silence, so Ray offered an alternative. "I could look at some other ideas where we could keep the discount. Maybe we could raise the Jobber price and cut margins. The Jobbers are making pretty good margins now."

"How would Jesse look at that?"

Ray had to answer honestly, "He won't like it. The Jobber is sacred territory for NAPA. Maybe we could raise the list price or the dealer price, or...no, Jesse wouldn't buy it. We could cut costs...advertising allowance or cut the thirty-three-man field force, or—"

"Damn it! I'm not going to make a decision on the field force and then have him reverse it through the back door. No, this has gone far enough. Look, I need a day to take care of a few things here. We can meet Wednesday to—"

"That's the Fourth of July."

"Damn. OK, Thursday. I'll set up a meeting on Thursday in Jackson. Don't say anything until Burch calls you."

"But Max," Ray protested. "I'm on vacation now with the family. I'm calling from the motel outside Washington. Can't we meet on Monday?"

"No, he might blow the whole thing by Monday. This is too important. And it's important for you too, personally. Maybe you can come in for the meeting and then go back. Let me check to see if we have a plane in the area. We usually have one around Washington someplace. Give me your number."

Ray waited, wondering how he could tell Dorothy. Simpson called back. "We're in luck," he said. "They're flying Senator Brock back to Illinois after some Fourth of July shindig. They can drop you off in Jackson Wednesday night and take you back on Thursday afternoon." There was a pause. "But be prepared. You might have to stay on, depending on what happens."

Ray did not ask what might happen and why he might have to stay on. One possibility was that he would have to stay to run the company, but he put that thought out of his mind.

When he told Dorothy, she was livid. "This is the worst thing you've ever pulled," she said angrily. "This was time reserved for us—you, me, and the kids. You should have told them you won't be back until Monday."

"I tried, honey," he tried to explain. "Honest. But Max said it was too important...that Burch might kill the whole thing by Monday."

"Then let him kill the damn thing."

Ray thought about telling her about this being important to him personally, but thought that would sound even worse...like he was trying to get Burch's job. He would make it up to her later, but knew she would not buy that reasoning now. He ended the argument temporarily, by saying, "It's my job. I could quit my job, but until I do, I have to do...what I have to do."

They did not shower together that night or Tuesday night. On Wednesday night he was flying to Springfield, Illinois, on the BAC111 with Senator Walter Brock. It was a strange flight, just Ray and the Senator on this big private aircraft with a crew of three. Commercially the BAC111 carried over 100 passengers, but the Untico plane sat 24 passengers in elegant comfort. Big cushioned seats and upholstered couches were grouped in various ways, with a large bar in the middle. The third crew member served them drinks and delicious, hot hors d'oeuvres.

At the airport, Bob Vernon, Untico's Vice President of Governmental Affairs had thanked Ray for hosting the flight. "If you weren't going, I'd have to fly out to Springfield with the Senator and come back alone. We have to have a Untico employee on every flight."

"Glad to help out," said Ray, not wanting to get into the reasons for his trip.

"You're a good guy," Vernon continued, putting his arm around Ray's shoulders. "First you give me that Jap story to tell around the beltway, then you lose $15 to me playing golf, and now this. Let me know if you ever need a favor."

Ray should have been thrilled, riding on this beautiful plane with a U.S. Senator, but all he could think about was his guilt on leaving his family. "Damn," he thought. "I wish now I hadn't gotten those separate rooms. Now she's all alone in our room with nothing to think about except what a prick I am for leaving. I hope she's not calling that damn lawyer."

He spoke socially with Senator Brock for about an hour. Then they both pulled out some paperwork for the rest of the trip. They dropped the Senator off in Springfield and flew into Jackson. Ray came home to a very lonely house and went right to sleep.

■ ■ ■

Ray had to be careful at Thursday's meeting. He had to be sure not to let on that he even knew Max Simpson had set up the meeting. Burch had called him and told him only that he should get back for this important meeting. His vacation would have to be interrupted.

When Ray entered Burch's office, Max Simpson had not arrived, and Burch made no mention that he would. So Ray just sat down with Buzzard, Wise, and Webb, and did not show any surprise. Burch opened the meeting by asking Ray, "OK, Pendleton, have you come up with a way to get up to a reasonable profit with NAPA?"

Ray wanted to answer, "My proposed discount gave us a reasonable profit level." But the way Burch had phrased the question already assumed they were not at a profitable level. Ray thought it best not to argue that point, at least until Max got there. He just answered the question.

"Well Ralph, I can't really say that I have. I've looked at some alternate pricing strategies that would meet your goal, but I don't think Jesse would buy them." Everyone just looked at him, so he continued. "We could squeeze the Jobber margin so that 22 percent off his new, higher Jobber price would be the same as 15 percent off the present price. The Jobbers are making over 35 percent now. Also, we could raise the NAPA list price to get the same dollar profit. Or, we could do a little of each."

Burch and Wise were taking notes, but no one said anything. They just looked at Ray, so he kept talking. "We could disguise some of this by raising the prices on fast movers and lowering the slow movers. Also, we could play with the discounts at various levels...you know, change the dealer price sheets and the do-it-yourself sheets. Every Jobber has a different mix of customers, so it's hard to tie down just what his margin is."

"So you think we might be able to muddy up the price structure?" asked Burch.

"No, not really," Ray answered discouragingly. "Not to this extent. If we were talking a point or two on the discount we might be able to. But not seven or eight points. I'd hate to have to go in and try to fool them."

"You think we might," asked Burch, somewhat sarcastically. "But you wouldn't want to lie to a customer?"

Ray was getting a little angry. "No, that's not what I'm saying. I can go in with whatever we decide. But I don't think we can fool them. They can add." He paused, then said, "I sure wouldn't want Dudley Graham to call Max again."

Burch bristled at Ray's remark, but did not comment. "What about cutting our other costs?" he asked.

"We could pick up a little in Vince's promotion program. But it's not that big to begin with. NAPA handles most of that themselves. That's why they expect the discount. And we've gone through the manpower issue. I mean, I don't think Simpson would allow us to cut much. But even if we cut ten men, that's only the equivalent of about one point of the discount."

Burch put his pencil down. "Then what you're saying is you don't think we can sell NAPA."

"Not without giving them a bigger discount than you're talking about…their regular discount."

"That's what I thought," said Burch, turning toward the others. "We have a problem."

Ray was glad that this was finally getting across to Burch. The offer to NAPA would have to be reasonable. Maybe they could get this resolved before Simpson got there, and avoid a big confrontation. Ray would be happy to get out of there and back to Washington to save some of his vacation…and maybe his marriage.

Burch, however, presented a different view of the situation. "We've gone ahead under the assumption that we would sell NAPA," he said to all of them. "We've expanded our Seward plant and we've bought a hell of a lot of equipment. Now we find that if we hold to a reasonable profit level, we won't get the NAPA business. So, at our present level of sales, we have overcapacity."

Ray wanted to protest the idea of "reasonable profit," but said nothing for the moment.

Burch continued, showing no emotion. "Our choice then, is to fill up the plants with low-profit business, or to reduce our capacity.

While the short-term solution might be to fill up the plants, I think that starts us on a path towards diminished profits. I think we have to guard against relaxing our profit discipline." He turned toward Buzzard. "Carl, what's the best way for us to reduce our capacity?"

Ray could not believe his ears. Was Burch going to throw away the chance to get NAPA? He started to protest, but Buzzard answered Burch emphatically, "Close Jackson! No doubt about it. Close Jackson and get rid of the UAW. We'll be much more profitable."

Ray had to jump in. "Wait a minute. You mean we're going to throw away NAPA? Just like that?"

"Just like what?" Burch said innocently. "You're the one that says we can't sell them at a reasonable profit margin."

"I never said that," Ray said angrily. "I think we could make a good profit with their normal discount."

"I don't see how," Dick Wise answered. "We'd be giving them 7 or 8 percent better than our other WD customers. That's right out of our pocket."

"But our selling costs are lower."

"Not that much," Wise countered. "You said yourself that it takes ten salesmen to take off a point. We could do a little better than 15 percent. But nowhere near 22."

"Well then, let's try 19 or 20 percent." Ray was very angry and frustrated, fighting all by himself.

"No!" Burch said emphatically. "We go in at the right level or not at all. We don't have to sell these guys. We can do very well at our present volume with Harrisonburg and an expanded Seward plant."

"Yeah, what about the Seward plant?" Ray said, searching for something. "We wrote that Seward appropriation to expand for the NAPA business."

"No, we didn't," Buzzard corrected him. "We had no insurance that we had NAPA at that time. So the justification was cost reduction and future expansion. NAPA was never mentioned."

"But NAPA is why Simpson got it through the Untico system so fast."

Burch almost smiled. "Maybe he did. I can't control what he does."

Ray was beginning to understand, but he could not believe that this was really a planned conspiracy. He said bluntly, "It sounds like you never had any intention to sell NAPA...that you only used the prospect of selling them to expand Seward. But why?" Then he answered his own question. "To close Jackson. The intent was to close Jackson."

Burch did actually smile. "The thought crossed my mind." Buzzard laughed, while Wise and Webb smiled.

"But you can't do this," Ray said, throwing caution to the wind. "Max will never let you."

Burch's smile disappeared. "Pendleton, you keep bringing up what Max will say or what he'll let us do. Is that what you two talk about all the time on the phone? Well let me bring you up to date. Simpson is no longer with the company. They had a reorganization as of this morning." He looked fiercely at Ray. "Possibly because of some changes Max was trying to put through on Tuesday. Anyway, there's a new 'Office of the President,' with Moore, Tracy, and Torres. Every Untico unit reports in to one of them. We report to Tracy. And Alan agrees with this sound financial approach."

Ray's jaw dropped. He looked at Wise, Buzzard, and Webb, who were smiling broadly. Then he looked back at Burch and said, "Huh?"

26. Peace at Last

When Ray left Burch's office, he was in a daze. The plane was waiting for him, and he flew back to Washington as the only passenger. He knew he was in trouble, and he was trying to figure out what had happened. That way, he could figure out what to do next. But his thoughts of Burch and Buzzard and Simpson and Tracy were all blurred. Apparently he had chosen the wrong side, and Burch knew that. He took a drink of scotch on the rocks, but nothing cleared up. So he took another. By the time he got back to the motel he was a little dizzy.

Dorothy was very cool to him, especially when she smelled his breath. But as he tried to tell her what had happened, she could see his confusion and his sadness. When he told her he was in serious trouble, she forgot her anger and acted more kindly to him.

They finished the vacation with Dorothy making all the decisions. Ray just followed along. The kids did not seem to notice anything different as they concentrated on their own social world. They went to Mount Vernon on Friday morning, said good-bye to their new friends that night, and were back home by Saturday night. The ride home was very quiet.

On Sunday morning, Dorothy watched her husband sitting in the backyard, just thinking. After a couple of hours she brought him out a ham sandwich and a Coke. "You should eat something," she said warmly, as she handed him the sandwich.

"Thanks, honey," he said sadly. "But I'm not really hungry."

"How about a scotch?"

That got his attention. He looked up at her. "That might be a good idea. But in the morning?"

"It's afternoon."

She went out and came back with a bottle of J&B, some ice, and two glasses. "Mind if I join you?"

"No. That would be nice."

They sat quietly sipping their drinks for awhile. Then Ray said, "I might not have a job tomorrow."

Dorothy just nodded.

"I mean, I don't know how much Burch knows," he said. "He knows I've been talking with Simpson, but he might just think Simpson was calling me to get information. And whatever it was that Simpson was doing on Tuesday was Simpson acting on his own...I didn't know about it. But then, why hadn't I told him about my conversations with Max?" Ray shook his head slowly. "But then, why didn't he fire me on Thursday? If he thought I was plotting against him, why didn't he fire me right away? And if he didn't, maybe he's just a little angry and I'll be all right."

"Why don't you ask him?" Dorothy asked.

"I can't just walk right in and ask him if he's going to fire me," Ray answered. He looked at Dorothy, who said nothing. Then he smiled. "But why not? I've got nothing to lose."

"And tell him what you think about the NAPA thing, too."

"Well, I don't want to push it. Besides, I've never kept that a secret. And I have to find out if I should still try to sell them, or if I should just tell them we're not interested. I mean, I have to keep doing my job as long as I have it."

"Sure. And if you don't have it, you might as well find out and we can get on with our lives."

Ray thought for a moment. "You know, it's not so frightening when you think about it that way. I mean, that's the worst that could happen. I could lose my job."

"It wouldn't bother me," said Dorothy as she sipped her drink. "I don't know if I ever told you, but I don't really like this job."

Ray managed a small laugh. "You've told me."

They were silent for a few moments. Then Ray asked, "How would you feel about going back to Harvard? My leave of absence is over, but I think I might still get back. I mean, I know everything that I used to know, plus what I learned these past three years... which is plenty."

"If it was all right with you, it would be fine with me. I think I'd like going back to Boston."

Ray reached over and took a bite out of the ham sandwich. "I should give Dean Harrelson a call. See if I could really get my old job back." He took a deep breath and slowly exhaled. "It would be a relief, wouldn't it."

Dorothy smiled. "It would be for me."

Ray sat back, munching on his sandwich. "That's what I'll do then. Call Dean Harrelson...and then talk to Burch. One way or another, I'll know where I am."

"Me too!"

He smiled at Dorothy. "This has been kind of a hectic ride, hasn't it. I'm glad you're on my team."

"I'm glad you noticed."

"I've noticed. I may not show it, but I noticed."

"I know."

He sipped his drink as they sat quietly. Then he said slowly, "You know, I think Max was trying to kick Burch out and put me in as President."

"Of course."

"I was almost President," he said, looking up at the sky. "President of the whole damn company. Can you imagine that?"

She reached over and put her hand on his knee. "And you would have been a good one, too," she said with a warm smile.

Burch was too busy to see him on Monday or Tuesday. Ray postponed a trip to Chicago to meet with Sears in order to get things straight with Burch, but Burch kept putting him off. He did get through to Dean Harrelson, who told him that they would love to have him come back.

"What's going on?" Harrelson asked. "Why are you thinking about coming back?"

"Well there's a lot of strange things happening," Ray answered, guardedly. "Political stuff. You know, not my strength. I'll fill you in when I know more myself. But it's good to know I'm still wanted at Harvard. I really appreciate your support. Thanks."

"Don't thank me," Harrelson replied. "Getting an executive from industry with the credentials to teach is very rare. We'd love to have you. Call me when you can talk more."

That conversation made Ray feel much better and strengthened his resolve to have it out with Burch. On Tuesday night, Ray received a strange call. It started out as a survey call about the stocks of several big companies, including Untico. But as the woman asked her questions, she focused in more and more on Untico. Ray was getting suspicious when the woman said, "By now you must realize that we are really asking about Untico. We want to find out how stockholders and executives feel about how the company is being managed." Ray wondered if this could be the "Untico CIA" testing his loyalty. It seemed farfetched, but there was too much coincidence. However, he was feeling brave as a result of his call to Dean Harrelson, so he decided just to tell the truth. He answered the woman's questions, leaving no doubt that as an executive he thought Management was getting too accounting oriented. Instead of growing, they were getting too conservative, and the result would be wasting the considerable assets of Untico. The company would not grow the way they could and there would be lower returns for the stockholders.

"Now let's see what happens," he thought.

The next afternoon, Art Webb came in to tell Ray he was being terminated. He was given no reason except that, "Burch wished to change the marketing direction." Webb stayed with him as he gathered a few of his things and he only had a chance to say good-bye to Betty as he left. Betty sent him the rest of his things a week later. He never spoke with Burch.

Ray was bothered by the fact that Burch did not fire him personally. It made him feel that he was not very important, just a tool that Burch had used until he was no longer needed. Dorothy said it was because Burch had no "class." While Ray agreed, he knew that Burch was never friendly with him while they were working together. Why should that change when he was firing him? Burch was a cold, calculating businessman with no interpersonal skills and no desire to learn any. Burch was consistent.

Ray was more irritated that he had to leave in such a hurry, like they were afraid he would steal some pens or something. He would have liked to say good-bye to several people and leave with some dignity. But Dennison had been forced to leave in the same way. Yes, Burch was consistent.

■ ■ ■

Dean Harrelson was true to his word. The job was waiting at Harvard, with an increase from his old salary. "It's nice of them to do that," Ray said to Dorothy. "But my bonus this year would have been more than that."

"They only promised you that," Dorothy answered. "We never actually got it. They only give that bonus to the ones who do exactly what Burch wants…the whores. I guess we're not whores."

"Damn right."

The only people who said good-bye to Ray before he left Michigan were Vince Procino and Mike Evans. They came over one night while Ray and Dorothy were packing. Mike had a bottle of Jack Daniels, which he opened and threw the cap in the garbage. "We won't need that," he said. Dorothy left the three of them alone and went on packing.

They sat around talking about customers and competitors and salesmen for a couple of hours. By the time the bottle was empty, Ray was emotionally telling them they were his only real friends in the company. Mike told Ray he was one of the best marketing men he knew. They were close to tears when Dorothy made them a pot of coffee and sent Mike and Vince on their way.

Those were the last Amsaco people he saw. When they moved back to Boston, it was as if they had moved to another world. They had no further contact with the Bermans or the Wilmots or the Blooms or any customer friends, much less their Amsaco friends. Life went on at Amsaco as if the Professor was never there. Soon Dorothy and Ray were back in Boston as if they had never left…almost.

27. The Right Horse

Ray was walking slowly across the campus, deep in thought. This did not keep him from enjoying the activity around him. It was the first really warm day and it seemed the entire school was outside along the Charles River enjoying the bright sunshine and the sweet smell of spring. He was planning his next class, the McCord takeover. The most enjoyable part of the case was analyzing the personal side of each executive's position...something that hadn't been "taught at Harvard" in the past. His immediate problem was figuring out which students he should put on which reverse advocacy team.

The rhythms of academic life were comforting; they allowed him time to enjoy what he had and what he was doing. At Amsaco it was always the anticipation of better things that kept him going—like the approval of his Foreign Car Plan, or the next National Sales Meeting, or almost any next event. He was always waiting for something to be over or something else to begin. The next step was always going to solve all the problems, and he and Dorothy would be happy—not now, but later. But there was always one more step, then another, like a dream in which he was trying to reach some destination but never could.

Dorothy and the kids had slipped back into the friendly world of Boston as if they had never been away. And Ray came back as something of a celebrity. Everyone knew of his rise through the ranks to the position of Executive Vice President. He told Dean Harrelson of his "fall," but the Dean made light of it.

"Everyone gets fired in industry," he said. "But look how far you've gone." Ray's success proved that academia could do very well in practical industry situations. The rest of the faculty could now claim that they too would do well in industry, if they so chose.

Ray was treated as a returning hero. At the many parties, brunches, and dinners he and Dorothy were invited to, they repaid their hosts with stories of plush airplanes, yachts, dinners, and some remarkable characters they had encountered in the automotive industry.

"Suddenly we're celebrities," Dorothy said, as they drove home from the first of a string of informal faculty parties.

"Well, enjoy it," said Ray. "It won't last."

"Oh, I don't know," Dorothy said. "You're not just a conquering hero. You're the expert on the real world."

"Amsaco's the real world?" Ray laughed. "The automotive replacement business? That's Disneyland. This is the real world. People speak the truth, and families spend time together, and couples have time to make love, and—"

"You don't miss corporate life?" Dorothy asked.

"Miss it? My God, Dot, it was a nightmare. I was Alice in Wonderland. When I think how miserable we were, I can hardly believe it. It was like we were caught in a whirlpool and—"

"Or floating down the rapids."

Ray laughed. "Yeah, I guess we've had this conversation before." He paused, thinking. "But now, looking back, it was just madness…madness."

"You don't want to hop on a plane? Or eat at fancy restaurants? Or sail on the yacht?"

"Well, honey, don't get me wrong," he said, smiling. "Some of that was pretty nice. And I'm glad we did it and got to know that world. But it's no way to live. This is what I really want. Being with you and the kids…having a normal schedule…having intellectual challenges again. Burch did me a big favor."

Dorothy smiled. "Are you sure you don't miss being in on things—knowing what's happening?…making big decisions?"

"I never really made any big decisions, you know." He thought about that for a moment. "Isn't that strange? With all my big titles and salary and bonus, I never made any important decisions. Isn't that something? And as far as knowing what's happening, I really didn't know that much either."

For eight months after leaving Jackson, Ray had not spoken to anyone from Amsaco and still did not know what was happening.

Then Vince called him to say he would be in the Boston area. Ray was looking forward to seeing Vince and catching up on the latest.

The only other person he'd spoken to was Emil, who had offered Ray a job running one of his stores. "We're looking to expand into Orlando," Emil told him. "It's a growing area. You could run our Mickey Mouse Division."

Ray laughed. "I've already done that at Amsaco. No...thanks Emil. I really appreciate the offer, but I think I'm in the right position here at Harvard."

Emil assured Ray he would make more money than he did as a Professor.

Ray made a mental note to concentrate more on getting some high-paying consulting jobs to augment his salary—besides the one he already had. He smiled as he remembered how he wound up on his brother-in-law Henry's Board of Directors.

When Ray explained everything that had happened with Sears and Burch and Simpson and NAPA, Henry thought for a moment. "You did pretty damn good with those guys," he admitted. "Just picked the wrong horse, that's all."

Henry looked at Ray thoughtfully. "I've got a problem," he said finally. "No one wants to lend money for mortgages anymore. The damned usury laws limit the interest on mortgages, so the banks want big money up front...15 or 20 percent. And I have homes the people can afford, but they don't have the down payment. I mean, with both of them working, a family can make big payments, but they don't have the savings for the down payment."

"Why don't you lend them the down payment?"

"I'm a builder," Henry explained. "Not a goddamn bank. I don't know anything about loans. Why don't you come in with me...run my Finance Division."

"I'm a teacher," Ray said laughing. "Not a goddamn banker."

"Well, I thought maybe you could think of something. There's got to be a way. Some smart angle. Actually, some banks will take a lower down payment if the buyer takes out mortgage insurance so there's less risk. But they still don't like it."

Ray thought for a moment as Henry looked at him and waited.

"Insurance," Ray said thoughtfully. "The insurance companies could lend them the down payment so they could sell them the insurance. They can make money both ways, the loan and the insurance. And if they don't make much on the loan, they sure as hell can make a lot of money on the insurance. They know how to do that."

Henry smiled. "Yeah, then the bank gets their secure loan, the insurance company does pretty good, and I can sell a house with 10 percent down...or even 5 percent. Everyone is happy. It might work."

A week later, Henry called Ray. "You've got some pretty good ideas, Professor," he said. "I bounced that insurance thing around with the Board, and we're working on it now with a couple of insurance companies. So we're thinking...if you want to be on the Board...you'd add some class and make a little money too. And you'd make some good connections."

Ray laughed. "I don't know if I need connections. But it might be fun."

"Life is fun," Ray thought as he walked slowly to his class.

28. Epilogue

"How would you and Dorothy like to get a free dinner on Burch?" Vince had asked Ray over the phone. "Anywhere in Boston. And I'm bringing a surprise guest."

They ate at Anthony's Pier Four and the surprise guest was Al Goldman. Over drinks Ray told them how happy they were to be out of the rat race and back in academia. Vince filled them in on events at Amsaco.

"Things keep changing," he said shaking his head. "Let's see, first of all, your replacement was from the outside. Name of Drew Farnham, a Marketing Executive from of all places, Coca-Cola." He emphasized *Drew*.

"Coca-Cola?" Ray was surprised. "Does he know anything about the automotive aftermarket?"

"Not much. But Mike and I are teaching him."

"Like you taught me."

"We're trying. But he doesn't listen that well. He's pretty smart, but he's got some crazy big corporation idea that a good marketing strategy is all you really need."

"Like a foreign car plan," Goldman interjected, winking at Ray.

Ray laughed. "How's that going? That was a good plan."

"It was a fine plan," said Vince. "And it's doing pretty well. Foreign sales are picking up and our competitors are copying it. Even the other suppliers, like the exhaust system guys, are doing something similar. It's doing fine, but it's just not that important in the overall scheme of things."

Ray turned to Al. "You said to go ahead with it because it would be years before anyone found out it wouldn't work," Ray corrected him. "I guess maybe you were right. Who really cares now whether the Foreign Car Program is working? Al's probably the smartest guy at Amsaco," he said to Dorothy. Then he gave Al a friendly push. "How are things going internationally?"

"I'm not international anymore," Goldman answered grinning. "I'm back in the states...Executive Vice President of Operations."

"Whoa," Ray exclaimed. "What happened to Buzzard?"

Vince too was smiling. "That's a long story," he said. "Let's order and then I'll fill you in."

They ordered their food and another round of drinks, and then chatted about life in the Boston area. Meanwhile, Ray was anxiously waiting to hear about Buzzard. Finally he blurted out, "Well, what the hell happened to Buzzard?"

Goldman and Procino looked at each other and Goldman said, "You tell him. You were there."

"OK," said Vince. "But stay with me. A lot happened. Let's see... right after you left, Burch announced he was closing Jackson. Of course, the UAW screamed, but Burch said it was his only choice. We had overexpanded, expecting the NAPA business. I understand he blamed you for getting Untico all fired up and pushing for the Seward expansion. But the NAPA business was not available unless we sold at way too low a price, and he had to maintain pricing integrity or we would have an industry price war."

"But that's not true," Ray protested.

"Of course not. But it made a good story for the union."

"And that's probably what he was selling to Untico too," Goldman added. "They don't know the automotive aftermarket. They probably accepted the pricing integrity story as fact. At least Tracy did. And Simpson couldn't have fought that."

"That's just not ethical," said Ray, adding, "But Burch sure was consistent."

"That son of a bitch," said Dorothy.

Vince laughed. "Wait until you hear the whole story. Well, you could imagine the sabotage that started as Jackson shipped equipment and tools down to Harrisonburg. But Burch thought we were ready for that. Buzzard thought he could make enough parts in advance and combine that with Seward's new part-making capability, so that even if there was some sabotage, they could keep shipping until Harrisonburg got up to speed. They knew what had happened to Blackwell, and they thought they were ready for it." Vince smiled, and repeated, "They *thought* they were ready. But the UAW was too smart for them. Buzzard made sure there were enough parts made to last them several months, but Jackson made sure that the parts wouldn't work."

"They purposely made bad parts?" Ray asked. "What about Quality Control? Didn't they catch it?"

"Try to get the whole picture," Vince explained. "If the whole plant was closing, the QC guys were losing their jobs too. They were just as angry as the union guys. They must have known, but they just let the parts go."

"The parts looked pretty good," Al added. "But the holes would be the wrong size, or moved over an eighth of an inch, or an angle would be off a few degrees. Just enough to make sure they wouldn't fit. It really took some ingenious engineering to make them look so good but be absolutely worthless. We must have scrapped a million dollars worth of parts."

"But what about Harrisonburg?" Ray asked. "Didn't they catch it?"

"Not until it was too late," Al answered. "First of all, these parts were coming in so fast that Harrisonburg just stored them away until they were needed. Then, a few months later, when they pulled them out to use, they found they wouldn't work. But it was too late by then. I suspect that some of the QC guys at Harrisonburg might have known, but they weren't exactly in love with Buzzard. Who knows?"

"Anyway," Vince continued. "When Buzzard did find out about it, he flew down to Harrisonburg and almost went berserk. I mean he went through that place with a 'fuckin' this' and a 'fuckin' that.' Sorry, Dorothy."

Dorothy laughed. "That's all right. I know about Buzzard."

Vince smiled and continued. "But of course, he couldn't do anything about it. He was in the same position that Blackwell had been, even worse. In addition, there was something else going on that he didn't know about. After his first trip down to Harrisonburg, the workforce started talking seriously with the UAW. The union already had a bunch of signed cards and were ready. When Buzzard came storming through threatening to fire everyone, that must have decided it. It didn't take three weeks and they had an election and brought in the UAW."

Vince stopped and chuckled. "I understand that Lyons called Buzzard and said, 'Congratufuckinlations, you've got a fuckin' union.' I guess he was past the point of worrying about losing his job."

They all laughed as the waiter brought them their salads. Ray was enjoying himself and ordered another drink. Vince continued. "Well, Buzzard could see the handwriting on the wall. Production and delivery were going to go down the tube. Within a week he had another job. He's President of a small cable company in Wisconsin."

"That's when Burch called me in," said Goldman. "Quite a situation to walk into, huh? And I wasn't asked. I was told to get this under control."

"This would make a great case study," said Ray. "What did you do?"

"Well, whatever I was going to do," Al explained. "One thing was very clear. I couldn't do it with the union fighting against me. So I got together with Sam Ambrosio, secretary of the UAW, and told him the truth. I've known Sam for twenty years. I told him we had to work together or we'd all be out of a job. And he understood that. He said they could get things running if we opened Jackson back up...or more accurately, if we didn't close it completely. It was still running a little. I said we didn't need three plants, and if we didn't get up and running pretty soon we wouldn't need two plants. He told me to close Seward. They were not about to agree to close a union plant when we had a nonunion one still running."

"I wouldn't think so," Ray said, interested in the intellectual aspects of Goldman's dilemma. "So what did you do?"

"Well, I thought of keeping the three plants open," Goldman explained. "But that really would be expensive, even if we minimized staff. Industry sales growth is beginning to tail off and we really don't need three plants. We won't even need two if we lose Sears."

"You might lose Sears?" Ray asked.

"Well, they've been getting angrier and angrier with our delivery. I think I might have it under control now, using Jackson, but it might be too late." Goldman held up his hand. "But let me finish. While I was thinking about the problem, I remembered something Dan McCormick had told me at the last Untico Management Meeting. Seems the Yard builds an awful lot of their own peripheral equipment. They can't find companies to build a lot of their precision parts, especially when they get into that nuclear stuff. So they've been developing their own in-house capabilities. And they're expanding this operation, opening plants along the eastern seaboard. Well, the thought hits me that maybe they can use a ready-made facility that's already staffed, if they can train operators in their processes. It's a long shot, but I called Dan. And he got all excited. They were looking to open an operation in Virginia, and Harrisonburg would fit right in. And that's what we did, switched the plant over to the Yard. The damn thing went so fast, it amazed me."

"Did all the people keep their jobs?" Dorothy asked.

"Every one of them," Goldman answered emphatically. "We agreed with the union to close Harrisonburg as long as the plant switched over to Commerce Yards and everyone kept their jobs. It worked out fine. Our Management stayed right on, too, and shipped our equipment back to Jackson. Then the Yard brought in high-tech equipment, along with a bunch of trainers, and a bunch of key technical people. In a month they were switched over like they had never built a shock in their lives. And since they stayed in the Untico family, everyone kept their benefits. It was almost perfect. The only problem was Jackson trying to get the equipment working...the stuff they sabotaged. But we're getting there... slowly."

"Boy, this really would make a great case study," said Ray, shaking his head. "It shows something good about a conglomerate, with all the employees switching to another Untico company." He paused. "I'll bet Ted Lyons is relieved to be out from under Buzzard. He was a pretty unhappy guy the last time I saw him."

Procino and Goldman looked at each other and grinned. "You tell him," said Vince.

Goldman paused to get his thoughts together. "There's another story," he said still grinning. "When I spoke with Dan, he brought me up-to-date on the events at the Yard. Seems our old buddy Chessman was really causing an upheaval, really putting on a show. He was fighting with every one of the unions—and they have quite a few—over the featherbedding work rules. Telling them we don't need four guys to sit around and watch one guy turn a wrench. Tom told the union guys that the old days as a family company were over and from now on they had to work for their day's pay. Untico would have a well-run, profitable operation or they would shut it down. Let the Navy get their ships from Electric Boat."

Ray laughed. "I can imagine Tom in action."

"Yeah, I guess he really put on a show. At least that's what Dan told me. And the unions fought back. They had wildcat strikes and Tom took them to court or brought in scabs. And they were late on deliveries and Tom said, 'So what? If you want to ruin the company, go ahead. I'll find another job. You guys won't.' The union even got Admiral Rickover to call Dan and chew him out over late delivery. Dan said that contact came through Jimmy Carter, but it didn't matter. Dan stuck to his guns and backed Tom. Tom even had to have a bodyguard. He got threats. But eventually he won out. They compromised with the unions, giving them higher wages, but making big strides in eliminating the ridiculous work rules. Dan said they paid the men 4 percent more, but got twice the work done."

Goldman stopped and winked at Procino. "But the unions threw in one other demand...or request. They agreed that there should be better relations between Management and Labor, and they could see the need for more efficient operation. But to foster better relations, they suggested that maybe Tom could be promoted out of the Personnel job."

"And Dan agreed to that?" Ray asked.

"Sure," said Al emphatically. "He brought Tom in to do a job, and he did it. He broke the featherbedding rules and gave the Yard the chance to manage the way they should...like a business. He did what he came to do. And Dan didn't just throw him out. He rewarded Tom with a better position, Vice President of Peripheral Operations. Tom heads up all the non-shipyard operations. It's a big job, and for the first time it gives Tom some direct line responsibility...some P&L responsibility."

"He can determine pricing?" Ray kidded.

"Yeah, and everything else he's criticized. I'm sure Tom's happy about it." Al thought for a moment. "Well, I'm not that sure. But he should be if he ever expects to run a company."

Ray laughed. "I could never be sure what Tom was thinking. He is unique. And now he's actually responsible for line operations?"

"Yeah, everything except the Yard," Al said, starting to grin somewhat wickedly.

Ray thought for a moment, trying to understand Goldman's grin. Vince had the same grin. Then a thought hit him.

"Wait a minute," he said slowly. "Tom's head of all non-yard operations...and they took over the Harrisonburg plant to build parts. Don't tell me! Chessman is Lyons' boss?"

Goldman and Procino burst out laughing. Then Ray and Dorothy joined in. Ray started to explain to Dorothy, who said, "I know, I know. You've told me about Chessman persecuting Lyons. This would have been his worst nightmare. The poor man."

"It was," said Ray, still laughing. "Until he got Buzzard. Can you imagine? Getting rid of Buzzard, just to get Chessman. Let's drink to Ted, who must be the unluckiest man in the world."

They all kept laughing as the entrees were served. Vince ordered another round of drinks and they talked about some of the other people. Jim Steele had taken another job running the manufacturing operations for a furniture company in North Carolina. "It's not the Shenandoah Valley," said Vince. "But it's pretty nice down there, and I understand he's pretty happy."

Dave Dennison had not found another job, but was talking with Eric Van Drew, Executive Director of AWDA. "I think he'll go with them," said Goldman. "As a Vice President of Industry Relations or something. The job doesn't pay much, but it keeps him in touch with everyone in the industry...like a goodwill ambassador."

"And Mike will stay on for another year," said Vince. "But no more. He says he'll be damned if he would train another Executive Vice President."

"He'll be there after we're all dead," Al commented. "Selling Amsaco shocks is his life. And there's no one better at it. If I were running the company, he'd be the top Sales guy."

"But he's not an accountant," Ray joked.

"We've got enough accountants," Al replied seriously. "My

replacement in international, Phil Schroeder, is financial. Specializes in acquisitions. But I guess that's what we need to grow internationally."

"Burch's whole staff is financial it seems. Is Farnham financial?" Ray asked.

"He's an MBA."

"The whole staff then."

"Yeah, but I don't think Art Webb will stay," Goldman predicted. "I think he wants to go back to auditing...probably at another company. We should really have a Personnel man to run Personnel. Art's OK with the benefit plans, but he's no good with the UAW. It was a bad move by Burch to put him in there."

"Sounds like Burch made a few bad moves," Dorothy observed.

"Yeah, he has," Al responded, then added carefully, "I think he's kind of shaky. He's not well thought of in the industry. Making these big moves and then having to back off and reopen Jackson is embarrassing. It makes him look weak. And Untico isn't that happy with him. The cost of all the moving and scrapping parts turned a big profit year into a break-even one. I wouldn't be surprised to see a change. Even Schroeder wasn't his pick. Tracy sent him in. Maybe he'll be the next President."

"Or maybe you," Ray pointed out.

Goldman smiled. "That would make sense, but I don't think so. I'm not that close to Tracy. Besides, who ever said that making sense had anything to do with corporate decisions."

"It seems to be exactly opposite," said Dorothy. Then she smiled mischievously and added, "I think I know who the next President of Amsaco will be."

"Who?" the other three asked.

"Tom Chessman."

"You might be right," said Vince as he laughed. "He could do it politically."

"And he has a big reputation right now," Goldman added. "Did a good job at the Yard. Maybe it's not such a joke." He laughed. "It sure would be a lot of fun if he was sitting in the corner office. Every day would be an adventure."

"I might enjoy being back at Amsaco under those conditions," Ray said jokingly.

"Don't even joke about that," said Dorothy, suddenly looking serious.

Goldman looked surprised. "You didn't like the life at the top?" he asked Dorothy. "You didn't enjoy the good life?"

"It wasn't a good life for me. You guys led the good life. I stayed home alone with the kids. It was a terrible life for me."

Vince asked seriously, "Was it that bad for you? Even with the fancy resorts and the yacht and stuff?"

"That part was interesting. But even that was work. We were entertaining people that we didn't really know...didn't really like in some cases. We were always under pressure not to say the wrong thing, not to offend anyone, not to reveal any secrets. And we had to listen courteously, even if the customer was boring or talking garbage. No, the good life wasn't that good."

"It might have gotten better," Ray interjected. "After you see the same people year after year, real friendships could develop."

Dorothy laughed. "Yeah, except that no one seems to be around year after year. The cast is always changing."

"That's true," Goldman agreed. "But it used to be different. Emil and Mike...and Dave, they were around for a long time. They all expected to work for Amsaco until they retired. Now it looks like only Mike will make it. These guys really did do what was best for Amsaco, because the better Amsaco did, the better they did...in the long run. We really were a team. But Burch or Buzzard or *Drew* Farnham, they couldn't care less about Amsaco. They're trying to build a good resume, with short-term results, and then move on to a bigger and better job."

"Why did things change?" Dorothy asked.

"Hard to say exactly," Goldman said. "It's partly because the big conglomerates aren't concerned much with the actual business, just with results. They have to report better results each year to please stockholders. And stockholders are really the pension funds or mutual funds...very impersonal. They just want steady growth in their investment." Goldman paused. "When the company is affected and jobs aren't secure, people don't get so tied to a company or a specific place to live. It's almost expected that an executive will move from company to company to gain experience. I know a search firm executive who discounts anything over five years with one company. Says you don't learn much after five years."

"I think the level you're at makes a difference," Vince added. "If you're low enough in the organization you can stay with the company in one location...if you don't get caught in a layoff or a plant closing. But executives have to keep moving."

"I'm so glad we're out of that rat race," Dorothy said. She looked at Ray and smiled.

"Yeah, me too," said Ray. He turned to Vince and Al. "Those three years with Amsaco almost ruined our marriage. I lost my perspective and got caught up in the corporate games. I don't know why."

"I know why," said Dorothy. "It was because you liked them."

Ray looked at Dorothy. "I never intended to ignore my family, but something kept pulling me in deeper and deeper. God, it was like a nightmare. And now it's like coming out of the nightmare, like waking up...like leaving Oz and coming back to Kansas."

Vince laughed. "Well, Harvard ain't exactly Kansas."

"It is to me," said Ray, smiling at Dorothy. "We're a family again. I take Paul to his basketball games and watch Barbara at her recitals. And Dorothy and I have real time to spend together, without Ron Berman ruining it, or Burch calling me to a meeting." He laughed. "It's like we kicked Burch out of our bed. And Dorothy's much warmer than Burch."

"And prettier," Vince added.

Ray reached over and took Dorothy's hand. "You guys might think this is kind of mushy," he said, looking into Dorothy's eyes. "But I really love this woman. When I think how close I came to losing her, it frightens me."

"I think maybe you've had too much to drink," Dorothy said, smiling lovingly back at him.

"Damn right I have," he agreed. "Let's have another round. Let's celebrate the Pendletons' return from Oz."

■ ■ ■

After dinner, Dorothy thought it best that she drive them home. Ray was not drunk, but he was feeling pretty happy. He hugged Vince and Al before getting in the car.

"You guys were my best friends at Amsaco," he said with tears in his eyes. "I really appreciate that. And thanks for the dinner too."

"You're welcome," said Goldman, laughing. "Just don't kiss me."

"And thank Burch for the dinner too," he yelled out the window as Dorothy drove away.

When they arrived home, Paul told them someone had called for Ray and wanted him to call back, no matter how late it was. "Go ahead," said Dorothy. "I want to clean up the dishes."

Ray looked at the name and number. "Honey, it's George Lorenzo in Dayton," he yelled.

"Oh? I wonder what he wants."

"I don't know. Never much cared for him. I didn't think he even knew who I was. Maybe he's coming out here or something. He's an alumnus, you know."

Ray dialed the number and got through to Lorenzo's wife, Janice. "Oh yes," she said. "George wanted to speak with you. I'll get him. Say hello to your lovely wife, Dorothy."

"Hello Ray," Lorenzo said a few moments later. "How have you been? We didn't see you at Distributor's Institute or the Academy dinner this year."

He sounded cordial, friendly. Ray hardly recognized his voice. "No," Ray said cautiously. "We've been on a different tour this year."

"So I've heard. A lot of people were asking about you though."

"Oh?"

"Yeah. You've got a fine reputation here...in the industry. That's part of the reason I'm calling. Look Ray, not to waste your time, I'd like to talk to you about an opportunity here at Crane for someone like you...for you."

"An opportunity? A job?"

"Yes." Lorenzo laughed. "A pretty good one."

"Oh, I don't know, George. I appreciate you thinking of me, but I'm really not interested in going back into the automotive industry...or industry in general." And the idea of working for George Lorenzo didn't appeal to him. "We're pretty happy here at Harvard."

"I'm sure you are. But this is a real opportunity. Let me explain what's happening."

"OK, but I really—"

"There are several things. Most important, it looks like we're going the way of the rest of the industry. We're being acquired by a big operation. This is confidential, and it's still not finalized, but Holt GMBH wants to expand its American operations and they're going to use our business as a major step. As part of the deal, Grady Leach, our President is going to head up all their American operations. He'll mainly be looking for new automotive acquisitions. Holt has a pretty aggressive plan for the States. I'll become President of Crane and I'll need some good people…like you."

"Well thanks, George, and congratulations. It sounds like a good move for you. and I appreciate your interest, but I—"

"Let me finish. It won't hurt to listen."

"Sure. OK," Ray agreed. He was curious. "It won't hurt to listen. What's the job?"

"It's the biggest job in the company." Lorenzo paused to let that thought sink in. "To be perfectly honest, Grady isn't going to be that active, or stay that long. He wants to retire and spend all the money he's going to make on this deal. So, his job is really where I'm headed, and I have to begin to groom someone for my job. And that's where you come in. I want to talk to you about becoming our Executive Vice President of North American Operations."

"North American Operations?"

"That includes everything, Sales, Marketing, Manufacturing—the whole operation."

"Wow."

"I'll be spending a good deal of time on the international side, and looking for good acquisitions here in the States. You'd be pretty much on your own, running North American Operations. More like President of Crane, USA."

"Wow," Ray said again. "Why me? I'm a college professor. I just teach some—"

"Don't give me that crap," Lorenzo interrupted. "I know your record at Amsaco. And the industry thinks you got a raw deal trying to keep your company from making a big mistake. You're well thought of with the customers, and you've got a good business background from Harvard. I know what I'm doing. I know you played a big part in taking the Sears account from us. And by the way, we're getting them back."

"You're getting Sears?"

"Yeah. And it would be your job to keep them this time. Plus anything else you could do. We'd like to penetrate the traditional end a lot more. Maybe you could get us the Bermans or the Goodmans...or Emil's ABW operation. Get us NAPA if you can." He laughed. "There are no secrets in this industry. I know what a good job you were doing with them."

Ray was in a daze, but something stopped him from saying that he got Sears only because of Crane's mistakes, and he'd had a chance with NAPA only because of Blackwell's mistakes. Lorenzo must have known something about that, but it didn't seem to matter to him. He knew Ray had been right and had tried to make the right moves. And George seemed a lot friendlier.

"Well, I don't know what to say, George. Sounds like a great opportunity, like you say, but I don't really want to—"

"Why don't we get together and talk about it," Lorenzo argued. "We can get into a lot more detail and go over salary and stuff. By the way, the salary would be well into six figures, with a generous bonus based on performance." Lorenzo paused.

"Six figures...?"

"And that's just to start. What do you say we talk?"

"Well, I guess we could talk."

"Good. I'm going to meet with the Holt people in New York on Thursday. I could come up to Boston on Friday. We could have lunch at Kresge. I'd like to see the old campus again."

"Kresge. Lunch. Friday..." Ray repeated numbly.

"Right. At twelve. And hold Friday night open. I'd like to take you and your wife to the Harvard Club. I know she'll play a part in this decision. And tell her Janice says hello."

"Harvard Club. Friday night."

"Great. See you then."

"Sure. See you—"

Ray hung up the phone slowly, his head spinning. He looked up and saw Dorothy, standing in the doorway, holding a half-dried dish and staring at him.